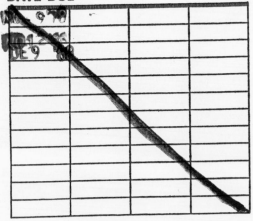

FOUNDATIONS OF MODERN POLITICAL SCIENCE SERIES

Robert A. Dahl, Editor

FOUNDATIONS OF MODERN POLITICAL SCIENCE SERIES

PRENTICE-HALL, INC., Englewood Cliffs, New Jersey

READINGS
ON
STATE
AND LOCAL
GOVERNMENT

Edited by

I R W I N   N.   G E R T Z O G

Yale University

FOUNDATIONS OF MODERN POLITICAL SCIENCE SERIES

Robert A. Dahl, Editor

READINGS ON STATE AND LOCAL GOVERNMENT
edited by Irwin N. Gertzog

13-761106-4

PRENTICE-HALL INTERNATIONAL, INC., London
PRENTICE-HALL OF AUSTRALIA, PTY. LTD., Sydney
PRENTICE-HALL OF CANADA, LTD., Toronto
PRENTICE-HALL OF INDIA PRIVATE LTD., New Delhi
PRENTICE-HALL OF JAPAN, INC., Tokyo

Current printing (last number) :

10   9   8   7   6   5   4   3   2   1

For Joshua and Rachel

CONTENTS

PREFACE

Several guidelines were employed in selecting the articles and excerpts reprinted in this book. First of all, an effort was made to include selections that arrive at concrete conclusions about important political relationships. Second, these conclusions were expected to lend themselves to further verification and elaboration, although they themselves might have been distilled from a unique set of circumstances or data. In other words, the inferences drawn by the authors should have been calculated to encourage additional inquiry by the serious, enterprising student. Third, an attempt was made to choose *recent* material. This was not always possible or desirable, however, and a few of the pieces chosen were written as much as a decade ago. These particular selections have, if anything, become more valuable with age, most subsequent treatments of the same subjects having added comparatively little to the older selections depth and breadth of insight. Finally, after choosing the material every effort was made to preserve its original integrity. Insofar as possible the full range of thought and scholarship that the author brought to his subject has been preserved intact, footnotes included, even though this has meant the republication of a few more lengthy selections.

Several of my colleagues provided me with helpful suggestions during the evaluation of the hundreds of books and articles that deserved consideration for an anthology of this kind. A special word of appreciation is extended to Peter Eisinger, James W. Fesler, Herbert Kaufman, Peter A. Lupsha, David R. Mayhew, and Russell D. Murphy, and to my research aide, Norman J. Resnicow. Their advice was not always heeded, however, and the responsibility for errors in judgment is entirely my own. I am also grateful to the authors and publishers who granted me permission to reprint their material.

Irwin N. Gertzog

PART ONE

INTER-
GOVERNMENTAL
RELATIONS

One popular conception of the American federal system assumes a fairly rigid bifurcation of power between the national and state governments. The Constitution's delineation of the functions of the central government and the language of the Tenth Amendment account in large measure for the popular acceptance of this image. Thus, Constitutional scholars, governmental practitioners, and the general public have often construed American federalism in terms of "layers of government," with each layer exercising mutually exclusive sets of functions. The Constitution makes no mention of local government, but the economic and political development of urban centers has forced observers to enlarge their conception of the federal arrangement and to acknowledge a set of functions for local agencies, as well.

While once it may have been useful to conceive of the federal system as comprising several layers of government (and there is considerable doubt that this conception has ever been entirely appropriate), this is no longer the case. The current interpenetration of national, state, and local agencies and officials has seriously undermined the usefulness of this frame of reference. Thus, the "layer cake" metaphor to describe the American political system is firmly and cogently rejected by the late Morton Grodzins in this reader's first selection. Carefully analyzing the distribution of power between central and peripheral units of government, Grodzins asserts that a "marble cake" image of American federalism best captures the spirit and workings of the federal system. He notes that functions are not assigned exclusively to any one level of government but rather that they are shared; most governmental functions, in fact, involve all three levels of government in some capacity.

This fundamental fact of political life, however, has not been sufficiently perceived by a number of committees created in recent years to reorganize the federal system. Each has been interested in minimizing the national role in governmental matters and in isolating functions that should be allocated exclusively to the states. But, as Grodzins points out, such goals ignore the principal feature of the American federal relationship, namely, *intergovernmental collaboration.* Grodzins discusses the conditions that promote dispersed power in the United States, focusing primarily on the role of American political parties. The absence both of party discipline and of coherent party programs makes the parties one of the nation's major decentralizing influences. Parties are most responsive when directives move from the bottom to the top of their hierarchies and least responsive when they move in the opposite direction. The centrifugal force parties exert both reflects and affects the distribution of power in the United States and their decentralizing influence, concludes Grodzins, is a highly desirable one.

The degree of collaboration among national, state, and local governments can be dramatized by examining the extent to which public funds collected by the national government are channeled into state and local agencies. Over the years the principal instrument through which Washington has distributed these funds has been the "grant-in-aid" program. But the tremendous growth in the number and size of these programs has altered the political and economic relationships among the parties to the federal system. Many observers have not been encouraged by these developments, and their objections, in turn, have stimulated a search for alternative means of redistributing the money. Richard P. Nathan, anticipating a leveling-off of defense expenditures in the post–Vietnam War period, examines five general approaches to the distribution of the additional revenues the national government is likely to have available for nondefense purposes. Nathan reviews the history and operation of the grant-in-aid concept and then turns to the workings and implications of the Heller-Pechman "revenue-sharing" proposal, the tax incentive plan, and the "model cities" and regional aid approaches.

The number of transactions associated with the American federal relationship is trifling compared to the millions of interactions among county and local officials each year. The social and economic interdependence of a major city and its suburbs, for example, has normally demanded political consultation and coordination among local governments. A major portion of their communications has been concerned with how to distribute the costs (social and political, as well as economic) of providing their residents with public services, and the intergovernmental collaboration that has often resulted has taken many forms. For example, governments in some areas have relied upon contractual arrangements. Occasionally, county and even state governments have been given the authority to perform functions previously regarded as municipal in nature. Some metropolitan areas have created area-wide councils—deliberative bodies composed of officials from local jurisdictions whose primary functions is the coordination of the public-service efforts of area governments but whose recommendations normally are not binding.

Los Angeles County's Lakewood Plan represents one of the best known instances of these intergovernmental arrangements, in this case based upon a set of county-local contractual agreements. The County negotiates contracts with local officials to sell services that community leaders feel their residents must have but which they are unable (for economic or other reasons) to supply for themselves. Richard Cion looks closely at the purposes of the Plan, the extent to which it measures up to the expectations of its participants, and some of its shortcomings. Cion is interested in the degree to which the communities retain control over the quality of the services provided by the County and the nature of the relationship between the communities and the County. He finds a multicentered decision-making process that, whatever else it may do, impedes greater political integration among the various governmental units within the County.

Cion, of course, is not alone in his interest in metropolitan reorganization. For years students of urban government have sought to promote political integration in metropolitan areas. Concerned with the efficient, economic, and equitable distribution of services, reform groups, public officials, and academicians have advanced hundreds of reorganization proposals, some of which have been adopted, but most of which have been rejected. Thomas M. Scott discusses several reorganization plans offered in recent years. He summarizes the conditions that seem to be associated with their adoption and the factors that appear to be related to their rejection. He finds that less radical reform proposals (e.g., intermunicipal cooperative agreements and transfers of functions to the county level) often require little more than ratification by local officials. More comprehensive proposals (e.g., large-scale annexations and metropolitan federation), on the other hand, normally require approval in a popular referendum. The large number of actors who see themselves as being adversely affected by radical change are usually able to mobilize sufficiently vigorous opposition to defeat these proposals. Scott concludes that far-reaching reorganization schemes are unlikely to receive support in the near future but that gradual changes in popular perceptions of what is radical may permit acceptance of these plans in the long-run.

CHAPTER ONE

THE FEDERAL SYSTEM

MORTON GRODZINS

Federalism is a device for dividing decisions and functions of government. As the constitutional fathers well understood, the federal structure is a means, not an end. The pages that follow are therefore not concerned with an exposition of American federalism as a formal, legal set of relationships. The focus, rather, is on the purpose of federalism, that is to say, on the distribution of power between central and peripheral units of government.

I. THE SHARING OF FUNCTIONS

The American form of government is often, but erroneously, symbolized by a three-layer cake. A far more accurate image is the rainbow or marble cake, characterized by an inseparable mingling of differently colored ingredients, the colors appearing in vertical and diagonal strands and unexpected whirls. As colors are mixed in the marble cake, so functions are mixed in the American federal system. Consider the health officer, styled "sanitarian," of a rural county in a border state. He embodies the whole idea of the marble cake of government.

From "The Federal System" by Morton Grodzins, in *Goals for Americans*. © 1960 by the American Assembly, Columbia University, New York, New York. Reprinted by permission of Prentice-Hall, Inc., Englewood Cliffs, New Jersey. Mr. Grodzins was Professor of Political Science at the University of Chicago before his death in 1964.

This paper is the product of research carried out in the Federalism Workshop of the University of Chicago. I am indebted to the workshop participants, particularly Daniel J. Elazar, Dennis Palumbo, and Kenneth E. Gray, for data they collected. I profited greatly in writing Part III of the paper from Mr. Elazar's prize-winning dissertation, "Intergovernmental Relations in Nineteenth Century American Federalism" (Chicago, 1959.)

The sanitarian is appointed by the state under merit standards established by the federal government. His base salary comes jointly from state and federal funds, the county provides him with an office and office amenities and pays a portion of his expenses, and the largest city in the county also contributes to his salary and office by virtue of his appointment as a city plumbing inspector. It is impossible from moment to moment to tell under which governmental hat the sanitarian operates. His work of inspecting the purity of food is carried out under federal standards; but he is enforcing state laws when inspecting commodities that have not been in interstate commerce; and somewhat perversely he also acts under state authority when inspecting milk coming into the county from producing areas across the state border. He is a federal officer when impounding impure drugs shipped from a neighboring state; a federal-state officer when distributing typhoid immunization serum; a state officer when enforcing standards of industrial hygiene; a state-local officer when inspecting the city's water supply; and (to complete the circle) a local officer when insisting that the city butchers adopt more hygienic methods of handling their garbage. But he cannot and does not think of himself as acting in these separate capacities. All business in the county that concerns public health and sanitation he considers his business. Paid largely from federal funds, he does not find it strange to attend meetings of the city council to give expert advice on matters ranging from rotten apples to rabies control. He is even deputized as a member of both the city and county police forces.

The sanitarian is an extreme case, but he accurately represents an important aspect of the whole range of governmental activities in the United States. Functions are not neatly parceled out among the many governments. They are shared functions. It is difficult to find any governmental activity which does not involve all three of the so-called "levels" of the federal system. In the most local of local functions—law enforcement or education, for example—the federal and state governments play important roles. In what, *a priori*, may be considered the purest central government activities—the conduct of foreign affairs, for example—the state and local governments have considerable responsibilities, directly and indirectly.

The federal grant programs are only the most obvious example of shared functions. They also most clearly exhibit how sharing serves to disperse governmental powers. The grants utilize the greater wealth-gathering abilities of the central government and establish nation-wide standards, yet they are "in aid" of functions carried out under state law, with considerable state and local discretion. The national supervision of such programs is largely a process of mutual accommodation. Leading state and local officials, acting through their professional organizations, are in considerable part responsible for the very standards that national officers try to persuade all state and local officers to accept.

Even in the absence of joint financing, federal-state-local collaboration is the characteristic mode of action. Federal expertise is available to aid in the building of a local jail (which may later be used to house federal prisoners), to improve a local water purification system, to step up building inspections, to provide standards for state and local personnel in protecting housewives against dishonest butchers' scales, to prevent gas explosions, or to produce a land use plan. States and localities, on the other hand, take important formal responsibilities in the development of national programs for atomic energy, civil defense, the regulation of commerce, and the protection of purity in foods and drugs; local political weight is always a factor in the operation of even a post office or a military establishment. From abattoirs and accounting through zoning and zoo administration, any governmental activity is almost certain to involve the influence, if not the formal administration, of all three planes of the federal system.

II. ATTEMPTS TO UNWIND THE FEDERAL SYSTEM

Within the past dozen years there have been four major attempts to reform or reorganize the federal system: the first (1947–49) and second (1953–55) Hoover Commissions on Executive Organization; the Kestnbaum Commission on Intergovernmental Relations (1953–55); and the Joint Federal-State Action Committee (1957–59). All four of these groups have aimed to minimize federal activities. None of them has recognized the sharing of functions as the characteristic way American governments do things. Even when making recommendations for joint action, these official commissions take the view (as expressed in the Kestnbaum report) that "the main tradition of American federalism [is] the tradition of separateness." All four have, in varying degrees, worked to separate functions and tax sources.

The history of the Joint Federal-State Action Committee is especially instructive. The committee was established at the suggestion of President Eisenhower, who charged it, first of all, "to designate functions which the States are ready and willing to assume and finance that are now performed or financed wholly or in part by the Federal Government." He also gave the committee the task of recommending "Federal and State revenue adjustments required to enable the States to assume such functions."[1]

The committee subsequently established seemed most favorably situated to accomplish the task of functional separation. It was composed of distinguished and able men, including among its personnel three leading

---

[1]The President's third suggestion was that the committee "identify functions and responsibilities likely to require state or federal attention in the future and . . . recommend the level of state effort, or federal effort, or both, that will be needed to assure effective action." The committee initially devoted little attention to this problem. Upon discovering the difficulty of making separatist recommendations, i.e., for turning over federal functions and taxes to the states, it developed a series of proposals looking to greater effectiveness in intergovernmental collaboration. The committee was succeeded by a legislatively-based, 26-member Advisory Commission on Intergovernmental Relations, established September 29, 1959.

members of the President's cabinet, the director of the Bureau of the Budget, and ten state governors. It had the full support of the President at every point, and it worked hard and conscientiously. Excellent staff studies were supplied by the Bureau of the Budget, the White House, the Treasury Department, and, from the state side, the Council of State Governments. It had available to it a large mass of research data, including the sixteen recently completed volumes of the Kestnbaum Commission. There existed no disagreements on party lines within the committee and, of course, no constitutional impediments to its mission. The President, his cabinet members, and all the governors (with one possible exception) on the committee completely agreed on the desirability of decentralization-via-separation-of-functions-and-taxes. They were unanimous in wanting to justify the committee's name and to produce action, not just another report.

The committee worked for more than two years. It found exactly two programs to recommend for transfer from federal to state hands. One was the federal grant program for vocational education (including practical-nurse training and aid to fishery trades); the other was federal grants for municipal waste treatment plants. The programs together cost the federal government less than $80 million in 1957, slightly more than two per cent of the total federal grants for that year. To allow the states to pay for these programs, the committee recommended that they be allowed a credit against the federal tax on local telephone calls. Calculations showed that this offset device, plus an equalizing factor, would give every state at least 40 per cent more from the tax than it received from the federal government in vocational education and sewage disposal grants. Some states were "equalized" to receive twice as much.

The recommendations were modest enough, and the generous financing feature seemed calculated to gain state support. The President recommended to Congress that all points of the program be legislated. None of them was, none has been since, and none is likely to be.

III. A POINT OF HISTORY

The American federal system has never been a system of separated governmental activities. There has never been a time when it was possible to put neat labels on discrete "federal," "state," and "local" functions. Even before the Constitution, a statute of 1785, reinforced by the Northwest Ordinance of 1787, gave grants-in-land to the states for public schools. Thus the national government was a prime force in making possible what is now taken to be the most local function of all, primary and secondary education. More important, the nation, before it was fully organized, established by this action a first principle of American federalism: the national government would use its superior resources to initiate and support national programs, principally administered by the states and localities.

The essential unity of state and federal financial systems was again recognized in the earliest constitutional days with the assumption by the federal government of the Revolutionary War debts of the states. Other points of federal-state collaboration during the Federalist period concerned the militia, law enforcement, court practices, the administration of elections, public health measures, pilot laws, and many other matters.

The nineteenth century is widely believed to have been the pre-eminent period of duality in the American system. Lord Bryce at the end of the century described (in *The American Commonwealth*) the federal and state governments as "distinct and separate in their action." The system, he said, was "like a great factory wherein two sets of machinery are at work, their revolving wheels apparently intermixed, their bands crossing one another, yet each set doing its own work without touching or hampering the other." Great works may contain gross errors. Bryce was wrong. The nineteenth century, like the early days of the republic, was a period principally characterized by intergovernmental collaboration.

Decisions of the Supreme Court are often cited as evidence of nine-teenth century duality. In the early part of the century the Court, heavily weighted with Federalists, was intent upon enlarging the sphere of national authority; in the later years (and to the 1930's) its actions were in the direction of paring down national powers and indeed all governmental authority. Decisions referred to "areas of exclusive competence" exercised by the federal government and the states; to their powers being "separate and distinct"; and to neither being able "to intrude within the jurisdiction of the other."

Judicial rhetoric is not always consistent with judicial action, and the Court did not always adhere to separatist doctrine. Indeed, its rhetoric sometimes indicated a positive view of cooperation. In any case, the Court was rarely, if ever, directly confronted with the issue of cooperation *vs.* separation as such. Rather it was concerned with defining permissible areas of action for the central government and the states; or with saying with respect to a point at issue whether any government could take action. The Marshall Court contributed to intergovernmental cooperation by the very act of permitting federal operations where they had not existed before. Furthermore, even Marshall was willing to allow interstate commerce to be affected by the states in their use of the police power. Later courts also upheld state laws that had an impact on interstate commerce, just as they approved the expansion of the national commerce power, as in statutes providing for the control of telegraphic communication or prohibiting the interstate transportation of lotteries, impure foods and drugs, and prosti-tutes. Similar room for cooperation was found outside the commerce field, notably in the Court's refusal to interfere with federal grants in land or cash to the states. Although research to clinch the point has not been com-pleted, it is probably true that the Supreme Court from 1800 to 1936 allowed far more federal-state collaboration than it blocked.

Political behavior and administrative action of the nineteenth century provide positive evidence that, throughout the entire era of so-called dual federalism, the many governments in the American federal system continued the close administrative and fiscal collaboration of the earlier period. Governmental activities were not extensive. But relative to what governments did, intergovernmental cooperation during the last century was comparable with that existing today.

Occasional presidential vetoes (from Madison to Buchanan) of cash and land grants are evidence of constitutional and ideological apprehensions about the extensive expansion of federal activities which produced widespread intergovernmental collaboration. In perspective, however, the vetoes are a more important evidence of the continuous search, not least by state officials, for ways and means to involve the central government in a wide variety of joint programs. The search was successful.

Grants-in-land and grants-in-services from the national government were of first importance in virtually all the principal functions undertaken by the states and their local subsidiaries. Land grants were made to the states for, among other purposes, elementary schools, colleges, and special educational institutions; roads, canals, rivers, harbors, and railroads; reclamation of desert and swamp lands; and veterans' welfare. In fact whatever was at the focus of state attention became the recipient of national grants. (Then, as today, national grants established state emphasis as well as followed it.) If Connecticut wished to establish a program for the care and education of the deaf and dumb, federal money in the form of a land grant was found to aid that program. If higher education relating to agriculture became a pressing need, Congress could dip into the public domain and make appropriate grants to states. If the need for swamp drainage and flood control appeared, the federal government could supply both grants-in-land and, from the Army's Corps of Engineers, the services of the only trained engineers then available.

Aid also went in the other direction. The federal government, theoretically in exclusive control of the Indian population, relied continuously (and not always wisely) on the experience and resources of state and local governments. State militias were an all-important ingredient in the nation's armed forces. State governments became unofficial but real partners in federal programs for homesteading, reclamation, tree culture, law enforcement, inland waterways, the nation's internal communications system (including highway and railroad routes), and veterans' aid of various sorts. Administrative contacts were voluminous, and the whole process of interaction was lubricated, then as today, by constituent-conscious members of Congress.

The essential continuity of the collaborative system is best demonstrated by the history of the grants. The land grant tended to become a cash grant based on the calculated disposable value of the land, and the cash grant tended to become an annual grant based upon the national government's superior tax powers. In 1887, only three years before the frontier was officially closed, thus signalizing the end of the disposable public domain, Congress enacted the first continuing cash grants.

A long, extensive, and continuous experience is therefore the foundation of the present system of shared functions characteristic of the American federal system, what we have called the marble cake of government. It is a misjudgment of our history and our present situation to believe that a neat separation of governmental functions could take place without drastic alterations in our society and system of government.

IV. DYNAMICS OF SHARING: THE POLITICS OF THE FEDERAL SYSTEM

Many causes contribute to dispersed power in the federal system. One is the simple historical fact that the states existed before the nation. A second is in the form of creed, the traditional opinion of Americans that expresses distrust of centralized power and places great value in the strength and vitality of local units of government. Another is pride in locality and state, nurtured by the nation's size and by variations of regional and state history. Still a fourth cause of decentralization is the sheer wealth of the nation. It allows all groups, including state and local governments, to partake of the central government's largesse, supplies room for experimentation and even waste, and makes unnecessary the tight organization of political power that must follow when the support of one program necessarily means the deprivation of another.

In one important respect, the Constitution no longer operates to impede centralized government. The Supreme Court since 1937 has given Congress a relatively free hand. The federal government can build substantive programs in many areas on the taxation and commerce powers. Limitations of such central programs based on the argument, "it's unconstitutional," are no longer possible as long as Congress (in the Court's view) acts reasonably in the interest of the whole nation. The Court is unlikely to reverse this permissive view in the foreseeable future.

Nevertheless, some constitutional restraints on centralization continue to operate. The strong constitutional position of the states—for example, the assignment of two senators to each state, the role given the states in administering even national elections, and the relatively few limitations on their law-making powers—establish the geographical units as natural centers of administrative and political strength. Many clauses of the Constitution are not subject to the same latitude of interpretation as the commerce and tax clauses. The simple, clearly stated, unambiguous phrases— for example, the President "shall hold his office during the term of four years"—are subject to change only through the formal amendment process. Similar provisions exist with respect to the terms of senators and congressmen and the amendment process. All of them have the effect of retarding or restraining centralizing action of the federal government. The fixed terms of the President and members of Congress, for example, greatly impede the development of nation-wide, disciplined political parties that almost certainly would have to precede continuous large-scale expansion of federal functions.

The constitutional restraints on the expansion of national authority are less important and less direct today than they were in 1879 or in 1936. But to say that they are less important is not to say that they are unimportant.

The nation's politics reflect these decentralizing causes and add some of their own. The political parties of the United States are unique. They seldom perform the function that parties traditionally perform in other countries, the function of gathering together diverse strands of power and welding them into one. Except during the period of nominating and electing a president and for the essential but non-substantive business of organizing the houses of Congress, the American parties rarely coalesce power at all. Characteristically they do the reverse, serving as a canopy under which special and local interests are represented with little regard for anything that can be called a party program. National leaders are elected on a party ticket, but in Congress they must seek cross-party support if their leadership is to be effective. It is a rare president during rare periods who can produce legislation without facing the defection of substantial numbers of his own party. (Wilson could do this in the first session of the sixty-third Congress; but Franklin D. Roosevelt could not, even during the famous hundred days of 1933.) Presidents whose parties form the majority of the congressional houses must still count heavily on support from the other party.

The parties provide the pivot on which the entire governmental system swings. Party operations, first of all, produce in legislation the basic division of functions between the federal government, on the one hand, and state and local governments, on the other. The Supreme Court's permissiveness with respect to the expansion of national powers has not in fact produced any considerable extension of exclusive federal functions. The body of federal law in all fields has remained, in the words of Henry M. Hart, Jr. and Herbert Wechsler, "interstitial in its nature," limited in objective and resting upon the principal body of legal relationships defined by state law. It is difficult to find any area of federal legislation that is not significantly affected by state law.

In areas of new or enlarged federal activity, legislation characteristically provides important roles for state and local governments. This is as true of Democratic as of Republican administrations and true even of functions for which arguments of efficiency would produce exclusive federal responsibility. Thus the unemployment compensation program of the New Deal and the airport program of President Truman's administration both provided important responsibilities for state governments. In both cases attempts to eliminate state participation were defeated by a cross-party coalition of pro-state votes and influence. A large fraction of the Senate is usually made up of ex-governors, and the membership of both houses is composed of men who know that their re-election depends less upon national leaders or national party organization than upon support from their home constituencies. State and local officials are key members of these constituencies, often central figures in selecting candidates and in turning out the vote. Under such circumstances, national legislation taking state and local views heavily into account is inevitable.

Second, the undisciplined parties affect the character of the federal system as a result of senatorial and congressional interference in federal administrative programs on behalf of local interests. Many aspects of the legislative involvement in administrative affairs are formalized. The Legislative Reorganization Act of 1946, to take only one example, provided that each of the standing committees "shall exercise continuous watchfulness" over administration of laws within its jurisdiction. But the formal system of controls, extensive as it is, does not compare in importance with the informal and extralegal network of relationships in producing continuous legislative involvement in administrative affairs.

Senators and congressmen spend a major fraction of their time representing problems of their constituents before administrative agencies. An even larger fraction of congressional staff time is devoted to the same task. The total magnitude of such "case work" operations is great. In one five-month period of 1943 the Office of Price Administration received a weekly average of 842 letters from members of Congress. If phone calls and personal contacts are added, each member of Congress on the average presented the OPA with a problem involving one of his constituents twice a day in each five-day work week. Data for less vulnerable agencies during less intensive periods are also impressive. In 1958, to take only one example, the Department of Agriculture estimated (and underestimated) that it received an average of 159 congressional letters per working day. Special congressional liaison staffs have been created to service this mass of business, though all higher officials meet it in one form or another. The Air Force in 1958 had, under the command of a major general, 137 people (55 officers and 82 civilians) working in its liaison office.

The widespread, consistent, and in many ways unpredictable character of legislative interference in administrative affairs has many consequences for the tone and character of American administrative behavior. From the perspective of this paper, the important consequence is the comprehensive, day-to-day, even hour-by-hour, impact of local views on national programs. No point of substance or procedure is immune from congressional scrutiny. A substantial portion of the entire weight of this impact is on behalf of the state and local governments. It is a weight that can alter procedures for screening immigration applications, divert the course of a national highway, change the tone of an international negotiation, and amend a social security law to accommodate local practices or fulfill local desires.

The party system compels administrators to take a political role. This is a third way in which the parties function to decentralize the American system. The administrator must play politics for the same reason that the politician is able to play in administration: the parties are without program and without discipline.

In response to the unprotected position in which the party situation places him, the administrator is forced to seek support where he can find it. One ever-present task is to nurse the Congress of the United States, that crucial constituency which ultimately controls his agency's budget and program. From the administrator's view, a sympathetic consideration of congressional requests (if not downright submission to them) is the surest way to build the political support without which the administrative job could not continue. Even the completely task-oriented administrator must be sensitive to the need for congressional support and to the relationship between case work requests, on one side, and budgetary and legislative support, on the other. "You do a good job handling the personal problems and requests of a Congressman," a White House officer said, "and you have an easier time convincing him to back your program." Thus there is an important link between the nursing of congressional requests, requests that largely concern local matters, and the most comprehensive national programs. The administrator must accommodate to the former as a price of gaining support for the latter.

One result of administrative politics is that the administrative agency may become the captive of the nation-wide interest group it serves or presumably regulates. In such cases no government may come out with effective authority: the winners are the interest groups themselves. But in a very large number of cases, states and localities also win influence. The politics of administration is a process of making peace with legislators who for the most part consider themselves the guardians of local interests. The political role of administrators therefore contributes to the power of states and localities in national programs.

Finally, the way the party system operates gives American politics their over-all distinctive tone. The lack of party discipline produces an openness in the system that allows individuals, groups, and institutions (including state and local governments) to attempt to influence national policy at every step of the legislative-administrative process. This is the "multiple-crack" attribute of the American government. "Crack" has two meanings. It means not only many fissures or access points; it also means, less statically, opportunities for wallops or smacks at government.

If the parties were more disciplined, the result would not be a cessation of the process by which individuals and groups impinge themselves upon the central government. But the present state of the parties clearly allows for a far greater operation of the multiple crack than would be possible under the conditions of centralized party control. American interest groups exploit literally uncountable access points in the legislative-administrative process. If legislative lobbying, from committee stages to the conference committee, does not produce results, a cabinet secretary is called. His immediate associates are petitioned. Bureau chiefs and their aides are hit. Field officers are put under pressure. Campaigns are instituted by which friends of the agency apply a secondary influence on behalf of the interested party. A conference with the President may be urged.

To these multiple points for bringing influence must be added the multiple voices of the influencers. Consider, for example, those in a small town who wish to have a federal action taken. The easy merging of public and private interest at the local level means that the influence attempt is made in the name of the whole community, thus removing it from political partisanship. The Rotary Club as well as the City Council, the Chamber of Commerce and the mayor, eminent citizens and political bosses—all are readily enlisted. If a conference in a senator's office will expedite matters, someone on the local scene can be found to make such a conference possible and effective. If technical information is needed, technicians will supply it. State or national professional organizations of local officials, individual congressmen and senators, and not infrequently whole state delegations will make the local cause their own. Federal field officers, who service localities, often assume local views. So may elected and appointed state officers. Friendships are exploited, and political mortgages called due. Under these circumstances, national policies are molded by local action.

In summary, then, the party system functions to devolve power. The American parties, unlike any other, are highly responsive when directives move from the bottom to the top, highly unresponsive from top to bottom. Congressmen and senators can rarely ignore concerted demands from their home constituencies; but no party leader can expect the same kind of response from those below, whether he be a President asking for congressional support or a congressman seeking aid from local or state leaders.

Any tightening of the party apparatus would have the effect of strengthening the central government. The four characteristics of the system, discussed above, would become less important. If control from the top were strictly applied, these hallmarks of American decentralization might entirely disappear. To be specific, if disciplined and program-oriented parties were achieved: (1) It would make far less likely legislation that takes heavily into account the desires and prejudices of the highly decentralized power groups and institutions of the country, including the state and local governments. (2) It would to a large extent prevent legislators, individually and collectively, from intruding themselves on behalf of non-national interests in national administrative programs. (3) It would put an end to the administrator's search for his own political support, a search that often results in fostering state, local, and other non-national powers. (4) It would dampen the process by which individuals and groups, including state and local political leaders, take advantage of multiple cracks to steer national legislation and administration in ways congenial to them and the institutions they represent.

Alterations of this sort could only accompany basic changes in the organization and style of politics which, in turn, presuppose fundamental changes at the parties' social base. The sharing of functions is, in fact, the sharing of power. To end this sharing process would mean the destruction of whatever measure of decentralization exists in the United States today.

V. GOALS FOR THE SYSTEM OF SHARING

The Goal of Understanding

Our structure of government is complex, and the politics operating that structure are mildly chaotic. Circumstances are ever-changing. Old institutions mask intricate procedures. The nation's history can be read with alternative glosses, and what is nearest at hand may be furthest from comprehension. Simply to understand the federal system is therefore a difficult task. Yet without understanding there is little possibility of producing desired changes in the system. Social structures and processes are relatively impervious to purposeful change. They also exhibit intricate interrelationships so that change induced at point "A" often produces unanticipated results at point "Z." Changes introduced into an imperfectly understood system are as likely to produce reverse consequences as the desired ones.

This is counsel of neither futility nor conservatism for those who seek to make our government a better servant of the people. It is only to say that the first goal for those setting goals with respect to the federal system is that of understanding it.

Two Kinds of Decentralization

The recent major efforts to reform the federal system have in large part been aimed at separating functions and tax sources, at dividing them between the federal government and the states. All of these attempts have failed. We can now add that their success would be undesirable.

It is easy to specify the conditions under which an ordered separation of functions could take place. What is principally needed is a majority political party, under firm leadership, in control of both Presidency and Congress, and, ideally but not necessarily, also in control of a number of states. The political discontinuities, or the absence of party links, (1) between the governors and their state legislatures, (2) between the President and the governors, and (3) between the President and Congress clearly account for both the picayune recommendations of the Federal-State Action Committee and for the failure of even those recommendations in Congress. If the President had been in control of Congress (that is, consistently able to direct a majority of House and Senate votes), this alone would have made possible some genuine separation and devolution of functions. The failure to decentralize by order is a measure of the decentralization of power in the political parties.

Stated positively, party centralization must precede governmental decentralization by order. But this is a slender reed on which to hang decentralization. It implies the power to centralize. A majority party powerful enough to bring about ordered decentralization is far more likely to choose in favor of ordered centralization. And a society that produced centralized national parties would, by that very fact, be a society prepared to accept centralized government.

Decentralization by order must be contrasted with the different kind of decentralization that exists today in the United States. It may be called the decentralization of mild chaos. It exists because of the existence of dispersed power centers. This form of decentralization is less visible and less neat. It rests on no discretion of central authorities. It produces at times specific acts that many citizens may consider undesirable or evil. But power sometimes wielded even for evil ends may be desirable power. To those who find value in the dispersion of power, decentralization by mild chaos is infinitely more desirable than decentralization by order. The preservation of mild chaos is an important goal for the American federal system.

Oiling the Squeak Points

In a governmental system of genuinely shared responsibilities, disagreements inevitably occur. Opinions clash over proximate ends, particular ways of doing things become the subject of public debate, innovations are contested. These are not basic defects in the system. Rather, they are the system's energy-reflecting life blood. There can be no permanent "solutions" short of changing the system itself by elevating one partner to absolute supremacy. What can be done is to attempt to produce conditions in which conflict will not fester but be turned to constructive solutions of particular problems.

A long list of specific points of difficulty in the federal system can be easily identified. No adequate congressional or administrative mechanism exists to review the patchwork of grants in terms of national needs. There is no procedure by which to judge, for example, whether the national government is justified in spending so much more for highways than for education. The working force in some states is inadequate for the effective performance of some nation-wide programs, while honest and not-so-honest graft frustrates efficiency in others. Some federal aid programs distort state budgets, and some are so closely supervised as to impede state action in

on any grounds of rational efficiency. Who, today, would create major governmental subdivisions the size of Maryland, Delaware, New Jersey, or Rhode Island? Who would write into Oklahoma's fundamental law an absolute state debt limit of $500,000? Who would design (to cite only the most extreme cases) Georgia's and Florida's gross under-representation of urban areas in both houses of the legislature?

A complete catalogue of state political and administrative horrors would fill a sizeable volume. Yet exhortations to erase them have roughly the same effect as similar exhortations to erase sin. Some of the worst inanities—for example, the boundaries of the states, themselves—are fixed in the national constitution and defy alteration for all foreseeable time. Others, such as urban under-representation in state legislatures, serve the over-represented groups, including some urban ones, and the effective political organization of the deprived groups must precede reform.

Despite deficiencies of politics and organizations that are unchangeable or slowly changing, it is an error to look at the states as static anachronisms. Some of them—New York, Minnesota, and California, to take three examples spanning the country—have administrative organizations that compare favorably in many ways with the national establishment. Many more in recent years have moved rapidly towards integrated administrative departments, state-wide budgeting, and central leadership. The others have models-in-existence to follow, and active professional organizations (led by the Council of State Governments) promoting their development. Slow as this change may be, the states move in the direction of greater internal effectiveness.

The pace toward more effective performance at the state level is likely to increase. Urban leaders, who generally feel themselves disadvantaged in state affairs, and suburban and rural spokesmen, who are most concerned about national centralization, have a common interest in this task. The urban dwellers want greater equality in state affairs, including a more equitable share of state financial aid; non-urban dwellers are concerned that city dissatisfactions should not be met by exclusive federal, or federal-local, programs. Antagonistic, rather than amiable, cooperation may be the consequence. But it is a cooperation that can be turned to politically effective measures for a desirable upgrading of state institutions.

If one looks closely, there is scant evidence for the fear of the federal octopus, the fear that expansion of central programs and influence threatens to reduce the states and localities to compliant administrative arms of the central government. In fact, state and local governments are touching a larger proportion of the people in more ways than ever before; and they are spending a higher fraction of the total national product than ever before. Federal programs have increased, rather than diminished, the importance of the governors; stimulated professionalism in state agencies; increased citizen interest and participation in government; and, generally, enlarged and made more effective the scope of state action.[2] It may no longer be true in any significant sense that the states and localities are "closer" than the federal government to the people. It is true that the smaller governments remain active and powerful members of the federal system.

Central Leadership: The Need for Balance

The chaos of party processes makes difficult the task of presidential leadership. It deprives the President of ready-made congressional majorities. It may produce, as in the chairmen of legislative committees, power-holders relatively hidden from public scrutiny and relatively protected from presidential direction. It allows the growth of administrative agencies which sometimes escape control by central officials. These are prices paid for a wide dispersion of political power. The cost is tolerable because the total results of dispersed power are themselves desirable and because, where clear national supremacy is essential, in foreign policy and military affairs, it is easiest to secure.

Moreover, in the balance of strength between the central and peripheral governments, the central government has on its side the whole secular drift towards the concentration of power. It has on its side technical developments that make central decisions easy and sometimes mandatory. It has on its side potent purse powers, the result of superior tax-gathering resources. It has potentially on its side the national leadership capacities of the presidential office. The last factor is the controlling one, and national strength in the federal system has shifted with the leadership desires and capacities of the chief executive. As these have varied, so there has been an almost rhythmic pattern: periods of central strength put to use alternating with periods of central strength dormant.

Following a high point of federal influence during the early and middle years of the New Deal, the post-war years have been, in the weighing of central-peripheral strength, a period of light federal activity. Excepting the Supreme Court's action in favor of school desegregation, national influence by design or default has not been strong in domestic affairs. The danger now is that the central government is doing too little rather than too much. National deficiencies in education and health require the renewed attention of the national government. Steepening population and urbanization trend lines have produced metropolitan area problems that can be effectively attacked only with the aid of federal resources. New definitions of old programs in housing and urban redevelopment, and new programs to deal with air pollution, water supply, and mass transportation are necessary. The federal government's essential role in the federal

[2]See the valuable report, *The Impact of Federal Grants-in-Aid on the Structure and Functions of State and Local Governments*, submitted to the Commission on Intergovernmental Relations by the Governmental Affairs Institute (Washington, 1955).

system is that of organizing, and helping to finance, such nation-wide programs.

The American federal system exhibits many evidences of the dispersion of power not only because of formal federalism but more importantly because our politics reflect and reinforce the nation's diversities-within-unity. Those who value the virtues of decentralization, which writ large are virtues of freedom, need not scruple at recognizing the defects of those virtues. The defects are principally the danger that parochial and private interests may not coincide with, or give way to, the nation's interest. The necessary cure for these defects is effective national leadership.

The centrifugal force of domestic politics needs to be balanced by the centripetal force of strong presidential leadership. Simultaneous strength at center and periphery exhibits the American system at its best, if also at its noisiest. The interests of both find effective spokesmen. States and localities (and private interest groups) do not lose their influence opportunities, but national policy becomes more than the simple consequence of successful, momentary concentrations of non-national pressures: it is guided by national leaders.[3]

[3]Messrs. Perkins and Redford state: "Professor Grodzins has made a significant contribution. The federal system has contributed to a "mild chaos" both administratively and financially. He accurately assesses the several quite futile attempts to disentangle the administrative and fiscal relationships of the states and the national government.

"At this juncture, however, it should be remembered that the present system of shared responsibility confuses rather than fixes responsibility. Ascertainable responsibility for policy, administrative performance, and financing is an essential feature of effective self-government. The possibility of achieving it needs to be explored.

"A reduction of the sharing of power would to some degree cause greater centralization of responsibility in the federal government. It would not necessarily result in loss of appropriate administrative decentralization and the loss of influence by the ordinary citizen over the activities of government. This is illustrated by what Mr. Grodzins himself says concerning the influence of the localized party structure on administration of centralized national functions.

"The chaos of party processes itself impairs leadership for national functions and national aims. Mr. Grodzins' conclusion that the costs of this chaos are tolerable may be drawn too easily. Whether the centrifugal pulls of party decentralization are so strong as to seriously threaten national leadership and responsibility in our government deserves careful assessment.

"Decentralization is an essential goal of American policy. So also are responsibility and leadership. Public concern needs to manifest itself about both of these goals."

CHAPTER TWO

FISCAL FEDERALISM: REVENUE SHARING AND ITS ALTERNATIVES

RICHARD P. NATHAN

This paper focuses on five major Federal aid policy alternatives which individually or in some combination could be a part of the Nation's post-Vietnam fiscal policy mix.

 I. The most obvious alternative for increasing Federal aid to States and localities would be for the Federal Government to devote additional resources to priority public needs by expanding existing Federal-aid programs or creating new aid categories.

 II. and III. As opposed to heavier reliance on categorical Federal-aid instruments, two methods are currently under consideration for providing broader and less conditional Federal financial aid at the State level. One is the general aid or tax sharing approach.[1] The second is the adoption of a Federal tax credit for State taxes as a means of channeling additional Federal resources to the States.[2]

---

[1]The term "tax sharing" is used here as synonymous with general aid as proposed in the Heller-Pechman plan and in subsequent legislative proposals. Some would use this term more broadly to include Federal tax credits for State and/or local taxes. It should be noted that tax sharing funds can also be channeled to local governments, either directly or by including a fixed minimum State-local pass through requirement in a tax sharing plan.

[2]See U.S. Advisory Commission on Intergovernmental Relations, *Federal-State Coordination of Personal Income Taxes*, October 1965.

Reprinted with the permission of the author from "The Policy Setting: Analysis of Post-Vietnam Federal Aid Policy Alternatives," in U.S. Congress, Joint Economic Committee, *Revenue Sharing and Its Alternatives: What Future for Fiscal Federalism?*, Vol. II, *Range of Alternatives for Fiscal Federalism*, 90th Cong., 1st Sess. (Washington: U.S. Government Printing Office, 1967), pp. 666–84. Mr. Nathan is a Research Associate at the Brookings Institution.

 The Brookings Institution, Jan. 19, 1967. The views and conclusions presented in this paper are those of the author and do not purport to represent the views of other staff members, officers, or trustees of The Brookings Institution.

IV. A basic alternative to these two new forms of general financial aid—both of which go primarily to the *States*—would be to rely upon a new and broader form of Federal aid for *local* governments. Demands for greater funding under the 1966-enacted "demonstration cities" program must be evaluated in relation to the Heller-Pechman plan. Mayors and other city officials generally favor this or a related approach as opposed to the tax sharing or tax credit approaches for providing new and additional Federal aid to the States.

V. A fifth, although less likely, Federal-aid alternative is a major expansion of the concept of the Appalachia program enacted in March of 1965. This program provides financial assistance for a wide range of economic development purposes on a *regional* basis. This approach too has its strong supporters who believe that a shift to the broad regional concept is the most appropriate policy direction in the Federal-aid field.

I. CONTINUED RELIANCE ON EXISTING TYPES OF FEDERAL-AID PROGRAMS

In evaluating any of the various proposals for major reliance on a new and broader form of Federal aid to States and/or localities, it is necessary to compare this approach with the existing Federal-aid "system" (if indeed it can be called a system). Thus, the policy option of increased reliance on the more traditional categorical-type Federal aids[3] is stressed and treated first in this paper. Although many readers may find it "old stuff" and may wish to skip over it, the next two sections review in quick fashion the historical development and major types of Federal-aid programs.

History of Federal Aids

The earliest form of Federal aid to the States was basically unconditional. The Northwest Ordinance, predating even the Constitution, provided land grants to the States for education and internal improvements. These land grants had to be used for these two broad purposes, "but had no other conditions and almost no plan for supervision and control."[4]

Growing out of the land grant, the next major Federal aid development was likewise unconditional. Under the surplus distribution program of 1837 (under Andrew Jackson), the Federal Government distributed to each State a share of the Federal budget surplus in excess of $5 million, with each State's share being based on its representation in Congress.[5]

---

[3]The term, "Federal aids," is used as a general term in this paper instead of the term, "grants-in-aid." The reason is that some Federal aid to States and localities is in the form of loans, guarantees, and payments in kind. The amounts under these aid forms are limited. The vast bulk of Federal aid to States and localities is in the form of cash payments, thus for most purposes the term grants-in-aid can be substituted for Federal aids in this paper.

[4]U.S. Commission on Intergovernmental Relations, *Final Report*, H. Doc. No. 198, 1955, p. 119.

[5]Daniel J. Elazar, *The American Partnership* (Chicago: The University of Chicago Press, 1962), pp. 200–210.

Although no conditions were placed on the use of this aid, it was widely believed that Congress intended it to be used for education and internal improvements. (In this period education and internal improvements accounted for the vast majority of State expenditures.) The 1837 surplus distribution plan was short-lived. The first three quarterly payments were made, but because of the panic of 1837 subsequent payments were suspended.[6]

Jane Perry Clark in reference to these early and basically unconditional aid programs (land grants and surplus distributions) concluded that they were unsuccessful precisely because of their broad and basically unconditional character. "There was no suggestion as to how the States were to spend the money, and they squandered their patrimony, or at best sold it for what many people think was a mess of pottage."[7]

The year 1862 was a major turning point in the development of Federal aids. The first Morrill Act was enacted in that year defining the objectives of Federal land grants more precisely than had previous statutes and introducing new conditions and supervisory procedures.[8] The 1862 Morrill Act donated lands to the States specifically for land-grant colleges. The second Morrill Act, passed in 1890, provided cash payments annually to the States for the same purpose.

From the Civil War to the beginning of World War I, new Federal-aid programs came slowly. Most of the new programs were for agriculture and were categorical-type grants, e.g., agriculture experiment stations (1887), forest fire protection (1911), and agriculture extension work (1914). All three programs are still in existence. The 1911 forest fire protection program was significant because it introduced for the first time "Federal approval of State plans and continued Federal inspection activities"[9] which have remained to this day key features of most Federal grants-in-aid.

The World War I period was important in the history of Federal aid for two reasons—the Federal highway grant-in-aid system was established on a comprehensive basis under legislation enacted in 1916 and new categorical Federal grants-in-aid were initiated for various public health purposes and for vocational education.

In the decade following the war, although existing aids were continued and in some cases expanded, no major new Federal aids were enacted. Emphasis was placed instead on initiative and experimentation at the State level. During this period several States adopted pioneering social legislation that was later used as a basis for new Federal aid programs.

[6]In the 1840's a variation of the surplus distribution plan was reinstated, but like its predecessor ended soon afterward. See Elazar.

[7]Jane Perry Clark, *The Rise of a New Federalism* (New York: Columbia University Press, 1938), p. 140.

[8]See U.S. Commission on Intergovernmental Relations, ch. 5, for a useful summary history of Federal grant-in-aid policies and regulations, including a discussion of the structure and impact of the various land-grant programs.

[9]Clark, p. 142.

The Depression, like the Morrill Act of 1862, marked a major turn-ing point in Federal aid policies.[10] It brought forth a virtual explosion of new Federal aids. This aid was generally provided on a basis which involved: (1) the precise definition of aided areas; (2) the requirement of State plans in conformance with Federal standards; (3) State matching of Federal funds;[11] and (4) the review and audit of aided programs by the relevant Federal officials. Among major examples of new categorical aid programs adopted during the Depression are:

—school lunch program (1933),
—old-age assistance (1935),
—aid to dependent children (1935),
—aid to the blind (1935),
—services for crippled children (1935),
—general health (1935),
—low-rent housing (1937).

The New Deal–initiated rise in the number and amount of Federal aid programs, although interrupted in the war years, continued in the postwar period under the Truman administration.

Coming into office in 1953, the Eisenhower administration sought to make basic changes in the scope and character of Federal-aid programs. Considerable emphasis was given to the work of various study and advisory groups set up in this field. The Eisenhower appointed Commission on Intergovernmental Relations (known by the name of its second Chairman, Meyer Kestnbaum) sponsored valuable research in this area and issued its own report in 1955. Later, in 1957 and 1958, an unsuccessful effort was made by the Eisenhower administration's Joint Federal-State Action Committee to eliminate certain Federal grants-in-aid in exchange for steps to turn over a compensating amount of Federal revenues to the States. The Action Committee recommended a specific tradeoff plan, whereby the Federal Government would turn over telephone excise tax revenues to the States in exchange for the elimination of Federal grants for vocational education and water pollution control. This proposal was adopted by the

[10]Historians differ on the degree to which the New Deal affected then existing Federal-State fiscal relationships. To some, the qualitative and quantitative impact of these new programs was so great as to basically alter the relationship between the Federal Govern-ment and the States. To others, such as Elazar, these new programs should be seen essen-tially as an extension of earlier Federal aid activities. While this paper does not go into an examination of this historical question, the view reflected here is that the New Deal pro-grams, with the involvement of the Federal Government in so many areas of State-local activity, does constitute such a distinct break with the past as to cast doubt on Elazar's view that there has been a steady and relatively continuous development of "cooperative feder-alism" since the late 19th century.

[11]During the Depression some hard-pressed States received loans for their matching share under various Federal aid programs. Some of these loans were later forgiven. See Clark, pp. 157–158.

administration, but differences in Congress as to how these limited goals should be achieved, resulted in its ultimate rejection.

Despite the Eisenhower administration's interest in strengthening the States and simplifying intergovernmental fiscal relations, total Federal aid increased to $7.3 billion in fiscal 1961, a threefold rise over the last year of the Truman administration. This increase is regarded by many as bipartisan validation of the New Deal extension of categorical Federal grants-in-aid into a wide range of traditionally exclusive State-local expenditure areas.

The history of Federal aid under the Kennedy and Johnson administrations is well known. Major new programs have been established in the fields of education, antipoverty, manpower training, mass transportation, mental health, air and water pollution control, and aid to the arts. Expenditures under a number of existing Federal-aid programs have increased substantially. The next result has been a rise in Federal aid to States and localities from $7.3 billion in fiscal 1961 to over $17 billion in fiscal 1968. Furthermore, commitments made by the 89th Congress in 1965 on President Johnson's "Great Society" programs are expected to produce major increases in Federal-aid expenditures in future years—barring, of course, a reversal of present policies. Estimates vary as to the eventual cost of these commitments. Projections range from $18.5 billion in fiscal 1970 based simply on the fulfillment of existing legislative obligations to $22 billion with the assumption of "normal" growth in Federal-aid expenditures.[12]

In this quick history of Federal aids, programs have been treated as if they are substantially alike. The fact of the matter is that there are distinct differences in the finances, administration, structure, and relative specificity of the various Federal-aid programs now in effect. *For purposes of this report, it is useful to group Federal-aid programs under four broad types of Federal-aid instruments.* These four classifications described below are defined in terms of the financial basis on which Federal aid is provided and the way in which the federally aided area is defined.

Types of Existing Federal Aids

In absolute dollar amount, the bulk of current Federal aid is paid to the States under grants-in-aid with Federal funds apportioned among the States according to a set formula. The various formula-type grants can be divided into three basic groupings, each of which is regarded here as a major type of Federal-aid instrument.

1. *Narrowly Defined Formula-Type Grants* The first grouping under formula-type grants is narrowly defined formula-type grants. It includes all Federal-aid programs which provide funds apportioned by formula for certain specific purposes within major functional expenditure areas. For example, until very recently there were a large number of narrowly

---

[12]Based on preliminary estimates provided by "Project 70," State-local finance project, Oct. 5, 1965. Prepared by Selma J. Mushkin and Robert Harris.

defined Federal grant programs in the health area.[13] Likewise, under agriculture, Federal aid is provided for narrowly defined purposes such as experiment stations and extension services. Federal formula-type grants are also available for certain specific forestry purposes, for example, tree planting, insect protection, and fire prevention.

2. *Highways and Public Assistance* The second grouping under formula-type grants includes just the two very large programs under which Federal aid is provided in broad functional areas, but is subdivided under various headings within the aided areas. The two programs are highways and public assistance. Together they account for more than half of the Federal-aid funds budgeted for 1968. Under highways, Federal aid is provided for the construction of interstate, primary, secondary, and urban highways. In the case of public assistance, Federal aid is provided for the aged, blind, disabled, and for families with dependent children.

3. *Broadly Defined Formula-type Grants* The third grouping of formula-type grants is of greatest interest in relation to new proposals for broader and less conditional Federal aid to State and local governments. Thus, a little more background is in order. This grouping includes those grants under which aid is given in major functional areas with relatively few conditions attached. Both of the illustrations under this heading are in the field of education—title I of the Elementary and Secondary Education Act of 1965 and the school aid for federally affected areas.

The purpose of title I of the Elementary and Secondary Education Act of 1965 ("Financial Assistance to Local Education Agencies for the Education of Children of Low-Income Families") is that of "broadening and strengthening public school programs in the schools where there are concentrations of educationally disadvantaged children."[14] It originally provides half of the average statewide cost of educating children from families with incomes of under $2,000 per year. Disbursements under title I in fiscal 1967 were approximately $1.2 billion. Compared to narrowly defined formula-type aids (above), this aid can be used flexibly for a wide range of new program purposes for the disadvantaged, except that it cannot be used for an across-the-board increase in teachers' salaries. This, of course, still falls short of the various education block-grant proposals under active consideration in the 90th Congress and as now proposed by the National Education Association.

School aid for federally affected areas has been provided since 1952 for school construction and current expenses in school districts where large Federal installations increase school costs or substantially reduce the local property tax base. This program has had a much longer history than title I and has retained its basically discretionary character over the years.

---

[13]Under a law passed in the 89th Congress, existing formula grants to the States for combating specific diseases were consolidated into "a flexible single grant to be awarded on a matching basis to assist in meeting public health needs." *House Report No. 2271*, p. 2. This move to a block grant for public health is an important new development.

[14]U.S. Congress, *S. Rept. No. 146*, pp. 5–6.

Residence of the parent, Federal employment, and student enrollment are the three factors which determine eligibility. Beyond this, as long as the public school is approved by the State department of education, it qualifies to receive aid and can use these funds at its discretion.

There is one important respect in which the Federal Government has recently exercised control over local school districts under *both* title I of the 1965 act and the federally affected areas program, that is, the prohibition against the use of Federal-aid funds for racially segregated schools. This prohibition applies to *all* Federal aid. Thus, the role of the U.S. Office of Education in this respect can be treated as a somewhat special case. Aside from this requirement (albeit a substantial one), Federal aid funds provided under these two programs come quite close to being discretionary aid for elementary and secondary education.[15]

4. *Project Aid*   In addition to these three groupings of formula-type Federal grants, there is an additional basic type of Federal aid—project grants. (Project aids can be further subdivided by type and purpose, e.g., demonstration, capital, program.) Project grants tend to predominate at the local level, whereas formula-type Federal aid in most cases is paid to the States. In recent years there has been a decided trend away from formula-type grants in favor of project grants. This applies both to revisions of existing programs and the adoption of new ones. While this trend may be beneficial in certain cases in terms of giving greater discretion and responsibility to the recipient jurisdiction, it has also meant that increasingly Federal-aid programs bypass the States.

To summarize, the four major types of aid instruments discussed here are listed below with key illustrations under each:

1. *Narrowly defined formula-type grants:*
   (*a*) Agricultural experiment stations and extension services.
   (*b*) Various forestry grants-in-aid.
   (*c*) National Defense Education Act (NDEA) title II (instructional equipment and materials) and title V (guidance, counseling, and testing).
   (*d*) Vocational rehabilitation.
2. *Highways and public assistance grants* (formula-type aid in broad functional areas, broken down into specific subcategories within the aided areas).
3. *Broadly defined formula-type grants:*
   (*a*) Title I of the Elementary and Secondary Education Act of 1965.
   (*b*) School aid for federally affected areas.
4. *Project aid:*
   (*a*) Urban renewal.
   (*b*) Public housing.
   (*c*) Open spaces.
   (*d*) Urban transportation.
   (*e*) Neighborhood Youth Corps.

[15]Now that a large, new aid for education program has been enacted, the administration is attempting to reduce appropriations for federally affected areas. Congress has strongly resisted this effort.

The Purpose of Federal Aid

It can be seen from the above history and classification of Federal aids that beginning with the Civil War period the basic concept of most Federal-aid programs has been to *stimulate* as efficiently as possible the achievement of certain fairly narrow Federal objectives. This is clearly true in the case of narrowly defined formula-type grants, the highway and public assistance Federal-aid programs, and most project grant programs. This stimulative character of Federal aid was stressed in the 1955 Kestnbaum Commission Report.

> The grant's widest use has been in *stimulating* the States to launch or expand services for which State and local governments are generally regarded as primarily responsible. National funds and leadership have *stimulated* State and local activity in agricultural education and research, welfare services, public health services, and vocational education, to cite some prominent examples. In some of these fields the States or localities had already made a start before the grant was made. Generally, though not always, the grants have produced notable spurts in State and local action, and the proportion of State and local expenditures to Federal aid has shown a steady and substantial overall increase.[16]

While there is agreement that categorical Federal aids stimulate States and localities to do things they would otherwise not have done, there is no such agreement as to whether this is a good thing. Here, it is useful to quickly review the theoretical underpinnings of current attitudes toward Federal aid and American federalism. One view of American federalism—the traditional or States' rights position—sees Federal-aid programs as tending to undermine the fundamental character of American federalism, in which there are two coordinate levels of government (National and State) each with its own assigned areas wherein it has basic responsibility or sovereignty.[17]

On the other side is an almost diametrically opposite school of thought. It views the achievement of national goals as more important than abstract

[16]Commission on Intergovernmental Relations, p. 125. [Italic added.]

[17]The philosophical base of this position was expressed in the Kestnbaum Commission Report. In its definition of federalism (which Wayne Morse, a dissenting member of the Commission, likened to the "ultra conservative point of view"), the Commission urged that "we should seek to divide our civic responsibilities so that we... *reserve National action for residual participation where State and local governments are not fully adequate, and for continuing responsibilities that only the National Government can undertake.*"

For a current statement of the "conservative" view, the reader is referred to several essays appearing in *A Nation of States, Essays on the American Federal System*, edited by Robert A. Goldwin (Chicago: Rand McNally & Co., 1961). Essays to note are: "What the Framers Meant by Federalism," by Martin Diamond; "The Prospects for Territorial Democracy in America," by Russell Kirk; and "The Case for 'States' Rights,'" by James Jackson Kilpatrick. The reader might also be interested in an essay on federalism by Alfred de Grazia in *The Conservative Papers* (Garden City: Anchor Books, 1964), pp. 228–249. Finally, for a more theoretical statement of the conservative view, see Part I of *Federal Government* by K. C. Wheare (New York: Oxford University Press, 1964).

political principles, like federalism.[18] The Federal Government, States and localities are seen as all working together, and there are therefore no limits as to the areas in which the Federal Government can provide financial aid to both States and localities.

The two proposed new Federal aid approaches discussed next in this paper (tax sharing and the tax credit) are relevant to this basic philosophic difference in attitude on American federalism and Federal aids in that they move in the direction of strengthening the States vis-a-vis the Federal Government. This is particularly true of the tax-sharing approach. It has been supported by Governors and others who favor a stronger role for State governments in American political life. By contrast, those with a more national orientation have tended to oppose this approach. This view was expressed sharply by Christopher Jencks in an article in the *New Republic*.

> The alternative to such idiocy (the Heller-Pechman plan) is to create, at long last, a national government which offers national solutions to the pressing domestic problems of the day.[19]

There is, however, a danger in overstating the philosophical significance of the differences between existing Federal aids and newly proposed broader aid approaches. There is presently underway something of a transformation of Federal-aid policies, deemphasizing the role of Federal grants as a means of stimulating the achievement of narrowly defined Federal objectives. A number of the new aid programs enacted under the Johnson administration provide aid in broad functional areas with considerable discretion to the recipient governmental jurisdiction. Title I of the Elementary and Secondary Education Act of 1965 is an obvious illustration. Likewise, community action project grants under title II-A of the Economic Opportunity Act of 1964 . . . can be used for a broad range of locally determined purposes. . . . Comprehensive plans for the use of community action funds must be approved by the Office of Economic Opportunity; however, local officials have wide discretion as to the types of expenditures for which they can submit applications. And, as already noted, the creation of a new block grant in 1966 by consolidating the old public health Federal aid categories represents a significant internal reform of Federal-aid programs.

. . . [T]he Johnson administration [made an effort] to give broad philosophical expression to these and other shifts in Federal-aid policies. The President in a speech in Ann Arbor, Mich., on May 22, 1964, called

[18]The concept of federalism implicit here was perhaps best expressed by the late Morton Grodzins of the University of Chicago. His definition of the Federal system likened it to a "marble cake, characterized by an inseparable mingling of differently colored ingredients, the colors appearing in vertical and diagonal strands and unexpected whirls." See: Morton Grodzins, "The Federal System," *Goals for Americans*, President's Commission on National Goals (New York: The American Assembly, 1960), pp. 265–282.

[19]Jencks, "Why Bail Out the States?" *New Republic*, Dec. 12, 1964, p. 10.

for "new concepts of cooperation, *a creative federalism.*"[20] While the meaning of "creative federalism" has not yet been fully spelled out, it is said to involve: (1) closer and more cooperative relationships between Federal, State, and local management-level officials; (2) broader and more flexible Federal-aid programs; (3) more reliance on direct Federal-local relationships; and (4) an effort to work through new types of structures, such as area-wide, regional, and public-private administrative units.[21]

The Heller-Pechman plan, the next Federal-aid approach to be discussed, goes much further than the various programs cited above as illustrations of "creative federalism." It did not specify any Federal-aid categories and it did not involve regulations or approval as to the actual expenditure of aid funds. Nevertheless, the above discussed recent Federal-aid policy developments must be taken into account in relating the tax sharing approach to the existing "system" of Federal aids for States and localities.

II. TAX SHARING

Walter Heller's recommendation to President Johnson in the spring of 1964 for supplementary general aid to the States gave the general aid approach greater public visibility than it has had at any time in recent history.[22] As discussed by Heller, his original concept was aid to the States with no conditions attached other than those applying to *all* Federal spending, such as the various Constitutional protections and civil rights laws.[23]

The Heller-Pechman Plan

The Pechman Task Force report to the President, submitted in the early fall of 1964, adhered basically to Heller's concept, althought it apparently

[20]Speech by President Lyndon B. Johnson, Ann Arbor, Mich., May 22, 1964, as cited in an article on "Creative Federalism," *Congressional Quarterly*, Apr. 22, 1966, p. 822.

[21]*Congressional Quarterly*, Apr. 22, 1966, pp. 822–823. See also: Max Ways, "Creative Federalism and the Great Society," *Fortune*, January 1966, pp. 120–123.

[22]Sources of background information on the original Heller proposal and the Pechman Task Force report are:

(a) Edwin L. Dale, Jr., "Subsidizing the States," *New Republic*, Nov. 28, 1964, pp. 33–34.

(b) Robert L. Heilbroner, "The Share-the-Tax-Revenue Plan," *New York Times Magazine*, Dec. 27, 1964, p. 8.

(c) Richard J. Jannssen, "Sharing Revenues," *Wall Street Journal*, Nov. 17, 1964, p. 1.

(d) "Library of Congress Analyzes Tax Sharing," *Congressional Record*, Aug. 25, 1965, pp. A4791–A4793.

(e) Alan L. Otten and Charles B. Seib, "No-Strings Aid for the States?" *Reporter*, Jan. 18, 1965, p. 34.

(f) Tom Wicker, "The Heller Tax Plan," *New York Times*, July 27, 1965, p. 9.

(g) Richard C. Worshop, "Federal-State Revenue Sharing," *Editorial Research Reports*, Dec. 23, 1964, pp. 943–960.

[23]In an interview in June 1964, Heller suggested Federal aid "without Federal control" as one way to relieve "fiscal drag" in the future. *U.S. News & World Report*, June 29, 1964, p. 59.

discussed a number of ways in which broad conditions could be placed on general aid. According to the press accounts, the task force recommended a plan to earmark a fixed percentage of the Federal income tax base to be set aside in a separate trust fund, the revenues of which would be allocated to States as general aid. (The tax base for these purposes was defined as the total taxable income of all Federal individual income taxpayers—approximately $250 billion in 1964.) Although no precise figure was endorsed, the Pechman Task Force is reported to have discussed a fund consisting of 1 percent of the Federal income tax base, which would have amounted to $2.5 billion in 1964 and an estimated $3.5 billion in 1970. This would have meant approximately $13 per capita in payments to the States in 1964.

The allocation system proposed by the task force was to divide the fund into two parts, the first part to be allocated to the States on a straight per capita basis, the remainder to be distributed among the lowest income States for equalization purposes. It was later estimated by Pechman in a speech before the American Bankers Association that—

> even if as little as 10 percent of the total were divided among the poorest third of the States (say, in proportion to population weighted by the reciprocal of per capita personal income), the grant to the poorest States would be almost double the amount it would obtain on a straight per capita basis.[24]

In addition to equalization, the task force apparently considered the inclusion of a tax effort factor. With this adjustment, States making an above average tax effort (measured in terms of State-local taxes relative to personal income) would receive a somewhat higher per capita allocation. States making a below average tax effort would be penalized.

A "pass-through" requirement for local governments has also been widely discussed in recent months. This feature is included in the Goodell bill (described below) and in other Republican and Democratic tax sharing bills introduced in the 90th Congress.

History of the Plan

Since its inception in 1964, the Heller-Pechman plan has had an uneven history. At first, President Johnson appeared to be getting ready to endorse the plan. Toward the end of the 1964 presidential campaign, the White House issued a Presidential statement which said that "intensive study is now being given to methods of channeling Federal revenues to States and localities."[25] In addition to promising "intensive study" of specific plans,

---

[24]Joseph A. Pechman, "Financing State and Local Government," paper prepared for the Symposium on Federal Taxation of the American Bankers Association, Mar. 26, 1965, p. 18.

[25]"Strengthening State-Local Government," Presidential Statement No. 6 on Economic Issues, Oct. 28, 1964, as reprinted in the *Congressional Record*, Aug. 25, 1965, p. A4816. Alan L. Otten and Charles B. Seib in an article in the *Reporter* said that this statement "was commonly interpreted as a Johnson endorsement of the Heller Plan."

the President's statement took a strong position in principle on the sharing of growing Federal revenues with States and localities.

> The National Government, as a constructive partner in creative federalism, should help restore fiscal balance and strengthen State and local governments by making available for their use some part of our great and growing Federal tax revenues—over and above existing aids.[26]

On the day that the Presidential statement was issued (Oct. 28, 1964) the main outlines of the Pechman Task Force report appeared in a page 1 story in the *New York Times*. Thereafter, strong opposition arose from labor groups and Federal officials in the agencies which administer Federal-aid programs and who regard the Heller-Pechman plan as a threat to their long-run program objectives. With this build-up of opposition and apparently unhappy about the premature release of the Pechman Task Force report, the President called a halt to speculation about the plan in mid-December 1964. He indicated at a background press briefing that the plan would be set aside.

Despite the fact that leading State officials (including governors of both parties)[27] have continued to support the basic concept of Heller's proposal, the administration has maintained silence on the Heller-Pechman general aid plan since the end of 1964. There were however two exceptions. Prior to a dinner at the White House for Governors in March of 1965, "informed sources" in the administration indicated that the President would be "receptive" to a plea by the Governors for the plan.[28] More recently,

---

[26]*Ibid.*

[27]Reporting from the Governors' Conference in Minneapolis, Tom Wicker said in the *New York Times*, "Virtually all the harried politicians who serve as Governors of American States liked the idea of the Heller Plan, but many have different ideas of what it is or ought to be." *New York Times*, July 27, 1965, p. 9. At their 1966 Interim Meeting at White Sulphur Springs, W. Va., the Governors again went on record favoring tax sharing. They said, in part:

Resolution No. 1:

"*Resolved*, That at the same time that we continue to work to modernize State and local governmental machinery, we believe it is essential that the Federal Government adopt new Federal intergovernmental fiscal policies which reflect a basic change in emphasis, giving more discretion and responsibility to State and local governments and moving away from the overreliance on national controls under the very large number of existing categorical Federal grant-in-aid programs; and be it further

"*Resolved*, That the National Governors' Conference specifically endorses the principle of tax sharing and the principle of block grants—consolidating existing Federal categorical grants-in-aid—to partially or wholly offset Federal categorical grant-in-aid programs which now exist or may be developed in the future."

Resolution No. 2:

"*Resolved*, That the National Governors' Conference authorize the Committee on State and Local Revenue to develop, in consultation with experts in the field and representatives of local governments, a Federal tax sharing plan for appropriate and timely consideration by the Executive Committee; be it further

"*Resolved*, That this plan include the allocation of additional revenue beyond present levels for use by the States and for distribution by the States to local governmental units."

[28]*New York Times*, Mar. 24, 1965, p. 18.

general aid was discussed in the 1967 Economic Report of the President in relation to post-Vietnam fiscal policy planning activities.

Republican Support for Tax Sharing

Strong pressure for the Heller-Pechman plan has also come from the Republican side. In July of 1965, the Republican Governors' Association and the Ripon Society issued a joint research paper strongly supporting the Heller-Pechman plan and lamenting the President's decision to set it aside.[29] Other Republicans in Congress have supported the plan. Senator Javits of New York, in September of 1965, proposed general aid to the States on the order of the Heller-Pechman plan, but specifically limited to health, education, and welfare purposes.[30] On the House side, Congressman Charles Goodell, chairman of the Republican Planning and Research Committee, proposed a tax sharing plan described briefly as follows:

> ... the sharing of a fixed percentage of revenues from the individual Federal income tax with State and local governments for purposes which would be determined by the recipient governments.
>
> Beginning at 3 percent of the receipts of the tax ($1.8 billion), the amount shared would be increased in steps to 5 percent.
>
> Under this proposal 50 percent of the Federal grant would be allotted to the States for purposes determined by the States, 45 percent would be allotted to States for unconditional allotment to local governments, and 5 percent would be devoted to strengthening State administrative machinery and practices. Local government includes local educational agencies.

Altogether, 25 Republican Members of the House of Representatives introduced some form of tax sharing or general aid legislation in the 89th Congress. This number increased markedly in the 90th Congress (59 bills in the House and 29 Senate Republican sponsorships to date). In all likelihood, this increase was a response to 1966 election gains, which many Republicans interpreted as a widespread voter rejection of the Great Society approach to intergovernmental fiscal relations.

The new popularity of the tax-sharing idea in 1966 is demonstrated by the results of a December 1966 Gallup poll. The poll asked a cross section of the adult population about the plan advanced by Congressman Goodell. Respondents were asked:

> It has been suggested that 3 percent of the money which Washington collects in Federal income taxes be returned to the States and local governments to be used by these State and local governments as they see fit. Do you favor or oppose this idea?

[29]*Government for Tomorrow*, Research Paper Sponsored by the Republican Governors' Association and the Ripon Society, July 1965.
[30]*Congressional Record*, Sept. 22, 1965, p. 23853.

The national results showed 70 percent favoring the plan, 18 percent against and 12 percent no opinion. Among independents, 60 percent favor the plan. The same percentage of support prevailed among the Democratic voters polled.

To be sure, the reemergence of the tax-sharing idea in 1966 was not simply a result of Republican efforts. Significant developments took place on Capitol Hill in the closing months of 1966 which gave bipartisan credence to a growing uneasiness about the rise in the number and specificity of Federal grants-in-aid. Senators Muskie and Ribicoff, both Democrats, conducted hearings in the late fall of 1966 which focused in large part on the problems of fragmentation and duplication in the administration of existing Federal aids for States and localities. Senate Majority Leader Mansfield indicated a similar concern about the impact of Federal aid in calling upon the chairmen of the major Senate legislative committees to give priority attention in 1967 to reviews of the organization and administration of existing Federal civilian expenditure programs.

To summarize briefly, the tax-sharing idea came to new prominence in 1964. It was rejected by the President late in 1964 and languished until the end of 1966. At this point, it reemerged as a major domestic policy issue because of (1) Republican interest in new policy initiatives, and (2) widespread concern about administrative rigidities and lack of coordination under the existing "system" of Federal aids.

III. FEDERAL TAX CREDIT APPROACH

Tax sharing is not the only way in which emphasis can be shifted away from existing particularistic Federal aids in favor of greater discretion and responsibility at the State level. Another means of providing broad financial support to the States is a Federal tax credit for various States and/or local taxes. As opposed to the Federal tax *deduction* for most State and local taxes as currently allowed, a *credit* would give the taxpayer a full dollar in savings for every dollar credited. This approach has been urged by the U.S. Advisory Commission on Intergovernmental Relations (ACIR), and the Committee for Economic Development (CED). The following numerical examples illustrate the effect of an optional credit for 40 percent of State personal income taxes as suggested on a tentative basis by the U.S. Advisory Commission on Intergovernmental Relations in October of 1965.[31]

[31]The ACIR used a 40-percent optional Federal tax credit for illustrative purposes in its report, *Federal-State Coordination of Personal Income Taxes*, October 1965. By optional, it is meant that the taxpayer has a choice between continuing to deduct his State personal income taxes for Federal tax purposes or taking the new credit for 40 percent of these taxes. Presumably, taxpayers in the plus 40 percent Federal personal income tax brackets would do better continuing to take a deduction. For a full analysis of the tax credit as an instrument for aiding State and local governments, see James A. Maxwell, *Tax Credits and Intergovernmental Fiscal Relations* (Washington: The Brookings Institution, 1962).

Numerical Example of the Effect of the ACIR Plan

If a State without an income tax levied a *new* income tax in response to an ACIR-type tax credit which cost a given individual $100, he would actually pay only an extra $60. Forty dollars (40 percent of his State income tax) would be subtracted from his Federal Individual income tax liability. Assume for the moment that his Federal income tax would have otherwise been $1,000. It would not be reduced to $960. His total income tax bill after the credit would now be $1,060 ($960 Federal plus $100 State). This is an increase of $60, yet his State would be far better off by $100.

In a State which already has a State income tax, the individual tax-payer would initially receive a net Federal income tax cut. The cut would be equal to the percentage of the Federal credit (40 percent under the ACIR suggested plan) times his State income tax liability. Total State income tax payments in 1965 were $3.6 billion. Until States with income taxes raised their rates, taxpayers in these States would receive the benefit of Federal income tax reductions totaling somewhere between $0.7 billion and $0.9 billion.

However, the tax credit approach in the eyes of many of its proponents assumes that the credit will be *"picked up"* by the States. Using the same dollar amounts as in the previous numerical example, a taxpayer who initially had $1,000 Federal and $100 State income tax liabilities before the credit could pay $66 more in State income taxes and still have the same total tax liability ($934 Federal plus $166 State) after the 40 percent credit has been put into effect and assuming it was "picked up" by his State.

The ACIR estimated that the net cost of this 40 percent optional credit in fiscal year 1967 would be about $730 million.[32] However, with the assumption that States would respond to the credit by relying much more heavily on income taxes, the cost could go considerably higher. For example, should States respond to the 40 percent credit by levying State individual income taxes equivalent to 3.5 percent of Federal taxable income (a very high rate by comparison), the cost of the credit would be an estimated $4.2 billion in fiscal 1968.[33]

Pros and Cons of the Tax Credit Approach

The main advantage of the ACIR tax credit approach over the general aid approach is that it can be used to stimulate States to rely more heavily on income taxation, which historically has been the least productive of the three broad based State-local tax sources (property, sales, income).

---

[32]U.S. Advisory Commission on Intergovernmental Relations, *Federal-State Coordination of Personal Income Taxes*, p. 117.

[33]*Ibid*. The ACIR calls this 3.5 percent rate assumption "most unlikely." Only a handful of States today have rates approaching this level. See Advisory Commission on Intergovernmental Relations, *Tax Overlapping in the United States 1964*, p. 116, for comparative State data on 1954 and 1964 State individual income tax effective rates.

Today, one-third of the States do not have any personal income taxes, and another third tax personal income at "relatively low effective rates."[34] State individual income tax revenues of $3.6 billion in 1965 accounted for only 14 percent of total State tax collections, excluding employment taxes.[35]

Another advantage claimed for the tax credit approach over the general aid approach is best expressed in terms of the effect of the credit in clarifying "political accountability." States would have to impose and administer their own income tax to derive any benefit from a credit. Thus, it is argued that there would be a stronger incentive to make certain that funds secured as a result of the credit were devoted to priority public expenditure purposes.

A Federal tax credit for a given proportion of State income taxes could also have advantages from the point of view of national tax policy. It would mean that even with a decline in the share of taxes collected at the national level, effective use would continue to be made of income taxation. Proponents of the credit see this as desirable for two reasons: (1) the income tax is more responsive to economic growth than other taxes; and (2) it is an agreed upon and workable means of incorporating a measure of progression into the Nation's global tax system.

Looking at the other side, one of the main general arguments against the credit is that it would not achieve its intended aim of strengthening State-local finances because some States with income taxes invariably would not choose to "pick up" the credit. Instead, they may decide to allow individual taxpayers to take advantage of this new provision, which would mean that in those States the credit would have much the same effect as another across-the-board Federal income tax reduction.

Additional arguments made against the ACIR credit are that it discriminates against taxpayers in nonincome tax States and at the [same] time that it coerces these States into adopting a personal income tax. In income tax States, some taxpayers would receive a net cut as a result of the credit, whereas in nonincome tax States many taxpayers would be forced to pay higher taxes in order for their States to take advantage of the credit.

The tax credit approach as a whole also raises difficult problems from the point of view of the lower-income States. A Federal credit for State taxes would tend to give proportionately greater tax relief to taxpayers in the higher income States because they have more taxable income. While it is possible to devise an equalization factor in the credit, this adjustment tends to make the credit so complex as to be almost unworkable on top of our already complex three-layer tax system.

Since its announcement in October of 1965, the ACIR tax credit

[34]U.S. Advisory Commission on Intergovernmental Relations, *Federal-State Coordination of Personal Income Taxes*, p. 11.
[35]*Ibid.*, p. 39.

proposal has not met with what could be considered wide acceptance, partly because of the disadvantages cited here and partly because it came at a time when increased Federal expenditures and inflationary pressures mitigated against any further programs which would add to the Federal deficit. The latter point, of course, also applies at present to the various tax sharing plans. There is always the possibility that when the Federal budgetary situation permits, the tax credit approach will have more political support than the Heller-Pechman or a similar tax sharing plan. . . .

IV. MODEL CITIES PROPOSAL

An obvious alternative to a new generalized aid instrument concentrating on the States, as in the case of tax sharing and tax credits, is more aid for the cities. For this reason, the background, administrative structure, cost, and rationale of the new model cities program are included in this paper.

On January 26, 1966, President Johnson sent a special message to Congress on "Improving the Nation's Cities." He recommended a $2.3 billion, 6-year "demonstration cities program that will offer qualifying cities of all sizes the promise of a new life for their people."[36] In the designated demonstration areas, the Federal Government would provide financial assistance under existing urban aid programs, *plus:* (1) 90 percent of the costs of planning and development; (2) special supplemental grants of "80 percent of the total non-Federal contributions required to be made to all projects or activities which are a part of the demonstration program and financed under existing grant-in-aid programs"; (3) Federal grants for relocation of families and businesses; and (4) "technical assistance to help carry out these programs."[37]

As to the administration of the demonstration (or model) cities program, the selection process and the role of the "Federal coordinator" in each demonstration area are of central concern. The President in his message listed 14 guidelines for determining eligibility under the new program. Among the most important are that the demonstration should:

—arrest blight and decay in entire neighborhoods;
—offer maximum occasion for employing residents of the demonstration area;
—provide for relocation of residents and businesses;
—be managed by a single agency with adequate powers;
—maintain or establish a residential character in the area;
—be coordinated with overall metropolitan plans, particularly for transportation; and
—maintain a schedule for the expeditious completion of the project.[38]

[36]U.S. Congress, House, *Message from the President of the United States Transmitting City Demonstration Program*, 89th Cong., second sess., Document No. 368, p. 4.
[37]Robert C. Weaver, Statement before the Subcommittee on Housing of the House Committee on Banking and Currency, Feb. 28, 1966, p. 1.
[38]*Message from the President*, pp. 4–5.

In testifying before Congress, Secretary Weaver of the Department of Housing and Urban Development indicated that these guidelines would be strictly interpreted.[39] The Secretary said that about a dozen cities would quickly qualify, and that by the end of 5 years he anticipated that 75 metropolitan areas would be involved covering 60 million people.[40]

Once an application has been approved, the next step would be the appointment of a "Federal coordinator." Referring to the coordinator, the President said in his January 1966 message that he would "assist local officials in bringing together the relevant Federal resources."[41] Secretary Weaver also stressed that the coordinator's role would be to provide "liaison services," and that he would have "no authority over local officials . . . and no power over the programs and activities of that locality."[42] Despite these assurances, many opponents of the program in the Congress concentrated on the centrality and power of the coordinator in the affected areas.

Financing Model Cities

As enacted in November of [1967], the cost of the model cities program (averaging $400 million per year) is well below that of the Heller-Pechman proposal ($2.5 billion estimated for 1964), and is roughly half of the low estimate of the ACIR tax credit ($730 million). Appropriations support has been at even lower levels. Nevertheless, it is quite clear that for the model cities program to achieve its intended long-range objectives will require major infusions of new funds in future years. Various organizations of municipal officials have already gone on record that the originally proposed $2.3 billion, 6-year program is not anywhere near large enough to meet current needs. Mayor Jerome P. Cavanagh of Detroit, in testifying before the Housing Subcommittee of the House on behalf of the National League of Cities and the U.S. Conference of Mayors said, "we should recognize that $2.3 billion is a start—*and nothing more*."[43] The National Housing Conference and National Association of Housing and Redevelopment Officials have also questioned the adequacy of the original $400 million per year figure.[44]

The model cities program is certainly not the same as a general aid plan for cities. Aid is limited to approved urban development projects, and then only in selected cities. However, because this program obviously

[39]*Congressional Quarterly*, Mar. 4, 1966, p. 493.

[40]*United States Municipal News*, United States Conference of Mayors, vol. 33, No. 4, Feb. 15, 1966, p. 14.

[41]*Message from the President*, p. 6. Italic added.

[42]Robert C. Weaver, p. 8.

[43]Jerome P. Cavanagh, statement before the Housing Subcommittee of the House Banking and Currency Committee, Mar. 2, 1966, p. 5. Italic added.

[44]*Nation's Cities*, Magazine of the National League of Cities, vol. 4, No. 4, April 1966, p. 28.

can be very expensive in the long run (thus detracting from the ability of the Federal Government to finance alternative major new domestic expenditure programs) and because it is intended to allow considerable discretion to local officials, it can be viewed as a new Federal-aid policy alternative on much the same footing as the Heller-Pechman plan. This, of course, does not rule out a *compromise*. Federal funds in the future could be provided for the two programs, thus satisfying both the central city and State factions. The types of considerations which must be taken into account in developing such a compromise are discussed briefly in the conclusions of this paper.

V. REGIONAL AID APPROACH

The fifth major Federal-aid policy alternative envisions that neither States nor localities, as such, would receive the lion's share of new Federal-aid funds. The funds would go instead to regional groupings of states and/or counties on a basis patterned after the Appalachia regional economic development program enacted in 1965. Other regions are already moving forward on plans for broad regional development programs. Moreover, should the Appalachia program succeed in its initial phase, there is every reason to anticipate that additional Federal funds would be sought for this region as well.

The Appalachia Plan

As enacted, the Appalachian Regional Development Act of 1965 provides $1.1 billion in new aid for depressed counties in 12 States.[45] Federal aid is designated for several major types of programs, by far the largest amount ($840 million over 5 years) being for highways. Aid is also provided for demonstration health facilities, land improvement and erosion control, timber development, mining area restoration, water resources, vocational education, sewage treatment, and for matching funds under existing Federal grant-in-aid programs.[46]

The supervision and coordination of the Appalachia program is vested in the Appalachian Regional Commission consisting of the Governor of each participating State, or his representative, and a Federal representative named by the President. Decisions in the Commission are made by majority vote of the States with the Federal representative concurring. This, in effect, gives the Federal representative a veto power.

[45]See Jerald Ter Horst, "No More Pork Barrel: The Appalachia Approach," *Reporter*, Mar. 11, 1965, p. 27.

[46]Funds for these programs are authorized for 2 years, whereas the highway funds are authorized for five. Taken together, the planned annual expenditure rate is approximately $200 million per year.

The 1965 EDA Act

In addition to the Appalachia program, the Federal Government has taken steps to encourage the development of the regional approach to economic development in the Public Works and Economic Development Act of 1965. This act extends and replaces the former Area Redevelopment Act. The new act emphasizes regional planning as opposed to the previous approach of relying entirely on individual communities or counties.[47]

Even though the regional approach is regarded as an important part of the 1965 EDA act, the funds involved for regional economic development purposes are small by comparison to the total. Title VI of the act of 1965, which directs the Secretary of Commerce to encourage the development of multistate regional planning commissions, makes an initial authorization for this purpose of $15 million.[48] This is less than .5 percent of the total $3.25 billion 5-year authorization under the Public Works and Economic Development Act of 1965.

It is probably safe to assume that until further experience is gained with these various multistate commissions the Federal Government will be reluctant to make large increases in appropriations for regional economic development purposes. Thus, it may be a while before this approach actually emerges as a major new Federal-aid alternative on a scale commensurate with the Heller-Pechman plan, the ACIR tax credit, and the model cities program.

VI. CONCLUSION

Taking all five of these Federal aid alternatives together, they point up the importance for the future of comprehensive and clearly thought-out post-Vietnam fiscal policy planning.[49] Should "fiscal drag" recur, and should support buildup for devoting additional Federal resources to domestic public expenditures at the State-local level, the need will be to strike some kind of a compromise which is regarded as fair from the viewpoint of the lower income States, the poverty areas of deteriorated central cities, developing economic regions, and the wealthier States as a whole. Tax sharing, model cities, tax credits, regional economic development aid, and expanded reliance on narrowly defined and more traditional types of Federal aids can be combined in any number of ways. It is therefore essential that attention be given on a comprehensive basis to the economic and equity aspects of policy decisions

[47]According to the *Washington Post* (May 14, 1967), the regions moving ahead the fastest on the development of regional economic plans are: New England, the Coastal Plains (North and South Carolina and Georgia), the Ozarks, the Upper Great Lakes, and the "Four Corners" (parts of Utah, Arizona, Colorado, and New Mexico).

[48]*Congressional Quarterly*, Aug. 20, 1965, p. 1635.

[49]It should be noted that [President Johnson] in his 1967 Economic Report called for the establishment of an interdepartmental committee for precisely this purpose, what might be called peace contingency planning.

in this area, as well as to the fundamental political questions raised about the future of American federalism. The amount of Federal aid now being provided to States and localities and the potential for the years ahead (if recent growth trends are any indication) are so large that the failure to plan ahead on a rational basis could result in serious discrimination against certain types of areas, whether it be the lower income States, the core areas of the large metropolitan areas, or some other grouping of States and/or localities.

CHAPTER THREE

THE LAKEWOOD PLAN

RICHARD M. CION

The City of Lakewood, California, presents a perfect example of instant suburbia. In 1950, what is now Lakewood was primarily bean fields. During the next four years, developers transformed the land into a community of 50,000. Its growth was typical of postwar expansion throughout the country. In a pattern repeated over and over, suburbia moved outward, turning farmland into development tracts and crossroads into shopping centers. In Lakewood the bean fields disappeared, on Long Island the potato fields, and outside of Chicago the corn fields; but everywhere the result was the same: new homes appeared to house a predominantly young population. In this sense, Lakewood was a typical community. However, the political conditions in Los Angeles County stimulated a unique response: the contract plan.

Under the plan, cities contract with the County of Los Angeles for a wide range of municipal services (see Figure 1). For example, a city may purchase police protection by reimbursing the County for its costs in providing a patrol car on continuous duty with attendant backup services; or the city may purchase the services of more than one car if it so desires. Thus, the city is given some control over service quality through its power to determine how many units of a given service it will buy. The plan is distinguished from other systems of interlocal agreements by its comprehensiveness; participating cities enter the arrangement with the intention of securing all

Reprinted with permission of publisher, editor, and author from Richard M. Cion, "Accomodation Par Excellence: The Lakewood Plan," in Michael N. Danielson (ed.), *Metropolitan Politics: A Reader* (Boston: Little, Brown and Company, Inc., 1966), pp. 272–80. Mr. Cion studied political science at Princeton. He is a graduate of Harvard Law School, and is currently an attorney associated with the firm of Kaye, Scholer, Fierman, Hays & Handler in New York City.

Figure 1. Services provided to cities by the county of Los Angeles, July 1,1964

CONTRACTS AND RESOLUTIONS	ALHAMBRA	ARCADIA	ARTESIA	AVALON	AZUSA	BALDWIN PARK	BELL	BELLFLOWER	BELL GARDENS	BEVERLY HILLS	BRADBURY	BURBANK	CLAREMONT	COMMERCE	COMPTON	COVINA	CUDAHY	CULVER CITY	DAIRY VALLEY	DOWNEY	DUARTE	EL MONTE	EL SEGUNDO	GARDENA	GLENDALE	GLENDORA	HAWAIIAN GARDENS	HAWTHORNE	HERMOSA BEACH	HIDDEN HILLS	HUNTINGTON PARK
GENERAL SERVICES AGREEMENT		●	●	●	●		●	●		●	●		●			●		●	●	●	●	●	●				●	●		●	●
AGRICULTURAL COMMISSIONER																															
Noxious Weed Abatement																															
ASSESSOR AND TAX COLLECTOR																															
Assessment and Collection of Taxes	●	●	●	●	●	●	●	●	●	●	●	●	●	●	●	●	●	●	●	●	●	●	●	●	●	●	●	●	●	●	●
CHARITIES DEPARTMENT																															
Emergency Ambulance Service		●	●	●	●	●	●	●		●	●	●	●	●	●	●		●	●	●	●	●	●		●	●	●			●	●
Hospitalization of City Prisoners	●							●				●	●	●		●				●	●			●			●		●	●	
CIVIL SERVICE COMMISSION																															
Personnel Staff Services*						●								●											●				●		●
DISTRICT ATTORNEY																															
City Prosecution Services*		●	●	●	●		●	●		●			●	●		●	●		●	●	●	●	●				●	●		●	
ENGINEER																															
Co. Eng. Appt. City Engineer		●	●				●	●		●			●			●			●		●				●			●			●
Building Inspection Services		●	●	●			●	●		●		●	●			●			●		●				●			●			●
Engineering Staff Services*							●	●		●			●			●			●	●					●			●	●		
Industrial Waste Regulation		●	●				●	●		●			●			●			●	●	●		●		●						●
Master House No. Map Service*		●					●	●		●			●			●			●					●							
Sewer Maintenance															●																
Subdivision Final Map Check	●	●	●	●	●	●	●	●	●	●	●	●	●	●	●	●	●	●	●	●	●	●	●	●	●	●	●	●	●	●	●
FORESTER AND FIRE WARDEN																															
Forester and Fire Warden Appt. Fire Chief		●			●		●	●		●			●			●		●			●				●				●		
School Fire Safety Officer																															
Weed Abatement															●																
HEALTH DEPARTMENT																															
State Health Law Enforcement	●	●	●	●	●	●	●	●	●	●	●	●	●	●	●	●	●	●	●	●	●	●	●	●	●	●	●	●	●	●	●
City Health Ordinance Enforcement	●	●	●	●	●	●	●	●	●	●	●	●	●	●	●	●	●	●	●	●	●	●	●	●	●	●	●	●	●	●	●
Mobil Home and Trailer Park Inspection			●	●	●	●	●		●				●		●	●	●	●		●		●	●	●	●	●		●			
Rodent Control	●	●							●					●	●		●					●	●	●	●			●	●		●
LIBRARY																															
Reciprocal Library Services	●																										●				
MENTAL HEALTH DEPARTMENT																															
Mental Health Services																									●						
PARKS AND RECREATION DEPARTMENT																															
Park Maintenance					●																										
Recreation Services			●														●														
Tree Trimming Services*			●				●	●		●			●			●			●	●											

* Resolution Pursuant To General Services Agreement

	INDUSTRY	INGLEWOOD	IRWINDALE	LAKEWOOD	LA MIRADA	LA PUENTE	LA VERNE	LAWNDALE	LOMITA	LONG BEACH	LOS ANGELES	LYNWOOD	MANHATTAN BEACH	MAYWOOD	MONROVIA	MONTEBELLO	MONTEREY PARK	NORWALK	PALMDALE	PALOS VERDES ESTATES	PARAMOUNT	PASADENA	PICO RIVERA	POMONA	REDONDO BEACH	ROLLING HILLS	ROLLING HILLS ESTATES	ROSEMEAD	SAN DIMAS	SAN FERNANDO	SAN GABRIEL	SAN MARINO	SANTA FE SPRINGS	SANTA MONICA	SIERRA MADRE	SIGNAL HILL	SOUTH EL MONTE	SOUTH GATE	SOUTH PASADENA	TEMPLE CITY	TORRANCE	VERNON	WALNUT	WEST COVINA	WHITTIER	TOTAL OF EACH SERVICE
	•		•	•	•	•	•	•				•	•	•		•	•	•	•	•	•	•		•		•	•	•	•	•	•		•		•		•	•	•	•	•	•	•	•		57
																•					•																									2
	•	•	•	•	•	•	•	•	•		•	•	•	•	•	•	•	•	•	•	•	•	•	•	•	•	•	•	•	•	•	•	•	•	•	•	•	•	•	•	•	•	•	•	•	74
	•		•	•	•	•	•				•		•	•		•	•	•		•	•	•	•	•	•	•	•	•	•		•	•	•	•	•	•	•	•			•	•			62
		•	•	•	•	•		•	•		•	•			•			•				•			•					•			•		•			•	•		•	•		•		32
											•	•	•		•		•		•				•			•				•					•					•					15
	•		•	•	•		•	•					•		•	•	•	•		•		•	•	•					•			•					•	•		43
	•		•	•	•		•	•						•		•		•		•	•	•				•	•	•		•			•		•		•	•	29
	•		•	•	•	•	•	•					•	•		•		•		•	•	•				•	•	•		•			•		•		•	•	31
	•		•	•	•		•	•			•		•	•		•		•		•	•	•				•	•	•		•			•		•		•	•	32
	•		•	•	•		•	•					•	•		•		•		•	•	•				•	•	•		•			•		•		•	•	31
				•												•		•		•	•	•				•	•	•		•			•		•		•	•	25
																				•																			2
	•	•	•	•	•	•	•	•	•	•	•	•	•	•	•	•	•	•	•	•	•	•	•	•	•	•	•	•	•	•	•	•	•	•	•	•	•	•	71
	•		•	•	•		•	•					•	•		•		•	•	•						•	•	•				•		•		29
	•																																	1
																•																	2
	•	•	•	•	•	•	•	•	•		•	•	•	•	•	•	•	•	•		•	•	•	•	•	•	•	•	•	•	•	•	•	•	•	•	•	•	73
	•	•	•	•	•	•	•	•	•	•	•	•	•	•	•	•	•	•	•	•	•	•	•	•	•	•	•	•	•	•	•	•	•	•	•	•	•	•	73
		•				•	•	•				•	•	•	•					•	•	•		•	•	•	•					•		•		45
	•		•										•	•	•						•					•	•	•	•	•	•	•	•	•		•	31
	•	•							•				•	•				•				•										•	9
																																	1
																					•						•	•				2
			•	•		•	•													•					•	•						7
	•		•	•	•	•										•		•		•					•	•			•			•	20

CONTRACTS AND RESOLUTIONS

	ALHAMBRA	ARCADIA	ARTESIA	AVALON	AZUSA	BALDWIN PARK	BELL	BELLFLOWER	BELL GARDENS	BEVERLY HILLS	BRADBURY	BURBANK	CLAREMONT	COMMERCE	COMPTON	COVINA	CUDAHY	CULVER CITY	DAIRY VALLEY	DOWNEY	DUARTE	EL MONTE	EL SEGUNDO	GARDENA	GLENDALE	GLENDORA	HAWAIIAN GARDENS	HAWTHORNE	HERMOSA BEACH	HIDDEN HILLS	HUNTINGTON PARK
POUND DEPARTMENT																															
Pound Services		●	●			●		●	●			●			●		●	●	●		●	●	●	●				●	●		●
REGIONAL PLANNING COMMISSION																															
Planning and Zoning Services*			●					●	●					●				●												●	
REGISTRAR OF VOTERS																															
Election Services	●	●	●	●	●	●	●	●	●	●	●	●	●	●	●	●	●	●	●	●	●	●	●	●	●	●	●	●	●	●	●
ROAD DEPARTMENT																															
Road Comm. Appt. City Superintendent of Streets		●						●				●		●		●		●		●		●						●			
Street Maintenance and Construction		●						●	●			●		●		●		●	●	●		●						●			
Bridge Maintenance		●						●	●			●		●		●		●	●	●		●						●			
Street Signing		●						●	●			●		●		●		●		●								●			
Street Light Maintenance	●	●						●	●			●		●		●		●	●	●								●			
Street Sweeping		●						●	●			●		●		●		●		●								●			
Subdivision Engineering		●						●	●			●		●		●		●		●										●	
Traffic Signal Maintenance	●	●			●			●	●		●	●	●	●	●		●	●	●					●				●	●		
Traffic Striping and Marking		●						●	●			●		●		●		●	●									●	●		●
SHERIFF																															
Sheriff Appt. Chief of Police		●	●					●	●			●		●		●		●		●								●		●	
Law Enforcement Services		●	●					●	●			●		●		●		●		●								●		●	
Business License Enforcement		●						●	●							●		●		●											
Maintenance of City Prisoners in County Jail	●	●	●	●	●	●	●	●	●	●	●	●	●	●	●	●	●	●	●	●	●	●	●	●	●	●	●	●	●	●	●
Crossing Guard Service		●						●	●					●		●		●													
Disaster Law Enforcement		●	●					●	●			●		●		●		●		●										●	
Microfilm Storage																							●						●		
Motorcycle Patrol								●	●			●																			
School Safety								●	●																						
Traffic Law Enforcement		●						●	●			●		●		●		●		●											
TAX COLLECTOR																															
Business License Issuance Service		●						●	●			●		●		●		●													
SPECIAL DISTRICTS																															
Fire Protection		●			●			●	●			●		1		●		●		●										●	
Library		●	●		●	●	●	●	●		●		●		●	●				●	●	●		●					●	●	●
Lighting and Lighting Maintenance Districts		●			●	●		●								●				●	●	●		●							
Recreation and Park					●																●										
Sewer Maintenance Districts		●			●			●	●		●			●				●		●		●				●	●				
TOTAL PAGES ONE AND TWO	9	10	38	15	12	18	11	41	41	7	32	11	12	38	13	14	39	10	32	22	32	14	11	16	11	13	29	11	11	22	14

* Resolution Pursuant To General Services Agreement

1 By Contract

INDUSTRY	INGLEWOOD	IRWINDALE	LAKEWOOD	LA MIRADA	LA PUENTE	LA VERNE	LAWNDALE	LOMITA	LONG BEACH	LOS ANGELES	LYNWOOD	MANHATTAN BEACH	MAYWOOD	MONROVIA	MONTEBELLO	MONTEREY PARK	NORWALK	PALMDALE	PALOS VERDES ESTATES	PARAMOUNT	PASADENA	PICO RIVERA	POMONA	REDONDO BEACH	ROLLING HILLS	ROLLING HILLS ESTATES	ROSEMEAD	SAN DIMAS	SAN FERNANDO	SAN GABRIEL	SAN MARINO	SANTA FE SPRINGS	SANTA MONICA	SIERRA MADRE	SIGNAL HILL	SOUTH EL MONTE	SOUTH GATE	SOUTH PASADENA	TEMPLE CITY	TORRANCE	VERNON	WALNUT	WEST COVINA	WHITTIER				TOTAL OF EACH SERVICE
●		●	●	●	●		●	●					●		●	●	●	●		●		●			●	●	●	●							●	●					●	●						38
		●	●	●			●	●					●					●		●					●	●	●	●								●			●			●						21
●	●	●	●	●	●	●	●	●	●	●	●	●	●	●	●	●	●	●	●	●	●	●	●	●	●	●	●	●	●	●	●	●	●	●	●	●	●	●	●	●	●	●	●	●				76
●		●	●	●	●		●	●										●		●		●				●	●	●								●			●			●						24
●		●	●	●	●		●	●									●	●	●	●		●				●	●	●				●				●			●			●						29
●		●	●	●	●		●	●										●		●		●				●	●	●								●			●			●						26
		●	●	●	●		●	●							●			●		●		●				●	●	●								●			●			●						24
●		●	●	●	●		●	●										●		●		●				●	●	●				●				●			●			●						28
●			●	●			●	●										●								●	●	●								●			●			●						20
		●	●	●	●	●	●	●										●		●		●			●	●	●	●								●			●			●						26
●		●	●	●	●	●	●	●									●	●		●		●	●			●	●	●				●				●			●			●	●					38
●		●	●	●	●		●	●			●				●	●		●		●		●				●	●	●						●		●			●			●						31
●			●	●	●		●	●									●	●		●		●			●	●	●	●				●				●			●			●						29
●			●	●	●		●	●									●	●		●		●			●	●	●	●				●				●			●			●						29
●			●	●	●		●										●	●		●		●				●	●	●				●																19
●		●	●	●	●	●	●	●			●	●	●	●	●	●	●	●	●	●	●	●	●	●	●	●	●	●	●	●	●	●		●	●	●	●	●	●	●	●	●	●	●				72
			●				●											●		●						●	●					●				●												13
●			●	●	●		●										●	●		●		●			●	●	●	●				●				●			●			●						27
			●						●			●										●																		●								7
			●				●													●							●												●									8
			●														●			●		●																										6
●			●	●	●		●										●	●		●		●			●	●	●	●				●				●			●			●						,25
							●											●									●									●			●									11
●		●	●	●	●		●										●	●		●		●			●	●	●	●								●			●			●						27
			●	●	●	●	●				●	●	●		●		●	●		●		●					●	●	●	●						●	●		●	1		●	●					41
●	●		●	●	●	●	●			●						●		●				●				●		●				●							●		●	●		●				27
																											●																					3
●		●	●	●			●											●	●	●		●			●	●	●	●				●				●			●			●	●					29
30	8	31	42	37	35	17	41	30	4	7	14	11	15	10	15	13	27	42	13	38	3	37	11	11	22	35	41	38	12	10	7	27	9	10	13	37	10	10	39	12	8	36	16	10				

GRAND TOTAL OF CONTRACTS AND RESOLUTIONS 1553

or most of their municipal services through contracting. The County acts as a clearing house, supplying specified services as they are demanded in the quantities requested by the cities.

At its inception, the Lakewood Plan represented the convergence of three conflicting forces. On the one hand, the older cities in Los Angeles County opposed what they called subsidization of the built-up unincorporated areas by the County's board of supervisors. As in most areas, the Board had been paying for the services rendered to unincorporated areas out of the County's general fund. Simultaneously, the board of supervisors and the County bureaucrats were anxious lest incorporation of large segments of unincorporated territory reduce the size and quality of the County's service establishment. And finally, the unincorporated communities themselves desired control over their own territory. They sought the ability to guarantee the character of their population and the directions growth would take within their boundaries. The Lakewood Plan accommodated all of these various interests. Through incorporation, it gave the unincorporated communities the control they desired. At the same time, it removed the threat that incorporation posed to the County bureaucracy by retaining County services in the areas already using them. And by providing for the incorporation of built-up unincorporated communities, the plan cut the substance out of the older communities' complaints about subsidization; no longer could the League of California Cities complain that its members were bearing the financial burden of rendering services to people living in those communities.

In terms of popular acceptance, the Lakewood Plan is a success. Its clientele regard it with a euphoric mixture of contentment and admiration. One County official says the plan "is a partnership of cities and the County to provide joint services at the least cost while both agencies retain the power of self-determination and home rule."[1] This attitude is echoed by officials and citizens of the twenty-nine cities which depend on contracting for provision of virtually all of their municipal services. Yet, satisfied though its subscribers may be, the Lakewood Plan raises a number of troublesome issues. Plan communities must pay a high price for control over their own destinies. While contracting does provide them with decent services, it also restricts their freedom of action, severely limits the alternatives open to their leaders in many fields, forces them to bargain with the County for changes in policy, and compels them to operate within the rather narrow constraints of the contract plan.

Under the contract arrangement, no unit is capable of acting independently for long; each is tied to the others by the workings of the plan. All of the relevant interests give up a significant measure of independence in return

---

[1]Arthur G. Will, *Lakewood Revisited: Six Years of Contract Services.* A paper presented to the First Annual Municipal Seminar of the California Contract Cities, Palm Springs, California, April 29, 1960, p. 1.

for what they perceive as the values to be derived from participation. Ultimately, the only considerations of importance in the policy making process become those connected with preservation of the system. System-maintenance criteria replace other, more appropriate standards in determining governmental action.

Because the system satisfies their major goals, metropolitan actors do not perceive the sacrifices which they make in order to obtain the benefits of participation. And these sacrifices are real and considerable. Contract cities give up control over their service functions. Consider the case of a County sewer maintenance district coextensive with three newly incorporated contract cities. Unless the three city councils agree on policy matters, one or more of them will be frustrated. In practice, the governing body of the district will tend to ignore the councils and set policy for itself. Or consider the case of the sheriff's department. Every contract relevant to law enforcement contains a "sheriff supreme" clause. In essence, the clause provides that in the event of conflict between a city's views on law enforcement policy and the sheriff's, the sheriff has the final word. The plan is replete with such instances in which cities have no formal opportunity to achieve control over their services while remaining within its framework. And because withdrawal is always expensive and often impossible the cities are forced to remain within that framework.

In some cases, the system does not even let a city find out what its problems are, or permit it to do anything about them if it knows what they are. For example, there is uniform dissatisfaction with the sheriff's system of reporting on police activities to cities. Several city managers have noted that they are unable to determine the extent of their juvenile problem. Moreover, as the contracts are presently drawn, a city could not hire additional juvenile officers if it wanted to. Under the contract plan, a city is unable to initiate or pursue a program directed at some particular problem in which it is especially interested. In part this is an administrative failure and in part it is a flaw inherent in the system. Communications could be improved; indeed steps are being taken to make the sheriff's reporting system more satisfactory. However, as long as law enforcement services are sold on a patrol-car-package basis, there will be no way for a city to attack specific problems—it will be able to hire only the prescribed package of services and will not be able to obtain greater numbers of specialized officers.

Finally, while contract cities have nominal control over service levels, they are unable to establish independent service policy. Only the willingness of the County departments to negotiate disputes and to alter established policy has preserved a measure of local control. As a case in point, in 1958 the sheriff's department agreed to abandon a long-standing prohibition against the use of one-man cars. Until that time it had been the sheriff's practice never to send a man out alone in a patrol car. Several contract cities felt that the sheriff was being unnecessarily conservative and that his policy was increasing the cost of police protection unreasonably. There followed a lengthy debate which ended in a compromise. The sheriff adopted the use of one-man cars during the day shift; the cities were satisfied. Thus a workable settlement was reached after each side had a chance to present its own position and to assess the importance of the issue to the other. The whole incident illustrates the willingness of County departments to negotiate when necessary.

But the statement that County departments are willing to negotiate, and if possible to accommodate the demands of the cities is not identical with the statement that the cities have control over service policies. Quite the contrary, the long and tortuous bargaining behind the sheriff's acceptance of one-man cars did not constitute an exercise of home rule. The city councils involved did not change service policy, rather they used political pressure to induce the sheriff to change policy. There is a vast difference between a city council adopting a resolution to the effect that procedures will be altered in the future and the same council voting to engage in negotiations with the County over future policy.

Cities are willing to give up immediate control over policy because they have to; for most plan cities, the economy of participation was a necessary prerequisite of incorporation. The contract city subscribes to the plan in order to preserve its independent existence and to protect itself from outside encroachment by undesirable groups. Through application of the land-use controls which become available to it upon incorporation, the contract city is able to insure the continuing homogeneity of its residents. Complete control over service policy is the price it must pay for the benefit of incorporation.

When asked about the shortcomings of the plan, contract-city officials observe that they can cancel any agreement upon sixty days' notice. This right, they assert, insures the city's ultimate control. As long as the County's commitment to the arrangement remains strong, and there is no reason why it should not, then the city's right of withdrawal will guarantee its strong position in the bargaining process. However, experience has shown that it is not always easy for a city to cancel a contract when it wishes. In 1958, the newly formed City of Norwalk revised its police service policy. The city administrator, E. Frederick Bien, felt that the sheriff's services were expensive and unresponsive. A resolution to form a municipal police department was proposed and eventually defeated by a three-two vote of the Norwalk council. Interestingly, the decisive vote was cast by the measure's author. According to one councilman, the sheriff applied strong pressure to the group to reject the resolution, a view supported by other knowledgeable observers. In this case, the sheriff used his powerful position in County politics to prevent a city from exercising its formal right of withdrawal from the plan.

One point emerges clearly—a city cannot always withdraw from the contract system if it wants to. Its actions are not internally controlled; rather they are subject to outside political influence, particularly from actors in the County government whose interests lie in the continuation of the status quo. The city's great power in the negotiation process is largely a myth. Moreover, the myth is preserved by County officials for purposes of public relations. As one high-ranking County official observed, if the cities felt they had no control, new cities would fail to subscribe to the plan and the County's interest in its expansion would not be served.

Thus, the cities' drive for independence paradoxically results in a gross restriction of their freedom of action in all fields save one. While left with the ability to control their own land-use patterns, Lakewood Plan communities are unable to set independent policy in other areas. This is the price they pay for the ability to retain their particular character in the face of the rapid growth of the metropolitan area.

City interests are not the only ones subordinated to the maintenance values surrounding the plan. The County's commitment to the arrangement derives from the fact that contracting assures the continued growth of its service departments. However, by supporting the Lakewood Plan, County officials place serious limits on their freedom of action. While the County does have a position of strength relative to contract cities, it would be impractical to use pressure every time a city made a request. Frequent use of pressure would arouse city resistance and would discourage new cities from employing the arrangement. Therefore, County policy is to work whenever possible within the framework of the plan.

This decision implies that the County is ever ready to negotiate its differences with a city and, if necessary, to yield ground in the face of determined requests. It further implies that the County will make all of its resource allocation decisions with contract services in mind. For example, when establishing a new district library, the board of supervisors is likely to put it in a contract city if possible. When constructing a fire station or other facility, it must consider the stability of its contracts with cities in the area. Hence, the County must work under a certain amount of uncertainty; there is always the possibility, however remote, that contracts will be cancelled. In order to minimize the possibility, the board of supervisors tends to be very solicitous of contract cities.

Government in Los Angeles is then carried out by means of a dialogue between the cities and the County. Neither is free to pursue its own interest, yet neither is explicitly aware of the limitations placed upon it. The result is what Roscoe Martin calls a "fluid federalism."[2] All participants work to further their own interests within the rather rigorously defined constraints of the contract plan. The fluid quality derives from the fact that the constitution is continually subject to change by negotiation. But by subscribing to the system, the participants agree to work within its limitations; each

[2]Roscoe C. Martin. *Metropolis in Transition: Local Government Adaptation to Changing Urban Needs*. Washington: Housing and Home Finance Agency, 1963, p. 23.

must curb its own potential in order that the system as a whole will work, and each does so.

In the process, limits are placed not only on city and County interests, but also on the interests of the metropolitan area as a whole. A significant result of the Lakewood Plan has been to stimulate the creation of thirty-one new cities in Los Angeles County. That in itself would be enough to discourage any hope of voluntary cooperation for the solution of regional problems. Moreover, if the character of these new communities is considered, it is immediately apparent that voluntary regional consent on any significant matter is most unlikely. For example, the City of Industry is a bizarrely shaped industrial center. Following the outline of the Union Pacific and Southern Pacific Railroad yards, Industry is a tax shelter for factories and warehouses. In order to meet the minimum population requirement for incorporation (500), the city counted the inmates of an insane asylum. A court challenge to the legality of this procedure was halted before a decision was reached when the plaintiff declared himself no longer interested by virtue of the fact that he had moved out of the area (and into a house somewhat more luxurious than the one which he had occupied at the beginning of the suit). Obviously, Industry is not interested in any scheme which would mean sharing its huge tax potential with the rest of the County.

Industry is neither an extreme nor an unusual case. The cities of Commerce and Santa Fe Springs are similarly composed. Dairy Valley is an agricultural enclave whose population is composed principally of cows. Other cities have their own peculiarities. Rolling Hills is a city without public streets; they are all owned by a private corporation. Hidden Hills is literally a walled city; its residents can close the gates and refuse to let anyone in.

But the proliferation of special interest cities, each an additional veto in the unit-veto system of regional government, is not the only result of the plan. A desperate need in the metropolis is planning for the future—planning for orderly development, for judicious use of resources, and for regional facilities. Each time a new city is launched, the ability of the County's planning organ, the Regional Planning Commission, to meet the challenges of urbanization effectively is further vitiated. Instead, the County, through the Lakewood Plan is forced to implement a variety of local land-use plans, each a design which stresses protectionism, preservation of particularistic values, and ignorance of regional needs. Although the Regional Planning Commission continues to construct master plans for the entire County, it is increasingly powerless to implement them.

Another of the plan's significant products is the subtle alteration it works on the role of County bureaucrats and officials. In most metropolitan areas, if there is a strong central government like a county, the officers of that unit generally have good reason to support area-wide government. Big government is in their interest; they are likely to be the recipients of whatever new powers arise out of metropolitan reform. But the Lakewood Plan has rechannelled County imperialism. Instead of supporting the formation of regional government, the County is committed to the status quo. Because the plan provides a means of insuring the County's position, the bureaucrats' natural tendency to seek widening of their power through a more general government is aborted. They live contentedly within the framework of the Lakewood Plan, their power already secure, their reason for seeking metro gone.

Far from strengthening the impetus toward regionalism, the Lakewood Plan actually vitiates it. By creating new and more aggressive enclaves of particularism in the County, each one protected by the home rule provisions of the state constitution, by strengthening the desire for status quo on the part of county officials, and by making the Regional Planning Commission totally ineffective, the plan builds the first line of resistance against metropolitan approaches to metropolitan problems. Moreover, the plan itself does not attempt to solve these problems. Planning, water supply, transportation, sewage, education, segregation—they are all beyond its scope. In so far as it eliminates the need for more local departments, the plan alleviates some of the duplication of functions which typically wastes metropolitan resources. But it avoids the hard problems. As a system of interlocal agreements, it cannot extend itself to regionalism; it is limited by the extent of consensual patterns among its subscribers.

It is interesting to note that the political system which emerges in Los Angeles County resembles politics in New York City as pictured by Sayre and Kaufman: "a loose-knit and multicentered network in which decisions are reached by ceaseless bargaining among the major categories of participants in each center, and in which the centers are partially but strikingly isolated from one another."[3] Thus, the nation's largest city, New York, and its most diffuse metropolis, Los Angeles, have developed curiously similar distributions of influence out of vastly different environments and institutional arrangements. In both areas, and indeed in all polycentric systems, three characteristics are consistently exhibited: First, by definition, there are many relevant actors, each invested with an independent base of power. Second, government is conducted by negotiation; no one actor is powerful enough to control policy alone, and no group of actors is motivated to unite on a large range of issues. And third, no actor is able to freely and completely pursue his own interest. The only interest which is fully served is that of the system itself; all others are subordinated to it.

[3]Wallace S. Sayre and Herbert Kaufman. *Governing New York City: Politics in the Metropolis*. New York: Russell Sage Foundation, 1960, p. 716.

CHAPTER FOUR

REORGANIZING METROPOLITAN GOVERNMENTS

THOMAS M. SCOTT

As metropolitan areas continue to expand and develop, attention is turned increasingly to governmental reorganization as a way of solving public problems. Most of the standard texts in American state and local government describe the various alternatives: annexation, consolidation, transferring of functions, special districts, "federated metro" proposals, etc.[1] In addition, a growing body of literature discusses the successes and failures of these alternatives in specific metropolitan areas.[2] The casual reader of these works, however, is likely to be struck by the seemingly haphazard manner in which alternatives have been proposed, accepted, rejected, and compromised in various metropolitan areas. What is needed at this point, and what this essay attempts to do, is to offer a tentative explanation of the pro-

[1]For example, see: Charles Adrian, *State and Local Governments* (New York: McGraw-Hill, 1960), chap. 12; Duane Lockard, *The Politics of State and Local Government* (New York: Macmillan, 1963), chap. 16; Russell Maddox and Robert Fuquay, *State and Local Government* (Princeton: Van Nostrand, 1962), chap. 22.

[2]John C. Bollens (ed.), *Exploring the Metropolitan Community* (Berkeley: U. of California Press, 1961); David A. Booth, *Metropolitics: The Nashville Consolidation* (East Lansing: Institute for Community Development and Services, Michigan State U., 1963); Winston Crouch and Beatrice Dinerman, *Southern California Metropolis* (Berkeley: U. of California Press, 1963); John C. Grumm, *Metropolitan Area Government: The Toronto Experience* (Lawrence: Governmental Research Center, U. of Kansas, 1959); Scott Greer and Norton Long, *Metropolitics: A Study of Political Culture* (New York: Wiley, 1963); Roscoe Martin and Frank J. Munger, *Decisions in Syracuse* (Bloomington: Indiana U. Press, 1961), parts 2 and 4; Henry Schmandt, Paul Steinbicker, and George Wendel, *Metropolitan Reform in St. Louis* (New York: Holt, Rinehart and Winston, 1961); Edward Sofen, *The Miami Metropolitan Experiment* (Bloomington: Indiana U. Press, 1963).

Reprinted by permission of the University of Utah, copyright owners, from Thomas M. Scott, "Metropolitan Governmental Reorganization Proposals," *Western Political Quarterly*, Vol. XXI (June, 1968), pp. 252–61. Mr. Scott is Associate Professor of Political Science at the University of Minnesota.

cess of governmental reorganization as it is occurring in the contemporary metropolis.

Once developed, metropolitan governmental reorganization may take many sizes and shapes, but it must come into being either by decision of the official governmental units involved (state legislatures, county boards, city councils, etc.) and/or by voter referendum. Experience to date suggests that relatively minor reorganization is likely to be consummated by the official governmental units while major changes require voter ratification. Experience also suggests that voter approval is hard to come by; indeed, when given the opportunity, voters have often turned down metropolitan governmental reorganization proposals, especially those involving radical change.

The May 1962 report of the President's Advisory Commission on Intergovernmental Relations, *Factors Affecting Voter Reactions to Governmental Reorganization in Metropolitan Areas*, describes efforts to reorganize government in eighteen metropolitan areas between 1950 and 1961 (see Table 1 for summary). Eight or nine proposals, depending on how one keeps score, were accepted by the voters during this period. The rest were defeated. Closer examination of the Commission report reveals important differences between the proposals accepted and those rejected. In all ten cases where voters turned down reorganization plans, significant, indeed radical, changes had been proposed. Five plans involved city-county consolidation which meant total political elimination of the core city and suburban communities.[3]

Table 1   Summary of metropolitan reorganization proposals and their acceptance or rejection

Radicalness of Proposal	Metropolitan Area	Voters Reaction yes	no
Minor Changes	Erie County–Buffalo	x	
	Denver Capital District	x	
	Oneida County–Utica	x	
	Onondaga County–Syracuse	x	
County Reorganization	Lucas County–Toledo		x
Metro–Federated	Cleveland		x
	Miami–Dade County	x	
	Nashville–1958		x
	Nashville–1962	x	
	St. Louis		x
Annex and Federation	Atlanta	x	
Annexation	Louisville		x
Consolidation	Albuquerque–Bernalillo Co.		x
	Durham–Durham Co.		x
	Knoxville–Knox Co.		x
	Macon–Bibb Co.		x
	Newport News–Warwick	x	
	Richmond–Henrico Co.		x

[3]The five were Albuquerque–Bernalillo County, New Mexico, 1959; Durham–Durham County, North Carolina, 1961; Knoxville–Knox County, Tennessee, 1959; Macon–Bibb County, Georgia, 1960; and Richmond–Henrico County, Virginia, 1961.

In three of these cases (Albuquerque, Durham, and Knoxville) the proposal was overwhelmingly defeated in the central city and in the surrounding county areas. In Bibbs County, Georgia (Macon), and Henrico County, Virginia (Richmond), the core cities passed the consolidation proposal, but it was defeated in the suburbs.

Three of the ten unsuccessful attempts (Cleveland, Nashville–1958, and St. Louis) involved variations of the federated-metro scheme which transferred some functions to a metropolitan-wide governmental unit and retained the remainder in the local municipalities. In Cleveland and St. Louis the plan was resoundingly defeated in the central cities and suburbs. In Nashville–1958, the proposal passed in the central city but was lost in the suburbs.

The last two of the unsuccessful reorganization attempts were unique. A basic feature of the Louisville "Improvement Plan" included the annexation of some 68,000 suburban residents to the central city. This proposal, while carrying in Louisville proper, was defeated overwhelmingly in 29 of the 31 suburbs. The Lucas County (Toledo), Ohio, attempt involved a "significant change in the structure of county government." It was voted down by a better-than-two-to-one margin in the central city and in the surrounding county areas.

On the other hand, many of the proposals receiving favorable voter reaction required *relatively* less radical governmental change. Three involved a reorganization of county government, but included strong safeguards for municipal autonomy; ". . . the charter stated that local governmental functions, facilities, and powers were not to be transferred, altered, or impaired."[4]

The 1961 Denver Metropolitan Capital Improvements District involved a metropolitan sales tax to facilitate the financing of capital improvements. It was defeated in the suburbs but carried well enough in Denver to give it the over-all simple majority required by state law. However, the Colorado Supreme Court later declared the enabling legislation under which the plan was passed to be in violation of the Colorado Constitution. The successful Seattle multipurpose district plan of 1958 is a modified and compromised version of an earlier unacceptable proposal, and its powers and functions are in reality quite modest.

Only four of the metropolitan reorganization attempts receiving voter approval appear to involve more or less radical change. In 1950, Atlanta with the approval of both city and county voters succeeded in annexing 87,000 suburban residents as part of the Fulton County Improvement Plan. The consolidation of the two first-class cities, Newport News and Warwick, Virginia, in 1957 appears to be another radical change, especially

[4]The three were Erie County (Buffalo), New York; Oneida County (Utica), New York; and Onondaga County (Syracuse), New York. See Advisory Commission on Intergovernmental Relations, *Factors Affecting Voter Reactions to Governmental Reorganization in Metropolitan Areas* (May, 1962), pp. 45, 59, and 61.

when the name of the newly created unit was to be Newport News. The Miami–Dade County federation and the 1962 metropolitan plan for Nashville–Davidson County are the other two radical reorganizations that have achieved voter approval.

This brief and sketchy review suggests the idea of a continuum based on the degree of "radicalness" of the various metropolitan governmental reorganization proposals. (See Figure 1.)

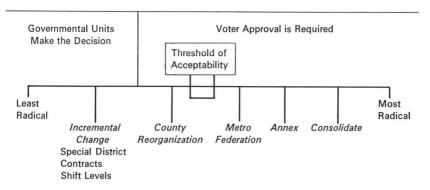

Figure 1   Continuum of radicalness of metropolitan governmental change

On the "least radical" end of the continuum are those proposals involving relatively minor changes, such as intermunicipal cooperative agreements, interunit contracts-for-services, transfers of functions to county and state levels, single-function special districts, etc. As Figure 1 indicates, these reorganizations, while not necessarily uncontroversial, are normally ratified by governmental decision-makers (city councils, county boards, state legislatures).

The more comprehensive proposals are located toward the more radical end of the continuum where state and/or local law requires voter approval. While county reorganization plans such as those in Syracuse, Buffalo, and Utica, are not especially radical and are likely to be ratified at the polls, metropolitan federations, large-scale annexations, and most consolidations represent more drastic change and, with the few exceptions noted, have been turned down by the voters. Experience to date suggests that voters are willing to accept moderate but not radical change. One might say that there is a "threshold of voter acceptability" located somewhere along the continuum of radicalness indicating the point beyond which, generally speaking, citizens are not likely to approve metropolitan governmental change.

Several questions are raised immediately by this formulation. What does it mean to say that some proposals are considered to be more "radical" than others, i.e., what is it about these plans that makes them more radical and thus, presumably, less acceptable? Is the "threshold of acceptability" fixed at a certain point, or does it vary over time and from one metropolitan area to another? How can this analysis explain the "deviant" cases; e.g., Atlanta, Newport News–Warwick, Miami, and Nashville–1962?

A radical reorganization proposal is one that involves (or is perceived as involving) substantial change in existing political arrangements for large numbers of people. It may affect elected, appointed, and civil service governmental positions. It may alter the citizenship status of residents of various municipalities. It may realign governmental services and the existing tax structure. In short, it threatens (or is perceived as threatening) the political-governmental world that citizens, governmental employees and officials, and political leaders have learned to live with and like. They know how the system operates, what to expect from it, and how to function within it. Change threatens their very existence. Thus, suburbs threatened with loss of identity and decision-autonomy, suburban business threatened with loss of patronage, suburban and county officials and employees threatened with loss of jobs and status, central city political leaders threatened with dilution of electoral support, etc., have usually resisted any and all kinds of metropolitan reorganization attempts.

Conversely, support for such proposals has generally come from civic groups, core city newspapers, and ideologically oriented, "good-government" organizations. The campaigns have been waged primarily in the mass media and not in the direct face-to-face, door-to-door style characteristic of hard-fought political struggles. The antagonists of reorganization see the proposals as directly threatening specific elements in their political-governmental lives and are willing to supply the effort needed to insure defeat, while the supporters of such plans, seeing them vaguely as providing a "better day ahead" do little more than reinforce each other through intellectual public debate and the editorial pages of the city newspapers.[5]

In fact, the similarities in the patterns of support and opposition to reorganization proposals in most metropolitan areas lead one to conclude that intensive opposition by actors directly affected is the *normal* way for the political system to respond to such plans. Furthermore, there is every reason to anticipate that this vigorous opposition will *normally* succeed in defeating the lukewarm ideological fervor and activity of the reorganization proponents. Incidentally, it should be noted that this struggle usually bypasses a large portion of the electorate who exclude themselves both from the pre-vote dialogue and from the decision at the polls.[6]

If the "normal" response to radical metropolitan reform proposals is vigorous reaction by those directly affected, ineffectual intellectual-oriented

[5]See especially, Bollens, *op. cit.*, Booth, *op. cit.*, Greer, *op. cit.*, Martin and Munger, *op. cit.*, and Sofen, *op. cit.*

[6]Advisory Commission Report, *op. cit.*, p. 71, shows that the average turnout for the 18 referenda was less than 25 per cent of the voting-age population and none exceeded 41 per cent.

activity by ideologues, and disinterest by most, why have some of these proposals been accepted; notably, Miami, Nashville–1962, Atlanta–1950, and Newport News? And, does this mean that radical change will not occur in other metropolitan areas?

The thesis advanced in this essay is that radical reorganization was possible in these four areas because special or unusual circumstances in each caused them to respond "abnormally" to the reform proposal. In other words, they must be treated as deviant cases and explained separately from what has been identified as the "normal" response pattern. Unfortunately, the literature of political science does not adequately discuss the Atlanta and Newport cases. However, available evidence does support the notion that both situations were unique. By 1950, the city of Atlanta had spread into two counties, Fulton and DeKalb, and much of the suburban population growth was in unincorporated areas surrounding the central city. While the counties were unable to tax the populated areas more heavily, they did provide them with city-level services. A survey conducted at the time indicated that only one area in Fulton County outside of Atlanta paid as much in taxes as it received in services from the county. This meant, of course, that Atlanta taxpayers were paying the lion's share of the cost of city-level services for suburban dwellers, and explains why the suburbanites resisted both incorporation and annexation by Atlanta. Among other things this situation had led to an extraordinary number of formal cooperative agreements between the city and the county in areas such as welfare, water, sewers, courts, libraries, fire, police, schools, bond programs, and hospitals as well as development of a general plan of improvement by the Local Government Commission of Atlanta and Fulton County.

The Commission's plan was a carefully worked out compromise and it avoided the main sources of anticipated resistance by: (1) excluding DeKalb County even though it was an integral part of the developing metropolitan area (because it did not want to be involved in the governmental integration proposals); (2) providing for the annexation of *unincorporated* areas to Atlanta and not disturbing existing municipalities; (3) judiciously dividing and arranging governmental functions and services and carefully providing for the job and salary protection and seniority and pension rights of existing municipal and county employees. The Commission Plan required an advisory election which carried in Atlanta by 90 per cent and in the unincorporated areas of Fulton County by 57 per cent.

The unusual features of the Atlanta case include the substantial development of unincorporated suburban areas and the compromised nature of the integration proposal which undercut the potential opposition of the recalcitrant county, existing suburban municipalities, and city and county employees.[7]

[7]See Lynwood M. Holland, "Atlanta Pioneers in Merger," *National Municipal Review*, 41 (1952), 182.

The Newport News–Warwick, Virginia, case is also unique. In 1950, the peninsula area of Virginia contained five units of local government; the cities of Hampton and Newport News, the counties of Elizabeth City and Warwick, and the town of Phoebus. A referendum to consolidate all five units failed at that time although it carried in Newport News and Warwick County. Subsequently, Newport News continued to annex unincorporated territory and the threat of such annexation led to the consolidation of Elizabeth City County, Hampton, and Phoebus into a new city of Hampton and the incorporation of Warwick County to Warwick City.

In 1956 a citizens' group proposal to consolidate the three remaining units of government failed to receive the required support in each of the units when Hampton defeated the proposal 7,048 to 6,192. The referendum had not received the wholehearted support of the three city councils and in addition there was some opposition to the proposed name of the new complex. (The vote on the integration proposal included a vote on the name as well.)[8]

Following the 1956 defeat with its demonstrated lack of support for integration in Hampton, the cities of Newport News and Warwick voted to consolidate. The referendum, which carried very strongly in Newport News and by 54 per cent in Warwick did *not* include a proposed name for the newly consolidated unit. In a subsequent election the name, "Newport News," was accepted despite some opposition from the citizens of Warwick.[9]

Again, while the analysis of the consolidation struggle is far from complete it is clear that the peculiarities of the geographical situation, the history of slow but steady governmental integration, and the willingness to compromise by excluding the reluctant unit were important conditions that contributed to the ultimate merging of Newport News and Warwick.

By contrast, the other two successful radical reorganizations, Miami and Nashville, have been thoroughly studied. Edward Sofen describes the unique social-political-economic characteristics of Dade County, Florida, at the time the "Metro" federated plan was approved. Tourism was the backbone of the economy, population turnover and mobility were high, community traditions were relatively low, and the number of established municipalities was quite small. Consequently, Sofen notes that

> Miami was able to create a metropolitan government with the very type of support that failed in other parts of the nation because of [these ecological conditions]—particularly the absence of powerfully established political parties, labor organizations, and ethnic groups—and because Miamians have long been accustomed to depend on such non-party sources as the newspapers for political leadership.[10]

[8]Weldon Cooper and Chester Bain, "Three-City Merger Sought in Virginia," *National Municipal Review*, 45 (1956), 443.
[9]See News and Notes, *National Municipal Review*, 46 (1957), 409 and 526.
[10]Sofen, *op. cit.*, p. 86.

Even under these unique circumstances, however, the "Metro" proposal received a slim majority of the 26 per cent of eligible voters participating in the election. One might conclude that any organized opposition such as would be found in a "normal" metropolitan area (labor, parties, municipal officials, etc.) could easily have caused the defeat of the plan. In other words, the success of the reorganization referendum in Dade County is the result of the county's being a unique metropolitan area responding in an abnormal way to the proposal.

The Nashville case is equally unique and interesting. David Booth first describes a normal metropolitan area responding normally in 1958 to a federated metropolitan reorganization proposal. The plan was supported by the city newspapers, the Nashville Chamber of Commerce, the League of Women Voters, the Citizen's Committee for Metropolitan Government, and other similar groups. Furthermore, "no attempt was made to organize a 'grass-roots' organization in support of the proposal. . . ."[11]

> The opposition to the consolidation plan was much more clandestine, remaining largely silent and hidden until about a week before the vote, when it unleashed a bitter whirl-wind attack. The plan was attacked on many grounds and was even alleged to be inspired by the communist plot to take over the world. Spot announcements on the radio were used to urge defeat of the proposal. Leaflets were given out on the streets and on buses and also through the county school teachers to their pupils. Apparently, most of the opposition came from some members of the Quarterly County Court [the county legislative body], from county school teachers' organizations and from private suburban fire and police companies which would have been largely driven out of business with the adoption of the plan. The proposal was also opposed by many suburban merchants and businessmen, who apparently feared renewed competition from the central business district, in the event of consolidation. . . .
>
> As has often been the case elsewhere, the defeat of Metro in the Nashville area was caused by an adverse vote outside the central city.
>
> The defeat was not surprising and, in many ways, was typical of the failures of other consolidation plans. . . .[12]

By 1962, however, the situation had changed radically. The city and county had raised taxes to meet immediate demands. The city had adopted a vehicle tax on all automobiles using city streets in an attempt to force suburban commuters to help finance city services. Needless to say, the county residents were not pleased. Soon after the 1958 metro referendum, the city annexed seven square miles of contiguous industrial and commercial property and in 1960 Nashville annexed 82,000 suburban residents without their approval. The annexations were very unpopular because they deprived the county of valuable human and commercial resources while forcing the

[11]Booth, *op. cit.*, p. 20.
[12]*Ibid.*, pp. 20–21.

original city taxpayers to pay for the upgrading of services required by the newly annexed territories. The annexees were extremely resentful since they did not want to be citizens of Nashville and they regarded the annexations as a "sell-out" by the Nashville mayor and his political organization.

Resentment over taxation and fear of annexation created renewed interest in the federated proposal as a modified way to protect suburban communities. The plan was reintroduced and a vigorous campaign for its adoption mounted. Booth compares the 1958 and 1962 campaigns:

> In 1958, the situation lacked urgency. The question was nebulous and hinged on the desirability of adopting an abstract solution to real and anticipated problems. In 1962, the issues were critical and clear-cut, though they varied for different groups. For the voter in the old core city, the question was whether or not to keep Ben West as mayor. A vote for the Charter was a vote against the mayor.
>
> For the voter in the newly annexed areas, the issue was whether to become a first-class citizen in a new metropolitan government, or to retain the second-class, under-represented status inherent in annexation. Another issue was whether to retain a mayor who had broken his pledge (to give the people a vote on annexation) or whether to drive him from office, in order to choose new political leaders.
>
> For the voter in the rest of the county, there were also two issues: whether he wanted to be liable to annexation at any time, yet receive no guarantee of better services, or whether he wanted to adopt Metro, which guaranteed services within one year.... The second issue was a choice between taxation without representation... (the vehicle tax) and between a new plan, wherein each voter would participate in the election... of the new council....[13]

The final vote was quite different from the outcome in 1958. Voting was heavy; the plan was defeated in the old core city, but won well enough in the newly annexed areas and in the county to assure adoption.

These four case studies support the basic argument of this thesis, namely that voter approval of more radical metropolitan reorganization will occur only in unusual or "abnormal" circumstances. In Atlanta, the final integration proposal represented a carefully conceived compromise that protected as many as possible of the existing social and political interests. In Newport News–Warwick, reorganization came only after a long history of consolidation proposals, defeats, counter proposals, and compromises. In Miami an amorphous social-economic-political structure did not provide the usual basis for organized opposition and the plan was approved by a largely disinterested electorate. In Nashville–1962 strong reaction to a series of political events caused a dramatic change of attitude on the part of city and county voters. The issues changed from the vague ideological speculations

---

[13]*Ibid.*, pp. 86–87.

of the "good government" groups in 1958 to the hard, tough, self-interest motivations of 1962, and in heavy voting the proposal won handily.

By contrast, the studies of the "normal" metropolitan responses to radical proposals (Cleveland, Nashville–1958, and St. Louis) give no indication of unique or special conditions that might have affected and altered the anticipated outcomes. Bollens and Schmandt in summarizing these reform campaigns suggest that "for the most part, the same classes of protagonists, the same evolutionary steps (from study commission, through official charter-drafting board to public vote), the same demographic and political factors, and the same type of public response were present in each instance."

They specify these common patterns: (1) metropolitan reform has been the product of good government groups and has not resulted from grass-roots dissatisfaction or leadership by public officials; (2) the general public is indifferent; (3) mass-based interest groups are rarely committed as either supporters or opponents; (4) major reorganization proposals are unlikely to succeed without organized political support; (5) voters who support metropolitan reform are usually drawn from higher socio-economic categories; and (6) campaigns conducted by good government groups and civic notables seldom establish effective communication with a mass audience.[14]

How then do "normal" metropolitan areas respond to their problems, if, as the evidence suggests, they are not capable of radical reorganization? As most observers have noted, they deal with their problems incrementally, preferring, for the most part, those responses at the "least radical" end of the continuum where voter approval is not required; e.g., single-purpose special districts, contracts for service, shifting functions to other units, etc. These solutions, along with increased federal involvement, mean that problems never develop to the point where they activate and mobilize large-scale public demands. Thus, in the "normal" metropolitan area support for radical change is not sufficient to overcome the active opposition of the various combinations of self-protecting interests and change is therefore relatively undramatic.

However, these facts of metropolitan political life are not necessarily permanently fixed. Indeed, there is evidence of an additional element in the process we have been describing, an element involving intergovernmental "learning." While Toronto, Miami, and Nashville–1962 have been described and explained as deviant cases, they also serve as functioning "showcases" or "experiments" of radical reorganization.[15] Newspapers, educators, associations of public officials and employees, civic groups, etc. become aware

[14]John Bollens and Henry Schmandt, *The Metropolis: Its People, Politics, and Economic Life* (New York: Harper and Row, 1965), pp. 521 ff.

[15]Toronto (and Winnipeg) has not been discussed, but it is here classified as a deviant case because the provincial government developed the federated plan and voter response was not involved in its implementation.

of, study, and disseminate information on these experiments. For example, in the Minneapolis–St. Paul area there is active interest in the Toronto and Dade County plans and various civic groups are supporting travel to these areas so that civic leaders may investigate their virtues on a first-hand basis. Even the experience of defeating such a proposal serves to educate the voting public. Greer cites evidence from St. Louis that suggests a "general friendliness to the notion of future efforts at metropolitan integration," following the 1959 defeat.[16]

As awareness and understanding develop, the radical reorganization proposals may begin to look less and less radical (assuming they do not fail in the experimental communities). Adjustments and compromises designed to fit the peculiar needs of a given metropolitan area may be made, and this may lead to a reduction of fears and perceived threats. If reorganization proposals become less threatening, anticipated opposition may be reduced, shifting the threshold of voter acceptability toward the more radical end of the continuum. When and if this learning and adjustment process occurs, "normal" metropolitan areas may be more likely to adopt major reorganization plans.

To summarize the analysis: normal metropolitan areas with central city–suburban conflicts, competing political parties, interest groups, governmental employees, etc., will tend to respond to governmental reorganization proposals in one of three ways: (1) relatively minor—incremental change will be accomplished without voter participation (depending on state and local law); (2) relatively minor changes requiring referenda will be approved; (3) relatively radical proposals will be defeated by the vigorous opposition of actors directly affected over the ineffective campaigns of ideologically committed "good-government" groups. With few exceptions recent metropolitan reorganization proposals have followed this pattern.

Radical reorganization plans tend to be approved only in areas with unusual social-economic-political characteristics, such as Atlanta, Newport News, Miami, and Nashville–1962. These cases are unique and must be explained as deviations from the normal patterns. However, they are also "living proof" of the viability and, perhaps, desirability of radical change and thus they function as innovators in the common political culture. As more and more individuals and groups learn of the innovation, the norms of this culture may change, resistance may be diminished and voter acceptance may increase. As this learning and diffusing process continues, metropolitan areas with more normal characteristics may find it politically possible to accept relatively radical reorganization proposals.

Practically speaking, this analysis suggests that in the near future radical metropolitan change will continue to win voter approval only under unique circumstances. In the meantime, "normal" metropolitan areas (as most are)

---

[16]Greer, *op. cit.*, p. 163.

will forestall crises by dealing with their problems in a piecemeal manner. Eventually, as awareness grows and new ideas become more widely diffused, what we now regard as innovative will become simply another of the many alternative solutions to modern urban problems and additional metropolitan areas will be more likely to reorganize their governmental structures.

PART TWO

POLITICAL
INTERESTS
AND POLITICAL
ORGANIZATION

Perhaps the cardinal attribute of democratic political systems is that their institutions in some way respond to the wishes and needs of their citizens. These institutions are not normally responsive to *all* public and private issues that are raised, however; nor do they immediately take note of demands registered by *all* individuals. In practice, they tend to be sensitive only to those conflicts that appear to affect a sufficiently large number of intensely involved citizens in a way that makes governmental attention and action appropriate. Obviously, the size of the affected citizenry, the intensity of its feelings, and the legitimacy of governmental concern are not static qualities. The same issue that on one occasion may break through the threshold of public consciousness (itself, an imprecise variable) may on another occasion stir not even a ripple of public interest. A great deal depends upon the resources and perseverance of the groups affected and how they organize to pursue their goals, as well as the nature of the issue involved.

These are some of the matters touched upon by James S. Coleman in his examination of community conflict. Coleman first treats the initiation of conflict, basing his discussion on examples of actual disputes. He outlines the variations in the types of incidents and events that tend to precipitate local controversy, the kinds of interests that are threatened, and the conditions that encourage the emergence of open controversy. He then turns to the dynamics of community conflicts and asserts that, once begun, these conflicts resemble one another to a remarkable degree. Social controversy has a dynamic of its own "which carries it forward in a path which bears little relation to its beginnings." Coleman charts this path, treating, among other things, mid-controversy shifts in the issues in dispute, the emergence of new leaders, the polarization of competing forces, and the formation of partisan organizations.

The selection by Donald R. Matthews and James W. Prothro shifts the emphasis from specific, concrete community controversies to variations in the strengths of political organizations whose function is to dramatize issues and to promote causes consistent with the values, interests, and goals of their members. The authors compare the extent and character of Negro political organization in four pseudonymous southern counties. They find significant differences in the stages of growth and effectiveness of Negro organizations, with the variations dependent in part upon the racial attitudes of whites and their leaders, the extent of economic diversity within the counties, and the nature of the county electoral systems. The effectiveness of these organizations depends in large measure on the closeness of the relationship between Negro leaders and their followers and on the extent of organizational continuity and cohesion.

Political organization is also the concern of Fred I. Greenstein, but his selection deals with the genesis, growth, and decline of the urban political "machine." Greenstein attributes the emergence of these organizations to the rapid population growth of America's cities and to the inability of city governmental institutions to handle either the needs of urban businessmen or the demands of the millions of immigrants who came to the nation's cities. Organizational decline, he suggests, has resulted from a depletion in the rewards old-style politicians have been able to offer and reduced voter interest in the traditional prizes these leaders have had at their disposal. Finally, Greenstein examines the development and impact of two new urban political styles: the politics of nonpartisanship and the ideologically oriented politics of recent reform movements in some major cities.

The tendency of local governments in both "machine" and "non-machine" cities to respond inadequately to the needs of their most disadvantaged residents has led to increased demands that poor people be encouraged to participate more actively in the public and private decisions directly affecting them. The national government's strongest effort to respond to these demands was institutionalized in the Economic Opportunity Act of 1964. Among the Act's most controversial provisions was one calling for "maximum feasible participation" by the poor; in practice, this provision encouraged participating cities to establish local poverty agencies whose elected members could speak for the poor in planning and implementing the federally financed, locally operated anti-poverty programs. One aspect of this step in the direction of greater participatory democracy is treated by Don R. Bowen and Louis H. Masotti. Bowen and Masotti inquire into the personal circumstances of those among the poverty-stricken in Cleveland who sought to represent the poor on the city's poverty agency. The authors find that most of the candidates were reasonably well established in the community they planned to represent, engaging actively in the group life of these communities and possessing many friends and a substantial personal following. The candidates manifested a high degree of trust in others and a willingness to help those with problems, even though they indicated a generalized disillusionment with and resentment toward local government. Finally, the authors suggest that the candidates were not motivated by a well integrated political ideology and, despite a generally optimistic outlook, did not feel that the poor would be well represented on the poverty board. This feeling did not seem to undermine the candidates' faith in representative democracy, however.

The needs of the disadvantaged have shaped the scholarly pursuits of many specialists in state as well as local politics. Recent investigations have considered the extent to which competition between the two major state political parties influences public policy. Some have suggested that states with one-party or weak two-party systems have been inclined to generate politics inimical to the interests of their poorer residents. These observers maintain that states with two strong political party organizations, on the other hand, are more likely to pursue "liberal" policies. Other analysts, including Thomas R. Dye, have argued that the degree of party competition is not so important a policy determinant as a state's socioeconomic characteristics. In the selection reprinted, Dye uses state expenditures in five policy areas (education, highways, welfare, public regulation, and taxation) as measures of a state's willingness to aid the disadvantaged. He finds that four variables associated with "economic development" (urbanization, industrialization, and income and education levels) are more significant influences on policy outcomes than the degree of party competition. Nevertheless, Dye cautions that policies in certain other areas may be affected by party competition, and elsewhere he has noted that the size of the expenditure alone may not be a measure comprehensive enough to evaluate policy outcomes.

CHAPTER FIVE

THE SETTING, INITIATION, AND DYNAMICS OF COMMUNITY CONFLICT

JAMES S. COLEMAN

THE SETTING AND INITIATION OF CONTROVERSY

Community Involvement and Controversy   Everybody knows that there are
no controversies where there is nothing to quarrel about. Yet it is often
overlooked that community disagreements are also a measure of community
life. If communities held only the physical things of existence for their members, there would be no disagreement.

Communities differ widely in the degree to which community life
is important enough to argue about. Within large cities, for example, there is
usually considerably less to involve the residents in civic affairs than there is
in a small, self-sufficient town. In a large city, a man's work is outside his
neighborhood; often his children go to school outside that neighborhood;
and in the extreme case, the neighborhood itself is hardly distinguishable as
a unit. Thus, in the large cities, involvement in controversy is usually least
widespread, often confined to a few activists.

This relationship between the degree of involvement of the members
of the community and the frequency of controversy is not confined to communities and cities. Other organizations exhibit the same tendencies. For
example, when trade unions play an important part in their members'
lives, one finds active internal politics, with lively factional fights, internal
disputes, and challenges from the ranks. "Business unions," on the other hand,
which do no more than carry out wage negotiations, and whose members are
little involved, are quiet, stable bureaucracies with little internal discord.

Reprinted with permission of The Macmillan Company from *Community Conflict* by
James S. Coleman. Copyright 1957 by The Free Press, a Corporation. The author's
footnotes have been omitted. Mr. Coleman is Professor of Social Relations at Johns
Hopkins University.

Even more extreme in their bureaucracy and mass apathy are such voluntary organizations as consumer co-operatives, automobile clubs, professional societies, business associations, and veterans' groups. Such organizations, of only segmental importance to their members, seldom have membership opposition to administrative policies or to a proposed slate of officers. Opposition, if it comes at all, is usually from within the ranks of leaders; there is no controversy on the membership level, merely a "circulation of elites."

Because controversy goes hand-in-hand with membership participation, the recent increase in community disputes should be not only a cause for concern about democratic processes, but at the same time an indication of a continued and perhaps reawakening interest in the local community. It may be that the movement to the suburbs, the increase in leisure time, and the consequent refocusing of life around the home and the neighborhood, have brought people back into community life, both psychologically and physically.

Kinds of Events and the Crises They Create

Not every kind of event which deeply affects people in a community will create a conflict. Communities are beset by many kinds of crises— floods, storms, factory shutdowns, school controversies, vigilantism, political disputes, religious contention, crime waves, etc.—which may result in many kinds of responses, including conflict.

Floods, for example, most often generate united action within a community. An extended drought, on the other hand, might well throw a community into despair; far from uniting, drought defeats, as the dust storms of the thirties defeated the most energetic families and communities of the southwest plains. Economic depression can have a similar effect. The shutdown of a steel plant in Marienthal, a small city in Austria, reduced a lively and active town to an apathetic one whose members were listless and hardly interested in the life of their community.

In contrast, such crises as the Supreme Court desegregation edict, for example, or the floating of a school bond, or the charge "Communist" leveled at a public official, may create real controversy and conflict.

As these examples suggest, the *type of event* helps determine whether a crisis will unite a community, defeat it, or cause controversy. A flood, as we have said, seldom divides a community; it affects all men much the same, pits them all against a common enemy. A school desegregation pronouncement, however, has diverse effects: it affects Negroes differently from whites, parents differently from people without children, prosegregationists differently from those who condemn segregation. Yet the crises are alike in that both permit action. In contrast, there arise problems for which communities have no solutions, such as the Okies' plight in the midst of drought or the Marienthalers' insoluble unemployment problem.

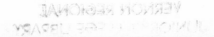

Not only the type of event shapes the nature of the crisis; the kind of community in which it happens is equally important. The charge "subversive" against a schoolteacher will divide some communities into opposing camps, other communities will unite to protect the teacher, while still others will unite against the teacher. Communities have widely different "styles of life" with which they approach problems and these are important determinants of the course of conflict. One author reports that a town faced with the removal of its major plant responded actively and in a unified way, in part because "the people are self-sufficient and self-reliant, supplying most of their own needs and standing on their own feet in the face of emergencies."

Yet the response cannot be wholly explained by a "self-sufficient and self-reliant" people. Two other towns, equipped with similar independence of spirit, responded with bitter internal strife when faced with a seemingly simpler problem: the arrival of industrialization. There are other factors, some psychological, others a matter of social organization. (In the city which successfully met a threatened plant removal the well-organized and active Chamber of Commerce was ready to meet the challenge.) In any case, numerous studies make evident that it is neither the kind of problem facing a community nor the community's characteristics which alone determines the pattern of conflict, but rather a conjunction of the two.

Events and Incidents Which Lead to Dispute

Criteria   If the differences in events and in communities which lead toward unification, division, or defeat are closely examined, the following three criteria become evident in the development of controversy out of an event: (a) The event must touch upon an important aspect of the community members' lives—education of their children, their means of livelihood, religion, taxes, or something similar. Obviously, *different* areas of life are important to different communities, to different people within a single community, and at different periods of time. . . . (b) The event must affect the lives of different community members differently. A tax proposal, for example, affects property-owners one way and non-property owners another. (c) Finally, the event must be one on which the community members feel that action can be taken—not one which leaves the community helpless.

Given these three critieria, then, it is possible to say something about the events which will lead a given community to conflict, to unified action, or to demoralization. But what are some examples of conflict-producing events? A few are listed below:

1. In Northampton, Massachusetts, a controversy over fluoridation of the water supply began after the mayor appointed a commission and, following its recommendation, initiated a plan for carrying out fluoridation. Here the event which set off the controversy was the publication of a complete plan for fluoridation without prior public discussion of the proposal.
2. In other cities (e.g., Cincinnati, Seattle, Williamstown [Massachusetts])

a similar pattern appears: controversy began *after* machinery had been set up to carry out fluoridation.

3. In Norwalk, Connecticut, a controversy arose over the announcement by a community organization (the VFW post) of a plan to report to the FBI the names of those persons in the community whose activities were "not related to a strong America."

4. In Athens, Tennessee, a group of World War II veterans attempted, as a reform group, to wrest political control from the entrenched regime. In other southern towns similar uprisings occurred in the early postwar years.

5. In a number of southern towns which underwent rapid change from rural to industrialized areas, intense industrial conflict occurred. Although the precipitating incidents differ in different cases, the event which really presaged conflict in all cases was the advent of industrialization.

6. In Scarsdale, New York, conflict over books in the public schools began when a local citizen became disturbed over what he felt to be the domestic menace of communism, and besieged the school board with complaints against books in the school library.

7. The Pasadena, California, conflict, which resulted in the ouster of the superintendent of schools, began ostensibly as a fight over a budget and tax assessment for the new school year. It had its real beginnings, however, soon after the superintendent arrived, in a number of small dissatisfactions with his administrative procedure, above all his inaccessibility to powerful persons in the community.

8. Other school controversies are precipitated by varied kinds of incidents. Some began by accusations from local citizens that a superintendent, principal, librarian, teacher, board member, or even P.T.A. member was subversive or suspect, or that "progressive education" was being practiced. In some of these cases, the initial information came from sources outside the community, that is, from one of the right-wing organizations which keep files on persons who have been members of left-wing groups, or from the files of a state or national investigating committee. But in most cases, it appears that the initial charges arose locally and only later, if at all, did material from the outside play a part.

9. Other school controversies began when a speaker with right-wing or left-wing affiliations was invited to the community. Characteristically, heckling occurred during the speech, and the speaker's past associations were revealed in the discussion periods after the speech.

10. A study of community conflict published in 1929 cited several examples of conflict arising when church-building and other activities by one church group in the community offended members of other churches.

11. A study of abandonment of the city-manager plan in four cities indicates that in each of the four, opposition to the plan was organized by a man on the fringe of the local business community who had been rebuffed in dealing with the city council. But this can hardly be called the sole precipitating incident; in all four cities, dissatisfaction had developed over the years, principally among the working class.

12. In one New York town, the Republican city fathers selected the location

of new water wells without going through the forms of democracy. Incensed community members held firmly to their democratic rights and an extended controversy ensued.

13. In Milford, Delaware, Bryant Bowles made inflammatory speeches against desegregation and led the parents, children, and other townspeople into mass picketing. In Clinton, Tennessee, John Kaspar and Asa Carter delivered speeches which provoked a wave of violence against the integration of twelve Negro children into the Clinton high school. All three were outsiders to the communities involved.

Internal and External Sources   These and the other conflicts studied allow some generalizations about the kinds of incidents and events which set off disputes. In the first place, there is a clear distinction between disputes which arise *internally* and those which are a consequence of some *external* incident. The most completely internal include: the fluoridation controversies (1, 2); the political uprising in southern towns (4); the church conflicts (10); abandonment of the city-manager plans (11); and location of the water wells (12). Not only were these incidents set off by community members themselves; the issues involved were purely local. A second group of conflicts were local in origin but fed on national issues: the Norwalk vigilantism (3); the Scarsdale and Pasadena school conflicts, and other school conflicts which centered around local school figures (6, 7, and 8). The incendiary incidents here came from sources within the community, though they did involve nationwide issues. Finally, a group of controversies must be laid primarily to external sources: industrialization in southern communities (5); conflicts resulting from the Supreme Court desegregation ruling implemented by state policies (13); and a few of the school controversies in which persons and propaganda from the outside began the controversy (9, 13).

This, then, is one important difference in the origin of community conflicts. Some need no external issue or incident to set them off, but are generated by processes internal to the community itself. In other cases, the community is more or less at the mercy of the world outside: a national climate of opinion like the recent fear of Communist subversion, industrial expansion or depression, a national law which contravenes the community's mores such as the Supreme Court ruling. This is not to say that a community can do nothing to affect the course of such controversies once they have begun. To be sure, it is a major premise of this report that much *can* be done, whether the conflict arises internally or externally. But when the problem arises from external sources, it is, in a sense, dumped on the community's doorstep.

As one might expect, community conflicts are now more often related to national affairs than they once were. . . . A great many present-day community conflicts—some of those cited above are indicative—have their sources outside the community. Whether we like it or not, the community is less often the locus of important social decisions than it once was. Even though school and church policy are still local matters, and community taxes remain important, the economic fate of a community often rests in the hands of men who have never passed through town. Similarly, there is a continual shrinkage of the jurisdictional areas of community-level laws by state and federal governments which find it necessary to have a consistent policy. Thus, the prospect for the future is toward an increase in the proportion of externally caused community controversies—although there are, and always will be, certain areas of social decision-making which are the province of the community or neighborhood.

The Content of the Issue and the Area of Life It Affects   A second difference among the incidents which set off community disputes is in the area of life they affect. Three general areas can be roughly distinguished.

One is *economic*. Many communities have been split down the middle by economic issues. Whether a matter of livelihood (e.g., the movement of a factory to town), or the payment of taxes, or still a different issue, economic issues are likely to produce strong response.

Power or *authority* in the community constitutes a second important area of life. In the four city-manager disputes which led to abandonment of the city-manager plan, the increasing dissatisfaction with the plan had its origin in certain groups (primarily the working class) which felt in effect disenfranchised. Similarly, in the rebellion of southern veteran groups, the possibility of taking political power away from the machine led the veterans to initiate conflict. The cases are many, but the motives appear to be the same.

Nevertheless, in the struggle for power, often only a few are affected: those who stand to gain office, and those who stand to lose it. The structure of political authority often remains the same, and only those who have something at stake feel their pulses quicken as events lead to a dispute. How the rest of the community becomes involved—and, to be sure, it often does—is another matter, and one which will be treated later.

The third "area of life" is less easily defined, but may be thought of quite generally as *cultural values* or *beliefs*. The current school controversies are most often disputes between conflicting values or philosophies of education; the desegregation disputes are conflicts between two deeply felt beliefs —ingrained attitudes toward Negroes and equally ingrained attitudes toward equality of opportunity. The fluoridation plans which have generated controversy in so many towns apparently touched on values of individualism and anti-scientism in provoking the resistance which has occurred. Differing values and doctrines may also be touched off by religious incidents, though these often include elements of community power and group hostility as well.

Besides these three major "areas of life," there is a fourth important basis on which people respond, deriving from attitudes toward particular *persons or groups* in the community, rather than from attitudes toward an incident, event, or policy. Existing antagonism between individuals, between clans, between ethnic groups, or between other groups in the community can lead people to take sides quickly—to say, "I'm against it because *he's* for it."

Many conflicts which appear to be centered around other issues are in fact a result of the existing hostility between two groups in the community. In such disputes, the particular issue involved can hardly be considered a unit in itself—it is only part of a continuing conflict, periodically active, the rest of the time languishing. These antagonisms are vestiges of previous disputes which often leave the community divided, and thus "load the dice" against peaceful resolution of future problems. The antagonism seems to keep the community alerted, open at any time to new dispute. . . .

There is no suggestion intended that any given community conflict feeds on a single basis of response. On the contrary, often a conflict widens to include many bases of response. Nor is it true that a single incident which sets off a community conflict—say, a school bond proposal—receives all its response from the same source. One side may be largely involved through its economic interests in keeping taxes low; its opponents may be motivated by a particular philosophy of education. Even on the same side, there may be different bases of response for different men: some may be motivated by economic interests, some by a philosophy of education, and still others by a chance for power in the community.

Thus far our implicit approach has been something like this: an incident, event, or problem requiring solution faces a community, and meets differing responses among the members as it touches upon areas of life which act as *bases of response* to the event. These bases of response, primarily economic interests, power, and values, provide the initial dynamics for the controversy. They drive a nucleus of adherents to carry forward the dispute, to expand and intensify it until perhaps the whole community is involved. The dynamics by which this intensification occurs—or fails to occur—will be discussed. . . . At this point, however, it is useful to examine variations in communities, that is, the social conditions underlying the response to one or another kind of incident.

Conditions for Controversy

Differences in Economic Structure   Communities differ widely in their economic systems. Some are self-contained in the sense that men both live and work there. These include towns with small and diversified industry, agricultural towns (which form an economic unit with the surrounding farmland), and one-industry towns. Others are towns in which most men (with the exception of the few merchants and others who provide the necessary community services) live but do not work. Suburban communities provide the best example. (Westchester County communities, for instance, have been called the "bedrooms of New York City.") Finally, there are towns which are largely economic service organs for nonresident groups, e.g., resort towns whose primary industries exist to serve vacationers.

Naturally, different kinds of economically related incidents arise in different kinds of towns and evoke different kinds of response. In economically self-contained towns it is economic disputes which are most common and most intense, for here economic disputes often concern men's livelihoods, not only their taxes or some other ancillary economic issue. Such disputes ordinarily begin within the plant—between workers and management— though they may be initiated by all sorts of incidents.

The diverse and often inconsequential nature of incidents which set off economic disputes suggests that the incident itself is hardly important, that there has already been a strong predisposition to controversy. As students of labor relations well know, the strength of the response is only partly based on economic interests. Often it is compounded by the antagonism generated through the day-to-day relationships of labor and management in the plant. This labor-management antagonism is a special and frequent case of the interpersonal and intergroup hostility which can arise between any two groups in the community. In some agricultural towns, farmer-merchant disputes similar to the quarrels of labor and management have broken out over similarly minor precipitating incidents. The farmers' distrust of merchants, particularly of banks and bankers, parallels the workers' distrust of management. The farmers' response, based both on economic interests and personal hostility, may help a trivial incident blossom into full-fledged conflict.

Thus, towns with a self-contained economy can generate a most intense response to economically related incidents, a response based in part on economic interests, and in part on the antagonism created between different parts of an economic system. Farmers and workers, neither of whom have much control over their economic destinies, are the groups in which this antagonism is most often generated. (Not all controversies originating in economically self-contained towns concern economic matters, of course. Cleavages over values—religion or "subversion"—can split such towns just as they split the suburbs.)

In towns which do not constitute an economic unit, towns where men live but do not work, this kind of division is not generated; controversies set off by economically related incidents seem to be less frequent and less intense. A man who lives in Long Island and commutes to work in New York will not take as the object of his economic frustrations the local merchant, businessman, or his next-door neighbor who works in another industry. It will be his employers, or perhaps "Wall Street financiers," but hardly others within his own community. It is true, however, that *tax* issues can be an important source of controversy in any community. [They seem] to be particularly important, in fact, in suburban communities where a high proportion of residents own their own homes.

The lack of economic class cleavage in many suburban towns does not imply that these towns are free from dispute. On the contrary, a high proportion of the community conflicts receiving national publicity in recent years have arisen in suburbs of large cities. But the incidents which have provoked these controversies, and the bases of responses which have drawn men into them, have often been quite different from those which divide economic classes. These controversies have centered around differing values: educational values, political beliefs, and patriotic concerns. There are several reasons why men who live side by side in suburban communities should hold such different values. One is the great mobility these people have; another is the fact that the communities have often been settled in two or more "waves," creating "old residents" and "newcomers" who are frequently of different age groups, different ethnic groups, and live in different sections of town. Finally, if men commute to work at diverse tasks in a large city, their values may wander apart, with nothing to pull them back within a "range of toler-ance." Suburbanites may live for years next door to someone with radically different views; they mind their own business until some important com-munity decision must be made, or until someone attempts to impose his views on a community institution like the school system.

The third general economic type mentioned—service towns, partic-ularly resort towns—are composed of "natives," a permanent, old-time group, and "outsiders," who are sometimes summer residents, sometimes year-rounders, but who in any case have come to town to rest or play, not to make a living. The responses which are touched off in these towns when an incident arises seem partly a consequence of economic resentments (for the "outsiders" are the primary customers of the "natives"), and partly a consequence of the extreme social barriers which isolate the two groups. . . .

Finally, another variation in economic structure must be mentioned —the variation between towns dominated by business interests and those dominated by political authority (through control of patronage, road con-tracts, and other local governmental contracting). In the latter, found most often in the nonindustrialized south, the absence of industry and the dominance of politics makes concern with politics much greater, and increases the likelihood that politically related incidents will set off controversy.

Thus, towns with different economic structures differ widely in the kinds of economic controversy they generate. At the same time, it can hardly be said that one kind of controversy is specific to a particular kind of com-munity.

Changes in Time   Certain bases of responses are more important at one time than another. . . . In the contemporary conflicts reviewed, none appears to be centered around the church (though there are, to be sure, such controversies still continuing—controversies, for example, over relo-cation of churches in residential areas populated largely by people of different faiths). Religion seems to be a less important value and a less frequent basis of community conflict than it once was. Few communities today, for example, are so split religiously that Baptists and Methodists feel compelled to organize separate banks in a town which can hardly support one bank! . . .

On the other hand, certain institutions, and the values which surround them, are just as strong today as they were thirty years ago. School controversies seem just as frequent . . . if not more so.

Besides long-run value changes, which affect the frequency of certain kinds of controversies, there is perhaps an even more important time effect —short-term changes in the social climate. A national climate of fear and distrust can provide a basis of response for numerous kinds of conflicts. After World War II, fear of Communist subversion acted as a kind of exposed "nerve"; when touched by an incident involving the schools, public health, and a host of other matters, it unleashed intense response. Of the conditions which tend to generate community conflict, such temporary climates of feeling seem to be among the most important. They appear to equip people with a kind of sensitivity to things which would leave them ordinarily unmoved. Often their greatest effect is on people who have been inactive in the community; that is, they bring into the controversy those community members who customarily remain on the sidelines.

Population Shifts and Heterogeneous Values   At some time or another, mass migration may deposit a whole new group of people into an existing community. Often, these newcomers differ from the natives in their "styles of life"; they may have different religions, different cultural backgrounds, different occupations. The resulting "community" consists of two very dissimilar parts, and unless extraordinary measures are taken to integrate them, they can remain distinct groups for as long as a hundred years. Probably the two most outstanding examples of this phenomenon are the New England villages of the nineteenth century whose native Americans faced immigrants of quite different backgrounds, and in our time, the small, quiet, suburban villages outside large cities which are suddenly mushrooming with migrants from the city. Dissimilar as these two groups of communities are in other respects, they are alike in this; and this similarity alone means that some of the same kinds of incidents divide the towns: school appropriations, churches, taxes. Whenever a difference in values and in interests is created by the influx of new residents, it becomes a potential basis of conflicting response and sets the stage for precipitating incidents. . . .

Existing Cleavages: The Residuum of Past Controversy   A final difference which leads some communities to respond to an incident with conflict and allows others to pass it by is the past history of controversy in the community, which may have created mutual antagonisms or fostered unity. We repeat this because of its extreme importance in predisposing a community to respond to *any* kind of precipitating event, be it one of economic interests, of values, or of political power.

General Patterns in the Initiation of Controversy

When a well-developed theory of community conflict is constructed, it will be possible to say much more about the initiation and early stages of controversy. In particular, it will be possible to show how several elements combine to set off a controversy, just as a boy, a match, and a firecracker combine to set off an explosion. Such a theory will show the specific role that each element plays and will make explicit the *different* kinds of elements which help initiate controversy.

One crude example may indicate how valuable this could be for reducing controversy. In a number of recent school controversies (not all, by any means, but the Pasadena and Houston controversies at least), three elements seem to have been crucial in the initiation of the dispute:

(1) the existence in the community of a few extreme activists, who gain moral support, and sometimes information, leaflets, etc., from national sources; (2) the existence of a national climate of fear and suspicion concerning internal subversion; (3) the lack of close and continued relations between school administration and community organizations representing conservative as well as liberal segments of the population.

Evidence (discussed more fully later) suggests that if any one of these elements had been absent, controversy would never have begun. Thus, such controversies, in theory at least, could have been prevented in three ways, that is, through eliminating any one of the three elements. Though the example is crude, it illustrates the potential value of such an approach.

Revolts Against an Administration: The Pattern of Initiation   There is one large class of conflicts which can be thought of as revolts against an administration. These disputes, which include some of the fluoridation controversies, the school disputes cited in the example above, the disputes over continuation of the city-manager plan, and many industrial disputes, are characterized by the following:

(1) *The administration in power becomes the defendant in the controversy which ensues.*

In the fluoridation controversies, this has been the town officials; in school controversies, the school administration (either the school board or the superintendent); in the disputes which led to abandonment of the city-manager plans, it has been the city-manager and usually the council as well; and in industrial disputes, the plant management.

(2) *A few active oppositionists, men who are continually in opposition, oppose the administration. These men are sometimes motivated by the hope of power, but often they are ideologically committed to a "cause."*

In the recent school controversies, these have often been men who are sincerely convinced the schools are subversive, men who are against all modern trends in education, or whose whole political philosophy is far to the right of present-day parties. Though their "causes" may differ, the men are fully dedicated. In labor-management disputes, the "oppositionists" are the active and ideologically-committed union leaders who never relax in their opposition to management. Like the dedicated right-wingers in the school controversies, their opposition to the "regime" is often based on a commitment to a cause which goes far beyond the immediate content of any dispute. In the four city-manager plan abandonments, the opposition leaders were evidently frustrated men on the fringes of the power elite. Their opposition appears to have been based completely on personal hostility and a desire for power. In the fluoridation controversies, the leader seems sometimes to have been a man with a desire for power; nevertheless, the leaders often included men who had little to gain personally but whose political philosophy moved them to oppose fluoridation as an infringement of individual rights.

(3) *A large group exists—often the majority of the people—who are ordinarily inactive, acquiescent to the administration, but not actively supporting it.*

In many school controversies, this is that large segment of the community, neither very liberal nor very conservative, which takes little interest or active part in school affairs. In the fluoridation episodes, the situation has been quite similar; the majority of the population is often apathetic, participating very little in community affairs. In the city-manager disputes leading to abandonment of the plans, voting statistics show that the working-class section of town, constituting the majority of the population, were ordinarily quite apathetic, content to let the city government be elected without voting. (It was the large increase in the *number* of these working-class votes, not in their *distribution*, which accounted for the final abandonment.) In labor-management disputes which became community conflicts, the workers as a whole, in contrast to their leaders, were usually apathetic.

(4) *An active group exists, usually a minority of the population, who continually support administration policies, and who were responsible for putting the administration in office in the first place.*

In school controversies, this includes the P.T.A., the school board, and other laymen who take part in school-community activities. In the fluoridation and city-manager controversies, these are usually the business and professional groups in town, organized and generally active in support of administration policies. In labor-management disputes, this is anyone from foremen on up who supports management within the company, and the community organizations which usually provide support for management from the community as a whole.

(5) *The large passive group, or a part of it,* [(3) *above*] *becomes active in one of two ways:* (a) a change in the general climate of opinion, reinforced by national mass media and by current events, mobilizes certain basic values and dispositions (e.g., patriotism and resulting fear of subversion) which the passive majority has held continuously, but which have been dormant. The current events and attendant publicity act, in effect, to create a completely new atmosphere of suspicion, where values which were well accepted only a short time ago are liable to attack. In this atmosphere, the administration needs to commit only one tiny misstep and the suspicion will be directed against it; it is operating under a set of values antagonistic to those who

brought it into power. (b) The administration commits a series of blunders in matters which are of considerable importance to the members of this passive majority, e.g., circumvention of democratic procedures by a city administration in setting up fluoridation plans or arbitrary exercise of power by management in industry.

Be it changes in a national climate of opinion or changes in the local climate of opinion brought on by specific acts of the administration, the effect is the same: the inactive majority is made ready for action.

(6) *The ideologically-committed, active oppositionist is now able to use this new hostile atmosphere to gain his ends.*

He can now lead the large, mobilized group against the administration and its supporting minority. Seldom are his objectives and values those of the majority, but he uses them for his own purposes while they are active and in opposition to his adversary.

In school controversies, for example, the majority seldom agrees with the educational or political philosophy of the right-wing leader even when it follows him. In the fluoridation controversies, the leaders are often chiro-practors and others on the fringes of the medical profession who have private grudges. In labor-management disputes, the active, ideological union leaders have left-wing political goals quite different from the immediate economic gains of their followers.

This process of initiation of controversy seems to be a very general one, accounting for many of the controversies examined in the literature. The general pattern is revolt against the group in power; the mechanisms through which the revolt occurs seem to be those above. Unfortunately, perhaps, these mechanisms suggest manipulation of the masses by "evil" opposition. But a sophisticated administration often manipulates just as effectively to prevent conflict. For example: In many southern border states, school boards, school superintendents, and city governments co-operated to bring about school inte-gration without incidents and without community conflict. During the period of integration, residents of these communities were asked, in conjunction with a national survey of attitudes toward Negroes, whether they favored integra-tion. Two-thirds of the white population in these areas which had quietly integrated said that they opposed integration. Thus the school and com-munity administration had skillfully initiated a policy—often with apparent widespread public support—which was at variance with the privately ex-pressed attitudes of a majority of the people.

Cases Which Lack One of the Elements   Some incipient controversies, which never really became true controversies or in which the administration was never seriously threatened, demonstrate why *each* initiating element must be present. In Scarsdale, New York, for example, dispute began when one citizen, sincerely convinced that books in the school libraries by Com-munists and leftists were aiding the cause of communism, attempted, first by himself, and then with the aid of a few fellow-citizens (a minister, a psychologist, a college professor, and others), to set up a watchdog committee to advise the Board of Education about books in the school library. After some controversy, during which the major governing organization and other organizations in town stood firmly against this committee, the Board of Education and the school superintendent repudiated all its efforts. At the next school board election, the incumbent members of the board were over-whelmingly re-elected by the community. Although the attacks continued, the opposition was never able to gain concessions from the school board, and the right-wing supporters never constituted more than a tiny minority of the community. At no time was there a divided community; the administration never lost community support.

In Scarsdale, two important elements were present: a national climate of opinion and a dedicated opposition leader. But a third, the passive major-ity aroused against the school, was not. Scarsdale, an upper- and upper-middle-class community, has probably a higher proportion of community members active in its organizations than other towns throughout the country. A close relationship existed between the community and its schools, as meas-ured both in individual interest and in community-school organizations. Thus the formula lacked one major ingredient, the passively acquiescent majority which could be mobilized against the administration. The actively-supporting group . . . was not a minority but the great majority of townspeo-ple.

Similarly, in Denver, Colorado, two of the ingredients which created full-scale controversy in Pasadena and Houston were missing. The climate of opinion existed, but there was no avid right-wing leader to take advantage of it, though there were less radical and less dedicated oppositionists. Also, relations between the school system and the community, though not as close as those in Scarsdale, were close enough that the school's active supporters . . . constituted a large segment of the Denver population.

These cases of controversy which never blossomed into successful revolt indicate the importance of each element in the genesis of controversy.

Patterns of Initiation in Other Types of Controversy   Not all community controverises develop along these lines. Port Washington, Long Island, for example, has been the scene of continual controversy between two factions —one favoring a traditional educational policy, the other a progressive one. Desegregation controversies do not fit this pattern either; here the central issue is the conflict of *new* policy with established community beliefs. Riots like those in Cicero and Peekskill do not constitute revolt against an adminis-tration. Many other controversies, e.g., the continued disputes between new and old residents in Yonkers and other fast-growing suburbs, or the ethnic-related controversies in New England towns, are also quite different. It is clear that the pattern of initiation we have discussed holds only for a certain class of controversy; other controversies follow other patterns. It is one task of a theory of community controversy to make these patterns explicit, to show (much more precisely than we have done) how they *combine* to initiate a conflict. Such a theory would be of considerable value for the practical problems of community decision-making.

THE DYNAMICS OF CONTROVERSY

The most striking fact about the development and growth of community controversies is the similarity they exhibit despite diverse underlying sources and different kinds of precipitating incidents. Once the controversies have begun, they resemble each other remarkably. Were it not for these similarities, Machiavelli could never have written his guide to warfare, and none of the other numerous works on conflict, dispute, and controversy would have been possible. It is the peculiarity of social controversy that it sets in motion its own dynamics; these tend to carry it forward in a path which bears little relation to its beginnings. . . .

One caution is necessary: we do not mean to suggest that nothing can be done about community controversy once it begins. To the contrary, the dynamics of controversy *can* be interrupted and diverted—either by conscious action or by existing conditions in the community. As a result, although the same dynamic tendencies of controversy are found in every case, the actual development in particular cases may differ widely. In the discussion below, the unrestrained dynamic tendencies will be discussed. . . .

Changes in Issues

The issues which provide the initial basis of response in a controversy undergo great transformations as the controversy develops. Three fundamental transformations appear to take place.

Specific to General   First, specific issues give way to *general* ones. In Scarsdale, the school's critics began by attacking books in the school library; soon they focused on the whole educational philosophy. In Mason City, Iowa, where a city-manager plan was abandoned, the campaign against the plan started with a letter to the newspaper from a local carpenter complaining that the creek overflowed into his home. This soon snowballed, gathering other specific complaints, and then gave way to the general charge that the council and manager were dominated by local business interests and had no concern for the workingman.

Most of the controversies examined show a similar pattern. (Even those that do not are helpful, for they suggest just why the pattern *does* exist in so many cases. Political controversies, for example, exhibit the pattern much less than do disputes based primarily on differing values or economic interests. The Athens, Tennessee, political fight began with the same basic issue it ended with—political control of the community. Other political struggles in which there is little popular involvement show a similar restriction to the initial issue.)

It seems that movement from specific to general issues occurs whenever there are deep cleavages of values or interests in the community which require a spark to set them off—usually a specific incident representing only a small part of the underlying difference. In contrast, those disputes which appear not to be generated by deep cleavages running through the community as a whole, but are rather power struggles within the community, do not show the shift from specific to general. To be sure, they may come to involve the entire community, but no profound fundamental difference comes out.

This first shift in the nature of the issues, then, uncovers the fundamental differences which set the stage for a precipitating incident in the first place.

New and Different Issues   Another frequent change in the issues of the dispute is the emergence of quite *new and different* issues, unrelated to the original ones. In the Pasadena school controversy, the initial issue was an increased school budget and a consequent increased tax rate. This soon became only one issue of many; ideological issues concerning "progressive education," and other issues, specific as well as general, arose. In another case, a controversy which began as a personal power struggle between a school superintendent and a principal shifted to a conflict involving general educational principles when the community as a whole entered in. A study of the adoption of the city-manager plan in fifty cities shows that in one group of cities, designated . . . "machine-ridden," the controversy grew to include ethnic, religious, political, and ideological differences. Political campaigns generally, in fact, show this tendency: issues multiply rapidly as the campaign increases in intensity.

There are two different sources for this diversification of issues. One is in a sense "involuntary"; issues which could not have been raised before the controversy spring suddenly to the fore as relationships between groups and individuals change. We see how this operates in an argument between two people, e.g., in the common phrases used to introduce new issues: "I hesitated to mention this before but now. . . " or, "While I'm at it, I might as well say this too. . . . " As long as functioning relations exist between individuals or groups, there are strong inhibitions upon introducing any issue which might impair the functioning. In a sense the stable relation suppresses topics which might upset it. But once the stability of the relation *is* upset, the suppressed topics can come to the surface uninhibitedly. We suggest that exactly the same mechanisms are at work in the community as a whole; networks of relations, however complex, act in the same fashion.

But in many other cases, illustrated best by political disputes, the diversification of issues is more a purposive move on the part of the antagonists, and serves quite a different function: to solidify opinion and bring in new participants by providing new bases of response. Again, this is evident in the two-person argument: each antagonist brings to bear all the *different* arguments he can to rationalize his position to himself and to convince his opponent. Just the same thing occurs in community conflict: each side attempts to increase solidarity and win new adherents from the still uncommitted neutrals by introducing as many diverse issues as will benefit its cause. Both these functions—increasing solidarity among present members, and gaining new members—are vital; the first aids in the important task of "girding for action" by disposing of all doubts and hesitancies; the second gains allies, always an important aim in community conflict.

The issues introduced must be very special ones with little potential for disrupting the group that initiates them. They are almost always "one-sided" in the sense that they provide a basis for response only in one direction, and they gain their value by monopolizing the attention of community members. In controversies where a challenge is offered to an incumbent administration, the issue of "maladministration" is, typically, a one-sided issue; the administration can only offer defense and hope that attention soon shifts elsewhere. In school controversies, the issue of Communist subversion in the schools is one-sided; as long as it occupies the attention of the community, it is to the advantage of school critics. In contrast, the issue "progressive education vs. traditional education" offers no differential advantage to either side (unless, of course, progressive education can be identified by its opponents as "Communistic") until one group can prove to the majority of the community that one approach is better from all points of view. . . .

Disagreement to Antagonism   A third change in the nature of issues as a controversy develops is the shift from *disagreement* to *antagonism*. A dispute which began dispassionately, in a disagreement over issues, is characterized suddenly by personal slander, by rumor, by the focusing of direct hostility. This is one of the most important aspects in the self-generation of conflict: Once set in motion, hostility can sustain conflict unaided by disagreement about particular issues. The original issues may be settled, yet the controversy continues unabated. The antagonistic relationship has become direct: it no longer draws sustenance from an outside element—an issue. As in an argument between friends, a discussion which begins with *disagreement* on a point in question often ends with each *disliking* the other. The dynamics which account for the shift from disagreement to antagonism are two: "involuntary," and deliberate. Simmel explains the involuntary process by saying that it is "expedient" and "appropriate" to hate one's opponent just as it is "appropriate" to like someone who agrees with you. But perhaps there is a stronger explanation: we associate with every person we know certain beliefs, interests, traits, attributes, etc. So long as we disagree with only one or a few of his beliefs, we are "divided" in our feelings toward him. He is not wholly black or white in our eyes. But when we quarrel, the process of argument itself generates new issues; we disagree with more and more of our opponent's beliefs. Since these beliefs constitute *him* in our eyes, rather than isolated aspects of him, his image grows blacker. Our hostility is directed toward him personally. Thus the two processes—the first leading from a single issue to new and different ones, and the second leading from disagreement to direct antagonism—fit together perfectly and help carry the controversy along its course. Once direct antagonism is felt toward an opponent, one is led to make public attacks on him.

Perhaps it would be fruitful to set down a little more precisely the "involuntary" processes which we suggest operate to shift issues from one disagreement to a multitude, ultimately to antagonism. In a diagram it might look something like this:

(1) Initial single issue } → (2) Disrupts equilibrium of community relations } → (3) Allows previously suppressed issues against opponent to appear } → (4) More and more of opponent's beliefs enter into the disagreement } →

(5) The opponent appears totally bad } → (6) Charges against opponent as a person } → (7) Dispute becomes independent of initial disagreement

Men have a strong need . . . for *consistency*. If I disagree violently with someone, then it becomes psychologically more comfortable to see him as totally black rather than gray. This drive for consistency may provide the fuel for the generalization processes in Steps 3 and 4 above.

Apart from these "involuntary" or "natural" processes, the use of personal charges by the antagonists is a common device to bypass disagreement and go directly to antagonism. Sometimes consciously, often unconsciously, the opposing nuclei attempt to reach new people through this means, drawing more and more of the community to their side by creating personal hostility to the opponent. In political disputes the degeneration to personal charges is particularly frequent. V. O. Key notes that in the South, state political campaigns are often marked by candidates' personal attacks on each other. He suggests that such attacks grow in the absence of "real" issues. This seems reasonable since the use of personal attacks may be an attempt to incite antagonism in cases where there is not enough disagreement for the natural processes of conflict to operate. In other words, the attacks constitute an attempt to stimulate controversy artifically—a "short-cut"—by bypassing a stage in the process which might otherwise let the conflict falter. Such actions would seem to occur only when community leaders need to gain the support of an otherwise apathetic community which has no real issues dividing it.

In another group of controversies, focused around certain value differences, the shift to personal attacks is sometimes immediate, and seems to be a result of real disagreement and incipient antagonism. School controversies often begin with personal charges against teachers or principals of moral impropriety, or, more frequently in recent days, subversion. Why is it that personal attacks in these instances succeed in creating immediate hostility within the community, while other kinds of personal attacks are viewed with disfavor by the community, that is, until the late, intense stages of controversy when all inhibiting norms and constraints are forgotten? The reason may be this: When a personal accusation refers to behavior viewed as extremely illegitimate by community members it outweighs the norm against personal attacks. Presumably the community members put themselves in the place of the attacker and say, in effect, "If I knew these things to be true, would I feel right about speaking out publicly?" When the charges concern sexual immorality or political subversion, many persons can answer "yes" to such a question; thus they feel unconcerned about making the kind of attacks that they would ordinarily never allow except in the heat of dispute. These attacks, in turn, quickly create the heat that might be otherwise slow in coming.

Changes in content and character of issues constitutes only one kind of change going on in the development of a controversy; at the same time, the whole structure of organizations and associations in the community is undergoing change as well. The nature of these changes is examined below.

Changes in the Social Organization of the Community

Polarization of Social Relations   As controversy develops associations flourish *within* each group, but wither *between* persons on opposing sides. People break off long-standing relationships, stop speaking to former friends who have been drawn to the opposition, but proliferate their associations with fellow-partisans. Again, this is part of the process of stripping for action: getting rid of all social encumbrances which impede the action necessary to win the conflict. Polarization is perhaps less pronounced in short-term conflicts, and in those in which the issues cut across existing organizational ties and informal relations. But in all conflicts, it tends to alter the social geography of the community to separate it into two clusters, breaking apart along the line of least attachment.

The Formation of Partisan Organizations   In many types of community conflict, there are no existing organizations to form the nuclei of the two sides. But as the controversy develops, organizations form. In a recent controversy in Cincinnati over the left-wing political history of the city planning director, supporters of the director and of the councilman who hired him formed a "Committee of 150 for Political Morality." This Committee used considerable sophistication in the selection of a name and in their whole campaign. Rather than remain on the defensive, and let the opposition blanket the community with charges of subversion, this Committee invoked an equally strong value—of morality in politics—and took the offensive against the use of personal attack by their opponents. This technique constitutes a way in which controversy can be held on a relatively high plane: by invoking community norms against smears, using these very norms as an issue of the controversy. If the norm is strong, it may keep the controversy "within bounds."

In general, as a dispute intensifies the partisans form *ad hoc* groups which have numerous functions while the controversy lasts: they serve as communication centers, as communication becomes more and more important within each side and attenuates between groups; they serve as centers for planning and organizing partisan meetings and other activities; and especially they can meet quickly—in a situation where speed is of utmost importance—any threat or challenge posed by the opposition.

The most common variation upon this theme is the union; in industrial disputes, the union is a defense organization *already* in existence; in a real controversy, it takes on all the aspects of the usual partisan organizations: secrecy, spirited meetings, pamphleteering, fund-raising.

The Emergence of New Leaders   As partisan organizations are formed and a real nucleus develops around each of the opposing centers, new leaders tend to take over the dispute; often they are men who have not been community leaders in the past, men who face none of the constraints of maintaining a previous community position, and feel none of the cross-pressures felt by members of community organizations. In addition, these leaders rarely have real identification with the community. In the literature they often emerge as marginal men who have never held a position of leadership before. A study of the fight against city-manager plans pictures the leaders of the opposition as men personally frustrated and maladjusted. The current desegregation fights have produced numerous such leaders, often young, one a former convict, usually from the outside.

The new leaders, at any rate, are seldom moderates; the situation itself calls for extremists. And such men have not been conditioned, through experience in handling past community problems, to the prevailing norms concerning tactics of dispute.

One counter-tendency appears in the development of these organizations and the emergence of their leaders. In certain conflicts, e.g., in Cincinnati, one side will be composed primarily of community leaders, men of prestige and responsibility in the community. Though such groups carry on the functions of a partisan organization, they act not to lower the level of controversy, but to *maintain* or raise it. As did the Committee of 150 (and the ADA in Norwalk, Connecticut, and other groups in other controversies), they attempt to invoke the community's norms against personal attacks and unrestrained conflict. Sometimes (as in Cincinnati) they are successful, sometimes not.

In the face of all the pressures toward increasing intensity and freedom from normal constraint this last development is puzzling. The source of the reversal seems to be this: in certain controversies (particularly those having to do with the accusation of subversion), one side derives much of its strength from personal attacks and derogation, that is, from techniques which, were they not legitimated by patriotism or sex codes or similar strong values, would be outlawed by the community. Thus, to the degree that such methods are permitted, the attackers gain; and to the degree that community norms are upheld against these methods, the advantage is to the attacked. The more the attacked side can invoke the norms defining legitimate controversy, the more likely it is to win.

Invocation of community constraints is almost the sole force *generated by the conflict itself* which acts in a restraining direction. It is a very special force, which appears to operate *only* under the conditions discussed above. Even so, it represents one means by which some controversies may be contained within bounds of normal community decision-making.

Community Organizations as the Controversy Develops   As conflict develops, the community's organizations tend to be drawn in, just as individual members are. It may be the American Legion, the P.T.A., the church, the local businessmen's association; if its members are drawn into the controversy, or if it can lend useful support, the organization will be under pressure from one or both sides to enter the controversy. This varies, of course, with the nature of the organization and the nature of the dispute.

At the same time there are often strong pressures, both within the organization and without, to remain neutral. From within: if its members hold opposing sentiments, then their disharmony forces the organization itself to remain neutral. And from without: the organization must maintain a public position in the community, which might be endangered by taking sides in a partisan battle threatening to split the community.

Examples of internal and external constraints on community organizations and leaders are not hard to find. In the Denver school controversy a few years ago, the county P.T.A. felt constrained to dissociate itself publicly from the criticisms of the school system made by their retiring president. In Hastings, New York, the positions were reversed: the school administration and teachers remained neutral while a battle raged over the P.T.A. election. Similarly, in the strike in Gastonia, North Carolina, local ministers felt constrained not to take a public position. If they had done so, the course of the strike might have been quite different as religious matters entered in explicitly. In some fights over the city-manager plan, businessmen's associations tried to keep out because the plan was already under attack for its alliance with business interests; and in at least one fluoridation controversy, doctors and dentists were reluctant to actively support the fluoridation plan, singly or as a group, because of possible community disfavor affecting business. In another case, union leaders who had originally helped elect a school board could not bring their organizations to support a superintendent the board had appointed when he was accused of "progressivism" and favoritism to ethnic minorities. Their own members were too strongly split on the issue. Ministers who were in favor of allowing Negro children to use the community house were influenced by the beliefs of influential members of their churches not to take a stand. Even in Scarsdale, which was united behind its school board, the Town Club incurred disfavor with a minority of its members, who supported the school's critics, for taking as strong a stand as it did.

In sum, both community organizations and community leaders are faced with constraints when a dispute arises; the formation of a combat group to carry on the controversy and the emergence of a previous unknown as the combat leader are in part results of the immobility of responsible organizations and leaders. Both the new leader and the new organization are freed from some of the usual shackles of community norms and internal cross-pressures which make pre-existing organizations and leaders tend to soften the dispute.

The immobility of organizations resulting from a lack of internal (or sometimes external) consensus is one element which varies according to the kind of issue involved. This is best exemplified by different issues in national politics: when the issue is an economic one, e.g., Taft-Hartley legislation, groups mobilize on each side of the economic fence; labor unions and allied organizations *vs.* the National Association of Manufacturers, trade associations, and businesses themselves. When the issue has to do with tariffs, the composition of each side is different, but there is still a mobilization of organizations on both sides. Sometimes the issue cuts directly across the organizations and institutions in society, thus immobilizing them, e.g., "McCarthyism," which blossomed such a short time ago. Labor unions never opposed McCarthy—their members were split. The Democratic party never opposed him—its constituency was split. Few of the powerful institutions in the country had enough internal consensus to oppose McCarthy. As it was, he drew his followers from all walks of life and from all levels of society. The cross-pressures resulting from lack of internal group consensus were reinforced by external pressures against opposing McCarthy, for all the values of patriotism were invoked by his forces. Almost the only organizations with neither internal nor external pressure against taking sides were the professionally patriotic groups like the American Legion and the DAR. If the issue had not immobilized labor unions and the Democratic party the opposition to McCarthy would have been much more effective.

The Increasing Use of Word-of-Mouth Communication   As the controversy proceeds, the formal media of communication—radio, television, and newspapers—become less and less able to tell people *as much* as they want to know about the controversy, or the *kinds of things* they want to know. These media are simply not flexible enough to fill the insatiable need for news which develops as people become more and more involved. At the same time, the media are restricted by normative and legal constraints against carrying the kind of rumor which abounds as controversy proceeds. Word-of-mouth communication gradually fills the gaps, both in volume and in content, left by the mass media. Street-corner discussion amplifies, elaborates, and usually distorts the news that it picks up from the papers or the radio. This interpersonal communication offers no restraints against slander and personal charges; rather, it helps make the rhetoric of controversy consistent with the intensity.

Summary

Several characteristic events carry the controversy toward its climax. The most important changes in *issues* are: (a) from specific disagreements to more general ones, (b) elaboration into new and different disagreements, and (c) a final shift from disagreement to direct antagonism. The changes in the *social organization* of the community are as follows: the polarization of social relations as the controversy intensifies, as the participants cut off relations with those who are not on their side, and elaborate relations with those who are; the formation of partisan organizations and the emergence of new, often extremist partisan leaders to wage the war more efficiently; and the mobilization of existing community organizations on one side or the other. Finally, as the pace quickens and the issues become personal, word-of-mouth communication replaces the more formal media. It now remains to examine some of the reciprocal causations constituting the "vicious circles" or "runaway processes" so evident in conflict. These should give somewhat more insight into the mechanisms responsible for the growth of conflict.

Reciprocal Causation and the Developing Dispute

The inner dynamics of controversy derive from a number of mutually reinforcing relations; one element is enhanced by another, and, in turn, enhances the first, creating an endless spiral. Some of the most important relations depend heavily upon this reciprocal reinforcement; if one or more of these cycles can be *broken*, then a disagreement already on the way to real conflict can be diverted into normal channels.

Mutual Reinforcement of Response   Relations between people contain a built-in reciprocity. I smile at you; if you smile back, I speak to you; you respond, and a relationship has begun. At each step, my reaction is contingent upon yours, and yours, in turn, contingent upon mine. *If* you fail to smile, but scowl instead, I may say a harsh word; you respond in kind, and another chain of mutual reinforcement builds up—this time toward antagonism. It is such chains which constitute not only the fundamental character of interpersonal relations, but also the fundamental cycle of mutual effects in controversy. Breaking that cycle requires much effort. The admonition to "turn the other cheek" is not easily obeyed.

The direct reinforcement of response, however, is but one—the most obvious—of the mutually reinforcing relations which constitute the dynamics of controversy. Others, more tenuous, are more easily broken.

The Mutual Effects of Social and Psychological Polarization   As participants in a dispute become psychologically "consistent," shedding doubts and hesitancies, they shun friends who are uncommitted, and elaborate their associations with those who feel the way they do. In effect, the psychological polarization leads to social polarization. The latter, in turn, leads to mutual reinforcement of opinions, that is, to further psychological polarization. One agrees more and more with his associates (and disagrees more and more with those he *doesn't* talk to), and comes to associate more and more with those who agree with him. Increasingly, his opponents' position seems preposterous—and, in fact, it *is* preposterous, as is his own; neither position feeds on anything but reinforcing opinions.

The outcome, of course, is the division of the community into two socially and attitudinally separate camps, each convinced it is absolutely right. The lengths to which this continually reinforcing cycle will go in any particular case depends on the characteristics of the people and the community involved. . . . It is these characteristics which provide one "handle" for reducing the intensity of community conflict.

Polarization and Intensity: Within the Individual and Within Each Side   As the participants become psychologically polarized, all their attitudes mutually reinforcing, the *intensity* of their feeling increases. One of the consequences is that inconsistencies within the individual are driven out; thus he becomes even more psychologically polarized, in turn developing a greater intensity.

This chain of mutual enforcement lies completely *within* the individual. But there is an analogous chain of reinforcement on the social level. As social polarization occurs (that is, the proliferation of associations among those who feel one way, and the attenuation of association between those who feel differently), one's statements meet more and more with a positive response; one is more and more free to express the full intensity of his feeling. The "atmosphere" of the group is open for the kind of intensity of feeling that previously had to remain unexpressed. This atmosphere of intensity, in turn, further refines the group; it becomes intolerable that anyone who believes differently maintain association within the group.

These are examples of reciprocal causation in community conflict, as they appear in the literature of these controversies. They constitute the chains which carry controversy from beginning to end as long as they remain unbroken, but which also provide the means of softening the conflict if methods can be found to break them. It is important to note that these reciprocal relations, once set in motion by outside forces, become independent of them and continue on their own. The one continuing force at work is the drive of each side to win, which sets in motion the processes described above; it carries the conflict forward "under its own steam," so to speak. But reciprocal relations also affect the initial drive, amplifying it, changing it; no longer is it simply a drive to win, but an urge to ruin the opponents, strip them of their power, in effect, annihilate them. This shift in goals, itself a part of a final chain of reciprocal causation, drives these processes onward with ever more intensity.

Gresham's Law of Conflict   The processes may be said to create a "Gresham's Law of Conflict": the harmful and dangerous elements drive out those which would keep the conflict within bounds. Reckless, unrestrained leaders head the attack; combat organizations arise to replace the milder, more constrained pre-existing organizations; derogatory and scurrilous charges replace dispassionate issues; antagonism replaces disagreement, and a drive to ruin the opponent takes the place of the initial will to win. In other words, all the forces put into effect by the initiation of conflict act to drive out the conciliatory elements, replace them with those better equipped for combat.

In only one kind of case—exemplified best by the Cincinnati fight in which one side formed the "Committee of 150 for Political Morality"— "Gresham's Law of Conflict" did not hold. As we have said, it was to the *advantage* of that side—not altruism—to invoke against the opponents the community norms which ordinarily regulate a disagreement.

Yet a rather insistent question remains to be answered: if all these forces work in the direction of increasing intensity, how is it that community conflicts stop short of annihilation? After all, community conflicts *are* inhibited, yet the processes above give no indication how. Forces *do* exist which can counteract these processes and bring the dispute into orderly channels— forces which are for the most part products of pre-existing community characteristics, and may be thought of here as constituting a third side in the struggle. Primarily this "third force" preserves the community from division and acts as a "governor" to keep all controversies below a certain intensity.

In part the variations in these forces in the community are responsible for the wide variation in the intensity of community conflicts. Thus, a conflict which reaches extreme proportions in one community would be easily guided into quieter channels in another.

Certain attributes of the community's leadership, techniques which are used—or not used—at crucial points to guide the dispute into more reasonable channels, also affect the development of conflict. These methods, along with the pre-existing community attributes, constitute the means by which a disagreement which threatens to disrupt the community can be kept within bounds. . . .

NEGRO POLITICAL ORGANIZATIONS IN THE SOUTH

DONALD R. MATTHEWS AND JAMES W. PROTHRO

Political organization and political power tend to go together. Unorganized masses of people have little impact on government action. Few men, no matter how ambitious or talented, are able to achieve enduring political power without the support of an organized following. Indeed, organization and power are so closely associated in America that the terms are often used as if they were synonymous.

This is a mistake. Power has bases other than political organization—wealth, prestige, and knowledge are the most important.[1] But southern Negroes have few of these other resources to translate into political influence. Their greatest potential asset in politics is the vote. And for the votes of Negroes to have a substantial effect on southern politics, they must be pooled rather than chaotically distributed among alternative candidates and policies. To pool them requires organization. Political organization is the best way for "underdog" groups of all sorts—workers, farmers, immigrants, Negroes—to overcome their poverty in other political resources.

The Negroes of the South can rarely use existing political organizations to promote their interests. The state and local political parties, dominated by whites, are in business to win elections in a region where being clearly identified as "pro-Negro" is still political suicide. "Yankees" often express surprise on learning that Republican candidates in the South are as committed to segregation as are their Democratic opponents. If the region's Re-

---

[1] See R. A. Dahl, *Who Governs?* (New Haven, Conn.: Yale University Press, 1961), chs. 19–23, for a discussion of different kinds of political resources.

From *Negroes and the New Southern Politics* by Donald R. Matthews and James W. Prothro, copyright © 1966 by Harcourt, Brace & World, Inc., and reprinted with their permission. Messrs. Matthews and Prothro are Professors of Political Science at the University of North Carolina at Chapel Hill.

publicans are serious about winning elections, they must conform to local attitudes and prejudices. Other voluntary organizations that play a part in southern politics—farm groups, local chambers of commerce, trade or professional associations, unions, and the like—are even more difficult for Negroes to infiltrate. If Negroes are to organize for political purposes, they must create their own organizations.

And they gave. Since *Smith* v. *Allwright* there has been a rapid growth of Negro associations in the South devoted to stimulating and directing Negro political activity.[2] These associations have taken a bewildering variety of forms and have developed at very different rates in different communities. They range in comprehensiveness and effectiveness from a handful of Negro organizations that compare favorably with the nineteenth-century political machines of the northern cities, to sporadic and confused organizations whose endorsement of a white candidate ensures his defeat.

We begin this chapter by examining the development of Negro political organizations in four different southern communities—Crayfish, Bright Leaf, Camellia, and Piedmont counties. This examination should give us an acquaintance with the wide range of organizational forms taken by Negro political groups in the South and an understanding of the conditions that must exist before Negro political organization can emerge. For, although Negroes must have organization to achieve political power, their chances of developing an effective organization depend heavily on the characteristics of the community in which the organization must operate.

NEGROES WITH NO ORGANIZATIONAL SUPPORT

Negroes in Crayfish County have no formal organization that could be described as even incidentally concerned with politics. The basic resource on which a political organization normally relies is the voting strength the organization can command. If an entire group is excluded from the franchise, it can hardly be expected to develop political organizations—unable to offer rewards or threats, it has nothing with which to bargain.[3] Any effort by Crayfish Negroes to establish a political organization would be taken as a revolutionary threat to the "closed society" of Crayfish County.[4] One elderly Negro leader, when asked about his organizational affiliations, proudly explained that he was a Mason, but he quickly added, "We never talk about voting and things like that at our meetings"!

In this atmosphere the few efforts Negroes have made toward polit-

---

[2]For a description of this early period see A. Heard, *A Two-Party South?* (Chapel Hill, N.C.: University of North Carolina Press, 1952), ch. 14.

[3]Of course, it could pose threats outside the formal channels of politics—through mass boycotts or demonstrations, for example. The lack of militancy among Crayfish's Negro leaders and the extreme hostility of local whites make this tactic most unlikely.

[4]The phrase was coined by James W. Silver, *Mississippi: The Closed Society* (New York: Harcourt, Brace & World, 1964).

ical organizations have assumed the form of underground conspiracies. Early in the 1950's Crayfish members of the NAACP invited a Negro attorney from a neighboring state to conduct classes on voter registration for Crayfish residents. The obstacles were monumental. Getting people to come to civic meetings is difficult enough when the meetings are well publicized, but these registration classes had to be kept secret from the whites! As a result, no sample registration forms could be secured, the site of the classes was changed from one meeting to the next, and the meetings were called at irregular intervals. Nevertheless, about 300 Negroes were trained over a three-year period.

Nothing could appear less blameworthy in most parts of the United States than classes for prospective voters. But in Crayfish County holding such classes was like trying to organize a new political party in the Soviet Union or trying to plan a jailbreak from Leavenworth. The training sessions ended when some whites learned about the classes from their Negro employees. The whites threatened to break up the meeting, and the visiting attorney escaped harm only when several domestics got help from the white housewives for whom they worked. Such incipient organization as the classes had inspired dissipated immediately. Indeed, the effort had probably been doomed from the outset. If Negroes could not openly conduct classes on registration procedures, they could hardly take advantage of the instruction they received. Prospective voters at that time had to pay a poll tax to the county sheriff, and in order to register they had to appear before the clerk of the criminal court; both officials would have assumed their roles as law enforcement officers if Negroes had approached them in their role as electoral officials.

Shortly after the Supreme Court declared state-enforced segregation in public schools unconstitutional in 1954, five Crayfish Negroes filed a petition with the school board seeking to get their children admitted to the white school. The action was ill organized—apparently a desperate gamble by a few individuals who entertained the wild hope that Supreme Court decisions might be respected even in Crayfish. They were quickly disabused of this notion. Crayfish whites, unaccustomed to formal demands from local Negroes, perceived the "threat" in highly unrealistic terms. They reacted as if they expected the Negro children to appear at the white school the next morning, without waiting for the school board to act on the petition, for court orders, for assignment to classrooms, or for any of the other procedures that would be required before the Negro children could transfer to the white school. The morning after the petition was filed, a number of heavily armed whites gathered around the school in automobiles. No Negro children appeared; nor have any appeared yet.

The show of force by whites seems ridiculous. No knowledgeable person should have expected Negro children to arrive at the school before any action had been taken on their petition. But if its purpose was to frighten the Negroes into withdrawing their petition, it was a well-conceived stratagem. Each of the Negro petitioners withdrew his name, claiming that he had been misled into signing what he thought was a request for the improvement of Negro schools. This self-debasement was also functional: for the white community, because it permitted them to continue thinking that "our" Negroes prefer segregation, even though care must be taken to keep them from being duped by outsiders; for the Negroes, because they suffered no physical harm. Well after the incident had been settled, the chairman of the county school board was willing to be frank. "They claimed they thought they were just petitioning for better schools," he said, "but they knew damn well what they were petitioning for."

NAACP activity in Crayfish County is necessarily covert. Even suspicious attire may be taken as evidence of membership. The president of the county board of supervisors, for example, learned that the justice department was planning to file a suit against the Crayfish registrar because not a single Negro appeared on the voting lists. He decided that he knew "a good nigger" who could be allowed to register and drove out to talk with him about it one Sunday. The Negro, when summoned,[5] came out of his house wearing a suit and necktie. The county official asked where he was going "all dressed up" like that, and the erstwhile "good" Negro lost his chance for the franchise by saying that he was going to visit his sister in a neighboring state. "When I go to see my sister I don't get all dressed up," the official charged. He concluded that the Negro must have been planning to attend a district meeting of the NAACP.

What harm comes to a Negro who is discovered to be a member of the NAACP? No direct evidence was secured on this question. "There have been a few niggers killed here in Crayfish," the president of the board of supervisors reported, "but they weren't killed by *responsible* people." Most white leaders emphasized the lack of violence in Crayfish. Indeed, this emphasis was so strong and distinctive as to suggest that an absence of violence cannot be taken for granted in Crayfish as it can be, for the most part, in the other three communities. Whatever the sanctions, Negroes seem to regard the accusation of NAACP membership with great trepidation. The president of the board of supervisors, explaining his role as a true friend of the Negro, said, "A nigger came to me yesterday—he had been accused of belonging to the NAACP by a white man, and he was right tore up by it. He had attended a meeting, but when he discovered it was an NAACP meeting, he left. He had never told me a lie before, so I straightened it out. . . ."

Another futile effort to organize Crayfish Negroes occurred in 1961. A representative of the Student Non-violent Coordinating Committee held

[5]Whites in Crayfish do not normally enter Negroes' homes; they call them out for conversation.

registration classes for Negroes, and this time the whites did not learn about the effort until the instructor appeared with two of his students before the registrar. . . . [T]he SNCC representative was clubbed with a pistol and arrested for disturbing the peace. The local Negroes did not succeed in registering, and no more efforts in that direction were taken until after a federal registrar was sent to the county in 1965.

Efforts at Negro organization in Crayfish have thus been sporadic and unsuccessful. Moreover, they have depended on outside leadership. Even the church fails to furnish an organizational base for political action by Negroes in Crayfish. Only 4 per cent of the churchgoers there say that elections are discussed at church. The message of the Negro preacher in Crayfish deals with the heavenly life of another world, not with the hell of his present world.

INTERMEDIATE STAGES OF ORGANIZATION

Although Bright Leaf has no local chapter of the NAACP or of such protest organizations as CORE, its organizational life looks rich indeed when compared with that of Crayfish. Four organizations in Bright Leaf have encouraged Negro political activity: the Civic Association, the Benevolent Brothers, the Progressive Voters League, and the Bright Leaf County Progressive Council.

The Civic Association, founded in 1935, is the oldest of these organizations. It began, not as a political-action organization, but as an elite group of professionals and businessmen who could bargain with whites for services to the Negro community. Specifically, it was designed to perform the traditional "gate-keeping" function between the Negro and white communities. Ostensibly open to any Negro in Bright Leaf County, the Association was actually controlled by leading members of the Ministerial Alliance and by a few Negro professionals and businessmen who had contacts with the white community. Nevertheless, the organization was directed toward the needs of Negroes in general rather than simply toward the needs of the leaders.

The style of the Civic Association and the nature of white responses to it are suggested by the way in which the first Negro policeman was hired by the city of Farmington in 1951. Without fanfare, members of the Association asked the chief of police and the city council to hire a Negro policeman. The council delayed action until it learned of public reactions to Negro policemen in the state's largest city. On the basis of this report, the council appointed the first Negro to the police force. Most of the work of the Civic Association has been this sort of practical action for limited welfare gains. Although its leaders have always been interested in getting more Negroes registered to vote, they are careful not to threaten the whites with full-fledged Negro political organization. One Negro leader close to the Association commented:

> Only the Civic Association has any resemblance to a Negro political organization in Bright Leaf County, and it speaks for very few. The only effort at organizing Negro voters in the county has been haphazard. . . . The main organized concentration of leadership has been on action-welfare programs.

The Benevolent Brothers was founded a year after the Civic Association, but it has been concerned with problems of the Negro community only, and has not sought to serve as a link between the Negro and white communities. It is a benevolent, fraternal order made up of businessmen and quasi-professional Negroes who do not belong to the "inner circle" of the Civic Association. The fraternity trappings include a limited membership (25), a $25 initiation fee, weekly dues of $1, and a system of "blackballing" any prospective member who is unacceptable to a current member. In its early years, the Benevolent Brothers concentrated on giving to the poor at Christmas time and on fraternal activities. In the last ten years, however, the Brothers have actively campaigned to increase Negro voter registration. And in 1961 they successfully challenged the political leadership of the Civic Association. Eight leaders of the Association, without consulting other Negroes, had hand-picked their own president as nominee for the Farmington City Council. The Benevolent Brothers called a meeting of representatives of all Negro organizations and clubs, and this group endorsed a young attorney instead of the Civic Association leader. In the face of this communitywide decision, the Association acquiesced and agreed to support the attorney.

As a way of promoting the Negro's candidacy, representatives of all the Negro clubs in Farmington formed an organization called the Progressive Voters League. Registration increased markedly in the predominantly Negro ward, and victory seemed likely under Farmington's system of district election. At the last moment, however, two members of the Civic Association accepted bribes to lead small blocs of Negro voters to oppose the Negro candidate, and he was narrowly defeated. The all-white city council responded to this near-victory by changing the electoral system to an at-large vote, which dims Negro prospects for success in the future. Nevertheless, the Progressive Voters League continues as an "umbrella organization" under which all Farmington Negroes can work together.

The Progressive Voters League is active only in Farmington. To encompass Negro groups from the entire county, a sister organization—the Bright Leaf Progressive Council—was also formed in 1961. The Progressive Council has pushed for such countywide goals as a bond issue to create an industrial school open to Negroes. Both the Voters League and the Progressive Council have been watched with sympathy by union leaders in Bright Leaf, who say that they supported the Negro candidate. It is unlikely that many rank-and-file white union members did, and no formal union-

Negro coalition has developed. Even so, if the enthusiasm and activity of the 1961 campaign can be sustained, the old style of bargaining between whites and the leaders of the Civic Association will change. "Because of the rise of organizations among Negroes," one leader said, "whites are finding they will have to deal with more Negroes."

Camellia County has a more complete range of Negro organizations than Bright Leaf, but there has been no coordination among them. Between the Second World War and the outbreak of mass protest in Camellia in 1956, the Capital City Civic League tried to provide political leadership by sponsoring petitions to public officials, organizing rallies at which Negro voters could "meet the candidates," and even endorsing slates of white candidates. But individual political entrepreneurs in the Negro community made their own separate deals, selling small blocs of votes to the highest bidder. Today another, rather nebulous organization, the Progressive Voters Council, operates only at election time. One respondent suggested that it was merely a "paper" organization that served as a front for getting handouts from naïve white candidates. None of the Negro leaders bothered to mention it in talking about political activities in the county.

The Capital City Civic League has tried to operate as a genuine "up-lift" organization, but it has failed to muster a strong following in the Negro community. Most of its officers have been from the staff of the Negro college, with which the mass of Negroes have little sense of identification. Militant protest has been unthinkable to the Civic League leaders, so its role has been restricted to negotiating with whites for welfare gains.

In 1956, however, Capital City Negroes suddenly entered—almost leaderless—into mass protest activity. Triggered by the arrest of college students who refused to observe the segregated seating practice on a city bus, a mass bus boycott developed. Behind this militant protest virtually the enitire Negro community rallied. Lack of organization was a severe handicap during the early days of the boycott. Organization was essential, not only for the immediate and complicated task of directing car pools but for the formulation and communication of plans within the Negro community—and, ultimately, with the white community. The conservative Civic League leaders were discredited early in the negotiations, and at that point the League was doomed as an effective representative body. (Efforts have recently been made to revive it as a negotiating body concerned with welfare gains.) In the absence of any organization capable of speaking for the Negroes, the Negro community was represented at an initial meeting with the city manager by a nine-man committee from the Capital City Ministerial Alliance. But this special group was not representative of the Negro public. That same day, the Inter-Civic Council (ICC) was organized as an executive body to serve as a bargaining agent with the whites.

Despite efforts to subvert the ICC—by displaced Negro leaders as well as by whites—its militant stance evoked great enthusiasm from the Negro public. For the first time since Reconstruction, Capital City Negroes were making open demands on the white community. Negro ministers on the ICC held mass meetings in their churches and invested the protest movement with revivalistic fervor. Despite harassment of Negroes driving for the car pool—"they'd arrest you for driving too fast if you got over the speed limit and for obstructing traffic if you got under it"—the organizational effort was successful. Solid support of the boycott from the entire Negro community bolstered the prestige of the militant new leaders. But the success was restricted to the satisfaction of openly defying the white community and demonstrating that the Negro masses wholeheartedly supported the demands of their leaders. The demands themselves were not met; the city commission enacted an ordinance that authorized bus drivers to assign each passenger to a seat, on grounds of "safety" in distributing weight rather than on grounds of race. Only the bus between the Negro college and the Negro ghetto on the opposite side of town was actually integrated, and it has few white riders.

The ICC tried to channel the public enthusiasm it had evoked into greater political power, but with little success. It cooperated with the State Voters League in registration drives, and in 1957 the vice-president of the ICC announced himself a candidate for the city commission. His candidacy, the first by a Negro in modern times, gave real impetus to the registration drive, and the election brought out a record number of voters for a local election in Capital City. White reaction to his candidacy was almost as intense as that of Negroes, and he was defeated by a two-to-one margin. This electoral effort marked the high-water mark politically for the ICC. The leaders have continued to talk politics and have tried to "pressure" elected officials, but with little evidence of success.

Other organizations have had no better luck in attempting to win a share of political power for Capital City Negroes. In the face of adamant city officials staunchly opposed to any desegregation, and of a white electorate that votes almost solidly against any local candidate with a liberal position on racial questions, the races communicate through mass protest and lawsuits rather than through political action. A local chapter of the NAACP has been active in recent voter-registration efforts, but it has made its greatest advances in the courts. It initiated suits resulting in token desegregation of the schools and of facilities at the municipal airport. Capital City also has an active chapter of the Congress on Racial Equality (CORE), which cooperated with the NAACP in desegregating facilities at the airport. But these and other organizations suffer from lack of coordination. In the spring of 1964, for example, a "freedom march" on the state capitol failed even to approach expectations because CORE and the NAACP could not agree on the route of march!

Except for the momentary successes of the Inter-Civic Committee, then, Negro organizational efforts have had little positive effect on the politics of the area. Even the ICC has not been able to eliminate the individual dealings of Negro "ward heelers"[6] with white politicians and the consequent proliferation of slates "approved by Negroes." In 1964, an integrated League for Better Government was organized by a few business and professional people, mostly professors, from the white and Negro community. When one of the candidates for the city commission received the League's endorsement, his long-time friends were incredulous at his refusal to repudiate the group. The endorsed candidate was soundly defeated. This group of "do-gooders" can hardly succeed where Negro efforts have failed. The charge made by one white leader about the NAACP applies even more to the League for Better Government: "The NAACP hasn't done the organizational job here it is capable of doing. There is too big a split between the college and the town. The NAACP is controlled by the college group, and they tend not to participate in the activities of the town and politics."

EXTENSIVE AND COORDINATED ORGANIZATION

Piedmont County has an even greater range of Negro organizations than Camellia. An NAACP chapter, various business-civic organizations, and labor unions appeared in Piedmont before 1954. Since then an NAACP youth group, the Student Non-violent Coordinating Committee, CORE, a Black Muslim temple, and special groups—such as those conducting spontaneous sit-ins—have added to the complex organizational structure of Urbania. But all these organizations, formal and informal, have been overshadowed by the Urbania League for Negro Activities (ULNA). Indeed, the activities of most of these other organizations are loosely coordinated by ULNA. The ULNA is far more than a Negro voting league; it is one of the most successful Negro efforts in any southern locality to combine elitist talents and mass support for the realization of broad political, economic, and social gains.

Urbania Negroes organized a formal voting league in 1935. The number of Negro voters in the city was already quite large by the standards of the time and the region. Negroes sent delegates to the Democratic county convention as early as 1932. Moreover, the Negro leaders enjoyed access to local party chieftains and to public officials as well. Why, then, was a general voters' league for Negroes established?

To begin with, all the public facilities of Urbania were segregated, as they were everywhere else in the South. Moreover, even in purely political terms, the registration of Negro voters was "selective," with the mass of Negroes excluded from registration. The Negro votes that were cast were

---

[6]This label has a special meaning in southern Negro communities: a "ward heeler" is an individual "wheeler-dealer" who sells votes to white candidates. He is in no sense a cog in a large and smoothly operating machine.

not used to bargain effectively with white leaders for a fair share of governmental services. The casual visitor did not have to ascertain the skin color of the residents to know when he had entered the Negro section—unpaved streets, poor lighting, and other evidences of public neglect told him where he was. Despite the great need for political bargaining power on the part of the Negro community as a whole, unscrupulous Negro "ward heelers" sold small blocs of Negro votes in each election. These political entrepreneurs generally exaggerated the number of votes they could deliver, and they often made no effort to deliver at all. Respectable Negro leaders were greatly concerned about this practice, because it reduced the chance of using the Negro vote as a resource in bargaining and because it gave the Negro community as a whole a reputation for dishonesty and irresponsibility.

A small group representing the Negro upper class met at their Tennis Club in 1935 to found the ULNA. Only successful businessmen and professional people attended the meeting. The first executive committee was composed of a local Negro insurance executive, the editor of the Negro newspaper, a professor, a leading minister, and a successful businessman. The leadership of the group has continued to be vested in the executive committee, and membership on this select committee is recognized as the reward for long and successful service to the Negro communtiy. But the composition of the executive committee has been broadened to include representatives from all the major Negro organizations. By 1945, Negro labor union officials and other leaders from less prestigious groups had won seats. In this way the ULNA has avoided the danger of becoming an upperclass clique without direct ties to the Negro masses.

Membership in the ULNA was originally described as open to "all people in the county who can't sleep or eat in the leading local hotel." It is doubtful that membership was ever so wide as that statement suggested. Largely because of the work of the ULNA, the hotel integrated all its facilities in 1963. If the old, half-humorous description had been taken seriously, the organization would have had to disband, killed by its own success. But the ULNA is a thriving organization that will continue to push for a better break for the local Negro community in hiring, job training, and— of course—governmental services.

At present, membership in the ULNA is of two types, as formalized by Article III of the organization's 1958 constitution: (1) personal memberships are open to those citizens of Urbania "who affirm their interest in and subscribe to the purposes" of the organization, and (2) organizational memberships are open to representatives of each organization in Urbania which shall apply to, and be approved by, the executive committee of the ULNA. Included in the latter category are churches, parent-teacher associations, civic clubs, fraternal and political organizations, labor unions, faculties of educational institutions, business and professional associations, and other organizations of like purposes. Actually, even the mass rallies periodically called by the ULNA attract only four hundred to five hundred people; and the active hard core of the group does not total over one hundred. This number includes the 12 members of the executive committee, currently elected at large; the representatives from the various constitutent organizations; the organization workers, who comprise the block and precinct organizations; and other activists who regularly help in the many activities of the group.

The formal organizational structure of the ULNA is thus similar to that of the United States Chamber of Commerce, with both individual and organizational memberships. Such an all-encompassing structure is well geared to the aims of the organization. The founders of the ULNA felt that it could perform two immediate political functions. First, it could act as a centralizing and coordinating agency to maximize Negro registration and voting. Second, it could serve as a means for deciding which white candidate the Negro community could most profitably support. In other words, it was to create and direct a Negro bloc vote in order to reward friends and punish enemies. No longer would individual Negroes make deals on small blocs of Negro votes with individual white candidates. Once ULNA's political committee had decided on a slate, the members were to support the slate as a group. A sample ballot would be printed (in a Negro-owned and Negro-managed print shop), the "correct" candidates marked, and the endorsed slate distributed to Negro voters as they went to the polls.

In order to win mass support, the ULNA organized the Negro community block by block. Fortunately, the local Negro insurance company had a large field staff in the city that sold policies door to door and collected weekly payments. The overlap between the insurance salesmen and the ULNA's block workers was substantial. The use of such existing, nonpolitical structures as the basis for organized political activity is a common practice in the white community, especially in areas where political party organizations are weak.[7] Rarely, however, does a Negro sub-community have such a "natural" base for block-by-block organization.

By the beginning of the Second World War, the ULNA had expanded its operations substantially. It had led a movement to found a similar organization on a statewide basis. Although this movement had failed, it is impressive that a group with such initiative and ability had managed to develop in the South before the war. Within Piedmont, the ULNA had extended its efforts beyond politics by organizing economic, social, civic, and educational committees for special work and responsibility.

During the Second World War the organization continued to work for broad goals favorable to Negroes and by 1945 had won important gains. Streets had been paved, and the schools had been improved. Some extra

[7]See Alexander Heard, *The Costs of Democracy* (Chapel Hill, N.C.: University of North Carolina Press, 1960); and Eugene C. Lee, *The Politics of Nonpartisanship: A Study of California City Elections* (Berkeley, Calif.: University of California Press, 1960).

police protection and better street lighting had been provided. The question of whether Negroes were to serve on juries was being considered. In addition, Negroes had won a more equitable distribution of federal relief funds and jobs, and the Urbania Police Department had hired Negro policemen.

ULNA representatives had gained access to the offices of public officials, and either the executive committee or its representatives met with the mayor of Urbania fairly frequently to discuss the needs and problems of the Negroes in the community. This was an improvement over the earlier relationship, in which only a few important Negroes had enjoyed access to city offices. In 1948 the statewide importance of the ULNA was demonstrated when the recently elected governor of the state came to thank them, in person, for their support in the election.

After the war ULNA stepped up its activity in all areas of community life, especially politics. It continued to select a slate of favorable white candidates, and it began openly to support Negro candidates for local public office. It had endorsed some Negro candidates early in its history but with no hope of victory. The endorsements were a device to stimulate Negro registration before there were any sympathetic white candidates to support. Now the ULNA began to back candidates to win. This, plus the fact that white candidates for such high offices as mayor, governor, and the United States House of Representatives now came willingly (if still covertly) to the meetings of the executive committee to solicit its support, was an indication of growing strength. Bloc voting might prove self-defeating in the long run, as many whites and a few Negroes argued, but the Negro community had bloc-voted themselves some voice in local public decision-making nonetheless.

The leaders of the ULNA, like Negroes throughout the South, were historically inclined toward the Republican party. And yet they set about trying to win influence in the Democratic primaries. The Negro precinct chairmen served on the Democratic county executive committee *ex officio*. In 1948 these Negro chairmen, all of whom were leaders in the ULNA, cooperated with the Democratic precinct chairmen from predominantly white labor precincts to wrest control of the Urbania County Democratic Executive Committee from the powerful faction that had controlled it for years.

Although the ULNA failed to elect one of its members to the Urbania City Council in 1949, its votes helped elect a new mayor and several members of the council. Before the municipal election of 1951, a faction of the ULNA Executive Committee—led by the college professor who had been one of the founders of the ULNA and was to be the Negro candidate in 1951—argued that joining with white labor to back a common slate was not the best way to get a Negro elected to the city council. This faction felt that the time had come for a Negro to be elected to the city council and that "bullet" or "single shot" voting by Negroes was the only route to victory.[8] Only the influence of younger, more party-oriented members of the ULNA Executive Committee saved the coalition with white labor at that time.

Unfortunately for the coalition, the white labor vote was harder to deliver than the labor leaders had anticipated, and the Negro candidate was defeated. This defeat was doubly disappointing to the Negroes, because they had thought their candidate was sure to win. The labor leaders came up with several explanations. A recent statewide election had engendered unusually strong racist feelings, they said; the strong advocacy of "don't let the Negroes take over the city government" by a newly developed committee of local whites had proved to be disruptive; and labor's victories in the prior municipal election had made the unions complacent. None of these reasons rang very true to Negroes. The whole affair looked like a "double-cross."

The next month, instead of accepting defeat with a philosophical "wait until next year," the ULNA held a mass meeting and reorganized itself. All positions on the ULNA Executive Committee were declared open for election. The current chairman managed to hold on to his position, but many of the faces were new. Only by increasing the membership of the Executive Committee to 25 was the chairman able to get an agreement on policies that would allow the Negro-labor coalition, and its strong support of the Democratic party, to continue.

In the municipal elections of 1953, a Negro was elected to the Urbania City Council for the first time in its history. The success was marred, however, by continuing conflict within the ULNA. The Executive Committee decided to back a candidate other than the college professor who had lost in 1951. The professor, rejecting the rejection, ran as an independent in the primary and was soundly beaten by the ULNA's candidate. Though factionalism continued in the ULNA, it did not again reach the point of an open break. The ULNA succeeded in getting its candidates elected in 1955, 1957, and 1959.

The school-segregation decision of 1954 proved very disruptive to the ULNA's relations with the white community. In May 1958, the friendly county Democratic chairman was defeated for reelection, and, in the same county convention at which he was defeated, only one Negro was selected as a delegate to the state convention. (In the past as many as 23 Negroes from Urbania had attended the state convention.) When the Piedmont County Young Democratic Club met in October, no members of the executive committee of the ULNA were invited. The ULNA leaders protested

[8]This "bullet" voting technique is a device for maximizing the advantage of the minority in an election in which more than one at-large vote is granted each voter. By voting for only one candidate, the minority group is able to increase the weight of its actual vote because the opposition presumably will vote for more than one candidate.

to the new Democratic county chairman, but he told them that the club was a private organization and could invite whomever it chose.

As it had in the past, the ULNA now closed its ranks. It set about recruiting new members and adopted a formal constitution. Several municipal bond elections were successfully carried in Urbania from 1945 to 1959, and impartial observers attributed the outcome to the Negro vote organized by the ULNA. These bond issues provided increased hospital, educational, and other public services of particular benefit to Negroes. One bond issue provided funds for building a fire station in the Negro community, and the ULNA was able to get it manned by Negro firemen. Negro deputy sheriffs, policemen, and election officials were employed for the first time. An integrated industrial school began to provide Negroes with training they had never been able to get before.

Thus even after the *Brown* decision greatly heightened local racial tensions, and thereby undercut the political effectiveness of the ULNA, the ULNA continued to serve as the bargaining representative of Urbania Negroes vis-à-vis the white community. Also the organization continued to value its coalition with labor and its ties with the local Democratic party— even when neither the party nor the rank and file of labor were particularly eager for Negro support.

The gubernatorial election of 1960 demonstrated that the ULNA could still direct the Negro vote toward its candidates. The ULNA experienced its most serious electoral split, however, in the municipal elections of 1961, when two of its long-time friends opposed each other in the mayoralty election. The former county Democratic chairman, who had headed the Negro-labor coalition and had often befriended the ULNA, ran against the incumbent, a man whom both the former chairman and the ULNA had supported for ten years. The ULNA Executive Committee met more than once to hear impassioned pleas for support from both sides. At last the committee abandoned the incumbent, though several members had serious misgivings. On election day, the Negro turnout was the lowest in years. Only 66 per cent of the total vote in the four heavily Negro precincts went to the ULNA-endorsed candidate. In other races in the same election, candidates endorsed by the ULNA received at least 80 per cent of the total vote in these precincts.

Apparently the break in the ULNA ranks had healed by the 1962 countywide election. The fact that an ULNA member was running for county commissioner helped rekindle the zest for battle. He led in the first primary but was defeated in the runoff. This campaign, though it ended in defeat, seemed to reestablish solidarity and confidence among the leaders and the Negro public. The wealthy, cosmopolitan, dignified chairman of the ULNA, according to his associates, spent 12 hours on election day driving voters to the polls. Later he said, speaking like the successful businessman he is, "The tremendous across-the-board team effort that hundreds of our people made in this campaign [is to be lauded]. It's an indication of growing community solidarity."

What gains have come from these years of labor by the ULNA? Perhaps the most significant is the respect that white community leaders have come to show for the organization. Sometimes this respect is grudging, but other times it is open and forthright. One white leader says, "The ULNA is the best race organization in the community and the most democratic."

Moreover, the ULNA has given the Negro public in Urbania a skillful and representative leadership structure on which it can depend. Its ability to organize a substantial Negro vote gives Negroes a loud enough voice to be heard in the Democratic party—the local majority party. Rising political strength has also brought welfare and status gains to Urbania Negroes. These gains, such as the desegregation of motels, hotels, and restaurants, cannot all be attributed directly to the ULNA. Many of them would probably have come anyway. But the ULNA hastened their coming by capitalizing on a relatively permissive environment and relatively strong Negro leadership and financial resources.

Other organizations, including the NAACP, CORE, fraternal and business organizations, youth groups at the college, and various special groups, have helped the ULNA to activate the Negro community. Often the NAACP and the ULNA have seemed to be one and the same organization in Urbania because of the widespread overlap in membership. For example, the chief counsel for the ULNA also directed the local NAACP legal redress committee. The two organizations cooperated closely in conducting voter-registration drives; the NAACP was always careful to remain nonpartisan, but it knew that the ULNA would channel most of the new registrants into the Democratic party. The legal approach to desegregation— long the policy of the NAACP—appealed to the business and professional men who dominate Urbania's Negro leadership. Negotiations, bargaining, and legal actions were techniques well fitted to their skills and general philosophy.

More militant organizations—CORE, for example—and student groups altered the techniques and pace of Negro efforts in Urbania. These groups, which relied on mass protest in the form of picketing, boycotts, and sit-ins, posed a threat to the ULNA leaders, who relied on less dramatic techniques. But the leaders adjusted to the new ways—not without some misgivings and tension—and brought the new groups into ULNA activities. In 1961, for example, cooperation between several groups led to the opening of sales positions in downtown Urbania stores to Negro applicants. In a neat division of labor, the youth groups furnished the pickets and the ULNA and NAACP handled the negotiations. All the groups used the threat of boycotts as their bargaining weapon. At the annual mass meeting of the ULNA in January 1962, speakers from the NAACP youth group at the college and from other, more militant groups appeared on the program. Later, in the drive to desegregate all Urbania facilities, the ULNA chairman promised the demonstrators that they would not languish in jail if arrested—the ULNA would come to their defense.

Even this comprehensive and coordinated program has not always met with success, however. Politically the ULNA has failed to get a Negro elected to the Piedmont County Commission. Urbania Negroes have occasionally been rebuffed by the very officials they helped elect to office; when the Mayor's Human Relations Committee recommended that the city-owned theater be integrated, the Urbania City Council refused to act. (After a siege of picketing, the theater was finally integrated.) The Urbania City School Board, even with a Negro member to prod the consciences of other members, moved slowly in desegregating the schools. Mass protest and an organized vote can be used only within the limits set by the dominant forces of the community. Even the most effective Negro organization must expect some setbacks in the South. But after each defeat, the Urbania League for Negro Activities has managed to inject new life and enthusiasm into the community and has reorganized for the next battle.

PRECONDITIONS FOR EFFECTIVE NEGRO POLITICAL ORGANIZATION: SITUATIONAL FACTORS

The four southern communities we studied in detail differ greatly in the development of Negro political organization. Good reasons can be found for this variation. In some communities, social, economic, and political factors tend to encourage—or at least not to inhibit—the growth of effective political organization. In others, these factors impose severe limits on the extent and effectiveness of Negro organization. These variables fall into two classes—those that are "external" to the Negro community and those that grow out of the Negro community itself. Let us look first at the "external" or situational variables.

The Racial Attitudes of Local Whites

White attitudes about the proper "place" of the Negro help determine the success or failure of Negro efforts to organize. In Crayfish County, for example, the white community is solidly opposed to any relaxation of rigid segregation. Given a choice between "strict segregation, integration, or something in between," every white Crayfish respondent except one said that he favored strict segregation. The exception was a young lady who had grown up in Los Angeles and who was living in Crayfish temporarily because her husband was driving a truck for a construction company.[9] Whites in the other counties are not unanimous in their dedication to rigid

[9]The resident white interviewer, recognizing the heretical nature of this respondent's views, commented that "she wouldn't last long in Crayfish County."

segregation: the proportion drops to 87 per cent in Bright Leaf, 65 per cent in Camellia, and 58 per cent in Piedmont. When we add Negro views to those of the whites, we find that a small majority of the total population of Piedmont rejects strict segregation.

More important, whites in Piedmont believe that Negro opinions *ought* to count in the community. On the proposition that "colored people ought to be allowed to vote," a majority of whites in Piedmont (69 per cent) and in Camellia (68 per cent) agree "quite a bit." Almost half the whites in Bright Leaf (49 per cent) but only 4 per cent of the Crayfish whites similarly endorse the principle of suffrage for Negroes. If we add those who agree "a little," white acceptance of the proposition becomes overwhelming in three of the counties: 90 per cent in Piedmont, 93 per cent in Camellia, and 82 per cent in Bright Leaf. But it reaches only 16 per cent in Crayfish! In the face of such determined opposition from those who control all the political and economic power, efforts to organize politically must assume the form of conspiracies.

White attitudes—either in themselves or as an index of other community factors—are not the only constraints on Negro efforts to organize. If they were, we would expect Camellia County to follow closely behind Piedmont in the scope and effectiveness of Negro political organization. Other situational factors, of varying importance and specificity, are suggested by a close examination of the four communities: the political style of white leaders, locally and statewide, in dealing with racial questions; the factional system peculiar to the community; the local electoral system; the relative homogeneity or heterogeneity of the community in nonracial terms; and the Civil War and Reconstruction experiences of the community. Added to public opinion on racial questions, these overlapping situational variables pretty much determine whether or not the Negro community can organize for political ends. And, taken together, they provide a reasonably clear and specific meaning to the ordinarily vague concept of "political culture."

The Political Style of White Leaders

The white leaders in Crayfish openly espouse white supremacy. Only there can the leaders pretend that they have no "race problem." Crayfish Negroes are so browbeaten that the whites can sing the old refrain about having "good, happy niggers," and can repeat the old joke about the local Negro who finds life so miserable in the North that he wires his old "boss man" for money to return to the happy life on the farm. One of the leaders commented: "We have the best colored people in the world . . . our colored people are not giving us any trouble." And if they do give trouble, it is not reported. Merely from reading the *Breedville Weekly* one might conclude that no Negroes lived in Crayfish.

In Bright Leaf, the white leaders express paternalistic attitudes sometimes mixed with genuine benevolence. The response of the superintendent of schools to a question about relations with "the colored community" is illuminating:

> Rather good, I think. There are some hotheads but a group of us are working to establish communication. I do what I can to show my love for them—get scholarships. Nigrahs come in the back door and stand—I tell them to have a seat, and suggest that they go out the front door—it's nearer. I call janitors in the schools "custodians." This is more than words and acts; they know I'll fight for them, for instance, give them money. The point is: treat them as humans, call them "Mister" and "Miss"; nothing special, just what human beings deserve.

The superintendent of schools is not typical of Bright Leaf's white leaders, most of whom hold more clearly anti-Negro stereotypes. But it is remarkable that we can find such a leader, who says that his prime objective is to prepare teachers for integration, in this community. This is not a transient, but an old and widely admired leader. The new high school in Farmington bears his name, and generations of graduates remember him with affection and respect.

Camellia County is more cosmopolitan and liberal than Bright Leaf, mainly because it is more urban and is the home of the state capitol and the state university. Although some Camellia whites, mostly from the university, have actively championed integration, the officials of Capital City have been virulently anti-Negro. Officeholders talk about the fine relations that existed with old-style Negro leaders before the bus boycott confronted them with the undeniable fact of mass Negro dissatisfaction. The chief of police, under whose direction the local police force has ruthlessly broken up demonstrations, says, "They want to be good, but the NAACP has caused friction—whites and colored are farther apart than in years. The college people and Negro preachers start things—they prey on younger niggers." The municipal judge, who has handed down stiff sentences to demonstrators, observes: "CORE is a Communist front, I'm convinced." Most Camellia leaders recognize that the two colleges in Capital City are the source of much racial agitation and regard them almost as alien institutions. They value the colleges as a source of entertainment (in the form of athletic events) and as a source of income, but they look on them with great suspicion. Crayfish's governing authorities can indulge themselves in the myth that neither Negroes nor whites in the community disapprove of the established system; Camellia's leaders are fighting against change, embittered by Negro defiance of segregation and infuriated by some white support of that defiance.

In Piedmont County the white leaders do not regard Negro demands as unreasonable in themselves. Although hard bargaining occurs and ill will exists, the right of the Negroes to work through the ULNA and other organizations is unquestioned. "The top leadership of Negroes is good, just top-flight," was the comment of the city manager.

Local Factional and Electoral Systems

In a study of Negro leadership in northern cities, James Q. Wilson found that the structure and style of Negro politics reflected the general politics of the city in which the Negroes lived.[10] We may similarly expect the factional systems and the electoral systems of southern communities to help determine the nature and extent of Negro political organization.

Crayfish County has a purely personalized politics, with no identifiable factional structure. The Negro community has no factional structure and no politics of concern to the general community. Public officials are elected on a district basis. Normally this system tends to give Negroes a good chance of winning public office, because segregated housing concentrates the Negro population in a few districts where they may constitute a majority. With Negroes excluded from politics, however, Crayfish whites can keep an electoral system that results in heavy representation of the county's numerous hamlets. The emerging Negro political organization of Bright Leaf County is facilitated by the loose bifactionalism of the county, which provides a limited number of factions with which the Negroes can deal. Like Crayfish, Bright Leaf once elected public officials on a district basis, but this arrangement was dropped as soon as the Negroes organized to take advantage of it.

Camellia County's politics are conducted through white factions at least as recognizable as those in Bright Leaf. But the Negro factions are semi-atomistic and personalized. Accordingly, we must explain the rivalry among Negro leaders and their inability to create any enduring political organization with mass support in some other way than to say that they are simply a reflection of white factionalism. Camellia officials are elected at large, an arrangement that has denied recent Negro candidates any real chance of success. Piedmont has the most clear-cut system of factional competition, and the Negro community there has organized to win recognition and commitments from the enduring white factions. Many public officers are elected by district in Piedmont, and the system was not changed when Negroes began to win office: too many white politicians were indebted to the organized Negro vote.

Diversity of Interests

The white population of Crayfish is extremely homogeneous. Almost the entire population depends, in one way or another, on the farming, cattle, and dairy interests of the county. The only industry of any consequence is absentee-owned and serves simply to supplement the incomes of poorer whites by giving work to the white women in the county. In Bright Leaf,

[10] *Negro Politics: The Search for Leadership* (Glencoe, Ill.: The Free Press, 1960), pp. 52ff.

which is almost as homogeneous, farming interests dominate the county and a chamber of commerce viewpoint dominates Farmington. Competing interests have arisen in Farmington, however, as "newer elements" jostle "older elements" for advantage. Should this factionalism crystallize, the incipient Negro organization may be stimulated to greater activity. Camellia County is similarly dominated by business interests and "old families" that have grown rich with Capital City's growth. The general provincialism is mitigated by the presence of professionals in the colleges and the state government, but they are an ill organized and "alien" interest.

Only Piedmont has enough industries and unions to furnish economic as well as social heterogeneity. Union leaders, for example, negotiate with Negro leaders in seeking common candidates to support; in the other communities white laborers generally oppose candidates who are known to have Negro support.

Local History

The history of each community is the final situational variable affecting political organizations. For example, a community that was the scene of long and bitter violence between labor and management as far back as the 1920's or 1930's might be expected to be organized politically along class lines to an unusual degree. In the South, the common experiences most important for a community's response to Negro political organizations are the Civil War and Reconstruction—or, more accurately, secondhand memories of "The War" and Reconstruction. These events have shaped all southern politics.

In Crayfish and Camellia counties, memories of that cataclysmic period are particularly bitter. The leading lawyer in Breedville (the only other lawyer is a drunk) delights in explaining how an outside land company exploited the corrupt legal system during Reconstruction by grabbing much of the land away from the people who had settled the Crayfish area. His delight appears to be enhanced by the violence used to drive the land company out and by the fact that he still gets an occasional fee from cases based on that period of confusion.

At the site of the state government, Camellia residents witnessed Negro and "carpetbag" control of the state government at first hand. A minor skirmish was fought near Capital City during the Civil War, and the townspeople stir up old memories every year in a formal celebration of the rout of the Yankees by a few old men and the brave young boys who were left in the university. At the turn of the century Camellia was still strictly a plantation county, with 80 per cent of its population made up of Negroes. Many "old family" leaders still act as if they were living in Crayfish rather than in a metropolitan area.

Bright Leaf residents have few exaggerated notions about an aristocratic past. The school superintendent explained,

I call this a new town and a new community. Some nearby counties have pre-Civil War aristocracy; this county developed *after* the Civil War, and new leaders are recognized. Bright Leaf is a plebian county. It has no old aristocracy to fight.

He suggested that this lack of an ante-bellum history explains why Bright Leaf has better race relations than neighboring counties. Piedmont residents have favorable recollections of the Reconstruction. Before the Civil War the county was populated by poor farmers with few slaves, so the war itself produced no violent change in the way of life. Moreover, the end of the war and the presence of Union troops in the area triggered a local industrial revolution in textiles and tobacco. The development of successful industry rather than concern about the new status of Negroes thus dominated the Reconstruction period in Piedmont.

PRECONDITIONS FOR EFFECTIVE NEGRO POLITICAL ORGANIZATION: THE NEGRO COMMUNITY

Favorable circumstances do not ensure effective Negro political organization, but they make it possible. The characteristics of the Negro community itself determine how well circumstances are exploited for political purposes. All the factors that we found in the preceding chapter to be conducive to high-quality leadership also tend to produce effective Negro organizations. More specifically, three factors seem to be particularly important for organizational effectiveness in the Negro communities examined: close ties between leaders and followers, organizational continuity, and organizational cohesion.

Most of the leaders of the Urbania League for Negro Activities won their positions through successful business, professional, or union activity *within* the Negro community. A few of the business leaders have Negro customers in a number of states. This economic relationship frees the ULNA leaders from dependence on whites; equally important, it demands that the leaders stay in close touch with the needs of ULNA members and non-members alike. In Camellia County the gap between leaders and followers is not so neatly bridged by economic ties; the largest pool of potential Negro leaders are employed by the college, and there is no economic incentive for them to remain in communication with the Negro masses. The "town-gown" division within the Negro community also tends to encourage leadership rivalry.

The continuity of the ULNA in Piedmont has resulted in experienced leaders and organizational prestige. The Inter-Civic Committee in Camellia was created to take over the direction of a single great effort—the bus boycott—and it has been unable to take on new functions. The Progressive Voters League in Bright Leaf grew out of the rivalry between two older organizations in the heat of an election campaign. This organization may be able to persist, but there are some indications that it may not survive for many other campaigns.

A high level of cohesion is necessary if political ambition and self-interest are to work for, rather than against, the racial cause. Southern whites traditionally assume that they can exploit individual Negroes, and it is easy for them to extend this assumption to politics. Moreover, many Negroes are highly vulnerable to economic inducements and threats. Urbania Negroes once competed for the largesse of white politicians seeking small blocs of Negro votes. Today such efforts are channeled through the ULNA, and Negro votes are "sold" for policy commitments, not for preelection payoffs. As we mentioned earlier, two Negro leaders in the Bright Leaf Civic Association, irritated because their candidate had been rejected by the Benevolent Brothers, were bribed to defect in a recent election. In Camellia County organizational rivalries produce competing slates of candidates endorsed by Negroes, with the result that white candidates refuse to place confidence in any Negro organization. One white politician explained that he was forced to rely on his personal organization:

> Three Negro groups were hauling to the polls on election day. . . and it was questionable as to whether they were getting them to vote correctly because they were handing out different lists even though CORE had distributed a list to the voters. I sent my own car with my name on the side and hauled Negro voters to the polls myself.

CHAPTER SEVEN

THE CHANGING PATTERN OF URBAN PARTY POLITICS

FRED I. GREENSTEIN

Highly organized urban political parties are generally conceded to be one of America's distinctive contributions to mankind's repertory of political forms. Just as the two major national parties in the United States are almost universally described in terms of their *dis*organization—their lack of an authoritative command structure—the municipal parties have, until recently, been characterized by most observers in terms of their hierarchical strength. E. E. Schattschneider once summarized this state of affairs in the memorable image of a truncated pyramid: a party system which is weak and ghostlike at the top and solid at the bottom.[1]

This essay deals with the disciplined, largely autonomous local political parties which sprang up in many American cities in the nineteenth century. Much of the literature on these political configurations is heavily pejorative, concerned more with excoriation than explanation. Even the basic nomenclature, "boss" and "machine," is laden with negative connotations, although recently there has been a turn toward nostalgic romanticization of the "vanishing breed" of city bosses.[2]

Here, for reasons which I shall indicate, the attempt shall be to delineate rather than to pass moral judgment: What was the nature of old-style urban

[1]E. E. Schattschneider, *Party Government* (New York, 1942), pp. 162–169.

[2]Among the better known accounts are Frank R. Kent, *The Great Game of Politics* (Garden City, N. Y., 1923, rev. ed., 1930); Sonya Forthall, *Cogwheels of Democracy* (New York, 1946); Harold F. Gosnell, *Machine Politics* (Chicago, 1937); and the many case studies of individual bosses. For a recent romanticization, see Edwin O'Connor's novel, *The Last Hurrah* (Boston, 1956).

Reprinted with permission of publisher and author from Fred I. Greenstein, "The Changing Pattern of Urban Party Politics," *The Annals of the American Academy of Political and Social Science*, 353 (May, 1964), 1–13. Mr. Greenstein is Professor of Political Science at Wesleyan University.

party organization? Why did this political pattern develop and how did it operate? What contributed to its short-run persistence in the face of reform campaigns? Under what circumstances have such organizations disappeared and under what circumstances have they continued into the present day— or even undergone renaissances? What are the present-day descendents of old-style urban party organizations?

Analytic delineation invariably involves oversimplification. This is doubly necessary in the present case, because our knowledge of the distribution of types of local party organization is scant. We have no census of local political parties, either for today or for the putative heyday of bosses and machines. And there is reason to believe that observers have exaggerated the ubiquity of tightly organized urban political parties in past generations, as well as underestimated somewhat their contemporary prevalence.

OLD-STYLE PARTY ORGANIZATION:
DEFINITIONAL CHARACTERISTICS

Ranney and Kendall have persuasively argued that the imprecision and negative connotations of terms like "boss" destroy their usefulness. What, beyond semantic confusion, they ask, can come from classifying politicians into "bosses" versus "leaders"? Such a distinction leads to fruitless preoccupation with the purity of politicians' motives rather than the actuality of their behavior; it overestimates the degree to which figures of the past such as Richard Croker, William Tweed, and Frank Hague were free of public constraints; and it obscures the fact that *all* effective political leaders, whether or not they are popularly labeled as bosses, use quite similar techniques and resources.[3]

Granting these points, it still seems that a recognizable and noteworthy historical phenomenon is hinted at by the venerable terms "boss" and "machine." If the overtones of these terms make us reluctant to use them, we might simply speak of an "old style" of party organization with the following characteristics:

(1) There is a disciplined party hierarchy led by a single executive or a unified board of directors.

(2) The party exercises effective control over nomination to public office, and, through this, it controls the public officials of the municipality.

(3) The party leadership—which quite often is of lower-class social origins— usually does not hold public office and sometimes does not even hold formal party office. At any rate, official position is not the primary source of the leadership's strength.

(4) Rather, a cadre of loyal party officials and workers, as well as a core of voters, is maintained by a mixture of material rewards and *nonideological*

[3]Austin Ranney and Willmoore Kendall, *Democracy and the American Party System* (New York, 1956), pp. 249–252.

psychic rewards—such as personal and ethnic recognition, camaraderie, and the like.[4]

THE RISE OF OLD-STYLE PARTY ORGANIZATION

This pattern of politics, Schattschneider comments, "is as American as the jazz band . . . China, Mexico, South America, and southern Italy at various times have produced figures who played roles remotely like that of the American boss, but England, France, Germany, and the lesser democracies of Europe have exhibited no tendency to develop this form of political organization in modern times."[5] What then accounted for the development of old-style party organization in the United States?

The Crokers, Tweeds, and Hagues and their organizations probably could not have arisen if certain broad preconditions had not existed in American society and culture. These include the tradition of freewheeling individualism and pragmatic opportunism, which developed in a prosperous, sprawling new society unrestrained by feudalism, aristocracy, monarchy, an established church, and other traditional authorities. This is the state of affairs which has been commented on by countless observers, even before de Tocqueville, and which has been used to explain such disparate phenomena as the failure of socialism to take hold in the United States, the recurrence of popularly based assaults on civil liberties, and even the peculiarly corrosive form which was taken by American slavery.[6]

It also is possible to identify five more direct determinants of the form that urban party organization took in the nineteenth century, three of them consequences of the Industrial Revolution and two of them results of political institutions and traditions which preceded industrialization.

Massive Urban Expansion

Over a relatively brief span of years, beginning in the mid-nineteenth century, industrial and commercial growth led to a spectacular rise in the

---

[4]This last definitional criterion explicitly departs from the characterization of a "machine" in James Q. Wilson's interesting discussion of "The Economy of Patronage," *The Journal of Political Economy*, Vol. 59 (August 1961), p. 370n., "as that kind of political party which sustains its members through the distribution of material incentives (patronage) rather than nonmaterial incentives (appeals to principle, the fun of the game, sociability, etc.)." There is ample evidence that for many old-style party workers incentives such as "the fun of the game," "sociability," and even "service" are of central importance. See, for example, Edward J. Flynn, *You're the Boss* (New York, 1947), p. 22; James A. Farley, *Behind the Ballots* (New York, 1938), p. 237; and the passage cited in note 8 below. The distinction between "material" and "nonmaterial" incentives would probably have to be discarded in a more refined discussion of the motivations underlying political participation. So-called material rewards, at base, are nonmaterial in the sense that they are valued for the status they confer and for other culturally defined reasons.

[5]*Op. cit.*, p. 106.

[6]See, for example, Edward A. Shils, *The Torment of Secrecy* (Glencoe, Ill., 1956) and Stanley M. Elkins, *Slavery* (Chicago, 1959, reprinted with an introduction by Nathan Glazer, New York, 1963).

number and proportion of Americans concentrated in cities. A thumbnail sketch of urban expansion may be had by simply noting the population of urban and rural areas for each of the twenty-year periods from 1840 to 1920:

	Urban Population	Rural Population
	(in millions)	
1840	1.8	15.2
1860	6.2	25.2
1880	14.1	36.0
1900	30.1	45.8
1920	54.2	51.6

These statistics follow the old Census Bureau classification of areas exceeding 2,500 in population as urban. Growth of larger metropolitan units was even more striking. In 1840 slightly over 300,000 Americans lived in cities—or, rather, a single city, New York—with more than a quarter of a million residents; by 1920 there were twenty-four cities of this size, containing approximately 21 million Americans.

The sheer mechanics of supporting urban populations of this magnitude are, of course, radically different from the requirements of rural life. There must be extensive transportation arrangements; urban dwellers are as dependent upon a constant inflow of food and other commodities as an infant is on the ministrations of adults. A host of new administrative functions must be performed as the population becomes urbanized: street construction and maintenance, bridges, lighting, interurban transportation, sanitary arrangements, fire-fighting, police protection, and so forth. Overwhelming demands suddenly are placed on governments which, hitherto, were able to operate with a minimum of effort and activity.

Disorganized Forms of Urban Government

The forms of government which had evolved in nineteenth-century America were scarcely suitable for meeting the demands of mushrooming cities. Governmental structures reflected a mixture of Jacksonian direct democracy and Madisonian checks and balances. Cities had a multitude of elected officials (sometimes they were elected annually), weak executives, large and unwieldy councils and boards. The formal organization of the cities placed officials in a position permitting and, in fact, encouraging them to checkmate each other's efforts to make and execute policies. Since each official was elected by appealing to his own peculiar constituency and had little incentive to co-operate with his associates, the difficulties caused by the formal limitations of government were exacerbated. In a period when the requirements for governmental action were increasing geometrically, this was a prescription for chaos.

Needs of Businessmen

A third aspect of mid-nineteenth-century American society which contributed to the formation of old-style party organizations was the needs of
businessmen. There was an increasing number of merchants, industrialists,
and other businessmen, licit and illicit, who needed—and were willing to pay
for—the appropriate responses from city governments. Some businessmen
wanted to operate unrestrained by municipal authority. Others desired street-
railway franchises, paving contracts, construction work, and other transactions connected with the very growth of the cities themselves.

Needs of Dependent Populations

The needs of the bulk of the nineteenth-century urban population were not
for profits but for the simple wherewithal to survive and maintain a modicum
of dignity. It is difficult in the relatively affluent society of our day to appre-
ciate the vicissitudes of urban life several generations ago: the low wages,
long hours, tedious and hazardous working conditions, and lack of security
which were the lot of most citizens. Even for native-born Americans, life often
was nasty and brutish. But many urbanites were first- and second-generation
immigrants who, in addition to their other difficulties, had to face an alien
culture and language. Between the Civil War and the First World War,
the United States managed somehow to absorb 25 million foreigners.

Unrestricted Suffrage

Urban dwellers were not totally without resources for their own advancement.
The American tradition of unrestricted male franchise was, in the long run,
to work to their advantage. Although it doubtless is true that few city dwellers of the day were aware of the importance of their right to vote, politicians
were aware of this. Because even the lowliest of citizens was, or could become,
a voter, a class of politicians developed building upon the four conditions
referred to above: the requirements of organizing urban life, the inability
of existing governments to meet these requirements, and the presence of
businessmen willing to pay for governmental services and of dependent
voting populations in need of security from the uncertainties of their existence.

The old-style urban party leader was as much a product of his time and
social setting as was the rising capitalist of the Gilded Age. Building on
the conditions and needs of the day, the politician had mainly to supply
his own ingenuity and co-ordinating ability in order to tie together the machinery of urban government. If a cohesive party organization could control
nominations and elect its own agents to office, the formal fragmentation of
government no longer would stand in the way of municipal activity. The
votes of large blocs of dependent citizens were sufficient to control nominations and win elections. And the financial support of those who sought
to transact business with the city, as well as the revenues and resources of

the city government, made it possible to win votes. The enterprising politician who could succeed in governing a city on this basis was a broker *par excellence;* generous brokers' commissions were the rule of the day.

The importance of out-and-out vote-buying on election day as a source of voter support can easily be overestimated. Party organizations curried the favor of voters on a year-long basis. In a day when "better" citizens espoused philosophical variants of Social Darwinism, urban politicians thought in terms of an old-fashioned conception of the welfare state. In the familiar words of Tammany sachem George Washington Plunkitt:

> What holds your grip on your district is to go right down among the poor families and help them in the different ways they need help. I've got a regular system for this. If there's a fire in Ninth, Tenth or Eleventh Avenue, for example, any hour of the day or night, I'm usually there with some of my election district captains as soon as the fire engines. If a family is burned out I don't ask whether they are Republicans or Democrats, and I don't refer them to the Charity Organization Society, which would investigate their case in a month or two and decide they were worthy of help about the time they are dead from starvation. I just get quarters for them, buy clothes for them if their clothes were burned up, and fix them up til they get things runnin' again. It's philanthropy, but it's politics, too—mighty good politics. Who can tell how many votes one of these fires bring me? The poor are the most grateful people in the world, and, let me tell you, they have more friends in their neighborhoods than the rich have in theirs.[7]

With numerous patronage appointees (holders not only of city jobs but also of jobs with concerns doing business with the city), party organizations could readily administer this sort of an informal relief program. And, unlike many latter-day charitable and governmental relief programs, the party's activities did not stop with the provision of mere physical assistance.

> I know every man, woman and child in the Fifteenth District, except them that's been born this summer—and I know some of them, too. I know what they like and what they don't like, what they are strong at and what they are weak in, and I reach them by approachin' at the right side.
>
> For instance, here's how I gather in the young men. I hear of a young feller that's proud of his voice, thinks that he can sing fine. I ask him to come around to Washington Hall and join our Glee Club. He comes and sings, and he's a follower of Plunkitt for life. Another young feller gains a reputation as a baseball player in a vacant lot. I bring him into our baseball club. That fixes him. You'll find him workin' for my ticket at the polls next election day. Then there's the feller that likes rowin' on the river, the young feller that makes a name as a waltzer on his block, the young feller that's handy with his dukes—I rope them all in by givin' them opportunities to show themselves off. I don't

[7]William L. Riordon, *Plunkitt of Tammany Hall* (originally published in 1905; republished New York, 1948 and New York, 1963; quotations are from the 1963 edition), pp. 27–28.

trouble them with political arguments. I just study human nature and act accordin'.[8]

This passage reflects some of the ways in which party activities might be geared to the *individual* interests of voters. *Group* interests were at least as important. As each new nationality arrived in the city, politicians rather rapidly accommodated to it and brought it into the mainstream of political participation. Parties were concerned with the votes of immigrants virtually from the time of their arrival. Dockside naturalization and voter enrollment was not unknown.

But if the purpose of the politicians was to use the immigrants, it soon became clear that the tables could be turned. In Providence, Rhode Island, for example, a careful study of the assimilation of immigrant groups into local politics shows that, within thirty years after the arrival of the first representative of a group in the city, it began to be represented in the councils of one or both parties. Eventually, both of the local parties came to be dominated by representatives of the newer stocks. Thus, in 1864 no Irish names appear on the lists of Democratic committeemen in Providence; by 1876 about a third of the names were Irish; by the turn of the century, three-quarters were Irish. In time, the Republican party became the domain of politicians of Italian ancestry.[9] Perhaps the most dramatic example to date of urban party politics as an avenue of upward social mobility was in the antecedents of President Kennedy, whose great-grandfather was an impoverished refugee of the Irish potato famine, his grandfather a saloon keeper and a classical old-time urban political leader, his father a multimillionaire businessman, presidential advisor, and ambassador to the Court of St. James's.

When the range of consequences of old-time party organizations is seen, it becomes apparent why moral judgments of "the boss and the machine" are likely to be inadequate. These organizations often were responsible for incredible corruption, but they also—sometimes through the very same activities—helped incorporate new groups into American society and aided them up the social ladder. The parties frequently mismanaged urban growth on a grand scale, but they *did* manage urban growth at a time when other instrumentalities for governing the cities were inadequate. They plied voters, who might otherwise have organized more aggressively to advance their interests, with Thanksgiving Day turkeys and buckets of coal. But, by siphoning off discontent and softening the law, they probably contributed to the generally pacific tenor of American politics. It seems fruitless to attempt to capture this complexity in a single moral judgment. One can scarcely

[8]*Ibid.*, pp. 25–26.
[9]Elmer E. Cornwell, Jr., "Party Absorption of Ethnic Groups: The Case of Providence, Rhode Island," *Social Forces*, Vol. 38 (March 1960), pp. 205–210.

weigh the incorporation of immigrant groups against the proliferation of corruption and strike an over-all balance.

WHY REFORMERS WERE "MORNIN' GLORIES"

Stimulated by high taxes and reports of corruption and mismanagement on a grand scale, antiboss reform movements, led by the more prosperous elements of the cities, became increasingly common late in the nineteenth century. Compared with the regular party politicians of their day, reformers were mere fly-by-night dilettantes—"mornin' glories."[10] They lacked the discipline and the staying power to mount a year-long program of activities. Perhaps more important, the values of the reformers were remote from—in fact, inconsistent with—the values of the citizens whose support would be needed to keep reform administrations in office. Reformers ordinarily saw low taxes and business-like management of the cities as the exclusive aim of government. To the sweatshop worker, grinding out a marginal existence, these aims were at best meaningless, at worst direct attacks on the one agency of society which seemed to have his interests at heart.

THE DECLINE OF OLD-STYLE PARTY ORGANIZATION

Although in the short run old-style party organizations were marvelously immune to the attacks of reformers, in recent decades the demise of this political form has been widely acclaimed. Because of the absence of reliable trend data, we cannot document "the decline of the machine" with precision. The decline does seem to have taken place, although only partly as a direct consequence of attempts to reform urban politics. Events have conspired to sap the traditional resources used to build voter support and to make voters less interested in these resources which the parties still command.

Decline in the Resources of Old-Style Urban Politicians

Most obviously, job patronage is no longer available in as great a quantity as it once was. At the federal level and in a good many of the states (as well as numerous cities), the bulk of jobs are filled by civil service procedures. Under these circumstances, the most a party politician may be able to do is seek some minor form of preferment for an otherwise qualified job applicant. Furthermore, the technical requirements of many appointive positions are sufficiently complex to make it inexpedient to fill them with unqualified personnel.[11] And private concerns doing business with the cities are not as likely to be sources of patronage in a day when the franchises have been given out and the concessions granted.

[10]Riordon, *op. cit.*, pp. 17–20.
[11]Frank J. Sorauf, "State Patronage in a Rural County," *American Political Science Review*, Vol. 50 (December 1956), pp. 1046–1056.

Beyond this, many modern governmental techniques—accounting and auditing requirements, procedures for letting bids, purchasing procedures, even the existence of a federal income tax—restrict the opportunities for dishonest and "honest" graft. Some of these procedures were not instituted with the explicit purpose of hampering the parties. Legislation designed deliberately to weaken parties *has*, however, been enacted—for example, nomination by direct primary and nonpartisan local elections, in which party labels are not indicated on the ballot. Where other conditions are consistent with tight party organization, techniques of this sort seem not to have been especially effective; old-style parties are perfectly capable of controlling nominations in primaries, or of persisting in formally nonpartisan jurisdictions. But, together with the other party weakening factors, explicit antiparty legislation seems to have taken its toll.

Decline of Voter Interest in Rewards Available to the Parties

Even today it is estimated that the mayor of Chicago has at his disposal 6,000 to 10,000 city patronage jobs. And there are many ways of circumventing good government, antiparty legislation. An additional element in the decline of old-style organization is the increasing disinterest of many citizens in the rewards at the disposal of party politicians. Once upon a time, for example, the decennial federal census was a boon to those local politicians whose party happened to be in control of the White House at census time. The temporary job of door-to-door federal census enumerator was quite a satisfactory reward for the party faithful. In 1960 in many localities, party politicians found census patronage more bother than boon; the wages for this task compared poorly with private wages, and few voters were willing to put in the time and legwork. Other traditional patronage jobs—custodial work in city buildings, employment with departments of sanitation, street repair jobs—were becoming equally undesirable, due to rising levels of income, education, and job security.

An important watershed seems to have been the New Deal, which provided the impetus, at state and local levels as well as the federal level, for increased governmental preoccupation with citizen welfare. The welfare programs of party organizations were undercut by direct and indirect effects of social security, minimum wage legislation, relief programs, and collective bargaining. And, as often has been noted, the parties themselves, by contributing to the social rise of underprivileged groups, helped to develop the values and aspirations which were to make these citizens skeptical of the more blatant manifestations of machine politics.

VARIETIES OF CONTEMPORARY URBAN POLITICS

Nationally in 1956, the Survery Research Center found that only 10 per cent of a cross section of citizens reported being contacted personally by political party workers during that year's presidential campaign. Even if we consider only nonsouthern cities of over 100,000 population, the percentage is still a good bit less than 20.[12] This is a far cry from the situation which would obtain if party organizations were well developed and assiduous. But national statistics conceal a good bit of local variation. A survey of Detroit voters found that only 6 per cent of the public remembered having been approached by political party workers; in fact, less than a fifth of those interviewed even knew that there *were* party precinct officials in their district.[13] Reports from a number of other cities—for example, Seattle and Minneapolis—show a similar vacuum in party activity.[14]

In New Haven, Connecticut, in contrast, 60 per cent of the voters interviewed in a 1959 survey reported having been contacted by party workers.[15] The continuing importance of parties in the politics of this municipality has been documented at length by Robert A. Dahl and his associates.[16] New Haven's Mayor Richard C. Lee was able to obtain support for a massive urban redevelopment program, in spite of the many obstacles in the way of favorable action on such programs elsewhere, in large part because of the capacity of an old-style party organization to weld together the government of a city with an extremely "weak" formal charter. Lee commanded a substantial majority on the board of aldermen and, during the crucial period for ratification of the program, was as confident of the votes of Democratic aldermen as a British Prime Minister is of his parliamentary majority. Lee was far from being a mere creative creature of the party organization which was so helpful to him, but he also was effectively vetoed by the party when he attempted to bring about governmental reforms which would have made the mayor less dependent upon the organization to obtain positive action.[17]

Further evidence of the persistence of old-style party activities came from a number of other studies conducted in the late 1950's. For example, in 1957 party leaders from eight New Jersey counties reported performing a wide range of traditional party services, in response to an ingeniously worded questionnaire administered by Professor Richard T. Frost.[18]

[12]Angus Campbell, Philip E. Converse, Warren E. Miller, and Donald E. Stokes, *The American Voter* (New York, 1960), pp. 426–427. The statistic for nonsouthern cities was supplied to me by the authors.

[13]Daniel Katz and Samuel J. Eldersveld, "The Impact of Local Party Activity on the Electorate," *Public Opinion Quarterly*, Vol. 25 (Spring 1961), pp. 16–17.

[14]Hugh A. Bone, *Grass Roots Party Leadership* (Seattle, 1952); Robert L. Morlan, "City Politics: Free Style," *National Municipal Review*, Vol. 38 (Novermber 1949), pp. 485–491.

[15]Robert A. Dahl, *Who Governs?* (New Haven, 1961), p. 278.

[16]*Ibid.;* Nelson W. Polsby, *Community Power and Political Theory* (New Haven, 1963); Raymond E. Wolfinger, *The Politics of Progress* (forthcoming).

[17]Raymond E. Wolfinger, "The Influence of Precinct Work on Voting Behavior," *Public Opinion Quarterly*, Vol. 27 (Fall 1963), pp. 387–398.

[18]Frost deliberately worded his questionnaire descriptions of these services favorably in order to avoid implying that respondents were to be censured for indulging in "machine tactics." Richard T. Frost, "Stability and Change in Local Politics," *Public Opinion Quarterly*, Vol. 25 (Summer 1961), pp. 231–232.

Table 1   Services performed by New Jersey politicians

The Service	Percentage Performing It "Often"
Helping deserving people get public jobs	72
Showing people how to get their social security benefits, welfare, unemployment compensation, etc.	54
Helping citizens who are in difficulty with the law. Do you help get them straightened out?	62

There was even some evidence in the 1950's of a rebirth of old-style urban party activities—for example, in the once Republican-dominated city of Philadelphia, where an effective Democratic old-style organization was put together. Often old-style organizations seem to exist in portions of contemporary cities, especially the low-income sections. These, like the reform groups to be described below, serve as factions in city-wide politics.[19]

Why old-style politics persists in some settings but not others is not fully clear. An impressionistic survey of the scattered evidence suggests, as might be expected, that the older pattern continues in those localities which most resemble the situations which originally spawned strong local parties in the nineteenth century. Eastern industrial cities, such as New Haven, Philadelphia, and many of the New Jersey cities, have sizable low-income groups in need of traditional party services. In many of these areas, the legal impediments to party activity also are minimal: Connecticut, for example, was the last state in the union to adopt direct primary legislation, and nonpartisan local election systems are, in general, less common in industrial cities than in cities without much manufacturing activity.[20] Cities in which weak, disorganized parties are reported—like Seattle, Minneapolis, and even Detroit (which, of course, *is* a manufacturing center of some importance)—are quite often cities in which nonpartisan institutions have been adopted.

SOME NEW-STYLE URBAN POLITICAL PATTERNS

In conclusion, we may note two of the styles of politics which have been reported in contemporary localities where old-style organizations have become weak or nonexistent: the politics of nonpartisanship and the new "reform" factions within some urban Democratic parties. Both patterns are of considerable intrinsic interest to students of local government. And, as

[19]James Q. Wilson, "Politics and Reform in American Cities," *American Government Annual, 1962–63* (New York, 1962), pp. 37–52.
[20]Phillips Cutright, "Nonpartisan Electoral Systems in American Cities," *Comparative Studies in Society and History*, Vol. 5 (January 1963), pp. 219–221.

contrasting political forms, they provide us with further perspective on the strengths and weaknesses of old-style urban politics.

The Politics of Nonpartisanship

The nonpartisan ballot now is in force in 66 per cent of American cities over 25,000 in population. Numerous styles of politics seem to take place beneath the facade of nonpartisanship. In some communities, when party labels are eliminated from the ballot, the old parties continue to operate much as they have in the past; in other communities, new local parties spring up to contest the nonpartisan elections. Finally, nonpartisanship often takes the form intended by its founders: no organized groups contest elections; voters choose from a more or less self-selected array of candidates.

In the last of these cases, although nonpartisanship has its intended effect, it also seems to have had—a recent body of literature suggests[21]—a number of unintended side effects. One of these is voter confusion. Without the familiar device of party labels to aid in selecting candidates, voters may find it difficult to select from among the sometimes substantial list of names on the ballot. Under these circumstances, a bonus in votes often goes to candidates with a familiar sounding name—incumbents are likely to be reelected, for example—or even candidates with a favorable position on the ballot. In addition, campaigning and other personal contacts with voters become less common, because candidates no longer have the financial resources and personnel of a party organization at their disposal and therefore are dependent upon personal financing or backing from interest groups in the community.

Nonpartisan electoral practices, where effective, also seem to increase the influence of the mass media on voters; in the absence of campaigning, party canvassing, and party labels, voters become highly dependent for information as well as advice on the press, radio, and television. Normally, mass communications have rather limited effects on people's behavior compared with face-to-face communication such as canvassing by party workers.[22] Under nonpartisan circumstances, however, he who controls the press is likely to have much more direct and substantial effect on the public.

Ironically, the "theory" of nonpartisanship argues that by eliminating parties a barrier between citizens and their officials will be removed. In fact, nonpartisanship often attentuates the citizen's connections with the political system.

The Reform Democrats

The doctrine of nonpartisanship is mostly a product of the Progressive era. While nonpartisan local political systems continue to be adopted and, in

---

[21]For a brief review of the relevant literature, see Fred I. Greenstein, *The American Party System and the American People* (Englewood Cliffs, N. J., 1963), pp. 57–60.

[22]Joseph T. Klapper, *The Effects of Mass Communication* (New York, 1960).

fact, have become more common in recent decades, most of the impetus for this development results from the desire of communities to adopt city-manager systems. Nonpartisanship simply is part of the package which normally goes along with the popular city-manager system.

A newer phenomenon on the urban political scene is the development, especially since the 1952 presidential campaign, of ideologically motivated grass-roots party organizations within the Democratic party.[23] The ideology in question is liberalism: most of the reform organizations are led and staffed by college-educated intellectuals, many of whom were activated politically by the candidacy of Adlai Stevenson. In a few localities, there also have been grass-roots Republican organizations motivated by ideological considerations: in the Republican case, Goldwater conservatism.

New-style reformers differ in two major ways from old-style reformers: their ideological concerns extend beyond a preoccupation with governmental efficiency alone (they favor racial integration and improved housing and sometimes devote much of their energy to advocating "liberal" causes at the national level); secondly, their strategy is to work within and take control of the parties, rather than to reject the legitimacy of parties. They do resemble old-style reformers in their preoccupation with the evils of "bossism" and machine politics.

There also is an important resemblance between the new reform politician and the old-style organization man the reformer seeks to replace. In both cases, very much unlike the situation which seems to be stimulated by nonpartisanship, the politician emphasizes extensive face-to-face contact with voters. Where reformers have been successful, it often has been by beating the boss at his own game of canvassing the election district, registering and keeping track of voters, and getting them to the polls.[24]

But much of the day-to-day style of the traditional urban politician is clearly distasteful to the new reformers: they have generally eschewed the use of patronage and, with the exceptions of campaigns for housing code enforcement, they have avoided the extensive service operations to voters and interest groups which were central to old-style party organizations.

---

[23] James Q. Wilson, *The Amateur Democrat* (Chicago, 1962).
[24] There is another interesting point of resemblance between old- and new-style urban party politics. In both, an important aspect of the motivation for participation seems to be the rewards of sociability. Tammany picnics and New York Committee for Democratic Voters (CDV) coffee hours probably differ more in decor than in the functions they serve. An amusing indication of this is provided by the committee structure of the Greenwich Village club of the CDV; in addition to the committees dealing with the club newsletter, with housing, and with community action, there is a social committee and a Flight Committee, the latter being concerned with arranging charter flights to Europe for club members. See Vernon M. Goetcheus, *The Village Independent Democrats: A Study in the Politics of the New Reformers* (unpublished senior distinction thesis, Honors College, Wesleyan University, 1963), pp. 65–66. On similar activities by the California Democratic Clubs, see Robert E. Lane, James D. Barber, and Fred I. Greenstein, *Introduction to Political Analysis* (Englewood Cliffs, N.J., 1962), pp. 55–57.

For example, when election district captains and other officials of the Greenwich Village Independent Democrats, the reform group which deposed New York Democrat County Leader Carmine DeSapio in his own election district, were asked the same set of questions about their activities used in the New Jersey study, strikingly different responses were made.

Table 2   Services performed by New York reform Democrats[25]

The Service	Percentage Performing It "Often"
Helping deserving people get public jobs	0
Showing people how to get their social security benefits, welfare, unemployment compensation, etc.	5
Helping citizens who are in difficulty with the law. Do you help get them straightened out?	6

The successes of this class of new-style urban party politician have vindicated a portion of the classical strategy of urban party politics, the extensive reliance upon canvassing and other personal relations, and also have shown that under some circumstances it is possible to organize such activities with virtually no reliance on patronage and other material rewards. The reformers have tapped a pool of political activists used by parties elsewhere in the world—for example, in Great Britain—but not a normal part of the American scene. One might say that the reformers have "discovered" the British Labor constituency parties.

It is where material resources available to the parties are limited, for example, California, and where voter interest in these resources is low, that the new reformers are successful. In practice, however, the latter condition has confined the effectiveness of the reform Democrats largely to the more prosperous sections of cities; neither their style nor their programs seem to be successful in lower-class districts.[26] The areas of reform Democratic strength are generally *not* the areas which contribute greatly to Democratic pluralities in the cities. And, in many cities, the reformers' clientele is progressively diminishing as higher-income citizens move outward to the suburbs. Therefore, though fascinating and illuminating, the new reform movement must at least for the moment be considered as little more than a single manifestation in a panorama of urban political practices.[27]

[25]Goetcheus, *op. cit.*, p. 138.
[26]DeSapio, for example, was generally able to hold on to his lower-class Italian voting support in Greenwich Village; his opponents succeeded largely by activating the many middle- and upper-class voters who had moved into new high-rent housing in the district.
[27]Probably because of their emphasis on ideology, the new reform groups also seem to be quite prone to internal conflicts which impede their effectiveness. One is reminded of Robert Michels' remarks about the intransigence of intellectuals in European socialist parties. *Political Parties* (New York, 1962, originally published in 1915), Part 4, Chap. 6.

CONCLUSION

The degree to which *old-style* urban party organizations will continue to be a part of this panorama is uncertain. Changes in the social composition of the cities promise to be a major factor in the future of urban politics. If, as seems possible, many cities become lower-class, nonwhite enclaves, we can be confident that there will be a continuing market for the services of the service-oriented old-style politician. Whether or not this is the case, many lessons can be culled from the history of party politics during the years of growth of the American cities—lessons which are relevant, for example, to studying the politics of urbanization elsewhere in the world.[28] In the nineteenth century, after all, the United States was an "emerging," "modernizing" nation, facing the problems of stability and democracy which are now being faced by countless newer nations.

[28]On the significance of the American experience with old-style urban politics for the emerging nations, see Wallace S. Sayre and Nelson W. Polsby, "American Political Science and the Study of Urbanization," Committee on Urbanization, Social Science Research Council, mimeo, 1963, pp. 45–48.

CHAPTER EIGHT

SPOKESMEN FOR THE POOR: AN ANALYSIS OF CLEVELAND'S POVERTY BOARD CANDIDATES

DON R. BOWEN AND LOUIS H. MASOTTI

In February, 1966, elections were held in five areas of Cleveland to select "representatives of the poor" for five newly created seats on the metropolitan area's official poverty agency, the Council for Economic Opportunities in Greater Cleveland. The election was the result of three more or less simultaneous pressures. The Office of Economic Opportunity (OEO) in Washington had been stressing the section of the basic act which called for the "maximum feasible participation" of the poor in the planning and implementation of federally funded, locally operated anti-poverty programs. Local civil rights groups protested that the composition of the Cleveland poverty board did not fulfill that provision.[1] Furthermore, some of the sitting

[1]Prior to the election in 1966, the Council's board of trustees, the official policy-making body of the Cleveland program, consisted of 25 members appointed jointly by the mayor of Cleveland, the president of the Cleveland School Board, and the president of the Cuyahoga County Commissioners. Observers close to the situation have alleged that these three officials in effect performed a veto function over selections made by the powerful, business-dominated and private Welfare Federation of Cleveland. The 25 appointees included several representatives of the civil rights groups, as well as public officials and civic notables. None were poor.

"Spokesmen for the Poor: An Analysis of Cleveland's Poverty Board Candidates" by Don R. Bowen and Louis H. Masotti is reprinted from *Urban Affairs Quarterly*, Volume IV, Issue 1 (Sept., 1968), pp. 89–110, by permission of the Publisher, Sage Publications, Inc., and the authors. Messrs. Bowen and Masotti are Associate Professors of Political Science and, respectively, Research Associate and Director of the Civil Violence Research Center, at Case Western Reserve University.

The authors would like to acknowledge the very able assistance of James Monhart and Joel Latner in seeking out and interviewing poverty candidates, and the cooperation of John Olson and Frank Catliotta of the Cleveland Council for Economic Opportunities. A grant from the Greater Cleveland Associated Foundation facilitated several phases of the project.

members of the Council's board of trustees felt that there was a need for involving representatives of the poor in the decision-making process.

In July, 1965, the board of trustees' committee on representation recommended and authorized five additional seats on the board to be filled with representatives of the target poverty areas. The specific technique used for selecting the five representatives, i.e., direct election,[2] was agreed to in November, 1965, when the board decided that each of five target social planning areas should be entitled to one representative. The target areas are geographical units comprised of Census tracts which were identified some time before the existence of the anti-poverty program as the areas of greatest deprivation in the metropolitan area. As with most areas of this kind, the Cleveland target areas constitute a ring which surrounds the downtown business district and are characterized by extremes of poverty, crime, social disorganization, and poor governmental services. Three of the areas are almost completely Negro, one is in the process of becoming so, and the other is populated by an eclectic group including long-time white ethnic groups, Southern mountain whites, Puerto Ricans, and a few Negroes.

The representatives to be elected had to fall within the official definition of "poverty." This meant that to be eligible, a candidate must have an annual income of less than $1,500 if single, $2,000 if married, with a maximum which increases in $500 increments for every child.[3] Thus a family with ten children might have an income of $7,000, and the parents would still be eligible to run. The election rules also specified that a candidate must be a resident of the social planning area which he sought to represent.

The Council's decision to hold the election was made public in mid-December, 1965. It was announced in a variety of media, and the Neighborhood Opportunity Center and Outreach workers made strenuous efforts to convey election information to the residents of the areas involved and to invite candidacies.[4] The election was originally scheduled for the latter part of January, 1966, but at the request of the candidates it was postponed until February 23rd to allow more time for campaigning. By the filing deadline

[2]The direct election is only one of three basic techniques for determining indigenous representation on the local poverty councils. The others are appointment (e.g., Chicago), and conventions attended by delegates from community organizations (e.g., New York City). Other councils which employed direct elections of one type or another include those in Philadelphia, Los Angeles, and Kansas City.

[3]Readers with a lively sense of the history of the suffrage movement will no doubt find the phenomenon of inverse property requirements ironic. Interestingly enough, it was rationalized by a kind of stake-in-society argument also inverted; e.g., the poor should run the program because they alone have the requisite experience and knowledge to govern in this area.

[4]In Cleveland the Neighborhood Opportunity Centers, located in each planning area, act as channels of communication between the residents and the local office of O.E.O. Outreach workers (indigenous non-professionals, Vista) perform the same function, but actively visit the homes of the poor and try to identify problems and convey to residents the kinds of help which are available to them. Both programs are federally funded.

(January 19th), 48 candidates had declared their intentions of standing for election.[5]

HYPOTHESES ON CANDIDATES' CHARACTERISTICS

Our interest in this election begins at this point. We wanted to know who the candidates were, where they came from, and why they decided to run. Specifically, we sought to answer the question of why a certain number of poverty-stricken persons would emerge as candidates for a public office in the face of the extremely well-documented proposition that the characteristic political behavior of the very poor is apathy. Plainly these people were not apathetic. What then, if anything, differentiated them from the vast mass of their fellow poor? One obvious explanation was ruled out immediately; the elected members of the Council were not to be paid. In fact, the candidates were not reimbursed for their expenses and were denied a campaign subsidy (although one was requested). Hence, a narrowly conceived self-interest was not the answer. Most of them, in fact, had to make minimal, but from their viewpoint heavy, expenditures.[6]

Our speculations along these lines led us to three different, although not necessarily contradictory, hypotheses to explain the decision on the part of the candidates to run for office. The first was simply that the candidates were located near the social center of a center-periphery continuum. We knew, of course, that they were by definition poor and that their socioeconomic status (SES) would be low. Hence we needed a measure of their social participation which did not rely exclusively on status or income. The center-periphery dimension fits this requirement nicely, because it incorporates such things as voluntary group memberships, length of time at a given residence, information, friendships, and integration in an established neighborhood.[7] Generally, the centrally located person has more and better information, partakes in more group activity, spends more time "neighboring," and likes and tends to be liked by other persons. We predicted that the candidates would be, so to speak, "socially available" to run by virtue of their relative centrality, as opposed to the peripheral status of the vast mass of the very poor.

Our second speculation, which led to the next hypothesis, was that the candidates' personal organization would be stronger and more effective

[5]This in itself took some effort on the part of would-be candidates. "Filing" meant turning in a petition signed by at least 100 residents of the "election district" who were eligible voters for this election (eighteen or older).

[6]In fact, we did discover one candidate whose motive for running was his belief that election to the board would give him the necessary leverage to get a loan to start a small business. This, however, was the only case where personal advantage was even remotely hinted among any of the respondents, who were extremely frank throughout the interviews.

[7]For a discussion of this concept, see Lester Milbrath, *Political Participation* (Chicago: Rand-McNally, 1965), pp. 110–114. The indices we have used here are virtually identical with those indicated by Robert Lane in *Political Life* (N. Y.: Free Press, 1959), p. 196.

than that of most of the poor generally. That is, we expected that their personal lives would not be as disorganized, fragmented, and disoriented as that of most of the very poor. Specifically, we expected that the candidates would be anchored in a relatively stable network of family and group ties and would evidence a fairly high amount of gregariousness or sociability and ego strength. The reverse of this, of course, is that we predicted that they would be low on measures of alienation, cynicism, and anomie. We expected, in short, that our candidates would not only be socially available but also personally able to run.[8]

Our third hypothesis was that this election had aroused and flushed out the ideologues among the poor. We speculated that, given the circumstances under which the election was agreed to in the first place and the undertones of class and racial conflict, the candidates would exhibit a reasonably coherent ideology concerning an inequitable distribution of property, political power, and governmental services. We further anticipated that they would view the poverty elections specifically and the whole thrust of the "War on Poverty" in general as a means of redressing this imbalance. As a corollary, we thought it probable that the Negro candidates would see a relation between being impoverished and being Negro and that they would view the elections as a means of attempting to correct this double deficiency.

CANDIDATES' CHARACTERISTICS

The candidates were interviewed in our offices at the University, at various neighborhood opportunity offices or community centers, or at their homes, depending on the preference and convenience of the respondent. The initial contact was made by telephone for two-thirds of the candidates. Those without telephones were contacted by letter and asked to call us. Ultimately we were able to interview 43 of the 48 candidates. Four we were unable to contact after four or five attempts, and one declined to be interviewed. The four we were unable to contact did not have telephones. In view of the fact that we did not pay the respondents, that we put them inevitably to some personal inconvenience, and that the interview generally required some affirmative response on their part to our initiative, we judge the response rate to be very good.

A brief composite picture will indicate the characteristics of the forty-three respondents:

There were 7 men and 36 women.

The median age is 42, ranging from 23 to 75.

16 of the candidates are married, 5 are single, 20 are divorced or separated, and 2 are widowed.

[8]The relation between personal effectiveness and political participation has, of course, been demonstrated before. See, for example, Gabriel Almond and Sidney Verba, *The Civic Culture* (Princeton, N. J.: Princeton Univ. Press, 1963), chap. 10.

The mean number of children is 4, ranging from 0 to 13.

35 are negro, 8 are white.

The median income falls between $2,000-$2,500 per year, ranging from less than $500 to between $5,500-$6,000.

35 are Protestants, 4 are Roman Catholics, and 3 profess no religious affiliation. Of the Protestants, 18 are Baptists and the remainder are spread among 14 other denominations.

The median years of schooling is 11.1 years.

25 have not completed high school, 17 have graduated from high school, and 7 have had some kind of schooling beyond high school.

14 were born and raised in Cleveland, 26 were born and raised in the South, 2 were born and raised in other parts of the United States and 1 was born and raised abroad. Of the 29 non-Clevelanders, 24 were born in rural areas or towns of less than 5,000 population.

20 were unemployed, 11 employed part-time, and 12 were employed full-time. Of the 31 unemployed or part-time employees, 24 were receiving some kind of public assistance. 3 are retired and living on pensions or social security.

Table 1   Selected characteristics of poverty candidates and a community sample of 500

Variable	Candidates		Sample	
	No.	Per cent	No.	Per cent
Sex				
Male	7	16	248	50
Female	36	84	244	50
	43	—	492	
Race				
Negro	35	81	388	78
White	8	19	101	20
Oriental	—	—	1	—
Spanish-speaking	—	—	9	2
	43		499	
Age				
20-29	5	12	115	23
30-39	18	42	113	23
40-49	13	30	106	21
50-59	2	5	71	14
60-69	4	9	59	12
70+	1	2	32	7
	43		496	
Religion				
Catholic	4	9	66	13
Protestant	35	81	396	79
Jewish	0	0	3	1
Other	1	2	19	4
None	3	7	11	2
	43		495	

Table 1—Continued

Variable	Candidates		Sample	
	No.	*Per cent*	*No.*	*Per cent*
Education				
0-8	0	0	152	30
9-11 (some H.S.)	25	58	170	34
H.S. Grad. or better	18	42	176	36
	——		——	
	43		498	
Marital Status				
Single	5	12	41	8
Married	16	37	323	65
Separated	15	35	50	10
Divorced	5	12	32	6
Widowed	2	5	53	11
	——		——	
	43		499	
Partisan Affiliation				
Republican	4	9	25	5
Democratic	33	79	366	77
Independent	5	12	83	18
	——		——	
	42		474	
Number of Dependent Children				
0	9	21	165	37
1-5	25	60	250	57
6 or more	8	19	27	6
	——		——	
	43		442	
No. of Times Moved Past Ten Years				
0	9	22	115	24
1-5	25	61	334	69
6-10	4	10	31	6
10+	3	7	6	1
	——		——	
	41		486	
Mean	3.1		2.2	
Years at Present Address				
1 or less	11	26	131	26
2-5	12	28	185	37
6-10	9	21	84	17
10+	11	26	99	20
	——		——	
	43		499	
Mean	6.4		6.7	

On the face of it, the candidates seem as a group to share most of the characteristics of the poverty-stricken. The central tendency is for them to be low-income Negroes from the rural South. Their families are large and, for the women at least, there is rarely a spouse to assist them. They are concentrated among lower-status religious denominations and, when they can get work, lower-status occupations. The sole exception to this picture is their educational level, which is comparable to that of the whole city.[9] They have, in fine, most of the social characteristics generally associated with political apathy and indifference.[10] But they are neither apathetic nor indifferent. They did choose to run under circumstances which are for many of them difficult, both personally and financially. It is to that choice that we now turn our attention.

A word of caution, however, is warranted before we proceed. These 43 people in no sense constitute a sample of the population of Cleveland, or even of the poverty population of Cleveland. Indeed, we argue that in many ways they are atypical. Moreover, our effort here is to descriptively analyze the candidates as a whole and we have, for the moment at least, eschewed inter-group comparisons. (The authors are currently analyzing the data from a carefully drawn sample of 500 residents from the nine officially designated poverty areas of Cleveland, which will allow us to make detailed comparisons. . . .) In short, our interests are descriptive and impressionistic, not analytic and rigorous. We offer the observations of two trained and (we hope) reasonably competent social scientists. We believe our observations to be provocative and suggestive; but, for the time being, they can be no more than that.

Social Centrality

To repeat our first hypothesis: We expected that the candidates would be, using measures which do not directly involve SES, near the center of a center-periphery social dimension (and would therefore be more likely to run than if they were located near the periphery). We regard the evidence to be overwhelming in support of this hypothesis. Our judgment rests on the following findings: First, the level of voluntary group activity is quite high. Only 6 of the respondents reported no group affiliation whatever. They were counterbalanced by another 6 who indicated 6 or more group activities. The mean number of memberships was 3.1, and the range was 0 to 10. In addition, of those who reported some group affiliation, well over one-half (22) replied that they had served as an officer or committee chairman in at least one of the groups to which they belonged. Another one-third indicated filling a leadership role in more than one group. It is apparent that many of the candidates became organizationally active through their church membership; 19 of the 37 who have some group membership report that at least one of these is affiliated with the church to which they belong. But the more important route is through a network of community and neighborhood clubs of the neighborhood improvement association variety, to which every one of the candidates who reports some group activity belongs. In fact, it

[9] In fact, the mean years of schooling for the candidates was 11.1, as compared to 10.8 for the City of Cleveland.

[10] See Milbrath, *op. cit.* note 7, for a summary of the social characteristics associated with non-participation.

is our impression that the vast majority of the candidates received their information about the election and the initial encouragement to run through these organizations, most of which have close institutional relations with the existing private and public welfare agencies.

In addition to their linkages with a net of voluntary groups, the candidates are settled in neighborhoods to which they appear to have definite loyalties. Their residential patterns are highly stable. None of the candidates, for example, has lived in Cleveland for less than six years, and well over one-half (27) have lived there longer than 20 years. Moreover, almost three-quarters of the candidates have lived at their present addresses for at least five years. Of the 12 who have moved in the past five years, five are Negroes who, we suspect, moved into one of the areas because it represents an upwardly mobile residential pattern among Cleveland Negroes.

The comparative stability of the candidates' residential patterns is reflected in the number of friends and acquaintances they have. Over three-quarters (33) of the respondents report that they have a very large number of friends (more than 50) and over 90% (39) indicate that they have at least two "very close" friends whom they see at least once a month and, in most cases, considerably more often. In particular, more than one-third of the group reported that they had friends in the opposite race, an outcome we viewed as significant in light of the rather tight patterns of residential segregation which obtain in the city of Cleveland.

A final indication of the degree of centrality on the central-peripheral dimension lies in the candidates' political participation. Normally, political scientists treat political participation as a dependent variable and look for other indicators to associate with it. We treat political participation here as another indicator of the social centrality of the candidates. One reason we believe the respondents decided to become candidates for the Economic Opportunities Board was because they had previous experience in participating in other areas of political activity. First, and most obviously, our candidates are voters. Over 60% of them have voted in all eight primary and general elections held in the last four years.[11] Almost 80% voted in all four general elections. Only one of the candidates has not voted at all in the last four years, and only seven have not voted in at least one primary election.

Beyond the level of voting, more than 40% of the candidates classify themselves as active members of a political party. This is supported by the fact that well over half of them have participated in some way in a political campaign, and 15 of them belong to groups classified by the interviewers as "political."[12] Furthermore, the candidates for the most part are partisans. Only six classify themselves as independents; the rest report a definite party

---

[11]These elections include one national, one statewide, and two that were strictly local.
[12]In 14 of the 15 cases, the "political" groups were ward clubs.

affiliation. Following Campbell and his associates, we believe that partisanship is indicative of a higher level of involvement in the political system.[13]

Stability and Organization

We turn now to a consideration of our second hypothesis: The candidates were personally able to run because their lives are not so disorganized and disoriented as seems generally to be the case among the very poor.[14] The evidence for this proposition does not appear to be as strong as for our first hypothesis. However, on balance, we believe that the findings bear out our original expectations. In the first place, as we have noted above, the candidates have a life-style rich in group ties and friendships. They are, by and large, a gregarious and sociable lot. For example, approximately two-thirds of the candidates report that a primary reason for their candidacies was a strong desire to help other people and an equally strong perception that they could be effective by, as one candidate put it, "going around the neighborhoods and talking about these problems." The remaining third reported, with few exceptions, major reasons for running which also seem to us to reflect a high degree of sociability. Some said quite frankly that they ran because they enjoyed talking to others; a number were equally frank in saying simply that they believed themselves more qualified than others by virtue of their other social activities. Only one or two left us with the impression that the whole process was personally painful to them because of the public exposure to which they were not accustomed.

On the other hand, the respondents show a higher amount of familial instability than we expected. Of the 37 who were ever married, more than one-half (21) are divorced or separated. Interestingly enough, none of the seven married male candidates have been divorced or separated. All those who have are women; a comment perhaps on the matriarchal nature of the Negro family structure. In any case, the divorce and separation rate is markedly higher than a comparable figure either nationwide or for the Cleveland metropolitan area; and, whatever the reasons for it, we must conclude that our original expectation in this regard was mistaken and that a goodly number of the candidates have a history of at least some familial instability.

Whatever their family situation, the candidates display a marked sense of their own ego strength and personal efficacy. There are, of course, a number of measures of this dimension of personality, and the ones we employ here are ones dependent on information gained without extensive psychological probing. However, we believe them indicative. We've already noted that well over 90% of the candidates listed, as a reason for running, some kind of statement which indicated that they thought they could effectively accomplish something. When we inquired if they had any trepidations about interacting

---

[13]Angus Campbell, Philip Converse, William Miller, and Donald Stokes, *The American Voter* (N. Y.: Wiley, 1964), pp. 52–55.
[14]Lane, *Political Life*, *op. cit.* note 7.

with the appointive members of the Council (overwhelmingly middle-and upper-middle-class professionals), over two-thirds indicated in one way or another that they did not believe there would be any great difficulty. As one elderly candidate succinctly put it, "They got to listen to us 'cause we're the only ones who know what this mess is really like."

Another way of probing feelings of personal effectiveness is to ask about one's time orientation and aspirations for the future. Our respondents generally have high hopes. In the first place, they are optimistic about the "War on Poverty." Most (39) gave at least some positive reply to the question as to whether the program would accomplish anything. The specific criticisms are legion (not enough money, dominated by politicians, poor not involved, etc.), but the overall expectation is favorable. Many (27) believe that the war on poverty can be won in the specific sense that "poverty can be wiped out completely." Of those who do not think poverty can be eradicated, the vast majority believe it can be ameliorated, although "the poor ye shall always have with ye" was quoted to us by several respondents.

Incredibly (to us), the candidates are not only highly optimistic about doing a great deal about poverty, but they think it can be done quickly. Twenty of them believe that poverty can be totally eliminated in less than ten years.[15] Two thought it would take less than six months, but most see three to five years as the requisite amount of time. Some of these estimates obviously raise questions about the ability of the candidates to make minimally realistic time projections and suggest that the replies are more fantasy and wish projection than anything else. However, examination of the replies in detail leads us to reject this explanation. Our respondents believe that, given the proper infusion of skills and resources and, above all, the involvement of the poor themselves in the planning and execution of the various programs, poverty can be eliminated—or, at a minimum, so ameliorated that we would no longer call it poverty. They may, of course, be mistaken in their estimates, but being wrong is a long way from being fantastic.

On a more personal level, the candidates generally expect to be better off five years from today than they are now. Over half indicated they thought so definitely. Looked at another way, only two envisioned being worse off, and in both cases these were the fears of elderly persons for the deterioration of their health. As one soft-spoken gentleman of 75 put it, "I might not be able to get around and see my friends as I do now. I might even be dead." Moreover, the aspirations of those who believe that the future holds much promise are concrete and rational. These people know what they want and they know how they are going to get it. Their goals are conventional (better

---

[15]The ten-year figure is interesting in the light of O.E.O. Director Schriver's more recent prediction that poverty could be completely eliminated in the United States by the Fourth of July, 1976 (*New York Times*, June 20, 1966). Congressional leaders quickly dismissed this as merely political rhetoric, because it has been estimated that a ten-year target date would necessitate a minimum expenditure of ten billion dollars per year; the current O.E.O. budget is less than two billion dollars.

jobs, more education, more income), but they are solidly based. In very large part, the candidates believe they will be able to take advantage of the training and educational programs offered by the anti-poverty program to achieve their ends.

We sensed in a few cases a vagueness about the future, an inability or unwillingness to project themselves that far; in fact, a projected five-year future lacked meaning for some. "Oh I can't answer that, I just live from day to day, you know what I mean," one woman replied to our query about what she thought she'd be doing five years from now. Others thought they'd be doing about the same thing that they are now, "you know, talking to people, helping them, raising hell downtown." But these are minority themes. For the most part, the candidates have ambitions, and plans to realize them. In particular, we sensed a desire to escape the designation "poor." As one young mother put it, "They [her neighbors in a low-income housing project] hate that word, 'poor.' And 'poverty' is no better. It's just a different word for the same thing." We do not think it amiss to suggest that "I" could be substituted for "they" in that statement. Viewed from this perspective, then, our candidates have status ambitions. Every one of the specific goals they mention would serve to separate them from the category of "the poor" and the attendant personal responsibility for failure that that designation implies in a competitive society.[16]

As an additional indicator, we gave the respondents a standard test for political efficacy, knowing that this too is linked to feelings of personal effectiveness.[17] The results are not as conclusive as we expected. Nine of the candidates were ranked as efficacious, 14 as inefficacious, and the remaining 20 as ambivalent. This suggests that, as a group, the candidates do not have as strong a feeling of personal efficacy as other indicators lead us to believe.

Why is it that our respondents seem overwhelmingly to think that politics and government are beyond their ken? We can suggest an answer from a related part of this inquiry: The candidates in good part do not know, do not understand, and are embittered by the workings of bureaucracy. Over and over again there occur references to "red tape," "all talk, no action," and "bungling." In particular, the governmental structures with which

[16]This seems to contrast with other attitudes among the poverty-stricken reported by other investigators. For the most part, status ambitions seem to be lacking. See, for example, Frank Riessman, "A Portrait of the Underprivileged," in R. E. Will and H. G. Vatter, *Poverty in Affluence* (N. Y.: Harcourt, Brace and World, 1966), pp. 74–78.

[17]The scale has four statements to which the respondent is asked to agree or disagree:

1. I don't think public officials care much what people like me think.
2. Voting is the only way people like me can have any say about the way the government runs things.
3. People like me don't have any say about what the government does.
4. Sometimes politics and government seem so complicated that a person like me can't really understand what's going on.

For an extended discussion of the use of this scale, see Campbell et al., *The Voter Decides* (Evanston, Ill.: Row, Peterson, 1954), pp. 187–194.

the poor are likely to have the most contact—the welfare departments and the courts—appear as remote and alien, operating on rules and procedures incomprehensible to the average man. Nowhere does this appear more clearly than in the answers of those candidates who argue that the War on Poverty will succeed if, and only if, its administration is not exclusively in the hands of professional bureaucrats. Repeatedly, the candidates argue that the program must be brought to the people free of the routinization and rationalization of bureaucracy.

A related aspect of personal organization and effectiveness is relative absence of alienated and anomic behavior and attitudes.[18] Simply put, our respondents are probably one of the most non-alienated group of people who exist. Their behavior is anything but disinterested or apathetic; indeed, as indicated previously, they are deeply involved in a network of social ties. Cynicism about the motives and actions of others was so conspicuously absent that, at times, we wondered if we weren't simply misled. The faith and trust which the candidates expressed in the capacities of man was overwhelmingly positive. For most of our respondents, this was clearly related to deeply held and strongly religious moral codes. The rule of "help thy neighbor" was a real and personal commandment for most of them.

Their behavior, then, is anything but anomic or "ruleless." They have an interrelated set of rules concerning the value and necessity of loving and helping others, and by far the greater part of the 43 perceived that running for a position on the board of the Council for Economic Opportunities was a straightforward application of the code which they had always held.

Within this general "faith-in-others" pattern, we probed for certain specific attitudes which we anticipated might reveal tendencies toward alienation, cynicism, or anomie. Specifically, we asked members of each race what they thought about "whites (Negroes) in general." The question invited stereotypical thinking, and in some cases that was the reply. One elderly white lady thought Negroes were overprone to violence, and four or five of the relatively younger Negro women charged that all whites had a noticeable degree of racial prejudice against Negroes, and in one case, "whites won't give an inch unless we take it from 'em."

But these are the exceptions. Over and over again we were told that "all men are created equal," that "color is skin-deep," that the problems of the poor affect both black and white, and that they (members of the other race) were "just like everybody else." In fact, in many cases the interviewers were informed that the question itself was illegitimate and, perhaps, not a little immoral. The question, many of the respondents forthrightly told us, implied there was some difference traceable to racial characteristics, which was simply untrue. The candidates then showed little, if any, discernible

---

[18]For an extended investigation and summary of this relation, see Murray Levin, *The Alienated Voter* (N. Y.: Holt, Rinehart and Winston, 1962).

racial prejudice. Few perhaps would go so far as one Negro matron who, in answering how she felt about whites in general said, "I love them," but they did not stereotype and they are not ethnocentric. The "faith-in-others" extends across racial lines in a city not exactly notable for its harmonious interracial relations.

We sought further for specific evidence of political alienation. We wanted to know if the candidates were cynical and mistrustful of government and politicians. The answer to this question is both yes and no, but it is decidedly not ambiguous. They regard the federal government as a friendly, indeed munificent, and powerful institution. The federal government (in many cases, specifically the "Johnson Administration") is peopled by "statesmen," men of good will and ability. It is powerful but responsive to the needs of the people. In those cases where some lack is perceived, it is ascribed to ignorance, not indifference or malevolence. If the problem is brought to the attention of the proper officials, they will respond. The federal government has the skills, and above all the resources, to "do what's right."

On the other hand, the city and county governments did not win from our respondents a single positive reference. The only relatively friendly response we received was an admission on the part of a few candidates that the organs of local government simply lacked the tax resources to do anything about the plight of the poor. More common were replies which described the reactions of local government to the problems of poverty in terms ranging from indifference to corruption. Local government is peopled by "politicians"; men who are either inept or corrupt, knaves or fools. Local government is unresponsive to the problems which the candidates perceive as *the* urban problems—slums, rising crime, inferior schooling, and differential governmental services. And local government is unresponsive because, for most of the candidates, it is hostile and indifferent. "Naw, they haven't done nothing and never will," said one candidate in reply to our question whether the city government had done anything to cope with "the problems of the poor." "They're too busy looking out for themselves and the big guys downtown," she concluded.

Can the candidates therefore be classed as politically alienated? Despite such statements as the one just quoted, we think not. They are not distrustful of government in general, only of local government. They are not cynical about all political actors, but only a certain class of them. "Politician" is a term of disapprobation, but they reserve it selectively for use against those officials they dislike. Above all else, they believe that government can do something about the problems of the poor and that the federal government, at least, is moving. Their strongly negative attitude toward local government is based on what they perceive as a failure of output functions, not on a generalized disillusionment with the possibility of responsible and responsive governance.

Prevalence of Ideology

Our third hypothesis was that this election, coming in the time and manner that it did, had aroused the ideologues among the poor. In keeping with this expectation, we sought to learn first if the candidates displayed a coherent, consistent, and well-integrated set of ideological propositions and, second, what their content and direction might be. The answer to these questions is briefly and bluntly that they possess no such set. This is not to say that our respondents have no beliefs about the political and social world around them. They do. But these are latent and diffuse; they are not an ordered whole. If there are ideologues among the poor—and most of the evidence seems to indicate that they are few and far between[19]—with one or two slight exceptions they did not choose to run in these elections.

We sought first of all to learn if there was anything resembling a class consciousness and, more to the point, a sense of being a member of a disadvantaged and exploited class. The answers here are ambiguous. Almost three-fourths of the candidates believe that the poor are not treated fairly. The three most numerous reasons given for this response are inadequate governmental services, discrimination against the poor (possibly against Negroes), and economic exploitation (low wages, high rent, high interest). But by far the greater part of these hold that these conditions can be abolished without resort to revolution. In fact, as noted earlier, they are extraordinarily optimistic about the "War on Poverty." Moreover, the candidates do not, by and large, believe that the poor are treated unfairly because of the antagonism of other economic classes. They perceive no irreconcilable class conflict. The indifference of the "big guys" is ascribed to a lack of knowledge. "We just have to tell 'em [appointed members of the Council] what it's like here, and they'll go along with what's right; they're good people" was typical of many comments.

A more subtle point seems to be that a goodly number of the candidates do not personally identify themselves with "the poor." Throughout the interviews, there are constant references to "they," but few indeed to "we." Another common theme is the denial of any essential class differences. All men are alike, and what makes the very rich different is simply that "they have more money." Of course, as Robert Lane has noted, the denial of class differences serves to protect the egos of those who perceive a sense of failure in a competitive economic system, and this is no doubt operative here.[20] But more important from our viewpoint is the degree to which the candidates sever (or protect) themselves from identification with an underprivileged or exploited class. Lacking such an identification, they are unlikely to perceive the ideology of an exploited class.

[19]Robert Lane reports similar findings in *Political Ideology* (N. Y.: Free Press, 1962). See esp. chap. 9.

[20]*Ibid.*, pp. 61–72.

Our second major inquiry into the candidates' ideology concerned their perception of the relations between themselves—the poor—and government. In particular, we sought to determine what the candidates believed concerning democracy, freedom, equality, and what seemed to us the manifest condition of inequality in which they found themselves. In part, this line of inquiry was vitiated by the views already reported; our respondents do not on the whole believe themselves to be part of "the poor." That is, they do not associate themselves with the attitudes and behavior which that word symbolizes for them. They do not, therefore, think of themselves as "unequal," as we had supposed.

Our questioning about their perceptions of the democratic process had two different but related foci. First, we asked if they believed that the poverty board would be adequately representative of the views of the poor, with the addition of the five elected "poverty" members. More than two-thirds of the candidates replied "no" to this question. This result is consistent with the general belief on the part of the candidates that the poor are not treated fairly, which we discussed above. If the poor are not treated fairly, then it is probable that they would not consider themselves adequately represented on the board. But detailed examination of the replies indicates that the candidates are not charging that the poor are underrepresented because of systematic discrimination and exploitation. True enough, a number of them point out that "those five will be outvoted by the appointed ones." But the real concern for most of the candidates is with the details of administration or the relevance of certain proposals. They find it difficult to relate the programs advanced by the Poverty Board to the real problems of the poor as they understand them. "What good is this legal aid project?" questioned one articulate young Negro. "What have we got to do with lawyers?"

The candidates think then that the poor are not adequately represented, but for those who think the elected representatives of the poor should be a majority on the Council, they believe so not because the poor should seize the instruments of government nor because administration should be under the control of its beneficiaries (or victims), but because the middle-class professionals who make up the current majority simply do not have the requisite knowledge. In addition, there are a great number of others who believe that the poor will not be adequately represented because the districts which those elected represent are simply too big, both in population and area. But this, too, is ascribed to lack of foresight, not to malice. "It's real funny," says one candidate, "you'd think them politicians who set this thing up would know that one person can't cover all the way from 23rd to 97th. I guess they're just not as smart as they pretend."

Although our respondents do not think that the poor are treated fairly, and they do not for the most part think that the election in Cleveland will result in adequate representation of the poor on the Anti-Poverty Council, they make little or no connection between these perceptions and their understanding of democracy or representative government in general.

This conclusion emerges from the second focus, in which we sought to probe their view of the democratic process. Asked what they understand by the word "democracy," the candidates respond with a catalogue of the Bill of Rights. "You know," said one young mother striving to articulate what she takes for granted, "it's the right to say, well, whatever you like, no matter what. To say things they'd throw you in jail for in Russia." In fact, the single most common reply to our query was that democracy means freedom of speech and press, followed closely by a more generalized evocation of "freedom," the right to think, act, do as one likes without fear of sanctions.

Interestingly, the Negro candidates do not identify racial equality as the central meaning of democracy. Some, of course, are concerned about this. A number mention "equal rights for all," but this is not the dominant theme for most. Their understanding of democracy is legalistic and conventional, and in Cleveland, Negroes have enjoyed for a long time the kinds of rights which are central in their view to the democratic process. It is somewhat surprising that the candidates are not concerned about the other major right in the First Amendment, freedom of religion. Only one mentions this as part of her understanding of democracy; and she is a Catholic, which is perhaps significant.[21] Although most of the candidates are deeply religious, the relation between church and state is, for them, not apparently salient in this context.

In speaking about democracy, the candidates speak the language of rights, rarely of opportunities, and never of substantive equality. For those who think of equality, it is the equality of rights. They do not, as we have said, believe that the poor are treated fairly; but they do not connect this with class stratification and they do not connect this with the workings of democracy. Our respondents define a democratic political system according to certain rules of the game, but that the rules might be stacked against them is, with very few exceptions, a perception they do not express.

This is not, of course, to say that the candidates believe all is right with the world. On the contrary, more than a few are deeply angry with what they regard as the failure of the institutions of local government. Many are apprehensive about the direction and administration of the "War on Poverty," and most are personally offended by the examples of grinding poverty and its effects, which they encounter in their everyday lives. But their prescriptions for these social ills (more jobs, better education, better

---

[21]Lane reports that the freedom of religion was central to his largely Catholic respondents in Eastport. *Ibid.*, pp. 22–23.

services) do not depend upon their understanding of democracy. In fact, the two seem mostly unrelated to each other.

Political Liberalism

Our third major line of inquiry concerning ideology was to determine if the candidates ordered their political and social views on a liberal-conservative continuum. We had supposed that if the candidates perceived themselves as members of a disadvantaged class, and if they understood democracy as a process whereby such discrepancies should be corrected by government, then logically they would fall on the liberal end of such a continuum, given the configurations of attitudes and issues concerning the distribution of property and advantages which hold in the United States.

In one sense this supposition was correct. Three-quarters of the candidates identify themselves as members of the Democratic party; over 90% of them voted for President Johnson in 1964, and in the city's 1965 mayoralty race, they voted for a Negro independent candidate (Carl Stokes) who was generally regarded in the community as considerably more liberal than his opponents. Their party affiliations and voting records indicate that they do tend toward the liberal end of the American spectrum. But in another and more fundamental sense, our supposition was wholly incorrect. To put the matter simply, the terms "liberal" and "conservative" have no meaning for our respondents.[22]

Thirty-four of the 43 were unable to classify themselves as either liberals or conservatives. "Ah, that's a tough one, I don't think I want to comment on that" is a typical response. "Well, I'm neither, I just believe in helping people" is another. These comments come from citizens who highly approve of social welfare measures, and who are, in a number of cases, direct beneficiaries of the welfare state. Indeed, their only criticism is that these measures do not go far enough, fast enough. But they do not place these measures or their support of them in the traditional ideological framework of liberal or conservative. Surveys generally indicate that attitudes toward the redistribution of property are among the most reliable predictors of placement on a liberal-conservative continuum and vice versa.[23] But not for our respondents. Such measures seem to them natural, right, and good. That liberal and conservative refer to attitudes reflecting support or nonsupport of social welfare measures is a perception of the political process they do not have.

This is even more clear when we examine the replies of the candidates who did identify themselves as either liberals or conservatives. There were 9 of these: 5 liberals and 4 conservatives. Asked what they meant when they

---

[22]For a similar conclusion, see Philip E. Converse, "The Nature of Belief Systems in Mass Publics," in David E. Apter (ed.), *Ideology and Discontent* (N. Y.: Free Press, 1964), chap. 6.

[23]At least for the "informed" segment of the electorate who have such attitudes. See Campbell et al., *op. cit.* note 13, chap. 7.

employed the terms "liberal" or "conservative" in self-description, the liberals indicated that to them it meant a willingness to help others, a "charity towards all," as one lady replied. Probed for specific political connotations of their replies, two of the liberals indicated opposition to the Presidential candidacy of Senator Goldwater as one of the hallmarks of liberalism. "If he's a conservative," said one, "well then, I'm a liberal." But these reflections do not immediately come to mind. The salient meaning of these most political of terms is simply not a political context for the candidates.

Equally instructive are the replies of the self-classified conservatives (of whom three out of the four have solid Democratic Party voting records). "I'm a conservative because I believe in getting something done, not a lot of talk." "I'm conservative because I like to save money; I'll squeeze a nickel until the eagle screams." It is, of course, possible that the first candidate, a Negro, is telling us that he is disgusted with the white liberals who seem to be characterized by all talk and no action about the specific demands of Negroes. It is also possible that the second candidate is telling us that he favors a deflationary tight money policy with less governmental spending, but there is nothing in the rest of our conversations with these candidates to indicate that this is the case. Our impression is overwhelmingly that the candidates use these terms, if they use them at all, in a personal sense quite divorced from the ideological foundations which lead some members of the society to order their political preferences according to what position on a liberal-conservative continuum they perceive themselves as occupying.

SUMMARY

To summarize: We hypothesized that the candidates would be socially available to run by virtue of their relative centrality on a center-periphery continuum, that they would be personally equipped to run by a relatively high sense of personal effectiveness and organization, and that they would be motivated to run at least in part by ideological considerations. The first two of these hypotheses seem to us confirmed by the results of the interviews. The third hypothesis, on the other hand, is not supported by our data.

The evidence in favor of the first hypothesis is that the candidates are involved in a very great deal of voluntary group activity. They are "wired in," so to speak, to a network of group associations centering on their church and immediate neighborhood, but by no means confined to it. Within this network, they have developed in many cases an extraordinary number of friendships, a number of which transcend a rather wide racial cleavage in the central city. They maintain their location in this network in good part because of the stability of their own living patterns. They are anchored, as it were, in a reasonably solid home base. Last, but by no means least, they have previous experience of more than minimal political participation, and a goodly number of them would be classified as political activists. In short, the candidates are poor, but their social lives are far from impoverished. Indeed, they appear to us rich in the associational activity normally attributed only to those much higher in SES.

In support of our second hypothesis, we found that the candidates are an extremely sociable and gregarious set. The high number of divorces and separations does not support our view that they display a greater amount of personal stability and effectiveness than the poor generally; but on the other hand, we judge their ego strength to be fairly high and other aspects of effectiveness to be strongly present. They have a fairly well defined and realistic set of personal goals, and a lively sense of the time and means needed to achieve them. As a group, they do not score particularly high on political efficacy, but it is possible that the test used here tapped a particular dimension of misunderstanding and bitterness among the poor. On the other hand, they are anything but cynical or apathetic. Indeed, perhaps the most outstanding characteristic of the entire group is a willingness and ability to trust and help other persons. Finally, the candidates indicate a certain kind of political alienation; namely, disillusion and resentment about the operation of local government. But these feelings are particular, specific complaints about particular, specific grievances. They have nothing to do with a diffuse and generalized resentment of all government.

We reject our third hypothesis on the grounds that the candidates do not appear to share a tightly knit, well-defined ideological view of their social world. What is absolutely certain, at a minimum, is that they do not have an ideology of a revolutionary redistribution of property for the benefit of an exploited and disadvantaged social class. They perceive that the poor are treated badly, but they do not associate this with a class stratification system and they do not appear to identify themselves personally with "the poor." They do not believe that the poor will be adequately represented on the city's poverty board, nor do they think that local government responds to the needs of the poor. But there is little connection made between these perceptions and their understanding of democracy. That the poor are underrepresented and mistreated seems to them the work of a few misguided or malevolent individuals, not of the workings of representative government itself.

Finally, the candidates do not regard themselves as members of the political left or right (as represented by the terms liberal or conservative). Indeed, we judge that this political spectrum has little or no meaning for the vast majority of them. Most share attitudes and behavior which would cause an outside observer to classify them as liberals in the American political context. But the candidates arrive at their political positions without reference to whether they are liberals or conservatives. For them the test of a position is whether it is right and good, and there is little doubt in their minds that all reasonable men will see it as they do.

CHAPTER NINE

PARTY COMPETITION
AND PUBLIC POLICY

THOMAS R. DYE

PARTY SYSTEMS AND PUBLIC POLICY

While the basic institutional and legal frameworks of the fifty state governments are quite similar, party systems in the fifty states are remarkably varied. For purposes of analysis, many of the institutional characteristics of state political systems may be treated as constants. However, because states differ considerably with respect to the division of two-party control and the levels of interparty competition, we have an excellent opportunity to observe the effects of differences in party systems upon public policy outcomes. Does the character of the party system have an independent effect upon public policy outcomes, mediating between socioeconomic inputs and these outcomes? Or are policy outcomes determined by socioeconomic conditions without regard to the character of the party system?... Does it make any difference in policy outcomes whether a state has a one-party or two-party style of politics, or do socioeconomic conditions determine policy outcomes regardless of the character of the party system? It is the task of this chapter to summarize our answers to these important questions.

Of course, in assessing the influence of the party system on public policy outcomes, it is necessary to take into account the effects of socioeconomic inputs, since these inputs have . . . been shown to be related to both party system characteristics and policy outcomes in the states. This chapter will focus upon the effects of the division of two-party control and the level of interparty competition on policy outcomes in . . . five policy-making areas,

Reprinted with permission of publisher and author from Thomas R. Dye, *Politics, Economics, and the Public: Policy Outcomes in the American States* (Chicago: Rand McNally & Co., 1966), pp. 238–39 and 251–58. Mr. Dye is Professor of Political Science at Florida State University.

while controlling for the effects of the economic development variables. This will enable us to summarize the complex relationships between the characteristics of state party systems (... level of interparty competition), economic development variables (urbanization, industrialization, income, and education), and public policy outcomes (in education, health and welfare, highways, taxation, and public regulation). . . .

PARTY COMPETITION AND PUBLIC POLICY

The relationship between economic development and state party systems has already been established in the literature on American state politics. Golembiewski, in a study of the relationships between a variety of socioeconomic factors and state party systems, reported statistically significant correlations between urbanism, income, and industrialization and several measures of party competition among the fifty states.[1] Ranney and Kendall, Key, and Schlesinger have also implied that one or more of the measures of economic development correlate closely with party competition in the American states.[2]

. . . Party competition in state legislatures is measured by one minus the percentage of seats in each house held by the majority party, whether Republican or Democratic, between 1954 and 1964. Party competition in gubernatorial elections is measured by one minus the average margin of victory posted by the winning candidates, whether Republican or Democratic. Legislative competition scores range from 49 (1–51 per cent) in the Pennsylvania and Illinois lower houses (most competitive), to 0 (1–100 per cent) in the houses and senates of Arkansas, Alabama, Louisiana, Mississippi, and South Carolina (least competitive). Gubernatorial competition scores range from 48 (1–52 per cent) in Illinois, Iowa, Delaware, Wyoming, Massachusetts, Montana, New York, Michigan, New Jersey, Minnesota, and Washington (most competitive), to under 10 (1–90 per cent) in Louisiana, Georgia, Mississippi, and South Carolina. . . . These competition scores have been shown to be significantly related to income, education, and urbanization.[3]

The linkage between system characteristics and policy outcomes in American state politics is *not* so well established in the literature. In the most thorough study of this relationship to date, Dawson and Robinson cite only the work of V. O. Key, Jr. and Duane Lockard as relevant research in state

[1]Robert T. Golembiewski, "A Taxonomic Approach to State Political Party Strength," *Western Political Quarterly*, XI (1958), 494–513.

[2]Austin Ranney and Wilmoore Kendall, "The American Party System," *American Political Science Review*, XLVIII (1954), 477–85; Joseph A. Schlesinger, "A Two-Dimensional Scheme for Classifying States According to the Degree of Inter-Party Competition," *American Political Science Review*, XLIX (1955), 1120–28; and V. O. Key, Jr., *American State Politics* (New York: Knopf, 1956), p. 99.

[3]See [the author's *Politics, Economics, and the Public* (Chicago: Rand McNally & Company, 1966), p. 58].

politics on the impact of system characteristics on policy outcomes.[4] In his *Southern Politics*, Key finds that states with loose multifactional systems and less continuity of competition tend to pursue conservative politics on behalf of upper socioeconomic interests.[5] In states with cohesive and continuous factions more liberal policies are pursued on behalf of less affluent interests. Duane Lockard observed among the six New England states that the two-party states (Massachusetts, Rhode Island, and Connecticut), in contrast to the one-party states (Maine, New Hampshire, and Vermont), received a larger portion of their revenue from business and death taxes, spent more on welfare services such as aid to the blind, the aged, and dependent children, and were better apportioned.[6] Neither of these studies, however, attempted systematically to hold constant for the impact of economic development while observing these different policy outcomes. It was Dawson and Robinson who first attempted to sort out the influence of party competition on policy outcomes from the influence of economic development. The focus of the Dawson and Robinson study was upon welfare policy outcomes, which were defined to include the percentage of state revenue from death and gift taxes, per capita state revenue, per pupil expenditures, average assistance payments to the blind, the aged, and dependent children, and average unemployment compensation payments. Rank order correlation coefficients among 46 states showed that both party competition and income, urbanization, and industrialization were related to these policy outcomes. When party competition was held constant, wealth continued to correlate closely with policy outcomes. However, when wealth was held constant, party competition did *not* appear to be related to policy outcomes. The authors concluded that "interparty competition does not play as influential a role in determining the nature and scope of welfare policies as earlier studies suggested. The level of public social welfare programs in the American states seems to be more a function of socio-economic factors, especially per capita income."[7] In short, party competition has been found to have little independent effect on welfare policies; whatever correlations do exist between welfare policies and competition, they are merely a product of the relationship between economic development and competition, and economic development and welfare.

Table 1 shows the relationship between party competition and 54 separate measures of education, welfare, highway, tax, and regulatory policies in the fifty states. In the simple coefficients, which do *not* control for the effects of economic development variables, party competition appears

[4]Richard E. Dawson and James A. Robinson, "Interparty Competition, Economic Variables, and Welfare Policies in the American States," *Journal of Politics*, II (1963), 265–89.
[5]V. O. Key, Jr., *Southern Politics in State and Nation* (New York: Knopf, 1951), pp. 298–314.
[6]Duane Lockard, *New England State Politics* (Princeton: Princeton University Press, 1959), pp. 320–40.
[7]Dawson and Robinson, p. 289.

Table 1   The relationship between party competition and state policy outcomes, controlling for the effect of economic development

| | Party Competition | | | | | |
| | Lower Houses | | Upper Houses | | Governorships | |
	Simple	Partial	Simple	Partial	Simple	Partial
Education						
Per pupil expenditures	.51*	.08	.48*	.00	.59*	.08
Average teachers' salaries	.36*	.11	.35*	.18	.50*	.12
Teachers with B.A.	−.38*	−.34	−.39*	−.34	−.32*	−.34
Teachers with M.A.	.16	.16	.13	.22	.35*	.05
Male teachers	.50*	.14	.41*	.03	.57*	.22
Pupil-teacher ratios	−.55*	−.21	−.50*	−.15	−.64*	−.34
Dropout rates	−.74*	−.53*	−.67*	−.40*	−.62*	−.38*
Mental failures	−.64*	−.37*	−.57*	−.36*	−.75*	−.63*
Size of school districts	−.51*	−.34	−.37*	−.18	−.43*	−.29
State participation	−.50*	−.31	−.42*	.21	−.47*	−.34
Federal participation	−.24	−.30	−.26	−.34	−.14	−.34
Welfare						
Per capita welfare expenditures	.01	−.12	.00	−.00	−.03	−.01
Per capita health expenditures	.20	.11	.27	.01	.20	.26
State participation in welfare	−.33*	−.20	−.30*	−.12	−.36*	−.17
State participation in health	.10	.06	.06	−.00	−.06	−.11
Federal participation in welfare	−.48*	.02	−.50	−.08	−.52	−.17
Unemployment benefits	.52*	.05	.51*	.04	.52*	.11
OAA benefits	.60*	.01	.57*	.02	.55*	.02
ADC benefits	.65*	.04	.60*	.03	.69*	.07
Blind benefits	.61*	.11	.59	−.11	.53	−.02
General assistance	−.56*	.16	−.51*	−.09	−.53	−.05
OAA recipients	.32*	.07	.34*	.09	.48*	.12
ADC recipients	.28	−.06	.27	−.06	.17	−.02
Unemployment recipients	−.17	−.13	−.22	−.20	−.30*	−.16
General assistance cases	−.32*	−.24	−.27	−.14	−.30*	−.12
Highways						
Per capita highway expenditures	−.20	.15	−.18	.10	−.25	−.05
State participation	.18	.06	.15	−.01	.09	.00
Federal participation	−.13	.02	−.10	−.02	−.08	−.09
Funds from highway users	.18	−.19	.05	−.11	.09	−.23
Highway fund diversion	.19	.20	.14	.18	.21	.23
Rural-urban distribution	.12	.08	.12	.04	.36*	.34
Public Regulation						
Governments per population	.31*	−.23	−.27	−.22	−.18	−.24
Number of bills introduced	−.09	−.08	−.15	−.10	−.02	.06
Number of laws enacted	.17	.19	.11	.14	.17	.20
Public employees	−.28	.22	−.26	.14	−.24	.21
State employees	.00	.26	.06	.10	−.19	.08
Public employees' salaries	−.42*	.05	−.37*	.15	.51*	.18
Correctional expenditures	−.25	.08	−.15	−.10	−.02	.06
Policemen	−.15	.23	−.22	.14	−.25	.16
Prisoners	.39*	.31	.40*	.34	.32*	.32

Table 1—Continued

	Party Competition					
	Lower Houses		Upper Houses		Governorships	
	Simple	Partial	Simple	Partial	Simple	Partial
Crime rate	-.18	.23	-.06	.28	-.10	.29
Gambling revenue	-.12	.14	-.10	.01	-.17	.01
Divorce rate	.13	.33	.03	.16	.02	.23
Parolees	.36*	.29	.32*	.20	.37*	.29
Taxation						
Total revenue per capita	.40*	.19	.40	.13	.47	.16
Total taxes per capita	.52*	.03	.53*	.02	.59	.07
Debt	.22	.02	.24	.01	.21	.02
State percentage of total revenue	-.53*	-.34	-.47*	-.30	-.44*	-.28
Federal percentage of total revenue	-.25	-.21	-.25	-.14	-.26	-.24
Income taxes	.12	.05	.10	.03	.18	.01
Sales taxes	.22	.13	.22	.15	.15	.00
Alcohol and tobacco taxes	.15	.04	.10	.02	.16	.02
Motor fuel taxes	-.15	-.06	-.05	-.03	-.10	-.10
Property taxes	-.61*	-.34	-.52*	-.31	-.48*	-.32

Figures are simple and partial correlation coefficients; partial coefficients control for the effect of urbanization, industrialization, income, and education; an asterisk indicates a significant relationship.

closely related to a number of important policy outcomes. States with a high degree of party competition tend to spend more money per pupil for public schools, pay higher teachers' salaries, attract more male teachers, enjoy lower pupil-teacher ratios, have fewer dropouts and mental failures, have larger school districts, and raise more school revenue from local rather than from state or federal sources. These same states tend to pay more liberal welfare benefits, and tend to rely more on local welfare monies than on state or federal sources. States with competitive parties also tend to raise more total revenue per capita and more tax revenues, and they also tend to rely more on local than on state sources of revenue. In all, 26 of the 54 policy measures are significantly associated with party competition in simple co-efficients. Party competition has been found to be unrelated to 38 policy measures, including per capita health and welfare expenditures and finance, public employment, police and correctional policy, and the relative reliance placed upon income, sales, alcohol and tobacco, and motor vehicle taxes as sources of state revenue.

However, when the effects of economic development are controlled in the partial correlation coefficients, almost all of the association between party competition and policy disappears. Of the 26 statistically significant correlations shown in simple coefficients, 24 of these fall below accepted significance levels, once urbanization, industrialization, income, and education are controlled. In short, party competition has *no apparent independent effect* on 52 of the 54 policy outcomes investigated.

Table 2 The relationship between economic development and state policy outcomes, controlling for the effect of party competition

	Economic Development							
	Urbanization		Industrialization		Income		Education	
State Policy Measures	Simple	Partial	Simple	Partial	Simple	Partial	Simple	Partial
Education								
Per pupil expenditures	.51*	.44*	.36*	.36*	.83*	.73*	.59*	.35*
Average teachers' salaries	.69*	.66*	.64*	.66*	.88*	.85*	.57*	.39*
Teachers with B.A.	.42*	.64*	.60*	.71	.11	.53*	-.04	.28
Teachers with M.A.	.54*	.52*	.42*	.38*	.55*	.49*	.42*	.30
Male teachers	.48*	.43*	.26	.25	.63*	.42*	.63*	.39*
Pupil-teacher ratios	-.13	.09	-.19	-.11	-.43*	-.39*	-.50*	-.11
Dropout rate	-.40*	.30	.09	-.21	.54*	.18	-.60*	.24
Mental failures	-.05	.30	.13	.38*	-.46*	.10	-.70*	.41*
Size of school districts	.06	.23	0.26	0.35*	-.18	.20	-.37*	-.27
State participation	-.10	.06	.18	.27	-.30*	.16	.35*	.50*
Federal participation	-.36*	-.35*	-.08	-.08	-.32*	.14	.27	.27
Welfare								
Per capita welfare expenditures	.19	.21	.07	-.09	-.01	.01	-.07	.11
Per capita health expenditures	.45*	.38*	.39*	.38*	.56*	.57*	.42*	.42*
State participation in welfare	-.11	-.16	-.15	-.13	-.35*	-.15	-.17	.13
State participation in health	-.30*	-.35*	-.07	-.12	-.08	-.15	-.15	-.19
Federal participation in welfare	-.43*	-.31	-.35*	-.35*	-.82*	-.74	-.59*	-.39*
Unemployment benefits	.55*	.47*	.30*	.31	.80*	.71*	.67*	.50*
OAA benefits	.49*	.41*	.15	.13	.63*	.41*	.61*	.35*
ADC benefits	.51*	.46*	.26	.27	.74*	.52*	.55*	.12
Blind benefits	.59*	.55*	.28	.32	.71*	.55*	.64*	.32*
General assistance	.58*	.54*	.39*	.45*	.76*	.65*	.43*	.08
OAA recipients	-.22	-.07	-.26	-.20	-.55*	-.35*	-.35*	-.10
ADC recipients	-.15	-.09	.16	.16	-.30*	-.23	-.42*	-.37*
Unemployment recipients	.39*	.32	.69*	.67*	.58*	.51*	.23	-.07
General assistance cases	.38*	.32	.34*	.35*	.40*	.27	.25	-.03
Highways								
Per capita highway expenditures	-.37*	-.49*	-.51*	-.58*	.02	-.21	.04	.27

	Col 1	Col 2	Col 3	Col 4	Col 5	Col 6	Col 7	Col 8
State participation	-.30*	-.27	.05	-.04	-.15	-.09	-.04	.07
Federal participation	-.45*	-.50*	-.42*	-.42*	-.10	-.19	.23	.22
Funds from highway users	.04	.00	.20	-.17	-.32*	-.36*	.26	-.30
Highway fund diversion	.42*	.52*	.29	.33	-.07	.29	.06	.13
Rural-urban distribution	-.35*	-.30	-.45*	-.40*	-.38*	-.24	-.07	.17
Public Regulation								
Governments per population	-.39*	-.51*	-.76*	.81*	-.19	-.47*	-.09	-.11
Number of bills introduced	.53*	.53*	.39*	.41*	.28	.33	.04	.02
Number of laws enacted	.40*	.48*	.30*	.32	.10	.29	-.03	.14
Public employees	.07	-.02	.26	-.30	.36*	.12	.61*	.59*
State employees	-.16	-.25	.02	-.05	.32*	.15	.36*	.39*
Public employees' salaries	.41*	.35*	.42*	.42*	.83*	.77*	.58*	.37*
Correctional expenditures	.32*	.21	.30*	.24	.69*	.62*	.58*	.50*
Policemen	.75*	.72*	.54*	.53*	.64*	.66*	.32*	.26
Prisoners	-.01	.14	.11	.60	-.11	.20	-.58*	-.37*
Crime rate	.61*	.61*	.45*	.43*	.49*	.58*	.38*	.46*
Gambling revenue	.34*	.30	.38*	.35*	.34*	.33	.19	.20
Divorce rate	.07	.06	.10	.06	.17	.26	.24	.42*
Parolees	.45*	.39*	.30*	.30	.35*	.14	.37*	.01
Taxation								
Total revenue per capita	.30*	.16	.03	-.05	.64*	.48*	.75*	.67*
Total taxes per capita	.59*	.52*	.23	.19	.76	.60*	.74*	.58*
Debt	.61*	.58*	.54*	.55*	.59*	.60*	.37*	.22
State percentage of total revenue	-.28	-.17	-.08	-.07	-.34*	-.03	.24	.16
Federal percentage of total revenue	-.59*	-.55*	-.32*	-.30	-.33*	-.20	-.07	.14
Income taxes	-.05	-.10	.02	-.01	.20	.12	.19	.10
Sales taxes	-.03	.11	-.19	.01	-.15	-.04	.19	-.08
Alcohol and tobacco taxes	-.10	-.07	-.01	.00	-.10	.00	-.22	-.14
Motor fuel taxes	-.32*	-.35*	-.35*	-.36*	-.27*	-.47*	-.10	-.27
Property taxes	.36*	.15	-.11	-.17	.32*	-.06	.43*	.06

Figures are simple and partial correlation coefficients; partial coefficients control for the effect of three measures of party competition; an asterisk indicates a significant relationship.

The only apparently independent effect of party competition on policy outcomes is the effect on dropout rates and mental failures. Yet even these relationships disappear when the southern states are removed from the correlations. In order to provide a check upon our findings that party competition has little independent effect on policy outcomes and that its association with these outcomes is merely a product of the intervening impact of economic development, the relationship between economic development and policy outcomes has been observed in Table 2 while controlling for the combined effects of three measures of party competition. The simple coefficients in Table 2, which do *not* control for party competition, summarize many strong relationships . . . between economic development and a variety of policy outcomes. Of the 54 measured policy outcomes, 49 are significantly associated with at least one of the measures of economic development.

But the most striking comparison between Tables 1 and 2 is in the partial coefficients. The significant relationships between socioeconomic variables and policy outcomes *do not disappear* when the effect of party competition is controlled. For the most part, the partial coefficients in Table 2, unlike those in Table 1, continue to identify statistically significant relationships even after controlling for the effect of party competition. Of the 49 policy variables for which significant simple correlations are obtained in Table 2, 45 remain significantly related to one or more socioeconomic variables, even after party competition is controlled. Controlling for party competition does *not* seriously affect the relationships between economic development and educational expenditures, teacher preparation, salary levels, the proportion of male teachers, pupil-teacher ratios, welfare benefit levels, or state and local government revenues or tax receipts. Controlling for party competition has some effect on the relationships between economic development and dropout rates, the state participation in highway finance, the state proportion of total revenue receipts, and reliance upon property taxation. In short, while party competition has little independent effect on policy outcomes after economic development is controlled, economic development continues to have considerable independent effect on policy outcomes after party competition is controlled. These operations suggest that party competition does not play as influential a role on determining policy outcomes as the level of economic development.

SOME CONCLUSIONS ABOUT PARTY COMPETITION IN THE STATES

Economic development in the American states is related to party competition and to many policy outcomes, but party competition itself appears to have little independent effect on policy outcomes. Differences in the policy choices of competitive and non-competitive states turn out to be largely a product of differences in levels of economic development rather than a direct product of party competition. Economic development—urbanization, industrialization, income and education—is more influential in determining policy outcomes than party competition. Most of the association between party competition and policy outcomes is merely a product of the relationships between economic development and party competition, and economic development and policy outcomes.

Of course, these conclusions are predicted on results obtained from analyzing selected measures of state policy in five separate fields—education, welfare, highways, taxation, and public regulation. Conceivably, party competition may have a more direct effect on some policy outcomes which have not been investigated. However, expenditures for welfare and education, the liberality of welfare benefits, teachers' salaries, the quality of public education, and the tax and revenue structure are certainly among the most important decisions that states must make. And party competition seems to have little impact on the outcome of these decisions. . . .

PART THREE

THE POLICY-MAKING PROCESS: LEGISLATIVE DELIBERATION AND RULE-MAKING

Perhaps the most compelling generalization that can be made about legislatures in democratic political systems today is that their roles in initiating and shaping the rules governing society have become less significant. American state and local legislatures are no exception. They, too, have suffered a comparative decline in the amount and the quality of resources available to them for gathering information, interpreting trends, formulating proposals, and convincing an often skeptical public to support innovation. Today, these resources are more than ever at the disposal of the executive branch of government, and they enable governors, mayors, and city managers both to initiate and to follow through on detailed legislative proposals. This is not to suggest that legislatures have become ineffectual institutions, capable only of supplying or withholding a rubber stamp. If their contribution to lawmaking has diminished appreciably, certainly their capacity for facilitating the expression of many points of view, for providing legislative oversight, and, more generally, for offering a forum for the resolution or diminution of conflict has not. Even in making law their role cannot be underestimated. They still must approve all bills that become law, and they frequently take the initiative in significantly modifying these measures. Often chided for paying undue homage to the *status quo*, state legislatures and city councils nevertheless pass thousands of bills each year, some of which receive a major impetus from forces generated within the legislative body itself.

In the following chapters attention is given to selected features of the decision-making process in state and local legislatures. Gilbert Y. Steiner and Samuel K. Gove view the legislative process as a maze of obstacles through which proposals must be guided. Standing committees represent one such impediment, with their importance varying from state to state. The authors find that in Illinois neither the committees nor their chairmen exercise a significant independent influence over public policy. The chairman's influence is reflected more in the fact that the legislative leadership has enough trust in him to award him the position than it is in the fact that he is able to exercise the perquisites of that position. In Illinois, few bills are bottled up by a committee or an uncooperative chairman. Most are ultimately reported out (provided their sponsors want them sent to the floor) and when this happens committee amendments are not likely to have the preferred status given such amendments in other states or in the U.S. Congress. Steiner and Gove, nevertheless, find the Illinois committees to be an important convenience. They are useful bill-screening devices at the very least, and at most they may be significant instruments through which the legislative or executive leadership works to resolve or reduce group conflict.

In his chapter on councilmanic decisions J. Leiper Freeman examines the forces that impinge upon and influence the legislative process in a medium-sized town in Massachusetts. Looking at a series of appropriations decisions, Freeman identifies four factors that could conceivably influence council decisions: the nature of the issue; the internal group structure of the council; the norms of the legislative system; and the relationship between council members and influential actors outside the council. In the case studied, Freeman found that whenever councilmen deserted their usual voting faction they did so largely in response to their perceptions of constituents' interests. He also discovered that the internal organization of the council, i.e., the emergence of clearly discernible factions, explained a great deal about councilmanic behavior. Because council members were keenly aware of the factionalism they frequently rejected the informal norms adopted by previous councils to reduce conflict and invoked instead the formal rules governing procedures and practices. Finally, Freeman found that the opposition of the mayor and the belligerence of the press played a significant role in initially crystallizing the cleavage between the two factions.

Wayne L. Francis utilizes questionnaire responses from more than eight hundred state legislators in attempting to explain the variations in "perceived policy success" and "policy outcomes" among the fifty state legislatures. The former term refers to the degree to which "legislators feel that the system has met its responsibilities," while the latter denotes the "objective structural changes in the environment which result from decisions of public officials." Francis finds that perceptions of policy success are greatest in states where the same party controls both the legislature and the governor's office and where the minor party provides more than token opposition. Perceptions of policy success also seem to be related to the extent of pressure group conflict within the states. The author next examines the connection between policy outcomes and political conflict by comparing the levels of party competition and the degree of malapportionment within the states. He finds that states exhibiting a high degree of interparty competition tend to have well-apportioned legislatures. Thus, while policy outcomes involving the expenditure of funds may have little to do with the degree of party competition within a state (as Dye and others have suggested), those in areas unrelated to expenditures, such as the distribution of seats within the state legislature, may correlate closely with political variables.

CHAPTER TEN

THE INFLUENCE OF STANDING COMMITTEES IN THE ILLINOIS LEGISLATURE

GILBERT Y. STEINER AND SAMUEL K. GOVE

A maxim of many legislators and political scientists is that debate and activity (or lack of activity) on the floor of a legislative body is not nearly as important as committee work—that it is in committees that the real work is done, that the key to legislative results is in committee activity, that legislative struggles are won and lost in committee. This chapter is devoted to an exploration of the actual role of standing committees in the Illinois General Assembly. The data are drawn principally from the 1957 session. The chapter is concerned with substantive results, with the role of committees on important legislation, and with a search for some determinants of committee influence on the legislative output.

GENERAL FRAME OF REFERENCE

If the process of public policy-making can appropriately be conceived of as a process of adjustment between a virtually infinite number of groups directly and tangentially concerned with the impact of that policy on them, it can be asserted that one method of reaching such an adjustment is through the ordinary technique of statute lawmaking. That technique, in the American system, habitually involves passage of a specific bill by each house of a bicameral legislature and approval by the chief executive, or, alternately, passage by each house by an extraordinary majority notwithstanding the disapproval of the executive. In this process, the legislative bodies and the executive themselves become part of the interest group structure. Since

Reprinted with permission of publisher and authors from Gilbert Y. Steiner and Samuel K. Gove, *Legislative Politics in Illinois* (Urbana: University of Illinois Press, 1960), pp. 58–83. Mr. Steiner is a Senior Staff member of the Brookings Institution. Mr. Gove is Professor of Political Science and Director of the Institute of Government and Public Affairs, University of Illinois.

they influence the relative effectiveness of groups, organization and procedure of the legislative bodies for formal consideration of proposals become an important matter of inquiry.

By constitutional requirement and by rule, legislative organization and procedure are designed to present a series of impediments to the easy enactment of laws. The Illinois constitution requires that a bill be read at large on three different days in each chamber, that it be passed by a majority of all the members elected to each house, that it be approved by the governor or by an extraordinary legislative majority, and that it not become effective until the July 1 next following passage.[1] On top of this, the General Assembly itself imposes rules for the printing of bills, for the appearance of bills on the calendar as a condition for action, and for committee consideration. Every technical requirement, whether imposed by rule or by the constitution, is a barrier which must be overcome before a law is enacted. This conception of the formal legislative process as a series of hurdles suggests the possibility of creating a kind of ranked order of hurdles, an order which may change with different sets of conditions and with different bills. Obviously, if both houses are overwhelmingly Republican, a Democratic governor may be a more imposing hurdle for some bills than is the requirement of passage by a constitutional majority. On the other hand, with strong Republican houses, a Republican governor may very well be less of an impediment to enacting legislation than, say, the technical requirement for three readings.[2] The committee process is a dynamic impediment to be evaluated in comparison with these other dynamic impediments, each of which presents an opportunity for bills to be killed by particular groups. It is important to identify the conditions under which the committee impediment is maximized and minimized.

Although legislative flow charts show the standing committee as a step between introduction and floor consideration of a bill, some legislation is advanced without committee reference. Moreover, the extent and nature of committee consideration of legislation varies significantly between legislative bodies, running the range from the Alabama constitutional requirement that no bill be enacted without reference to and action by a standing committee of each house, to the disposition of the English House of Commons to restrict the share of committees "to that stage in the process where the principles of the bill have been determined and lie outside the ambit of the committee."[3]

[1] *Illinois Constitution of 1870*, Art. IV, Sec. 13.

[2] In June 1955, perhaps two weeks before adjournment, a bill to impose a property tax rate ceiling for Chicago was introduced in the Illinois Senate and advanced to second reading without reference to committee. Although there is little doubt that there were plenty of votes to secure passage, its sponsor decided that he was really not sympathetic to the proposal and declined to call the bill on subsequent readings. Here the three readings requirement was far more significant than the need for a constitutional majority.

[3] K. C. Wheare, *Government by Committee* (Oxford: The Clarendon Press, 1955), p. 122.

The implications of two evident facts—that there are variations in the use of committees and that there are variations in the scope and intensity of committee activity—would be important even if such variations were observable only in comparisons between legislative bodies. Actually, however, these variations exist within individual legislative bodies. Accordingly, it may follow that there is a relationship between the substance of legislation and the role of standing committees, that the committee function is a greater determinant of the ultimate disposition of some kinds of legislation that it is of others. It may also follow that there are conditions in any legislative situation which control the varying significance of committee activity.

In short, committees are a part of the total legislative mechanism, but they play no part under some conditions, a small part under other conditions, and under yet other conditions are critical determinants of the legislative output. Obviously, both the content of legislation and the characteristics of the particular legislative process create the appropriate conditions.

THE CONSEQUENCES OF COMMITTEE REFERRAL

One of the first strategic decisions to be made by the sponsor of any bill in either house of the Illinois General Assembly is whether to follow the so-called regular order of business and permit the bill to be referred to a standing committee for consideration, or to attempt to bypass the committee stage by securing either unanimous consent or a suspension of the rules in order to advance the bill on the calendar without committee reference. The great majority of bills are allowed to follow the regular order, but a large percentage are advanced without reference. What are the likely consequences of pursuing each course of action? Is there a real danger that legislation will be lost in committee, a danger sufficiently great to merit an initial effort to bypass committee action? Is there a reluctance to advance bills without reference? What is the prudent course of action to be followed at this stage of the legislative proceedings by a member who earnestly seeks to pass a bill?

Before any effort is made to deviate from the established order which calls for committee reference, a sponsor must assure himself that his bill does not face organized opposition. An objection to a unanimous consent request or a debate on a motion to suspend the rules spotlights the legislation under consideration and activates members who believe the legislative interest to be best served by following a regular procedure. Such a course of action would be well worth the risks, however, if the dangers attendant upon committee reference were significant. In fact, objections and debate of this sort are most infrequent. The absence of controversial efforts to advance without reference suggests that the dangers of committee reference are less profound than an alternative course of action, that a standing committee is not an effective impediment to the passage of a bill. A consideration of the validity of this suggestion merits attention.

In the first place, permitting a bill to be assigned to a committee carries with it no danger that the bill may be pigeonholed by an unsympathetic chairman. Committee chairmen do not kill bills, do not delay bills, do not ignore bills, and rarely make a parliamentary ruling that will have an important effect on the future of a bill. The major legislative role of the chairman is to receive requests and act in accord with those requests. A bill, once assigned to a committee of either house, will lie in committee until its sponsor either orally or by note requests the chairman to set a hearing on a particular date. Under the practices of the General Assembly, every chairman will accede to such a request, albeit if necessary suggesting an alternate date if a large number of bills have already been set for the proposed time. No matter how firm the opposition of the chairman may be to the legislation under consideration, he will not refuse a hearing, and he is not likely to attempt to delay or prolong a hearing once scheduled. By the same token, the chairman will not act as a screening agent for frivolous legislative proposals. The fact that a member who is its sponsor requests that a bill be heard is sufficient to guarantee the hearing. Moreover, Illinois committees habitually conclude hearings with a vote on a recommendation that the bill either "Do Pass" or "Do Not Pass." In very rare instances a bill is reported without recommendation, and even in such a circumstance, it leaves the committee and is placed on the desk of the presiding officer pending a motion from the floor. Inaction, then, is not a likely cause of death in committee.

Even more important is the fact that committees tend to be unwilling to assume responsibility for formally killing a bill. Although a former Speaker of the House has openly criticized this state of affairs, his criticism is a recognition of its existence. "I think," he has stated, "we would be able to conduct more business more efficiently if the committees would find a bad bill bad and say so at the committee level."[4] Time and again a member will explain an affirmative committee vote by saying that he believes the bill "to be important enough to merit consideration by the whole House" although he may vote "No" on the floor. The sponsor of a bill cannot be certain, but he can feel confident that, even in the face of organized opposition, his bill will be reported out favorably. Committee members tend to be anxious to share with the whole house the responsibility for negative action just as they must share the responsibility for positive action.

To state it pointedly, even beyond the guarantee that action on a bill can be achieved, the odds are all on favorable committee action. In most cases where favorable committee action is not forthcoming, it is understood

---

[4]Warren L. Wood, then Speaker of the House, in a lecture at the University of Illinois, April 23, 1953.

Table 1   Number and per cent of all bill referrals recommended "do not pass" by standing committees, 1955 and 1957

Session	Origin of Bills	"Do Not Pass" Recommendations			
		Senate Committees		House Committees	
		Number	Per Cent	Number	Per Cent
1955	Senate	26	3.2	10	2.2
	House	18	3.0	49	4.0
1957	Senate	50	5.9	9	1.6
	House	34	4.7	54	3.9

in advance by all participants that the bill is to be killed in committee. When the Senate Democratic leader who was Mayor Daley's legislative spokesman offered a bill in 1957 to expand the licensing power of the City of Chicago, he expected the measure to be killed in the Senate Municipalities Committee. Indeed, except for the persistence of a private civic group, the sponsor would never have called the bill for a hearing. In prehearing discussions, he stated that "We will make our presentation and take our licking." The outcome was exactly as predicted. Again, after the Mayor and the Governor agreed on a plan to subsidize the Chicago Transit Authority, legislative leaders on the majority side balked. The bills were finally offered by the minority, and an elaborate committee presentation was arranged. The committee listened and then proceeded to kill the legislation, a result that all members knew was inevitable. Committee voting produces few surprises.

The general reluctance of Illinois legislative committees to report a bill with a "Do Not Pass" recommendation is demonstrated by a study of the committee output in the 1955 session. In that session, there were a total of 1,666 referrals to standing committees of the House and 1,408 referrals to standing committees of the Senate, or 3,074 referrals to standing committees of the General Assembly. There were 103 "Do Not Pass" recommendations. Only 3.3 per cent of all referrals resulted in a "Do Not Pass" recommendation. The 1957 session shows a similar pattern. The accompanying Table 1 shows in detail the extent to which "Let the Bill Live" is the guiding philosophy of the committees.

A "Do Pass" recommendation by a committee in the Illinois legislature is considerably less conclusive an indicator of ultimate disposition of a bill than is a "Do Not Pass" recommendation. Half of the bills defeated during the 1953 session were killed on the floor after having received favorable committee action.

On the other hand, unfavorable committee action urging that bills "Do Not Pass"—either in the form of recommendations or by postponement of consideration—is generally upheld without challenge. Only fifteen motions to non-concur in unfavorable committee action were made in

1957. Other bills unfavorably reported were allowed to die without a fight. No bill on which a motion was made to non-concur became law, although one passed both houses but was vetoed. An important 1953 administration-sponsored House bill—to create a Committee on Equal Employment Opportunities—died in the Senate after a non-concur motion was defeated.

Plainly the committees do not kill many bills in a formal fashion. A legitimate corollary inquiry is whether they pointedly defer action on bills until such time late in the session when the bills are lost by a general tabling motion. Is the small percentage of bills formally killed by a "Do Not Pass" recommendation deceptive as to the actual "killing potential" of the committees? The conventions of procedure in Illinois, which support the principle of control by the sponsor all the way through the legislative mill, suggest a negative answer. No member of the General Assembly in Illinois will be denied a hearing on a bill he has sponsored, and no member other than the sponsor can insure a hearing on such a bill. The sponsor determines whether there shall be a hearing; he suggests the date and will be accommodated if it is at all practical. If he chooses to postpone the hearing, he is free to do so. If a committee vote is going against him, he may keep the bill alive by postponing further consideration until he is able to build up strength. He chooses the sponsor in the second chamber, but he may make a personal appearance before the committee in the second house.

All of this must be understood before drawing conclusions from the fact that between 20 and 30 per cent of all bills introduced habitually die in committee in the chamber of origin. Most bills that die in Illinois legislative committees are not killed; rather, they are made to commit suicide by their sponsors. The committees have no role in the loss of this large number of bills other than to serve as convenient receptacles, as custodians, as it were, for proposals that members of the legislature feel constrained for a variety of reasons to introduce but which these same members do not seek to have enacted into law. For many years, one minority member, now a congressman, had regularly introduced a bill calling for a referendum on a statewide bond issue to finance construction of buildings at mental hospitals and institutions of higher education. In 1957 the bill was introduced as usual and referred to the Senate Revenue Committee. When queried about the fact that it provided funds for a building at the University of Illinois which had already been constructed out of a 1953 capital appropriation, the sponsor was undisturbed. "That's all right," he said, "this is one of those bills that you put in to establish a principle. I don't try to bring it to a hearing. It couldn't move without administration support anyhow." The existence or absence of standing committees would have no bearing on the future of this kind of bill. If the committee system were to be eliminated in some future session of the legislature, such bills could just as effectively sit on the presiding officer's desk until adjournment. The formal procedure would be a little different; the substantive result would be the same.

The notion that homicide does not account for any great loss of bills in committee is not disturbed by an examination of the loss of bills in committee in the second chamber. Whereas 20 to 30 per cent of all bills introduced in each house die in committee in the chamber of origin, only 2 to 3 per cent of bills that pass the chamber of origin die in committee in the second chamber. Some of these bills, moreover, fall in the "suicide" category. This is the circumstance when identical bills are offered in each house and each bill passes the house of origin. One bill or the other will be allowed to die in committee in the second chamber without a hearing. In general, a sponsor who has carried a bill through one house does not permit the bill to die in the second house without a struggle. If the strategy calls for a committee hearing rather than an attempt to advance without reference, that hearing usually results in a "Do Pass" recommendation.

A significant percentage of all bills introduced in the legislature are subjected to proposed committee amendments. As much as one-fifth of the total number are amended by committees before legislative action is completed, and the recommendation of a committee as to the adoption of a committee amendment is ordinarily accepted by the chamber. In the House of Representatives, in 1957, the Speaker found it possible to expedite the business of the House by calling for a vote on committee amendments without permitting the amendments to be read or explained. This technique presumed that the House would be disposed to accept committee amendments and that any objectors would be alert without having to hear the text of the amendment read by the Clerk.

Committee amendments are not as important substantively as might appear at first blush, however. Because the conventions of the legislature anticipate that action in committee will generally be completed on a single day, the amendments that are most likely to be forthcoming with committee endorsement are amendments that have been formally prepared in advance of the hearing. The great bulk of these proposals are either technical corrections in the printed bill or agreed amendments that have been discussed by the sponsor and affected groups in advance of the committee hearing. Both classes of amendments are noncontroversial, and neither class can be said to grow out of committee consideration and discussion of the bill involved. In those instances where an amendment does develop out of committee discussion and consideration, it is frequently suggested that since the terms of the amendment have been determined, the bill should not be held up, but rather that it should be reported out favorably with the understanding that the bill will be amended on second reading in the full chamber. It is the bills which fall into this last group on which the committee impact is most important, and these bills often show no formal committee amendatory action. This latter group, however, and the relatively small group of bills which are substantively amended in committee tend to be amended to meet the objections of an affected group which has not theretofore been involved in the development of the legislation. In short, the committee is a formal forum to do things which might otherwise have been done earlier and informally or later by formal action on the floor. In this respect, committee action is a procedural convenience, although admittedly a convenience of a high order.

SOME CONDITIONS FOR BYPASSING THE STANDING COMMITTEE

The circumstances under which this procedural convenience is easily dispensed with are evident in a consideration of the legislation that never sees the inside of a committee room, legislation that is advanced on the calender without reference to committee. In quantitative terms, substantially more bills are advanced on the calendar without reference to committee than are recommended "Do Not Pass" by the various committees. In recent sessions each house has advanced no less than 9 per cent of all bills without reference, and the Senate, in 1955, so advanced 13 per cent of all Senate bills.

In the two weeks before adjournment nearly all bills that have passed the house of origin are advanced in the second chamber without reference to a committee. Advancement without reference is critical to passage of a bill after motions have carried to clear the calendars and to table all bills in committee, because any bill pursuing the normal legislative steps at that point is automatically defeated when sent to committee.

The figures showing bills advanced without reference by the second chamber have been especially high since 1953 when House, Senate, and Governor have all been Republican. Acting as a second chamber, each of the houses had advanced without committee reference one-quarter of all the bills coming from the house of origin. In terms of substance, the bills so advanced are noncontroversial only in the sense that it is believed that the groups directly and tangentially affected have been consulted, have acquiesced in the terms of the legislation, and would have nothing to contribute to a committee hearing other than a statement of acquiescence. They are not unimportant bills, they are not minor matters. They are agreed bills which virtually all of the interest groups involved either accept or choose not to oppose.

An illustration of this is seen in legislation enacted by the 1957 session of the General Assembly to permit the creation of a Chicago Railroad Terminal Authority which may result in a consolidation of the heretofore numerous railroad terminals in Chicago. Similar legislation had been introduced in the 1955 session at which time, as its sponsor wryly put it, "The bill got one vote in committee—my own." Just before and during the 1957 session, however, the Mayor of Chicago and Chicago legislative leaders entered into a series of conferences with representatives of the railroads involved. The conferences resulted in agreement, and the railroad lobbyist in Springfield proceeded to throw his considerable influence behind the legislation. The bill, introduced in the Senate, was referred to the Committee on Public Utilities and Railroads from which it was recommended "Do Pass" by unanimous vote. In response to a query about its likely fate in the House, the railroad lobbyist said that "If there are twenty-five members of the committee, the bill will get twenty-three votes since I assume that two members may be unavoidably absent." In fact, the legislation was advanced in the House without reference to committee and subsequently passed without opposition.

Again in 1957, the Illinois Municipal League, cooperating with an interim legislative commission concerned with metropolitan area local government service problems, offered a comprehensive amendment to the existing garbage and refuse disposal statutes. Among other things, the legislation granted municipalities eminent domain powers to acquire garbage disposal sites, authorized the imposition of a service charge in lieu of a tax, and permitted the creation of an intermunicipal or municipal-county garbage disposal agency. After the legislation was passed by the House, its Senate sponsor suggested that "there is no practical purpose to be served by letting the bill go to committee over here. Municipal governments and municipal employees are the only groups affected and they are satisfied." Accordingly, the bill was advanced without committee reference.

The important field of protective labor legislation—unemployment compensation, workmen's compensation, and industrial diseases—has traditionally been the subject of agreed legislation in Illinois. Labor and employer spokesmen meet informally and attempt to agree on the terms of legislation, transmit any such agreement to the appropriate tripartite advisory board, and the result is incorporated in legislation.[5] A broad area of agreement was reached in 1955 in the unemployment compensation field involving benefits, disqualifications, and eligibility periods. The bill incorporating the agreement was passed by both houses without reference to committee in either. Similarly, in 1957, legislation dealing with the subject of workmen's compensation and occupational diseases was offered on an agreed basis and adopted without committee reference.

Thirteen bills were offered in 1955 as part of a package overhaul of the Illinois Civil Practice Act. Prepared with the cooperation of the Illinois Bar Association, the bills all went to the House Judiciary Committee, were favorably reported, and passed the House. In the Senate they were all moved on the calendar and passed without benefit of committee reference. Here again, the members of the fraternity involved—the bar—had acquiesced,

[5]For a detailed analysis of the agreed bill process, see [Gilbert Y. Steiner, *Legislation by Collective Bargaining* (Urbana: University of Illinois, Institute of Labor and Industrial Relations, 1951)].

and there were no other important groups claiming an interest. Committee reference presumably would have served no useful purpose.

A very different situation existed in the extensive debates over reorganization of the Illinois judiciary by an amendment to the judicial article of the constitution. Here the affected groups were multitudinous, and the bar, the political parties, the justices of the peace, ethnic minority groups, and incumbent members of the judiciary found no common meeting ground in preliminary discussions. Ultimately a dominant coalition was formed as a consequence of neutralizing the bar and overriding the justices of the peace, but all of these groups participated in committee activity. Significantly, the standing committees of the respective houses were finally abandoned as forums, and the whole vexing question of development of a judicial reform resolution was transferred to an *ad hoc* joint committee. The cycle runs full in that the standing committee has no utility as a decision-making agency when all of the parties agree or when all of the parties disagree.

There is evidence to suggest that the legislature has recognized the limitations of the standing committee as a point at which to resolve extensive group conflict. The special *ad hoc* committee created to consider the judicial article had a counterpart in 1955 in a special *ad hoc* committee created by the House of Representatives to undertake the reapportionment made necessary by a constitutional amendment. Hearings before the House or Senate as a Committee of the Whole have increased. More and more the General Assembly has moved toward the creation of continuing interim commissions—on Pension Laws, School Problems, Municipal Problems, County Government, Motor Vehicle Laws—and has charged these commissions with responsibility for recommending legislation in their respective fields. The commissions are composed of members from both houses and often include public members as well. By operating fairly leisurely over an 18-month period and by operating in a general area without a specific proposal befor them, the interim commissions can be made to feel the impact of the numerous interest groups concerned with these questions. The standing committee holds its hearings and takes a vote; the commission takes soundings, and more and more problems seem to demand soundings before decisions are made.

Additional comment is in order on the relationship between the absence of committee reference and the political composition of House, Senate, and the executive branch. Table 2 shows that the tendency to advance bills without reference is most pronounced under conditions of total partisan homogeneity and least pronounced under conditions of partisan heterogeneity.[6] Thus, in the 1953 and 1955 sessions when House, Senate, and Governor were all Republican, neither chamber was reluctant to advance

---

[6]An incidental point of interest shown by the figures is that, in this state at least, bicameralism may be less likely to result in duplicate committee consideration of the same bill than is often supposed.

Table 2   Bills advanced without committee reference as percentages of all bills considered by the legislature, 1949–57

| Session | Politics of Governor | Politics of Legislature | | Per Cent of All Bills Advanced Without Reference | | | |
| | | | | In Chamber of Origin | | In Second Chamber | |
		House	Senate	House	Senate	House	Senate
1949	Democratic	D	R	7	4	17	7
1951	Democratic	R	R	7	5	8	4
1953	Republican	R	R	9	10	25	25
1955	Republican	R	R	9	13	27	25
1957	Republican	R	R	7	12	14	23

without committee reference, and each chamber was especially willing when acting as a second house sandwiched between a chamber of origin and a governor of the same political persuasion as a majority of the house.

The evident inference is that the partisan character of the governor is one of the elements that bears heavily on the role of the committees in the total picture. The uses of committees tend to be emphasized when there is partisan diversity among the participants in the legislative struggle. The uses of committees tend to be diminished when the governor and a majority of each house are of the same party so that life-and-death power over legislation is kept under party control.

This point was neatly emphasized in the 1957 session in a colloquy between a member of the Senate and the majority whip. The Senate Municipalities Committee was considering a bill to create a permanent commission on city and village affairs. It was pointed out by the whip that a very large number of commissions were being approved by the legislature. "I was under the impression," said a member, "that the general practice is to push these through and let the Governor's red pencil decide which of them will survive." He was told that "This is exactly correct. Accordingly, if any member has strong feelings about any particular commission, he should communicate with the leadership."

Almost exactly the same point was made by an influential senator who was having difficulty with an appropriation bill which was opposed by the Illinois State Chamber of Commerce. "We don't know," he told a House committee, "what the Governor will do with this, but let's get it over to him and let him decide." The committee, which had postponed the bill the previous week, accepted the wisdom of the argument and sent the bill to the floor. Ultimately, it was vetoed by the Governor.

STRATEGIES OF ACTION

The legislator, lobbyist, or private citizen who supports legislation pending before the Illinois General Assembly and who has studied the odds should anticipate favorable standing committee action. There are, however, techniques of minimizing controversy and thereby further insuring that the committee stage will be a formality.

The fact that Illinois committees act on bills submitted rather than on general topics sometimes makes it difficult to avoid controversy. In all standing committee hearings, consideration is focused on a bill as drawn, and the various groups involved are concerned with supporting or opposing the specific proposal. Maneuverability is more limited than it is in a situation where the precise terms of legislation grow out of general hearings. In the latter case, legislators and interest groups can adjust their positions as a result of their appraisals of what is required to achieve a dominant coalition of groups. Where a specific proposal is before a committee, many groups and many members are committed for or against. They tend to turn the hearing into a vehicle for strengthening their pre-existing positions, and the legislative sponsor must search for a solution that minimizes controversy. As one Chicago member put it during a session of the House Municipalities Committee, "I don't want to be caught in the middle of anything. I'm not voting for anything that makes some people glad and some people unhappy."

A further illustration of this point stems from the action of an Illinois committee in rejecting a bill that would have given to the governor or a designated subordinate subpoena powers to aid in investigations of all boards and departments of state government. The bill plainly had its genesis in the Orville Hodge scandal and the Governor's assertion at the time that he lacked power to investigate the constitutional office of auditor of public accounts. However, the Senate Judiciary Committee, at the conclusion of the sponsor's brief explanation of the purpose of the bill, indicated some unwillingness to support a delegation of the subpoena power to a subordinate named by the governor. If the committee had been conducting a public hearing on the general question of the adequacy of the governor's investigatory power, a bill would have been brought to the floor with committee sponsorship. As it was, the bill was reported out with a "Do Not Pass" recommendation when the sponsor was reluctant to accept an amendment striking the authority to delegate subpoena powers. Subsequently the bill was reintroduced by another member who deleted the delegation of the subpoena power. It passed out of the Judiciary Committee without significant opposition, and was actively supported by the sponsor of the original bill, who, when pressed for an explanation of why he refused to amend the measure in the first place, replied, "I produced that bill, and I had to defend it because I thought that it was in the best possible form when I introduced it. Obviously, I could have passed it out of committee with the amendment but then it would have had a history as a controversial bill."

The hearing process can become a kind of game in which the experienced legislator seeks to find the most propitious moment for presenting his bill to a committee. One element in the timing question is the ability of the legislative proponents or opponents of a bill to arrange to have their spokesmen heard. Members are usually reluctant to prolong a committee session, but when a constituent comes to Springfield to speak for or against a bill, no legislator is willing to let it appear that he cannot guarantee a hearing for his constituent. A prolonged session invariably results in an agreement to limit speakers to three, five, or at the most, ten minutes. A bill is more likely to receive a complete hearing if a chairman can be prevailed upon to call it early in the committee session. Where it is not a matter of impressing a constituent, most members prefer to bide their time. Few committee meetings close with as many members in attendance as were present at the outset. One constitutional executive officer, therefore, made it a point in 1957 to arrange to have some supposedly controversial legislation called at the end of a committee docket after most members had tired of the proceedings and left the committee room.

A sponsor's ability to gauge the temper of a committee accounts for the frequency of decisions to postpone consideration of a bill until a later date. Consideration is sometimes postponed by a sponsor because he has decided that the committee is not then willing to favor any bill that provokes opposition. Postponement is also likely to occur if a committee schedules for hearing on the same day bills that would lead to incompatible lines of public policy. No veteran member would permit a bill of his sponsorship to be heard before a committee at a time when favorable action could, in any way, embarrass the committee. Thus, when a series of bills providing for a so-called "functional" consolidation of the Chicago city and park district police passed out of the House Municipalities Committee, the sponsor of legislation that called for an "organic" consolidation of the two forces wisely postponed the hearing on his bill. A committee will often report contradictory measures, but it is understood that it will not be asked to do so on the same day. In fact, the "organic" consolidation was later recommended "Do Pass" by the Municipalities Committee with an agreement that its sponsor would make no effort to advance the legislation once it appeared on the House calendar, an agreement that was carried out.

Preparation for and the actual hearing of a bill in committee are handled in the most casual manner. Hearings are scheduled at the request of the sponsor or at the request of a lobbyist acting in the name of the sponsor. Notice that a committee meeting will be held on a regularly scheduled day and a list of the numbers of bills to be heard are duly publicized. When the committee assembles, however, neither the chairman nor any of the members are likely to have much knowledge of what is forthcoming. In a loose sort of way some chairmen try to insist that all persons who expect to be heard on a bill register with the committee clerk at the time of the hearing and show affiliation as well as name and address. The content of a witness's presentation is, however, unknown unless a member with a particular interest in a bill makes it a point to interrogate witnesses privately—and this is dependent on his ability to identify and to locate witnesses as well as on the witnesses' willingness to cooperate. Most members avoid this kind of activity lest it stir up organized group support or opposition. More frequently, committee personnel prepare their interrogations as witnesses are making their presentations to the committee. The unusual spectacle of a prepared interrogation of a witness on the lobby regulation bill by the Senate minority leader in 1957 provoked admiration from other members and from the press. The advantage that might accrue to the witness over the committee member as a consequence of preliminary preparation is largely nullified by the absence of prior knowledge of the direction in which any member may lead him. The general understanding is that the hearings process will make no preliminary demands on anyone, least of all on the committee itself.

Proponents and opponents of obviously controversial legislation make it their business to solicit votes from committee members prior to a committee hearing. The form of the solicitation or canvass will vary with the formal role of the group interested in the measure. The governor's office, for example, overtly canvasses in two ways. Once a decision is reached that a bill is to be deemed "an administration measure," committee members of the governor's party are informed by card that the bill will be heard before the committee involved at such and such a time. The card notes that the bill is an administration bill, and that "your support will be appreciated." In the House, the card goes out over the signature of the party whip. On the Senate side, the majority whip has handled the canvass personally in recent sessions. The sponsor will reiterate the fact of administration support in his explanatory statement, and the presence of one of the floor leaders at the committee session further emphasizes the point unless a specific disclaimer is entered. Only in extreme cases does the Speaker participate in this activity at the committee level. His presence at a hard-fought hearing on a bill to merge Chicago and Cook County welfare services was understood as a signal that the administration was "all out" in support of the legislation. In addition, as an ex officio member of all committees, he is privileged to cast a vote which, on the particular question, might have been important. One of the factors that strengthens the hand of the administration is that control over the creation of committees and over committee appointments rests in the party leadership in each house and both questions are considered *de novo* each session.

Under conditions of Republican control of the Governor's Mansion, solicitation of committee votes on the Democratic side is handled by party leaders, and much of the follow-up work including the problem of insuring attendance of friendly committee members—at least long enough to leave a signed proxy—is left to the lobbyist for the City of Chicago. The latter is also in a position to recommend either to the corporation counsel or to the mayor's acknowledged spokesman in the legislature that a committee be canvassed. For the Democrats, the chairman of the State Central Committee is principally concerned with party bills. His liaison with the Chicago lobbyist is a close one, however, and the latter not infrequently undertakes a canvass of a committee on behalf of the party as well as on bills dealing specifically with Chicago government and administration. The Chicago lobbyist is also expected to familiarize himself with committee procedures and to be alert to the appropriate motion at the appropriate time. He will, in addition, undertake routine checks to assure that bills are reported properly by committee clerks.

If a bill is administration-sponsored or administration-opposed and all participants have done their jobs, the potency of the governor is such that the results of the committee vote are predetermined. Deviations or defections, if they occur, are likely to occur on the floor of the House or Senate rather than in committee. No committee member is in a position to say that he was unaware of the administration attitude. Similarly, the minority party bloc is organized prior to the committee hearing on a bill in which its leadership is interested, and the occasional defection is not an unexpected one.

Logrolling explains most committee votes in Illinois. The committees are able to move at a fast, amiable clip because they do not go seeking controversy when no controversy is brought to them. In the absence of opposition, most members automatically and cheerfully support the colleague who is sponsoring a bill. Votes in favor of a contested bill are traded for support on other bills in the same or in a different committee or even on the floor. Many bills which reach the formal hearing stage are obviously trival and many others are clearly noncontroversial. Unless the sponsor is personally unpopular with his colleagues, such bills are moved along without discussion. This practice is frequently extended to cover more important bills to which there is no overt opposition. A common scene in many committees of both houses is for the sponsor's explanation to be cut short by an inquiry from a committee member, "Is there anybody here in opposition to this bill?" Unless opposition presents itself, a motion that the bill be reported with a "Do Pass" recommendation will follow.

This easy approach to committee life makes it possible for committees to schedule relatively large numbers of bills on a single day. On May 28, 1957, for example, when the legislature was at peak activity, the House Committee on Public Aid, Health, Welfare and Safety had 28 bills scheduled to be heard at its afternoon session. The previous week, the House Municipalities Committee had 26 bills on its call, and the Appropriations Committee had 21. On that same day, the Senate Committees on Pensions and Personnel and on Education had 16 and 14 bills scheduled respectively.

Committee hearings are public and committee votes are matters of public record, so that members always face the possibility of being confronted with a request for an explanation of a vote or votes. Consequently, a sponsor will not take advantage of strength and push a bill through committee without observing certain delicacies. No matter how extensive the support may be for a particular bill, and no matter how certain the result, once a bill is set for a committee hearing, its sponsor is expected either to demonstrate that the measure has provoked no opposition, or to provide arguments that will serve as justification for his colleagues' votes.

One of the most competent committee performances of the 1957 session was that of a former employee of the Legislative Reference Bureau, presently a professor of law at the University of Illinois, who appeared in opposition to a bill that would have fixed a limit on the property tax that is levied for corporate purposes in the city of Chicago. Long experience with the Illinois legislature and considerable familarity with the subject enabled the witness to make an extremely persuasive argument. He indicated privately, however, that he had no illusions about swaying votes on the basis of his argument. The legislator who led opposition to the bill concurred in the judgment that votes did not fall one way or the other on the basis of the argument. "However," the legislator pointed out, "do not undersell the significance of the presentation. Our arrangements [for votes] were concluded before the hearing ever started, but it was absolutely essential that members who had agreed to vote against the bill be furnished with a 'cover'—with an impressive witness whose competence was unquestioned so that they could offer an explanation of their votes. The professor furnished that 'cover.' When we return the favor on legislation in which others are interested, we shall expect to be furnished with a 'cover.' The more consistently a legislator can furnish a good 'cover' to support his position, the easier it is for him to enter into logrolling arrangements."

This practice of the "cover," which takes diverse forms, helps to account for the ease with which some of the most seemingly controversial legislation moves through or past standing committees. One such "cover" or formal justification for a vote is the designation of a measure as an administration bill. This is paralleled on the minority side by labelling a bill as "a party measure." Another kind of "cover" is exemplified by the lucid, compelling argument referred to above. Finally, there are a number of broad principles to which some members insist they adhere. Other things being equal, certain legislators, in committee and on the floor, wish always to work for the "home rule" principle, for bills that include referendum provisions, for maximum support for the schools and universities, and for bills which bear the endorsement of one of the specialized continuing interim commissions. Occasionally, two or more of these "covers" will clash, and the clash is likely to produce the most agitated committee sessions, and subsequently, the most agitated floor debate.

APPROPRIATIONS BILLS AND THE APPROPRIATIONS COMMITTEES

Much of the most elaborate formal testimony before committees is forth-coming in connection with major appropriations bills on which the result is predetermined. The committee hearing is thus transformed from a session designed to inform and influence legislators to a session designed to dra-matize, for public information, the policy that is to be pursued. In hearings before the Appropriations Committees on bills implementing the executive budget, the responsibility is on the agency or department of state govern-ment to make a case that will engender popular support for the work of the unit involved. Committee scrutiny is perfunctory. Appropriations committees of House and Senate, confronted with bills assigning millions of dollars to various state agencies, raise questions only about specific items covering relatively small sums. Thus, debate and discussion in the House Appropria-tions Committee on the 1957–59 budget of the Illnois Public Aid Commission was concerned not with criteria for public aid nor with the philosophy of the Commission. Instead, several efforts were made by committee members to determine whether the Commission planned to add to its public relations staff.

An indication of the casual character of Appropriations Committee hearings on the Senate side in 1957 was that, despite the fact that the budget was submitted to a Republican legislature by a Republican governor, motions to recommend that the appropriations bills be reported "Do Pass" were consistently made by Democratic senators. This activity became so marked that the Democratic Senate leader instructed his colleagues in caucus that they were to let the majority side make the motions on appropriations bills and thereby assume responsitility for that which neither most Repub-lican nor most Democratic legislators were in a position to comprehend.

Routine appropriations for smaller amounts, and especially those not specifically provided for in the budget, tend to be more closely scruti-nized. One veteran senator attempted to secure Appropriations Committee approval for an allocation of some $25,000 to rebuild an historical mansion in his district and found himself subjected to intense questioning about the details of the sum requested. Ultimately he found it necessary to postpone consideration for a week in order to acquire detailed information. Similarly, a request for less than $100,000 to replenish a World War I veterans' chil-dren's scholarship fund at the University of Illinois was objected to, and the committee would take no action until particulars on the history of the fund and its purposes were made available.

Occupying a sort of middle ground are those appropriations items which emanate from some agency of the state although they are not in-cluded as a formal part of the governor's budget. The tendency here is for the committees to be torn between the desire to accept the validity of the

legislative proposals. A frequent corollary assumption is that the most careful and the most intensive legislative work is done in committee. Perhaps because of the documentation available at the national government level, it has sometimes been supposed that standing committee chairmen in state legislatures have llife-and-death control over legislation.

Any understanding of the state legislative process or any theory of public policy-making at the state level must consider these generalizations. The following summary assesses the role of standing committees in the Illinois legislative process:

1. The individual member of the Illinois legislature is detached from the mainstream of legislative policy-making. Except for the leaders, few members are able to have an awareness of the origin and development of legislation. This detachment and this unawareness carry over to the committee life of the individual legislator. Consequently, the expectations of most members as to the importance of their committee work rarely come up to the actualities.

2. Standing committees of the General Assembly are part of a total complex of impediments to the enactment of law. As an independent determinant of the fate of legislative proposals, the standing committee is of scant importance.

3. Committee appointments, and particularly appointments to committee chairmanships are valuable as indications of confidence by the legislative leaders. Virtually no actual legislative power attaches to a chairmanship, but legislators regard chairmen of particular committees as part of an influential circle. Being a chairman is not a source of power, but being designated a chairman very well may be a source of informal power.

4. There are several substitutes for the standing committee as a focal point for the resolution of group conflict. Such a substitute can even exist outside of the formal legislative process, but it will be accepted by legislators if it is shown that no group with a direct interest has been excluded from the negotiations.

5. The governor is one substitute for the standing committee under appropriate conditions. The disposition to advance bills without reference is most pronounced under conditions of total partisan homogeneity and least pronounced under conditions of partisan heterogeneity. More bills are advanced without reference when House and Senate control and the governor are all in the same party, and fewer bills are so advanced when the governor and the legislative majority are not of the same party.

6. Bills are not advanced without committee reference unless the sponsor of a bill is relatively certain that a request to advance without reference will not provoke opposition. However, controversial and important legislation, as well as noncontroversial and unimportant legislation, is so advanced. The determinant appears to be whether the affected groups have had an opportunity to contribute to the terms of the bill.

7. Elaborate committee presentations are rarely developed for the purpose of influencing committee votes. The more important the bill, the more likely it is that the voting pattern is predetermined. The presentation is designed to afford a justification for votes.

CHAPTER ELEVEN

THE LEGISLATIVE PROCESS IN MUNICIPAL GOVERNMENT: A CASE STUDY

J. LEIPER FREEMAN

This study of the legislative process in municipal government focuses upon a city council's decisions involving the public works budget submitted by the mayor for the ensuing fiscal year. The data were collected through a series of intensive interviews with participants and an examination of the pertinent documents, several months after the action occurred. The study was exploratory, followed by a much larger project intent on illuminating community decision-making in "Bay City," a Massachusetts industrial center of nearly 50,000 persons.[1]

The basic objectives of the public works appropriations study were (a) to learn as much as possible about public decision processes and the kinds of influence impinging upon members of a public legislative body in a city, and (b) to determine the effectiveness of the technique of *ex post facto* interviews-in-depth with participants. The researchers were convinced that the technique can provide considerable evidence on the subject. At the same time, they felt that *ex post facto* interviews obviously furnish qualitatively different data from those provided by direct observation and on-the-spot

[1]The "Bay City" project was conducted under the auspices of the Harvard Graduate School of Education with funds from a grant by the W. K. Kellogg Foundation. The author is particularly indebted to the other two principal researchers, Peter H. Rossi and James M. Shipton, whose ideas and comments have been invaluable for preparation of this article. Others who took part in this phase of the research in some fashion were Leo Barry, Alice Bauer, Eugene Belisle, Jim Davis, Russell Davis, George Flower, Carl Freudenreich, Tom Guilford, Andrew Manges, Austin McCaffrey, Kermit Morrissey, Sam Morse, Cyril Sargent, and Claire Zimmerman.

interviews. The first type brings forth those more generalized events and relationships which are recalled as significant from the perspective of a later date. The second approach leads to more emphasis upon the idiosyncratic and momentary and is less likely to let minutiae slip through the net of recollection.[2] In the balance, despite limitations in the technique, the researchers felt that they had probed sufficiently to illustrate some significant elements in decision-making by municipal lawmakers. It was felt that willful deception, deliberate distortion, and the like were minimal. The biases of the findings were chiefly those inherent in the perceptions and recollections of the participants even after they had been stimulated to talk freely and to recall with thoroughness.

BASIC STORY OF THE PUBLIC WORKS APPROPRIATIONS PROCESS

Bay City in 1952 had a government which political scientists would classify somewhere between a "strong mayor" and a "weak mayor" type. Its mayor was elected for a two-year term and paid a salary of about $5,000 annually, for which he was supposed to spend most but not all of his time on the job. He had to share his executive powers in some cases with commissions or boards, but he usually named the members of these, subject to council confirmation, as vacancies occurred or terms ended. Department heads were for the most part under civil service and therefore generally immune to "spoils" reprisal either from the mayor or the council. Nevertheless, most department heads tended to feel that the mayor was the "boss" of the municipal enterprise within limits, and they generally did not like to be at cross purposes with him. Even those municipal administrators with separate boards or commissions to shield them were not insensitive to the mayor's status as the chief political officer of the city and to his budgetary controls. The mayor had the authority to determine the budget requests for each department, except the schools, and to submit them to the council. The council could either approve or lower the amounts requested, but could not raise them. The mayor also had considerable authority over the transfer of funds from one budget category to another. In the case of public works, he had special authority to alter the priority of expenditures for authorized projects of similar nature, thereby being able to push ahead the laying of a sidewalk in a favored neighborhood and to retard the laying of another in an unfavored area.

The council was composed of eleven members, also elected for two-year terms, five from the city at large and one each from the six wards of the municipality. They were paid nominal sums, and their councilmanic duties were not envisioned as consuming a major part of their time. They annually

[2]Furthermore direct observation also produces data of a sort different from any kind of interview data.

elected one of their number as president of the council and divided themselves into ten different standing committees on special subjects for the conduct of much of their work. The most important of these committees, playing a vital part in the appropriations process, was the finance committee, which was always composed of the council president and two other members.

In the boiling pot of Bay City's municipal politics, the "Progressives" (local counterpart of the national Democratic party) held a nearly two-to-one majority, as long as they could hold together. At the time of this study, traditional local party lines were in a state of some fluidity, occasioned by the formation of a "Coalition" composed of most of the "Non-Partisans" (local counterpart of the Republican party) and significant elements of their traditional opponents. The Coalition was pictured in the press as the answer to a need for respectability, economy, and less partisanship in city hall. In the 1949 election it had defeated a staunch Progressive mayor whom some compared to Boston's James M. Curley, using a third candidate to help split the Progressive vote. That Progressive had won the mayoralty in 1947 by galvanizing his party into a crushing majority, and it had been in reaction to this event that the Coalition was formed. The Coalition in 1951 re-elected its mayor, again defeating the Progressive "boss" with the help of a third candidate. The Coalition also elected a majority of six members to the council. The local newspaper, the *Bugle*, which was bed-rock Republican in outlook and had taken a leading part in devising and promoting the Coalition, looked forward to another two-year regime in which their mayor would be able to pursue the policies advocated by the newspaper with the support of the legislative body.

Shortly after the election and long before the mayor's budget was to be submitted to the council for consideration, however, three of the Coalition members of the new council joined with three members from the anti-Coalition faction to form a new majority. They named one of their men council president and reserved for themselves the choicest council committee posts, including especially the finance committee. The other three Coalition members of the council and the two remaining members then became a loyal minority in support of the mayor. Managers of the Coalition and representatives of the *Bugle* tried in vain to stop the revolt of the insurgents and to hold a majority together which would follow their leadership. They even suggested that the leader of the revolt flip a coin with one of the loyal members of the Coalition on the council to determine the presidency. But the insurgents remained adamant and resorted to their majority power. Thereupon, the *Bugle* complained vigorously that the mayor had received a "double-cross" from the new majority leaders of the council.

Facing this hostile majority led by defectors from his cause, the mayor went about the business of preparing his budget in a pattern that differed somewhat from previous years. As usual, the budget requests for public works were initially set up by the commissioner, relying largely upon the previous year's figures. Then the mayor together with the auditor worked out a final form for presentation to the council, reducing nearly half the items in the commissioner's requests. In contrast with previous years, however, at this point the mayor did not work informally with the finance committee of the council, now composed of three of the majority who had turned against him. Instead, when he had finished his budget preparations, the mayor simply turned the document over to the council, or, as he put it, he "dumped it on their desks."

The finance committee therefore held its own hearings on the budget instead of working with the mayor, and finally in its executive sessions it cut the mayor's public works requests in 17 out of a total of 29 items. When the report of the finance committee came to the whole council for vote and adoption, 12 of the reductions in the mayor's requests were sustained by a vote of six to five, while five of the reductions made by the finance committee failed to be sustained, losing five to six. All other items, reported by the committee in the same amounts as requested by the mayor, were approved by a unanimous vote.

In the eyes of much of the community, this represented a substantial reversal for the mayor and a vigorous exercise of sheer power by the legislative majority. Many citizens of Bay City, like residents in other contemporary American communities, had become accustomed to executive leadership in budgetary matters. They had also been accustomed to collaboration and communication between the executive and legislative branches in working out many details of government. The separation of powers was usually moderated by the practice of informal consultation.

The *Bugle* coined a name for the council majority, the "Sasser Six," an epithet intended to connote that they followed the dictates of the council president, Robert Sasser. The newspaper depicted the Sasser Six as an obstructionist group concerned only with self-interest and playing "irresponsible politics" with the budget.

The Sasser group had no real opportunity to explain their position to the public through the newspaper, although they did have some opportunity to get their position across via the radio, since the council meetings were broadcasted. The majority members of the council tried to argue that the mayor had not been sufficiently economical in devising his budget. The *Bugle* and other Coalition spokesmen had to contend that the mayor, whom they had avowedly helped to get elected to establish more economy in city affairs, should be allowed to spend more money than the council was willing to permit. The Coalition's rationale for this somewhat anomalous position was that the mayor had formulated an efficient and economical budget, but that the insurgent council majority had made irresponsible cuts in order to make political capital.

The aftermath of the budget fight was that the *Bugle* continued to hound the Sasser Six on many issues, particularly in a drawn-out struggle

by the mayor to secure the passage of a bond issue to expand the water supply of the city. Finally, in the latter part of the year, individual members of
the Sasser Six one by one switched to vote with the mayor on the water bonds.
Then in the autumn elections Sasser was badly defeated in a race for the state
legislature. By the end of the year when the time had come to reorganize the
council, the insurgents had lost their cohesion. But their actions prior to their
dissolution provided valuable insights into the legislative process.

LEGISLATIVE DECISIONS AND VOTING ALIGNMENTS

In the decisions on the public works budget, three patterns of voting alignments occurred. First, there were *non-controversial* decisions which were represented by *unanimous* votes in the council. Second, there were *controversial*
decisions settled by a vote of the *organized majority*, defeating the minority
by six to five. Third, a different type of *controversial* decision entailed a *factional alliance* of the council minority and one member who defected from the
organized majority. The *unanimous* decisions were the ones taken on budget
items where the finance committee had recommended the same amounts as
the mayor. The *organized majority* decisions were those in which the finance
committee's reductions in the amounts requested by the mayor were adopted.
The *factional alliance* decisions were those in which the finance committee's
reductions in the amounts requested by the mayor were not adopted, allowing the mayor's requests to stand.

These three types of decisions are variations of three logical and empirical types which one might find in any American legislative body. There are
first those decisions which are beyond controversy and are taken in an
atmosphere of consensus attributable either to overwhelming agreement or
indifference. Second, there are decisions taken in conformity with the pattern of majority vs. minority organization of the body. These are often called
"party-line" votes where the organization of the legislature has been accomplished on the basis of party affiliation in a two-party political system.
Finally, there are many types of combinations of minority factions which
on given issues can form a voting majority, even though the members of the
particular voting alliance have not stood and would not stand together to
organize the legislative body.

Historically, in American legislative bodies, a vast proportion of actions
taken are not controversial, but are accomplished by unanimous consent or
without objection.[3] Most of the controversial decisions are normally taken
by majorities composed of alliances of factions, even though "party affiliation appears to be the factor more closely associated with individual legislator's votes than any other."[4] In other words, relatively few decisions appear

---

[3]Avery Leiserson, *Parties and Politics*, New York: Alfred A. Knopf, 1958, p. 339; V. O.
Key, Jr., *Politics, Parties, and Pressure Groups*, New York: Crowell, 1952, p. 706.
   [4]Leiserson, *op. cit.*, p. 340.

to be determined by straight, down-the-line votes between organized majorities and minorities in American legislatures. More often, while a predominant number of the organized majority may vote on one side and a predominant number of the minority organization may vote on the other side controversial decisions are made by an *ad hoc* alliance of factions, with those who cross organization lines tipping the scales.

Obviously, the proportions among the three types in the 29 decisions made by the Bay City council in this study are not representative of the historic proportions found in American legislative bodies generally. In the first place, the proportion of non-controversial decisions was much lower than might have been expected. In the second place, the proportion of organized majority decisions was much higher among the controversial decisions than might have been expected. The conditions contributing to these phenomena are of interest and will be explored.

Furthermore, the three types of decisions noted in the literature on legislative processes are sufficiently represented in this study to permit an attempt at explaining the factors which seem basic to each type. The factors to be considered are as follows: (a) the nature of the issue (i.e., relative values attached to the rational objective sought by the legislation); (b) the internal group structure of the legislature; (c) the norms of the system; (d) external relationships of the legislators, including those with constituency, party, pressure groups, the press, and the executive.

THE NATURE OF THE ISSUE AS A FACTOR

The nature of the issue in most instances where the members of the council voted upon the 29 items of the public works budget was not perceived in terms of the relative values of the designated objectives but more often tended to be a question of human relations. The values of specific objectives in most cases were subsumed in questions about group relations within the council, about norms of council behavior, or about relations with the mayor, the newspaper, or other external factors.

For example, there was no discernible pattern of either controversial or non-controversial support for all "salary" items or all "expense" items, nor was there any consistent pattern of voting peculiar to most of the substantive objectives of the budget such as highways, bridges, sewers, snow removal, rubbish disposal, and the many other kinds of services performed by a public works department.

Certain exceptions should be noted. First, the mayor's requests for general administrative costs and engineering costs, both in personnel and expenses, were treated in a non-controversial manner. This set of facts proves nothing about the legislative process except that on these particular items, which the mayor had already cut to levels existing two years previously, the Bay City legislators were able to agree unanimously. The items may have been of such indifference to the legislators that they were treated without controversy. The values reflected in these objective *per se* which made them non-controversial are difficult to find.

Second, all of the mayor's requests for purposes of sidewalks and for water supply were upheld in controversial decisions by factional alliances despite the recommendations of the finance committee that they be reduced. In each of these issues, one member of the Sasser Six defected from that group to join with the minority in support of the mayor, producing a factional alliance of six councilmen on that particular vote. Since the loyal minority of the council voted in every instance to support the mayor, they were not demonstrably swayed to do so in these cases by the nature of the objectives at issue. Each council member who defected from the Sasser Six, however, could be said to have done so because of the particular objective of the item concerned. On the other hand, it was not clear from the evidence that they, as individuals, attached more intrinsic value to sidewalks or to water supply than did any of the other councilmen as individuals. Instead, the more demonstrable fact was that the councilman placed sidewalks or water supply higher in his priority of values because of the constituency interests he represented. Each of the two councilmen who switched from the Sasser Six did so because he was "very interested in sidewalks" or "very interested in water supply," but further investigation supported the view that his special interest was a derivative of ecological needs widely recognized in his ward.[5]

THE INTERNAL GROUP STRUCTURE OF THE COUNCIL AS A FACTOR

A key which unlocked the problem of understanding the division between the Sasser Six and the council minority, thereby serving to explain the organized majority votes and much other council behavior was to be found in the internal relationships of the council itself. Once elected to the council, the legislator became part of an organization in which members had different roles to play and different degrees of prestige, participation, and authority. Which roles he played and how much prestige, participation, and authority he enjoyed depended in considerable measure upon the committee posts assigned him. As in most other legislative bodies in the United States, the criterion of seniority was a traditional basis in the Bay City council for determining committee assignments.[6] Of course, the actual power to organize the council was in the hands of whatever majority was formed to exercise it, but usually the majority had recognized experience and seniority when organizing councils in the past.

[5]This point will be further discussed under the topic of "Constituency Relationships."
[6]This theme is strongly stressed in W. S. White, *Citadel*, New York: Harper, 1957. See also Roland Young, *The American Congress*, New York: Harper, 1958, ch. 3 and related references at pp. 289–94; Leiserson, *op. cit.*, pp. 333–39 and references cited.

In the formation of the Sasser Six, a group of junior members of the council, only two of whom had served a previous term, banded together and used the power of majority rule to prevent senior members from occupying the higher positions. This bargain struck at the outset of the legislative year constituted the foundation of the Sasser Six. Once founded, they held together in reaction to the criticism directed at them by the newspaper, the mayor, and the senior councilmen throughout the decisions on the budget and for over half the legislative year, until they finally disintegrated in the latter part of the year under the pressures previously noted.

The importance of the cohesion of the Sasser Six in terms of boosting their power in the structure of the council is demonstrated in the evidence which follows. First, a consensus ranking of the preference for and prestige of the ten committees of the council was obtained from the council members, showing the following results: (1) Finance; (2) Public Works; (3) Public Safety; (4) Legislative Affairs; (5) Claims; (6) City Property; (7) Printing; (8) Records; (9) Election Returns; (10) Hospital. By taking the committee memberships of each councilman and weighting them according to their rankings above, each legislator was assigned a score reflecting his position and rank in the structure of the council during 1952, the year that the Sasser Six dominated the organization. For comparative purposes, the same scores and rankings were made in a follow-up study of the council in 1953, the year after the Sasser Six had disintegrated. The relative scores and the relative rankings for the two years are presented in Table 1.

It can readily be seen that the six members who grouped around Robert Sasser obtained for themselves positions of much greater importance within the council than the five minority members and much higher than they were

Table 1   Committee position scores and ranking of councilmen in Bay City: 1952 and 1953

| | | Committee Position Scores | | Rank | |
Councilman	Senior or Junior Mem.*	1952	1953	1952	1953
Sasser	Jr.	Pres.	15	1	9
Mullins†	Jr.	43	30	2	4
Martin	Jr.	40	14	3	10
Kelly	Jr.	33	22	4	6.5
Wrenn	Jr.	26	13	5	11
Jauno	Jr.	25	15	6	8
Lafevre	Jr.	17	29	7	5
Blais	Sr.	13	22	8.5	6.5
Arnett	Sr.	13	Pres.	8.5	1
Galloway	Sr.	12	43	10	2
Sideburns	Sr.	11	31	11	3

*Senior members are those with more than one prior term on the council.

†Mullins made a crucial switch during the latter part of 1952 which helped restore the power of the mayor's loyal group and appeared to prevent Mullins' slipping far in rank after the Sasser Six fell apart.

able to obtain when their majority no longer held together. It is also evident that the junior members used their majority power to subordinate seniority as a criterion of leadership. Once committed to this internal structure, the organized majority resisted giving it up. They realized that if they did not stick together their political gamble and their revolt against the mayor, the newspaper, and tradition would probably come to naught. They seemed to hope that they would be able by their cohesive behavior to use council power to win public approval.

The organized majority decisions of the council in this situation were not "party-line" decisions in the ordinary meaning of a party which had won a majority at the polls. They were the product, instead, of an intra-legislative group formed after the election to seize council power, which operated in the pattern of party government without the external reinforcement that a majority party can usually command.

THE NORMS OF THE SYSTEM AS FACTORS

Surrounding the legislative process were expectations of both a legal and extra-legal nature which conditioned the action of the councilmen. For example, it was well recognized that by law some of the appropriations decisions to be taken by the council members lay within narrow ranges of alternative, if indeed there were alternatives. There were explicit legal requirements that prevented the council from curtailing the salaries of persons under civil service. Another law prohibited the council from increasing the amounts of budget items above the mayor's requests. An additional law was very exact in fixing the time of decision. On the basis of these, one could explain why certain items were non-controversial, why no items were raised above the mayor's figures, and why the decisions of the council were made within a specified time. In studying the legislative process, it would be a mistake to overlook the formal, legal requirements because participants do many things simply because the laws say that they should be done.

Other norms were less explicit, but were widely acknowledged by councilmen as usually applying to budget legislation. They were informal and extra-legal adaptations that guided the process at several stages, under ordinary circumstances. These norms involved expectations of (a) executive limitations upon the ranges of choice available to councilmen; (b) cooperation and communication between the mayor and the council in working out the budget; and (c) a maximum of public harmony in the council in making budget decisions. Note that these informal norms set forth much more limited roles for councilmen in this process than even the somewhat limited roles allowed by law.

Despite the legal restrictions previously mentioned, councilmen *legally* and *formally* were in a position to deal independently and even harshly with the mayor's budget. *Informally*, however, they expected under ordinary circumstances to be limited by the calculations of the department head, the auditor, and the mayor who would present a budget strongly shaped by the figures of previous years. At the outset, then, they expected the budget to be tied to an inscrutable and somewhat authoritative past. Furthermore, the councilmen expected the budget presented to them to have been carefully examined by the auditor whom they regarded as a "watchdog" with twenty years of experience in the mysteries of budget laws and figures. Normally, he and the mayor were expected to make up much of what would turn out to be the final budget.

Legally, there were no requirements that the mayor and the finance committee confer. Yet an expectation had grown up that they would get together informally and work out most of the executive-legislative differences, so that the council's challenges of the mayor's requests would be largely delivered in a quiet and compromising atmosphere.

Legally, there were no requirements that the finance committee's and the mayor's recommendations be supported. But there was an informal expectation that, under ordinary circumstances, the most important actions in council would be taken in the finance committee, followed by closed meetings of the whole council at which the committee might present its recommendations and most of the remaining differences might be resolved. Thus, controversy in public meetings on most budget items was not ordinarily to be expected.

Generally speaking, the longer a person had been a member of the council, the more he accepted these informal norms. Especially, he seemed to view controversy on budget items between the executive and legislative branches or within the legislature itself as *exceptional* rather than as the *dominant mode* of making decisions. The disparity between the senior and junior members in their endorsement of these norms was dramatized by the respective answers of an extreme representative of each group to the question: "If the council has several informal meetings on the budget and then is ready to take formal action, should the debates on some items be opened up in a formal public meeting?"

> *Senior member:* "After decisions have been agreed upon in the committee of the whole, then *differences should not be aired in public.* Give the committee of the whole four nights—then four more if necessary. Then come out and adopt the budget as a whole. This is a small city. You got to have harmony."
>
> *Junior member:* "The council meetings on the budget should be *open to the public* so that the real issues can be heard. And *never mind the friction* that the older members want to avoid. They and the mayor would like to have star chamber preliminary meetings called to avoid friction. This results in a cut-and-dried procedure."

Of course, not all of the senior members of the council felt as strongly as the oldtimer quoted above that budget decisions should be non-controversial and according to informal traditions, nor did all of the junior men feel as strongly in favor of open controversy as did the newcomer quoted. But the senior members, under ordinary circumstances regarded as the elder statesmen and custodians of the standards of the council, seemed to view the council as a body whose functions were to negotiate, to work things out cooperatively with the mayor and among themselves, and to avoid public divisions as much as possible. This conception stands in contrast to the formal notion of a legislature as an extremely independent body dedicated to crystallizing issues, focusing debate, and deciding by divided votes. The junior members seemed to have more of this formal but less sophisticated view of the council's functions, less appreciation of the informal norms, and a belief that the council should function with greater independence from the executive, with more public debate, and with public divisions in its votes.

In the decisions made by the council in this study, the informal norms had little effect, and therein lies one value of the inquiry. The fact that the informal norms were inoperative in this case does not demonstrate that they are ordinarily unimportant for an understanding of the legislative process. Rather, one should expect that in the majority of cases an understanding of the norms should lead to an understanding of the process. In fact, the follow-up study of the Bay City council on the budget process for the year subsequent to the one presently under analysis demonstrated that the informal norms were highly operative, once the senior members of the council had been restored to their "normal" positions of leadership. In this follow-up study, the actions of the council on the budget were explainable to an overwhelming extent on the basis of the same informal normative system that had been rejected under the leadership of the Sasser Six.

In the 1952 budget decisions, the operation of the informal norms was disrupted initially by the insurgence of the organized majority led by Sasser when they denied important posts to senior councilmen, thereby forestalling the leadership of those most clearly attached to and most familiar with the informal system. The insurgence in itself was regarded by the senior members and the mayor as a signal that informal procedures were not operative. Once started, it reduced the likelihood that most budget items would be decided in a non-controversial fashion.

The mayor reacted by violating the informal custom of working with the finance committee. The committee in turn used this violation as a basis for contending that the mayor was the aggressor in destroying executive-legislative cooperation and asserted its power to cut the mayor's requests. The finance committee ignored the views of the council minority defending the mayor. The loyal minority in turn reacted to this rebuff by voting solidly against every recommendation of the finance commitee which differed with the mayor's requests.

In short, a chain reaction was set off by an unusual political maneuver in which the norms most firmly espoused by the elder statesmen of the council were violated not only by their antagonists but by themselves. As a consequence, the proportion of controversial decisions rose sharply. Non-controversial decisions became matters largely of coincidence or legal compulsion. Both sides in the controversy resorted to more formal and legalistic procedures. Finally, the feelings of the two groups about the way things ought to be run served to reinforce the conflict, as the senior members were constantly irate with the junior members for violating the traditions of harmony, while the junior members took refuge in the notion that they were fighting to open up a closed shop.

EXTERNAL RELATIONSHIPS AS FACTORS

Three aspects of the external relationships of council members will be considered as they affected the appropriations decisions. They are, respectively, as follows: (a) constituency relationships; (b) relationships with the press; and (c) relationships with the executive. Party differences and pressure group contacts, ordinarily considered major factors in the decision-making process, were found to be of such negligible influence as not to merit detailed discussion in this case.

Constituency Relationships

There was no clear effect of constituency interests cutting across all patterns of decisions on the public works budget. Ruling out non-controversial, unanimous decisions, since they showed no divisions, consideration of the two types of controversial decisions indicates that constituency relationships were effective primarily in making individual members of the Sasser Six switch on particular issues to vote in factional alliances with the loyal minority.[7] Organized majority votes did not seem to have any clear relationship with constituency patterns. Two of the Sasser Six had been elected by the city at large, while three of the loyal minority had been elected at large, so that the majority-minority cleavage in the council was not based on an at-large vs. ward division.

In terms of the wards in which the councilmen *resided*, but which were not necessarily the only constituencies they represented, there was a pattern which coincided rather closely with the majority-minority cleavage, but it was not complete nor was it prominent in the calculations of the legislators. All of the members of the loyal minority lived in two of the six wards in the city, while all but one of the organized majority lived in the four other wards of the city. However, in view of the facts that the residential alignment was not complete and that ward alignments were not prominent in the calculations

[7]See Julius Turner, *Party and Constituency: Pressures on Congress*, Baltimore: Johns Hopkins Press, 1952; Duncan McRae, "Roll Call Votes and Constituencies in the Massachusetts House of Representatives," *American Political Science Review*, Vol. 46, December, 1952, pp. 1046–55; Leiserson, *op. cit.*, pp. 344–46.

of the councilmen, the conclusion is that this residential phenomenon was secondary and incidental to other considerations in maintaining the Sasser Six in opposition to the council minority. Certainly, since residence was not coincidental with constituency for the at-large councilmen, the residential alignment could not be used to buttress the contention that the majority-minority cleavage was based on differences in constituency.

Relationships with the Press

General pressures by the press and mass communications media constitute another type of external relationship which might affect the legislative process. It might be regarded as basically of the same gender as pressure group relationships, yet a newspaper is sufficiently different from other community organizations so that it deserves separate treatment. Legislators are not "members" of newspapers in any ordinary sense.

As the only daily newspaper in Bay City, the *Bugle* performed a significant function in the legislative process, but it was difficult to determine the effect of the other media of mass communication, especially the radio station which broadcasted the council meetings. As nearly as one could ascertain, broadcasting the meetings served primarily to make the members of the Sasser Six more cohesive and more aggressive against the mayor. They viewed the broadcasts as unique opportunities to make appeals to the general public and to offset the *Bugle's* very unfavorable portrayals of their actions.

The newspaper accounts of the council meetings and the slanting of the news and issues by the *Bugle* in general were calculated to make the Sasser Six villains in a municipal drama. The effect of this constant barrage appears to have been as follows: (a) First, it reinforced the defensive cohesion of the Sasser Six, at least for several months. By giving them a name and making them more conscious of themselves as a majority caucus, the newspaper helped to encourage the Sasser Six to act as an organized majority during the budget decisions and for some time afterward. (b) Second, the effect of the *Bugle* upon the councilmen it attacked did not come from any mass antagonisms demonstrably stirred up by the publicity. Instead, the things the besieged councilmen read directly about themselves in the newspaper led to their feeling defensive and eventually dismayed and frustrated. For all they knew, a majority of the people were for them, but the main channel of publicity was against them, and this raised great anxieties as they read the *Bugle* and speculated about its influence. As one of the leaders of the Sasser Six stated, after he had finally switched to vote with the mayor late in the year on the water bond issue: "There wasn't no protests to the council. I didn't get a call, but the paper kept at it until I was saying 'water, water, water' in my sleep." (c) Finally, the newspaper attack seems to have played an important part in wearing down the members of the Sasser Six so that they fell apart several months after the budget was adopted. Even though their initial reaction was toward more cohesion, eventually the six majority councilmen began to feel isolated and demoralized as the newspaper attack continued month after month. Despite their righteous indignation against the *Bugle's* journalism and their cognizance of its biases, they appeared ultimately very dependent upon the paper for obtaining some sort of public images of themselves.

Relationships with the Executive

Of course, the mayor became in this action by the council a prominent symbol serving to stabilize the differences between the organized majority and its opponents. All of the six-to-five votes in which the Sasser Six held together were votes against the mayor. The loyal minority on the council never deviated from a position in which they voted to uphold the mayor's budget requests. But it would be inaccurate to conclude that the formation of the Sasser Six was primarily a product of legislative antagonism toward the executive. To be sure, the revolt of the three insurgent Coalition members leading to the formation of the Sasser Six necessitated a break with the mayor as long as the latter chose to stand by the three senior Coalition councilmen and the newspaper. However, their antagonism toward the executive was more a product of the formation of the Sasser Six, which was organized to satisfy the ambitions of the newer members of the council and to forestall the domination of municipal politics by senior politicians working in collaboration with the newspaper and the managers of the Coalition. Of course, once the insurgent majority had been formed and the mayor chose to remain as the symbol of the Coalition, then the Sasser Six proceeded to play the role which their political situation seemed to dictate, and they opposed the mayor on many counts almost automatically.

SUMMARY

The foregoing case illustrates three major types of legislative decisions and furnishes some insights as to the way several kinds of factors affected the legislative process. The three major types of decisions, as expressed in terms of alignments in the voting patterns of the councilmen, were (a) non-controversial, unanimous decisions; (b) controversial, organized majority decisions; (c) controversial, factional alliance decisions. They were similar to those that might be found in any legislative body, although they were not present in the same proportions in this case as one might expect in the "typical" American legislative body.

Considering the nature of the issue as a factor, the following propositions were supported by the analysis of this case: (a) The nature of the issue *per se* was not a strong factor in determining council voting alignments. (b) Although many issues may be matters of such indifference or such overwhelming acceptability to legislators that they produce non-controversial voting patterns, this study did not indicate that they were necessarily so.

(c) The nature of the issue seemed most clearly a factor in producing legislative alignments of the factional alliance type. However, the particular issue did not seem to sway marginal legislators because of their personal values as much as because of the needs of their constituencies. Factional alliances appeared to be built *ad hoc* around issues according to constituency interests as perceived by legislators. This observation supported the argument for analyzing legislative behavior in terms of constituency characteristics rather than probing into individual motivation. (d) Otherwise, the nature of the issue in this case seemed to become enmeshed in the web of relationships—the internal structure, the formal and informal norms, and the external relations—of the legislative body.

In this study, the council's internal structure was shown to be one of the most important factors in the legislative process. (a) The organized majority, operating in a manner similar to a majority party caucus, was founded upon the agreement by which committee posts and legislative power and prestige were distributed after the members were elected. (b) This majority caucus cohered over a lengthy period of time, voting a "party-line" in most instances (except in several cases where some member defected on a particular issue affecting his constituency to vote in a factional alliance) even though members of the caucus differed as to party affiliation and had been elected on different tickets. (c) The desire for power and prestige within the council was so strong that the junior members were willing and able to use their majority to overrule the normally accepted principle of seniority as a basis of assigning council positions. As long as they stuck together, they preserved their positions within the council, but once they lost their cohesion, they lost their power.

Furthermore, certain general contentions were supported about the effect of norms upon the legislative process. (a) Formal, legal requirements furnished norms having a direct effect upon legislative behavior, and they had to be understood in order to explain certain kinds of decisions. They particularly explained, for example, why some decisions were non-controversial, since the councilmen felt that the law simply would not allow them to alter the mayor's proposal. (b) Other informal and extra-legal norms would have, under ordinary circumstances, explained a great deal about the legislative process in the Bay City council. Many of these informal norms, cultivated by senior members of the council, were designed to minimize open controversy and to maximize non-controversial decisions. Had the senior members been in positions of leadership in the council, these norms would have probably had more effect than they did in this case. (c) The fact that the informal norms were rendered inoperative by the insurgence of the junior members of the council produced two consequences. First, it increased the proportion of controversial decisions. Second, it forced the council to rely more upon legalistic methods of operating and resolving conflicts.

A brief recapitulation of the effects of external relationships upon the legislative process in this study of the Bay City council shows the following: (a) Constituency relationships were most important in the decisions of marginal legislators who crossed organizational lines to vote in factional alliances on particular issues. (b) At-large vs. ward constituencies did not show any unusual tendency to line up against each other. Other factors furnished more important, competing bases of alignment. (c) Party differences were fragile foundations for the maintenance of an organized majority. This in part was due to the unstable condition of party alignments in the community where the Coalition had urgd an attempt at bipartisanship. The weakening of traditional two-party lines furnished an environment in which the council could organize on the basis of the internal distribution of council positions of power and prestige, ignoring partisan differences. (d) Pressure group contacts appeared to be very highly overrated factors in legislative decisions. They seemed to be neither as numerous nor as effective as some conceptions of the legislative process might have led one to believe. Nor did this case demonstrate any great relevance of group memberships, either organizational or categorical, for the kinds of decisions made by the councilmen. (e) Of all the external relationships considered, those with the press and with the chief executive appeared to have the greatest consequences, especially in maintaining a voting cleavage between the organized majority and minority on the public works appropriations. The majority caucus, once it had organized and seized control of the council, was committed to maintaining its position, and it reacted defensively to the public image portrayed by the press and to the leadership symbolized by the chief executive. (f) The influence of the press appeared to be direct, i.e., the councilmen reacted to what they had themselves read in the newspaper rather than to any demonstrable pressures from others whom the press had stirred up. (g) The effect of attacks in the press upon the council majority was at first to produce more cohesion, so that in the appropriations decisions external attacks helped to reinforce the organized majority decisions. Eventually, the effect of a prolonged attack in the press was to frustrate and demoralize the organized majority, since they lacked adequate alternative ways of supporting themselves in the community. (h) Hostility of the majority caucus toward the mayor was not the cause of the formation of the caucus so much as it was an outgrowth of the organization of the caucus. Once the alignment of the council had taken place, however, the executive became an important symbol in the process of making decisions on the budget. Wherever the leaders of the majority caucus differed with the mayor, a controversial decision ensued. Wherever they did not differ, no controversy occurred.

CHAPTER TWELVE

POLICY SUCCESS AND POLICY OUTCOMES IN STATE LEGISLATURES

WAYNE L. FRANCIS

A legislative system has at least two basic kinds of output. The first may be called "perceptions of policy success," and the second, "policy outcomes." Perceptions of policy success are specific units of perception shared by members of the environment as a result of decisions by public officials. Policy outcomes are all of the objective structural changes in the environment which result from the decisions of public officials. Political scientists have perhaps given greater attention to policy outcomes.[1] In this chapter, however, I will discuss perceptions of policy success before turning to outcomes.

POLICY SUCCESS

The notion of perceived policy success is closely related to a number of concerns and concepts in the social sciences. Simon and others have given considerable attention to perceptions in satisfying models of corporate behavior.[2] In essence, it is assumed that there are certain levels of satisfaction to be reached in the fulfillment of a perceived goal. Individuals may mark out

---

[1]For the most extensive work on policy outcomes in the states, see Thomas R. Dye, *Politics, Economics, and the Public* (Chicago: Rand McNally, 1966). Several additional studies of policy outcome will be discussed presently. This is not to say that the psychological aspects of legislative policy-making have been ignored.

[2]H. A. Simon, "A Behavioral Model of Rational Choice," *Quarterly Journal of Economics*, LXIX (1955), 99–118, reprinted in *Models of Man* (New York: Wiley, 1957), pp. 241–260. Also see Charles Bonini, *Simulation of Information and Decision Systems in the Firm* (Englewood Cliffs, N.J.: Prentice-Hall, 1963).

Reprinted with permission of publisher and author from *Legislative Issues in the Fifty States: A Comparative Analysis* by Wayne L. Francis (Chicago: Rand McNally & Co., 1967), pp. 51–71. Mr. Francis is Associate Professor of Political Science at the University of Washington.

specific criteria (profit margin, volume of sales, the passage of a bill, etc.) by which they judge their progress, or they may carry with them some vague notion of what should be accomplished. Legislators no doubt arrive at a legislative session with a set of expectations about what should be accomplished, or else they acquire expectations after a few days of legislative business. Whether or not such expectations will be satisfied will depend upon both the level of expectation and the way in which they perceive the concrete events of the session.

The concept of perceived policy success is to be distinguished from the concept "sense of political efficacy," employed in the voting studies and in *The Legislative System.*[3] A legislator may have a high sense of legislative efficacy and still observe low policy success, or he may have a low sense of legislative efficacy and perceive high policy success. The efficacy measure is concerned with the degree to which the individual legislator feels that he is a part of the system or the degree to which he feels his individual actions are effective in the system. Perceived policy success refers to the degree to which legislators feel the system has met its responsibilities, but, of course, the concept could be expanded to include other legislative participants or even the electorate. The concept is really closer to "effectiveness," as Seymour Martin Lipset uses the term.[4] Lipset discusses the perceived effectiveness of political systems and implies that the stability of a political system will depend in part upon the degree to which members of the system consider its policies to be effective in relation to their expectations.

Evaluations of policy success in the legislative context are puzzling. Legislators choose among a wide range of alternatives. In some states these choices lead to generous social welfare programs, apportionment by population, and widespread school construction. In other states they may lead to comparatively little government activity, unapportioned legislative chambers, and limited support for schools. In every policy area, the alternatives are numerous. For almost every important bill and appropriation, the choice is one of degree; it is rarely a simple "yes or no" decision. Denial of an increased appropriation usually means acceptance of a lower level of appropriation, whether it is in regard to the entire budget or some specific department or agency. A defeat of one bill may spell the success of a similar bill. But nothing is ever fully resolved. The same problems creep up again and again. And each time the legislature meets, it must decide "more" or "less" on a host of familiar measures.

Although a legislator's personalized expectations may be quite tangible, because of the complexity of the legislative situation his generalized

[3]Angus Campbell, Philip E. Converse, Warren E. Miller, and Donald E. Stokes, *The American Voter* (New York: Wiley, 1960); Angus Campbell, Gerald Gurin, and Warren E. Miller, *The Voter Decides* (Evanston: Row, Peterson, 1954); and John Wahlke, Heinz Eulau, William Buchanan, and Leroy C. Ferguson, *The Legislative System* (New York: Wiley, 1962).

[4]Seymour Martin Lipset, *Political Man* (Garden City, N.Y.: Doubleday, Anchor Books, 1963), p. 64.

expectations are probably somewhat vague. He may have a pet bill or two, or a committee to manage; if he can obtain passage of the bills or win majority solidarity in the committee, he may fulfill his personalized goals. But what should the legislature accomplish as a representative body?

Suppose we assume that before a legislature is in session too many days, a large number of legislators build up notions about what the important issues of the session are; as a result, they *expect* that some sort of legislation must be implemented to settle the issues at least tentatively. Something must be done; everyone is interested. . . . The environment calls for legislation. And the passage of legislation leads to policy success, the defeat of legislation to dissatisfaction or policy frustration. Under these assumptions, policy success may be indexed by a passage-defeat ratio on important issues.

Each policy area and each state may be described by a passage-defeat ratio that is calculated from responses to the following questionnaire items:

1. *Strong legislation was passed in this area.*
2. *Legislation was passed, but in a considerably modified form.*
3. *Legislation was defeated, but then passed in a special session called by the governor.*
4. *Legislation was defeated either in the legislature or by a veto.*

For each policy area and each state, the total of the responses to all four items is divided into a subtotal based on the responses to the first two items. The index is crude, but it serves to point up some interesting relationships. Caution must be taken to interpret the passage-defeat ratio as an index to policy success, only as viewed by legislators, and not by the general population. Since the items above were at the end of the questionnaire, some respondents did not get that far, and others did not respond to one of the items for every issue they named. Approximately 80 per cent of the issue-mentions were described by one of the above items. Of course, the concrete points of interest are those that mark the passage of legislation on important matters of policy. It is possible that some legislators did not perceive these events for some issues they named.

Policy success, as indexed by the passage-defeat ratio, was highest in the areas of health (.84), education (.81), agriculture (.79), gambling (.78), business (.76), administration (.75), social welfare (.75), local government (.75), finance (.73), and highways-transportation (.70). The overall passage-defeat ratio ws .67. Likewise, policy success was lowest in the areas of elections-primaries-conventions (.32), constitutional revision (.39), courts-penal-crime (.50), liquor (.56), land (.58), water resources (.59), taxation (.60), labor (.60), civil rights (.60), and apportionment (.64). When examined in relation to the various forms of conflict for the policy areas, no linear associations of any significance were observed. It is relevant to point out, however, that in three of the four areas in which relatively little conflict of any type was observed (health, education, and highways-transportation), the index of policy success tended to be higher; and in the two areas experiencing high conflict of all types, taxation and apportionment, the index values were below the mean. Also, it might be pointed out that policy success is lowest in the area of constitutional revision, not surprising in view of the well-known difficulties in achieving constitutional change.

An examination of the states reveals that perceptions of policy success are related to three important variables—party control, the distribution of seats, and the degree of pressure group conflict. All of these relationships have significant implications for democratic theory and the conduct of democratic politics.

Political analysts have often expressed their concern over the consequences of divided control. What happens to the outputs of a legislative system when the system is forced to labor under the chains of *divided party control?*[5] Generally, it is argued that the party of the governor should have a majority in both chambers of the legislature; otherwise, no clear legislative program can emerge. The voting public is apt to become confused and will be unable to tell which party is responsible for policies it does not like. Normally, about one-third of the states are under divided control. In 1963 there were sixteen in which at least one chamber of the legislature was controlled by the party to which the governor did *not* belong. Since divided control is so common among the states, the consequences of such a situation need not remain a matter of total speculation.

In addition to the question of divided control, there remains the question of how much one party should dominate the seats of the legislature. Even if one party controls the office of the governor, the senate, and the house, it may have such overwhelming control that the legislature ceases to put forth policies of merit as often as it should. There is no loyal opposition to spur the majority party into action.

An examination of party control and the distribution of seats in the 48 states where the party identification of the legislators is made known yields at least three distinct groups of states. There are those in which control of the policy-making machinery is divided; those in which one party is almost totally dominant; and those in which there is party competition, although the legislature is still controlled by one party. A sketch of these groups (Table 1) makes it evident that perceived policy success is highest in the third group, those states where the parties share legislative seats but not legislative control. Policy success is lowest under the condition of divided party control, but it is also low in the states where one party dominates.

More detailed information on this point, listed in Table 2, suggests that divided control hampers the passage of legislation more markedly when the parties are closely matched in the legislature. The mean index values of policy success (calculated from passage-defeat responses) are lowest when the

---

[5]For example, V. O. Key, Jr., *American State Politics* (New York: Knopf, 1956); and also Malcolm E. Jewell, *The State Legislature* (New York: Random House, 1962), p. 7.

Table 1   Policy success under three conditions of legislative control (IRV for 1963)*

Condition	Index of Policy Success	Number of States[a]
Divided Party Control: Either the senate, house, or both are controlled by a party other than that of the governor	.63	16
One-Party Dominant: One party controls both chambers and the office of the governor; minority party has no more than 17 per cent of house seats and no more than 14 per cent of senate seats	.67	11
One-Party Competitive: One party controls both chambers and office of governor; minority party has more than 17 per cent of house seats or more than 14 per cent of senate seats.	.75	21

*Editor's Note: IRV denotes "Issue Respondex Value." The Issue Respondex Value is a frequency percentage calculated by dividing the number of positive responses made to a given statement by the total number of possible positive responses that could have been made by any group or sub-group of legislators. Thus, in Table 1, 63 per cent of the respondents serving in states with "divided party control" considered their legislatures to have been successful in the enactment of legislation in policy areas in which they thought legislation should have been forthcoming.

[a]Nebraska and Minnesota are not included; the IRV for these two states is .63. Alaska is included among the One-Party Competitive states, although house seats were evenly divided between the two parties.

legislature labors under both divided control and a close distribution of seats (.53 and .49). Divided party control seems to make less difference when the legislature is held firmly in the hands of one party. Perhaps the governor from a minority party tends to resign himself to a program of cooperation with the legislative majority.

The data in Tables 1 and 2 represent one year of legislative experience. We would need to examine data for several years in order to have full confidence in the results; however, these results do represent more than just accidental findings. They confirm many long-held suspicions about the consequences of divided control and the absence of two competing parties in the legislature. The extent to which such hindrances impair policy-making is difficult to estimate, but the data clearly show that legislators are less likely to come up with legislation when the cards are stacked against them. In 1963 Rhode Island was the classic example of a state plagued by divided control, among other things (.22). Pennsylvania under Scranton exhibited the opposite situation; it experienced a narrow, but solid, legislative majority (.925).

The consequences of pressure group politics for the states may also be evaluated in terms of policy success. We might suspect that, as conflict became more intense in the state legislature, legislation would be passed less frequently. Partisan, factional, regional, and pressure group conflict were all examined . . . , but, of these four types of conflict, only pressure group

Table 2   Policy success, party control and the distribution of seats (1963)

	Minority Party: Percentage of Seats	*House:* Divided Control	*House:* Solid Control	*Senate:* Divided Control	*Senate:* Solid Control
House:	.39–.50	Ariz.	Alaska	Ind.	Colo.
Senate:	.40–.48	(.660)	(.808)	(.351)	(.915)
		Ill.	Idaho	Nev.	Del.
		(.390)	(.640)	(.697)	(.818)
		Ind.	N.Y.	N.J.	Hawaii
		(.351)	(.806)	(.690)	(.639)
		Mont.	Pa.	R.I.	Idaho
		(.692)	(.925)	(.220)	(.640)
		Ore.	Utah		N.Y.
		(.482)	(.800)		(.806)
		Wis.	Wash.		Pa.
		(.586)	(.383)		(.925)
					Utah
					(.800)
					Wyo.
					(.736)
	Group IRV	.53	.73	.49	.78
House:	.32–.38	Conn.	Calif.	Conn.	Calif.
Senate:	.28–.40	(.673)	(.571)	(.673)	(.571)
		Nev.	Colo.	Ill.	Mass.
		(.697)	(.915)	(.390)	(.727)
		N.H.	Mass.	Mont.	Mich.
		(.792)	(.727)	(.692)	(.650)
		N.J.	Mich.	Ore.	Mo.
		(.690)	(.650)	(.482)	(.770)
		N.D.	Mo.	Wis.	Ohio
		(.767)	(.770)	(.586)	(.829)
			Ohio		Wash.
			(.829)		(.383)
			Wyo.		W.Va.
			(.736)		(.897)
	Group IRV	.72	.74	.56	.69
House:	.18–.31	Iowa	Del.	Ariz.	Alaska
Senate:	.14–.26	(.667)	(.818)	(.660)	(.808)
		Okla.	Hawaii	Iowa	Kan.
		(.756)	(.639)	(.667)	(.698)
		R.I.	Kan.	N.H.	Ky.
		(.220)	(.698)	(.792)	(.882)
		S.D.	Ky.	N.D.	Me.
		(.895)	(.882)	(.767)	(.800)
			Me.	S.D.	Md.
			(.800)	(.895)	(.689)
			Md.	Vt.	Tenn.
			(.689)	(.791)	(.844)
			Tenn.		
			(.844)		
			W.Va.		
			(.897)		
	Group IRV	.62	.78	.76	.79

205

Table 2—Continued

	Minority Party Percentage of Seats	House: Divided Control	House: Solid Control	Senate: Divided Control	Senate: Solid Control
House:	.00–.17	Vt.	Ala.	Okla.	Ala.
Senate:	.00–.14	(.791)	(.605)	(.756)	(.605)
			Ark.		Ark.
			(.578)		(.578)
			Fla.		Fla.
			(.825)		(.825)
			Ga.		Ga.
			(.833)		(.833)
			La.		La.
			(.448)		(.448)
			Miss.		Miss.
			(.667)		(.667)
			N.M.		N.M.
			(.519)		(.519)
			N.C.		N.C.
			(.712)		(.712)
			S.C.		S.C.
			(.825)		(.825)
			Tex.		Tex.
			(.640)		(.640)
			Va.		Va.
			(.757)		(.757)
Group IRV		.79	.67	.76	.67

Index values for Nebraska and Minnesota are .603 and .655 respectively.

conflict yields a strong negative correlation with policy success (r' = −.39).* States with high pressure group conflict rank low in policy success, and states with low pressure group conflict rank high in policy success (Table 3). When there was apparent pressure group conflict over the major issues of a state, the state had great difficulty in creating legislation that would resolve the issues.

Enough has been said in the literature about the relationship between the pressure group system in the states and the type of party system in operation. Strong pressure groups and weak parties are said to appear in the same states. Conversely, weak pressure groups seem to accompany strong, competitive parties. A legislative party is said to be strong if it exhibits a substantial amount of *cohesion* in the legislature. Cohesion is often measured by the degree to which Democrats vote together and Republicans vote together on roll call votes.[6]. . . Pressure group strength in one case was based upon answers to a questionnaire that was sent to, and returned by, at least one respondent in each state who was classified as an expert.[7]

If the degree of pressure group *conflict*, as defined by this study, is any reflection of the *strength* of pressure groups in the various states, then the

[6]Measures of cohesion vary from application to application; Jewell, pp. 49–53, discusses the most common procedures.

[7]Belle Zeller, ed., *American State Legislatures* (New York: Crowell, 1954).

Table 3   **Policy success and pressure group conflict in the fifty states**

	Very High Pressure Group Conflict	High Pressure Group Conflict	Low Pressure Group Conflict	Very Low Pressure Group Conflict
High Policy Success (Passage-defeat ratio)	2	5	8	10
Low Policy Success (Passage-defeat ratio)	10	8	4	3

N = 50 (Fifty States)

*Editor's Note: The degree of presssure group conflict within a given state over a given issue is determined by the frequency with which that state's legislators responded positively to the statement "There were at least two major interest groups who were at odds with one another over this matter."

findings of this survey do *not* confirm the reports of Zeller (editor) and Zeigler.[8] For example, the correlation between a ranking of states by partisan conflict and a ranking of states by pressure group conflict is slightly positive (r' = .20 . . .), certainly not what one would expect from a reading of the earlier studies. It is possible that pressure group *conflict* on important issues is not a necessary concomitant to strong pressure group activity. But an attempt to determine pressure group *interest* through the responses to the statement, "*At least one or two fairly important pressure groups made it known that they had a vital interest at stake*," gives similar results. The rank correlation coefficient for pressure group interest compared to partisan conflict is .12. Partisan conflict was shown previously to be strongly related to interparty election competition. Still it is possible that *important* issues are not the matters that indicate strong pressure groups, and we could stretch the argument to say that, where pressure groups are really strong, legislators will simply act as a ratifying body for the things the pressure groups demand.

The findings of this study would suggest that the extent, or strength, of pressure group activity is relatively independent of party conflict, competition, and perhaps cohesion, and that, regardless of party conditions, pressure group activity may be strong enough to precipitate low policy success. Alternatively, regardless of party conditions, pressure group activity may be weak. Where pressure group activity is weak, policy success tends to be higher. Some states are exceptions, however. Tennessee, for example, is described by both high pressure group conflict and interest (ranking 9 and 6 respectively) and high policy success. A key to this unusual situation may be the degree to which Tennessee legislators resist the demands of pressure groups. The results of *The Legislative System's* four-state study and a later article would both suggest that such an explanation might well apply to

[8]*Ibid.;* and Harmon Zeigler, "Interest Groups in the States," in Herbert Jacob and Kenneth N. Vines, eds., *Politics in the American States* (Boston: Little, Brown, 1965), pp. 113–114.

Tennessee.[9] In other words, the internalized dispositions of legislators make a difference. There are other states which experienced a low level of pressure group conflict along with low policy success; examples are Connecticut, Montana, and Nevada, all of which underwent divided control of the policy-making machinery. Other states which demonstrated a low level of pressure group conflict and low policy success but did not experience divided control are Idaho, Louisiana, New Mexico, and Texas; the latter three were dominated by one party, and perhaps Idaho legislators tended to facilitate interest groups.

POLICY OUTCOME

Does the nature of political conflict in a state show any relationship to the outcomes of state policy-making? One way to secure an answer is to compare states experiencing different kinds of conflict configurations, to see if corresponding differences in policy outcomes become apparent. The process of comparing outcomes among states has been hampered in the past by the coincidence of high industrialization and urbanization with vigorous party competition, and of low per capita income with one-party legislative systems. Dawson and Robinson met this problem when they examined the extent of public social welfare programs among the states.[10] The level of development in these programs seemed at first to be related to both socioeconomic factors and interparty competition, but, further examination revealed that socioeconomic factors were much more significant; when socioeconomic factors were held constant, interparty competition showed little relationship to the extent of public social welfare programs.

In a recent book, Thomas R. Dye raises a similar problem in considering the effects of malapportionment upon legislative outcome.[11] Does malapportionment lead to policy choices that aid the overrepresented areas at the expense of the underrepresented areas? If the best apportioned states tend to be the large industrial states, then it is very difficult to know whether it is industrialization or enlightened apportionment that leads to higher teachers' salaries, higher per pupil expenditures, and higher welfare payments. Dye and Hofferbert, in separate articles, have attacked this problem.[12]

[9]Wahlke, Eulau, Buchanan, and Ferguson, *The Legislative System;* and Wayne L. Francis, "The Role Concept in Legislatures: A Probability Model and A Note on Cognitive Structure," *Journal of Politics,* XXVII (1965), 567–585.

[10]Richard E. Dawson and James A. Robinson, "Inter-Party Competition, Economic Variables, and Welfare Policies in the American States," *Journal of Politics,* XXV (1963), 265–289.

[11]Thomas R. Dye, "State Legislative Politics," in Jacob and Vines, especially pp. 157–160.

[12]Thomas R. Dye, "Malapportionment and Public Policy in the States," *Journal of Politics,* XXVII (1965), 586–601; Richard I. Hofferbert, "The Relation between Public Policy and Some Structural and Environmental Variables in the American States," *American Political Science Review,* LX (1966), 73–82.

Both have concluded that malapportionment has very little direct effect upon the extent of state spending programs. In another instance, Herbert Jacob arrives at a similar conclusion.[13]

In all of the above works, the authors have given great emphasis to economic variables such as wealth and the various forms of state expenditures. The political variables such as party competition and apportionment have been shown to have little direct relationship to the economic variables when the associations between economic variables are controlled. In a society bent upon achieving greater and greater material wealth, it is thus tempting to minimize the impact of political variables upon the larger population. It would be interesting at this point, however, to compare the above conclusions with what legislators say about the important issues that confront them. Responses to the following four statements would appear relevant:

1. *The proposed legislation involved a large amount of money.*
2. *Proposed legislation involved many levels or branches of government.*
3. *Proposed legislation meant a long-term government commitment, if passed.*
4. *I felt the proposed legislation would have a direct impact upon a large number of people in this state.*

Issue Respondex Values for the first statement may be regarded as an index of the degree to which each policy area is related (directly) to the economy of the state. Table 4 shows how the policy areas rank on this score.

The measures of policy output selected by Dye, Jacob, and Hofferbert are all included in the seven top policy areas listed . . . (excluding gambling), although they do also deal with the apportionment question in light of the output measures and party competition. The apportionment area falls at the bottom of the imaginary scale set up here; it may be considered the least related to the economy of the state. Since education expenditures normally constitute about one-third of the state budget, and closer to one-half the budget when federal grants-in-aid are removed, it is not surprising to find education issues ranking first. Although this analysis is based upon the primary classification of issues into policy areas . . . , it is relevant to point out that a large number of education issues were given a secondary classification under finance.

The output measures selected by Dye, Jacob, and Hofferbert fall into areas that are above the IRV of .43 for all responses to the statement. All other policy areas fall well below the mean, with the exception of gambling. The six matching areas include 54 per cent of the issue-mentions utilized in this study. The results of this research do point out that earlier measures capture a significant proportion of what is identified here as important in

[13]Herbert Jacob, "The Consequences of Malapportionment: A Note of Caution," *Social Forces*, XLIII (1964), 256–261.

Table 4   Relationship between the policy areas and the economy of the states

Policy Areas	Amount of Money Involved IRV
1. Education	.77
2. Finance	.76
3. Taxation	.67
4. Social welfare	.66
5. Highways-transportation	.61
6. Gambling	.54
7. Health	.44
All responses	.43
8. Land	.33
9. Water resources	.30
10. Labor	.28
11. Local government	.27
12. Liquor	.24
13. Agriculture	.22
14. Administration	.19
15. Business	.17
16. Courts-penal-crime	.10
17. Constitutional revision	.07
18. Civil rights	.04
19. Elections-primaries-conventions	.03
20. Apportionment	.01

the legislature, that they do have very much in common, but that they may or may not be typical of other types of legislative output.

To avoid judging a political system strictly on economic terms, responses to the last three statements mentioned above can be evaluated. The policy areas described most frequently as involving many levels or branches of government were local government, administration, constitutional revision, finance, elections-primaries-conventions, water resources, and taxation, in that order. Those said to involve a long-term government commitment were education, water resources, local government, highways-transportation, social welfare, health, constitutional revision, administration, and finance. In a full ranking of policy areas, the correlations were —.06 between "amount of money involved" and "levels or branches of government involved," and .38 between "amount of money involved" and "long-term government commitment"; both correlations are certainly low enough to suggest a differentiation of resources among the twenty policy areas.

The perceived impact of proposed legislation in the twenty policy areas, as evidenced by whether legislators said a specific proposal would have a "direct impact upon a large number of people," also does not relate very strongly to the "amount of money" index ($r' = .32$). While the "amount of money" index had a wide range, .01 for apportionment issues and .77 for education issues, the "perceived impact" values demonstrated a small range, from .44 for administration issues to .83 for tax issues. The perceived impact of proposed legislation may also be examined from the responses to the statement, "*I felt the proposed legislation would represent or result in a marked departure from present practices.*" Here it is significant to note that, for the six policy areas corresponding to the output measures used by Dye, Jacob, and Hofferbert, the Issue Respondex Value was much lower (.31) than it was for the remaining areas (.48). In other words, legislators felt that in the areas involving large amounts of money, proposed legislation tended to represent simply a continuation of ongoing activities, and not a marked departure from existing practices. The corresponding rankings of policy areas on the two indices expressed a negative correlation of −.59.

The thrust of the evidence indicates that there is reason to reexamine what constitutes the output of a state legislative system. Measures of expenditure and taxation relate to part of that output and, in the short run, appear to be nothing more than products of the state's wealth. To a large extent, the diminishing marginal utility of dollars for every increase in individual income can explain the state's ability to raise revenue for those activities that have become part of the government's responsibility. These activities are perpetuated in familiar form, even increased, year by year, by an extensive bureaucracy with well-defined vested interests. Perhaps it is in the less moneyed policy areas that issues have the greatest chance to reflect the political characteristics of the system.

A system has many kinds of output, such as the perceived effectiveness of the system itself, sometimes called employee satisfaction, public satisfaction, or, as in this chapter, legislator policy success. An index to legislator policy success has been shown to be related to party control and the extent of pressure group conflict. Then too, some of the political variables need to be approached as ends in themselves, rather than as means to other more important things. It is too often assumed, for example, that apportionment involves nothing more than the reshuffling of lines in a complex game; whereas other policy areas, such as education, welfare, and highways, require the distribution of real dollars. In reality, apportionment involves the distribution of seats—just as other matters involve the distribution of dollars. It is not our intent to assess the value of a legislative seat in dollars, but legislative seats are central to the political process and their distribution should show some relation to other political characteristics.

An Example: Apportionment

Recently Dye has shown that urban underrepresentation in the states, as indexed by the David and Eisenberg technique, is correlated with the degree of party competition in both the upper and lower chambers of the legislatures (r = .50 and .44).[14] Controlling for the effects of urbanization, industrialization, income, and education, however, the associations calculated by Dye are less impressive, giving partial coefficients of .38 and .35.

---

[14] Paul T. David and Ralph Eisenberg, *Devaluation of the Urban and Suburban Vote* (Charlottesville: Bureau of Public Administration, University of Virginia, 1961).

Like David and Eisenberg, Glendon Schubert and Charles Press have also developed a technique for assessing how well the states have managed the apportionment problem.[15] They summarize their conclusions in a convenient set of scores and rankings of states, from the "best" apportioned to the "worst" apportioned, as indicated by selected population measures. Their results do not imply that the best apportioned states necessarily have the most responsive legislative or apportionment machinery. In some states population shifts are staggering, whereas in other states the population concentration is relatively stable. Florida, for example, has experienced an astounding influx of new inhabitants, while North Dakota has had very few. The stress and strain upon Florida legislators is surely greater than the stress and strain upon the legislators of North Dakota. To examine the performance of states, the Schubert-Press results must be modified by what knowledge we can gain of population movement.

Certain types of population shifts put pressure on the apportionment system of a state. Whenever population movement results in unequal net gains and losses in district populations, the demands for reapportionment come to the forefront. States undergoing great change will have difficulty adjusting their policies on schedule. In recent years, people have tended to migrate toward urbanized areas, creating conditions whereby rural legislators are left with small populations in their districts. Simultaneously, central cities and their suburban counterparts grow in population at a rate that is often too rapid for the legislature to deal with. Migration within each state, or from one state to another, will have the same overall effect.

When shifts in population concentration occur rapidly, severe strains are placed upon local party organizations. When state legislators are able to make minor adjustments through apportionment as the need arises, party leadership in the legislature will probably successfully withstand internal criticism. If a state, however, becomes so malapportioned that a large number of districts must be altered, agreement upon a plan becomes nearly impossible. In some states population changes outrun the abilities of the states' party leaders to force a decision. If reapportionment were to take place every two years, population changes would be less significant, but most state constitutions require that apportionment take place only every ten years. After ten years have passed, the state may no longer be accurately described by its apportionment map. To change maps quickly and extensively after such a long period is more than most parties can bear.

The amount of *population stress* may be indexed by reference to two types of information:[16]

---

[15]Glendon Schubert and Charles Press, "Measuring Malapportionment," *American Political Science Review*, LXIII (1964), 302–327, with corrections, 966–970.

[16]U.S. Bureau of the Census, *1960 Census of Population* (Washington, D.C.: U.S. Government Printing Office, 1960), Vol. 1, Pt. 1, U.S. Summary, Table 112, pp. 1–257. In Table 112 there are several indices of intrastate population movement. Net increase or loss in state populations is available in several sources, including the U.S. Bureau of the Census publications.

1. Percentage of net increase (or loss) in state population from 1950 to 1960; and
2. Percentage of population in a state moving from one dwelling unit to another between 1955 and 1960.

For the general purposes of this section, the percentages for each state are totaled, and these serve as the basis for ranking the states by population stress. Considered in conjunction with population stress, the Schubert-Press apportionment ranks are more meaningful. The Schubert-Press ranks are based upon the degree to which the population assigned to each legislative seat deviates from the population figure derived from:

$$\frac{\text{Total Population of State}}{\text{Number of Seats in Chamber}}$$

Population movement has tended to accentuate deviations from the ideal district population.

States ranking above the median in both the Schubert-Press scale and in population stress may be considered to approximate most closely the condition set down by the United States Supreme Court ("one man—one vote"). These states are Alaska, Colorado, Delaware, Hawaii, Indiana, New Jersey, Ohio, Oregon, Utah, Washington, and Wyoming (see Table 5). These eleven adaptive, well-apportioned states also fall, without exception, above the median in partisan conflict as identified by the Issue Respondex Values, and they are also among the 25 two-party states in a recent classification made by Austin Ranney.[17] Like Dawson and Robinson, Hofferbert, and Schlesinger, Ranney focused upon the amount of interparty election competition.[18]

Table 5   Party conflict in adaptive, well-apportioned states (by rank[a])

States	Population Stress	Schubert-Press Apportionment[b]	Partisan Conflict
1. Alaska	1	23	25
2. Colorado	7	21	2
3. Delaware	8	22	16
4. Hawaii	9	14	9
5. Indiana	24	9	3
6. New Jersey	19	17	10
7. Ohio	15	1	21
8. Oregon	16.5	2	22
9. Utah	11	5	8
10. Washington	13	15	1
11. Wyoming	16.5	16	13

[a]Ranks can range from 1 to 50.
[b]Slight adjustments have been made in the Schubert-Press ranking. The United States as a whole is omitted, thus changing all ranks following it by one. Nebraska is also reranked, without giving it extra credits for having only one chamber.

[17]Austin Ranney, "Parties in State Politics," in Jacob and Vines, eds., Table 1, p. 65.
[18]Ibid., pp. 63–70.

In essence, the two-party competitive states, or states where partisan conflict in the legislature is most apparent, include the adaptive, well-apportioned states.

At the next level are those states that are well apportioned but have had relatively stable populations. Table 6 illustrates that a majority of these states have experienced high partisan conflict in the legislature, but that a substantial number are those without closely matched parties, such as Arkansas, North Carolina, and South Carolina. When there is low population stress, party make-up in the legislature would seem to make less difference.

Table 6   Party conflict in well-apportioned states of stable populations (by rankᵃ)

States	Population Stress	Schubert-Press Apportionment	Partisan Conflict
1. Arkansas	36	11	43
2. Illinois	26	24	19
3. Maine	45	6	18
4. Massachusetts	40	4	17
5. New Hampshire	33	3	30
6. New York	38	10	14
7. North Carolina	29	19	41
8. Pennsylvania	49	8	4.5
9. South Carolina	28	20	44
10. South Dakota	46	13	36
11. Tennessee	34	7	38
12. Vermont	48	25	24
13. West Virginia	43	12	23
14. Wisconsin	31	18	4.5

ᵃRanks can range from 1 to 50.

At the third level are those states with high population stress and malapportionment. They are malapportioned partly because they have undergone substantial population relocation through the years, and, as a consequence, have been unable to keep step with the apportionment-by-population requirement. Ten out of fourteen, or over 70 per cent, of these states rank low in partisan conflict (Table 7). Only the competitive two-party states (Table 5) were able to achieve well-apportioned systems under the strain of high population movement. A few two-party states, like California and Connecticut, did not achieve high apportionment ratings in the face of high population stress, but they were exceptions.

At the fourth level are states with stable populations and poor apportionment systems. In this group are Alabama, Iowa, Kansas, Kentucky, Minnesota, Mississippi, Missouri, Nebraska, North Dakota, Oklahoma, and Rhode Island. These maladaptive, malapportioned state legislatures tend to experience relatively little partisan conflict. The only exceptions are Rhode Island and Minnesota (Table 8). Ranney calls Alabama and Mississippi

Tdble 7   **Party conflict in unadaptive, malapportioned states (by rank^a)**

States	Population Stress	Schubert-Press Apportionment	Partisan Conflict
1. Arizona	4	36	37
2. California	5	42	15
3. Connecticut	14	39	7
4. Florida	3	43	40
5. Georgia	22	50	47.5
6. Idaho	23	28	29
7. Louisiana	20	34	47.5
8. Maryland	10	38	39
9. Michigan	21	29	6
10. Montana	25	26	12
11. Nevada	2	40	26
12. New Mexico	6	41	33
13. Texas	12	35	42
14. Virginia	18	30	47.5

^aRanks can range from 1 to 50.

"one-party Democratic," Oklahoma and Kentucky "modified one-party Democratic," and Kansas, Iowa, and North Dakota "modified one-party Republican." Although Ranney classifies Minnesota and Nebraska as "two-party," political parties are deemphasized in both their legislatures. Missouri is a borderline case, both in this study and in the Ranney classification. Rhode Island remains the only real exception. A closer look at the Rhode Island legislature reveals that, in 1963, it suffered pronounced conflict of all types, having a mean rank of 1 when partisan, factional, regional, and pressure group conflict are considered simultaneously. Rhode Island appears to have been a victim of an unusual cross-section of conflicting interests. Moreover, it was shown earlier that Rhode Island respondents ranked lowest in "policy success" for 1963.

Table 8   **Party conflict in maladaptive, malapportioned states (by rank^a)**

States	Population Stress	Schubert-Press Apportionment	Partisan Conflict
1. Alabama	37	46	47.5
2. Iowa	44	44	31
3. Kansas	27	48	35
4. Kentucky	41	45	34
5. Minnesota	32	49	20
6. Mississippi	47	31	47.5
7. Missouri	30	27	27
8. Nebraska	39	33	45
9. North Dakota	50	37	28
10. Oklahoma	35	47	32
11. Rhode Island	42	32	11

^aRanks can range from 1 to 50.

In conclusion, the degree of legislative party conflict does seem to be closely related to the kind of apportionment system generated by the states. In Table 9, the strength of the relationship is illustrated. Apportionment outcomes are more tolerable in the more competitive states. There

Table 9   Relationship between apportionment typology and partisan conflict

	Adaptive Well-Apportioned	Stable Well-Apportioned	Unadaptive Malapportioned	Maladaptive Malapportioned
High Partisan Conflict	11	8	4	2
Low Partisan Conflict	0	6	10	9

N = 50 (Fifty States)

are, of course, many types of outcome, of which apportionment is only one. But since reapportionment does not involve taxation or finance, economic wealth may be regarded as a minor factor in the explanation of apportionment outcomes. Apportionment, as modified by population stress, is a function of party system, party conflict, or party competition. A well-apportioned state can be poor, and a malapportioned state can be rich in industry and economic capacity.

Why should reapportionment by population be more successful when party conflict is more pronounced? As was explained in the last chapter, the fairness of an apportionment plan by the standards of population enumeration, as evidenced by the David-Eisenberg and the Schubert-Press techniques, is only coincidentally related to the fairness of a plan by party standards. The ideal situation for majority party leaders occurs when they have narrow majorities in both chambers of the legislature and control of the governorship. Then they are more able to satisfy the legislative members of their party and still meet a loosely constructed standard of population equality. When one party is dominant, or when parties are less important, factions are fluid and tend to solidify and decompose in response to the rise and fall of each apportionment plan. There are too many members to please, and some of them must suffer. It is easier for apportioning officials (an appointed board or a committee of the legislature) to satisfy the majority party when that majority is not too large. In most states, when the majority party is satisfied, the plan will be accepted, subject perhaps to a court ruling. Even when control is divided in the state, it is possible that the House plan will satisfy its majority party and the Senate plan its majority party, to the detriment of minority party members in each chamber; of course, in this situation it may be much more difficult to settle upon a plan.

To illustrate the flexibility of apportionment under the population standard, the author gave one of his classes district maps of a hypothetical state with a fifty-member legislative chamber. Students were given the population of each county and told that, by employing multi-member single-county districts, single-member single-county districts, and single-member multi-county districts, they were to devise an apportionment plan that would adhere as strictly as possible to the population standard of one seat for every P/S people, where P is the total population and S the number of seats in the chamber. Districts had to be drawn along county lines. After the 25 students had drawn up their plans individually, with more than usual obedience to the Supreme Court ruling, they were given the normal vote of each county in order to see how the parties would fare in the upcoming election. Predictions based on the 25 plans were anything but consistent. One plan predicted that the Democrats would win 38 of the 50 seats, while another plan predicted that the Republicans would win 35 of the 50 seats, in spite of the fact that the total votes for each party were contrived to be equal!

In conclusion, the remarkable degree of latitude that exists when only the population principle is applied means that an apportionment outcome can be and is sensitive to the party make-up of the legislature. A final word of caution is in order, however. The data for this analysis apply to 1963 only, and, thus, are subject to modification. The performance of individual states may change markedly, but we would expect that the general relationship will hold true over time.

SUMMARY AND CONCLUSIONS

Two indices of policy output have been employed in this chapter: the first is based upon legislator perceptions relating to the passage of legislation; the second is based upon a standard external to the legislature, described as the Schubert-Press scale of apportionment. The essential question is one of determining to what extent various forms of legislative behavior relate to the output criteria. The first index is described as an index of policy success; it is defined as the number of times legislators perceive that legislation relating to the issues they name is passed, divided by the number of times they perceive that this legislation is defeated, in the most recent regular session of their legislature.

An examination of legislator perceptions yields the following results:

1. Index values of policy success are highest in the areas of health, education, agriculture, gambling, business, administration, social welfare, local government, finance, and highways-transportation.
2. Index values of policy success are lowest in the areas of elections-primaries-conventions, constitutional revision, courts-penal-crime, liquor, land, water resources, taxation, labor, civil rights, and apportionment.
3. Index values of policy success tend to be low in those states experiencing divided party control.

4. Divided party control has less effect upon policy success when the same party has a large majority of seats in both chambers of the legislature but does not win control of the office of the governor.

5. Index values of policy success tend to be low in those states where one party is dominant.

6. Index values of policy success tend to be high in those states controlled by one party which has only narrow majorities in the legislature.

7. There is a negative correlation between the index of policy success and the index of pressure group conflict ($r' = -.39$). The evidence suggests, however, that for important issues the strength of pressure group activity is relatively independent of the degree of party conflict and competition.

The second index of policy output, the Schubert-Press apportionment scale, is to be distinguished from output measures of expenditure. Judging by legislator perceptions, policy areas "involving a large amount of money" tend to be those areas in which proposed legislation does *not* reflect a "marked departure from present practices" ($r' = -.59$). Since the most recent literature dealing with levels of expenditure as policy outputs has shown the relative insignificance of party competition in determining such expenditures, it may be expected that policy areas not involving money, such as apportionment, will exhibit a closer relation to political variables. If we control for population movement, or population stress, we are likely to find well-apportioned systems in states experiencing a high degree of election competition and a high degree of partisan conflict in the legislature.

THE POLICY-MAKING PROCESS: EXECUTIVE LEADERSHIP

Perhaps the most fundamental attribute of government in mid-twentieth-century America is the enormously increased responsibility that has been imposed upon national, state, and local executive leaders. In good times and bad, during months of calm and moments of crisis, presidents, governors, and mayors, far more than any other officials, are expected to forge as well as to implement responsive policies and programs. Many are well armed for these responsibilities in their control of significant resources that are by-products of their positions and personal talents. Normally executive leaders are backed by sizable public bureaucracies, and often they command the support of political party loyalists inside and outside government. They are also in a position to capitalize upon the considerable attention they receive in the media and in popular discourse. On the other hand, they must always work within a set of constraints based upon formal and informal limitations on their authority, their own personal shortcomings, and the severity of the political conflict they seek to manage. Each chapter in Part Four focuses upon the influence of either state or local chief executives and the leadership patterns that emerge when they try to govern.

Robert A. Dahl considers five possible leadership patterns that conceivably could apply to the structure of influence in the city of New Haven: "covert integration by Economic Notables," "an executive-centered 'grand coalition of coalitions,'" "a coalition of chieftains," "independent sovereignties with spheres of influence," and "rival sovereignties fighting it out." He asserts that the first of these is not applicable to New Haven and describes how at one time or another in its recent history the city has experienced each of the other four patterns. From 1931 to 1953, for example, the city was governed by "sovereign" decision-making agencies, each more or less autonomous within its own sphere of influence. There was no dominant centralizing influence exercising control over these agencies, and although the mayors were not unimportant, they did not seek to develop their influence over the executive departments. Following the election of Mayor Richard C. Lee in 1953, however, a new pattern, an executive-centered coalition, was established. Ultimately Dahl is interested most in the relationship between leaders and followers, and on the basis of his observations of New Haven he concludes that the city is ". . . a Republic of unequal citizens—but for all that a republic."

Thomas J. Anton's treatment of gubernatorial leadership is embedded in a more general examination of expenditure decision-making by state officials. He suggests that there are sufficient similarities in the behavior of budget-making officials in the fifty states to permit the development of a decision-making model, one that may have relevance beyond the specific decisional process he is observing. He defines the roles major actors in the budget-shaping process are expected to play by the audiences for whom they must "perform": e.g., agency heads are expected to request more money each year, budget officers are expected to reduce these requests, and governors are expected to pursue balanced budgets at higher expenditure levels. Anton then examines the contrast between what state officials actually do and the statements or symbols they use to rationalize their behavior. He holds that these symbols often mask the true meaning of their actions, primarily because many important influences on the budget-making process are often beyond the control of state officials. Nevertheless, the relevant actors must urge "fiscal responsibility," or "economy," or "improved service," for at stake is "the symbolic satisfaction among the actors and the audiences which observe this stylized behavior."

The final selection in Part Four examines the role of the city manager —in particular, the variations in the perceptions of that role as expressed by city councilmen on the one hand and city managers on the other. Ronald O. Loveridge based his study on interviews with 338 city councilmen and 59 city managers serving in the nine-county, San Francisco Bay area. Loveridge finds that most city managers believe their proper roles include those of policy innovator and policy advocate. In fact, a majority of managers in his sample felt that a manager should not deliberately avoid taking unpopular positions on controversial community issues. He finds that city councilmen, on the other hand, regard the city manager more as a staff administrator than as a political executive. The councilmen feel that the manager should assure competent administration of the city's affairs and provide the council with "neutral" advice and information, taking care to avoid direct involvement in the policy and political process. Thus, there were two sharply dissimilar sets of expectations about the proper role of the city manager, and, given the power of the councilmen, the frequent interaction between the two sets of officials, and the relative visibility of the manager's policy activities, the conflict in role perceptions becomes particularly critical. Loveridge notes

that the manager tries to resolve this conflict in two ways: first, by camouflaging his policy activities or confining them to behind-the-scenes discussions
and, second, by limiting his involvement to "safe" policy areas while deliberately shunning more controversial matters. He suggests that these tactics
seriously handicap the extent to which managers can provide innovative
public leadership at a time when increased social conflict requires it.

CHAPTER THIRTEEN

PATTERNS OF POLITICAL LEADERSHIP IN NEW HAVEN

ROBERT A. DAHL

FIVE PATTERNS OF LEADERSHIP

The number of theoretically possible patterns of integration is almost infinite. However, because of their familiarity and generality, five possibilities were considered in our study of New Haven. These were:

1. Covert integration by Economic Notables.
2. An executive-centered "grand coalition of coalitions."
3. A coalition of chieftains.
4. Independent sovereignties with spheres of influence.
5. Rival sovereignties fighting it out.

The first of these, covert integration by the Economic Notables, is a common answer suggested by studies of a number of other cities. In this pattern the top leaders consist of a unified group of private citizens who arrive at agreements about policies by covert negotiations and discussions carried on in the privacy of their clubs, homes, business firms, and other private meeting places. Leaders gain their influence from their wealth, high social standing, and economic dominance. Usually the leaders are wealthy executives in important business firms; if this pattern fitted New Haven, presumably the top officers of Yale would be included because the university is one of the largest property owners and employers in the city.

A revealing aspect of this hypothesis is its insistence on the essentially clandestine or covert exercise of influence by the "real" leaders. Why? Because in most cities today the overt, public incumbents in the highest official positions—the mayors and other elected politicians, city officials, party chairmen, and so on—are rarely drawn from the ranks of wealth, social standing, and corporate office. By contrast, the patricians of New Haven were an *overt* political elite. They made no bones about their dominance. They not only openly occupied key positions in the religious, educational, and economic institutions of New Haven, but they also held a visible monopoly of all the important public offices. This . . . is indisputably not so today. If individuals of wealth, status, and corporate position dominate politics, evidently they *must* do so covertly.

The hypothesis of covert control by the Economic Notables is both widely popular and strongly supported by many scholarly studies, from the Lynds' monumental examination of Muncie, Indiana in the twenties and thirties to Floyd Hunter's more recent analysis of the "power structure" of Atlanta.[1] Indeed the term "power structure" has so much passed into the vocabulary of the informed man that it has become a current bit of jargon among educated inside-dopesters. Although careful analysis has shown that the conclusions about influence contained in the academic studies often rest upon dubious evidence and even that some of the data found in the works themselves actually run counter to the conclusions,[2] some communities do seem to have conformed to this pattern in the past and some may today. Certainly some citizens of New Haven believe firmly in the existence of a covert elite and offer plausible evidence to support their view.

I believe the evidence . . . is sufficient to warrant the rejection of the hypothesis that this pattern applies to New Haven. In every city where Economic Notables are alleged to rule covertly, it is important to note, evidently they do so by means sufficiently open to permit scholars and newspapermen to penetrate the veil; indeed, an inspection of the information contained in descriptions of these cities indicates that the job of probing into the clandestine structure of power has presented few barriers to the assiduous researcher. It is all the more improbable, then, that a secret cabal of Notables dominates the public life of New Haven through means so clandestine that not one of the fifty prominent citizens interviewed in the course of this study—citizens who had participated extensively in various decisions—hinted at the existence of such a cabal; so clandestine, indeed, that no clues turned up in several years of investigation led to the door of such a group.

To abandon the hypothesis of covert integration by Economic Notables

[1]Lynd and Lynd, *Middletown* and *Middletown in Transition;* Hunter, *Community Power Structure* and *Top Leadership, U.S.A.*

[2]For a detailed analysis of this point, see the forthcoming companion volume by Nelson W. Polsby, *Community Power and Political Theory.*

does not mean that the Economic Notables in New Haven are without influence on certain important decisions. . . . [But] if one wants to find out how policies of different leaders are coordinated in New Haven, one must consider some pattern other than covert integration by Economic Notables.

A second pattern is envisioned in an alternative hypothesis: that today the top leaders are more likely to comprise a coalition of public officials and private individuals who reflect the interests and concerns of different segments of the community. In this view, a coalition is generally formed and the policies of the coalition are coordinated largely by elected leaders who draw on special skills and resources of influence that leaders without public office are not likely to have. This pattern of integration is usually associated with vigorous, even charismatic elected chief executives; presumably it was characteristic of the presidencies of FDR and Truman.[3]

In its implications the hypothesis of an executive-centered coalition is radically different from the first possible pattern. Where covert domination by Economic Notables reflects relatively stable social and economic factors, the executive-centered coalition may be more ephemeral; the coalition may fluctuate greatly in strength and even dissolve altogether when the coalition's leaders can no longer reconcile their strategies and goals. Moreover, in the pattern of covert domination, influence derived from public office and popularity with the electorate is completely subordinate to influence derived from wealth, social standing, and corporate position; in the executive-centered coalition, the prerogatives of public office, legality, legitimacy, and electoral followings are independent sources of influence with a weight of their own. Finally, the hypothesis of a covert elite logically leads to a certain pessimism about popular government. If government officials and elected politicians are merely handmaidens of the upper classes, one cannot expect much in the way of peaceful reform via politics. Change must come about either through the gradual action of outside factors, like changes in industrial organization or technique, or else through a revolutionary seizure and transformation of the state by leaders of social segments who for some reason cannot win elections and attain public office. The hypothesis of integration by an executive-centered coalition, by contrast, allows for the possibility that reformist or radical coalitions (as well as conservative ones) may, by peacefully winning elections, obtain control of the powers of government and introduce durable changes in the distribution of access to influence, wealth, education, and social standing.

The third pattern is seen as integration of policies in different sectors by a coalition of chieftains. Something like it fits the various party and nonparty coalitions that control policy-making in Congress and particu-

[3]See Arthur M. Schlesinger, Jr., *The Coming of the New Deal* (Boston, Houghton Mifflin, 1959), Part VIII; James M. Burns, *Roosevelt: The Lion and the Fox* (New York, Harcourt Brace, 1956); Richard Neustadt, *Presidential Power* (New York, John Wiley, 1960).

larly in the Senate.[4] The difference between the second pattern and this one is of course only one of degree; in marginal cases it would be impossible to say whether a particular pattern of integration should be called executive-centered or a coalition of chieftains.

A coalition of chieftains, like the executive-centered coalition, is consistent with the hypothesis that nowadays top leaders are likely to be public officials and private individuals who reflect the varying and even conflicting interests and concerns of different segments of the community. In the executive-centered coalition, integration of policy is achieved largely by means of the skills and resources of an elected leader; in a coalition of chieftains, integration takes place mainly by negotiations among the chieftains that produce exchanges of information and eventuate in agreement. The executive-centered pattern contains a sizable degree of hierarchy in the distribution of influence among the leaders. The chief executive is at the center of a "grand coalition of coalitions"; in the extreme case he is the only leader with great influence in *all* the allied coalitions, perhaps the only leader who even *participates* in all of them. Moreover, his special resources mean that every other leader in the grand coalition is more dependent on the executive for perpetuation of his influence than the executive is dependent on him. In a coalition of chieftains, on the other hand, if hierarchy appears, it is weak and may rest almost exclusively on a central position in the network of communications occupied by a particular leader or set of leaders. Thus, although a few chiefs may be somewhat more influential than others, they are all highly dependent on one another for the successful attainment of their policies. There is some specialization of influence by issue-areas; a chieftain in one area may be deferred to on matters lying in his domain, and he in turn defers to other chieftains in matters lying in theirs. But the chiefs actively coordinate their policies through extensive interchange of information and reciprocal favors. An awareness that their most important policy goals do not conflict and a predisposition for similar strategies provide a basis for agreement on strategies.

Since a coalition of chieftains depends almost entirely on likemindedness, reinforced by the arts of negotiation and compromise, the life of a coalition may be short or long depending on the state of agreement and the negotiating capacities of the chiefs. A coalition may reflect persistent goals held among durable social and economic segments or the ephemeral goals of social elements in flux.

With some reservations as to historical accuracy, the fourth and fifth patterns might be regarded as analogous to a system of independent city-

---

[4]Recent observers describe Congress in terms that would fit the pattern here, although each offers highly important differences of emphasis and interpretation. Cf. David B. Truman, *The Congressional Party* (New York, John Wiley, 1959), Ch. 4. William S. White, *Citadel, The Story of the U.S. Senate* (New York, Harper, 1956), Chs. 8 and 14; Roland Young, *The American Congress* (New York, Harper, 1958), Ch. 3.

states or petty sovereignties. This is the pattern of congressional action dominated by virtually autonomous committees that was described by Woodrow Wilson in his classic *Congressional Government*. It is approached in some ways by what two recent observers find to be the pattern of decision-making in New York City.[5] In this system of petty sovereignties each issue-area is controlled by a different set of top leaders whose goals and strategies are adapted to the particular segments of the community that happen to be interested in that specific area. As long as the policies of the various petty sovereignties do not conflict with one another, the sovereigns go about their business without much communication or negotiation. When policies do conflict, the issue has to be settled by fighting it out; but since the sovereigns live within a common system of legal norms, constitutional practices, and political habits, "Fighting it out" means an appeal to whatever processes are prescribed, whether voting in a legislative or administrative body, decision by judges, executive approval, or elections. The practice of fighting it out increases the likelihood of appeals to the populace for support, and hence the extent to which leaders shape their policies to what they think are the predominant preferences of the populace. However, since fighting it out is mutually costly and the results are highly uncertain, strong spheres of influence may develop with a relatively clear understanding as to the limits of each sphere; in this case, fighting it out is avoided, appeals to the populace are less likely, and policies are shaped more to meet the goals of leaders, subleaders, and special followings.

Thus the way in which petty sovereignties integrate their policies tends to assume one of two patterns, depending on the extent to which the policies of the one sovereign are consistent with those of the other. If the petty sovereigns perceive their policies to be strictly inconsistent, in the sense that a gain for one means an equivalent loss to the other, then conflict is unavoidable and fighting it out is likely to be the method of settlement. This is the case, for example, if the sovereignties are two highly competitive parties, both intent on winning office for their candidates.

However, if the petty sovereigns perceive their policies to be consistent or even complementary, in the sense that a gain for one entails no loss for the other and may even produce a benefit, then fighting it out is likely to be avoided. Possibility of conflict is minimized by mutually accepted spheres of influence, combined with a strong presumption that the status quo must be adhered to; it is also understood that if disagreements arise they are to be resolved by implicit, or occasionally explicit, bargaining among the petty sovereigns without an appeal to the populace or other external authorities.

These five patterns of coordination seemed to us most likely to cover

[5]Herbert Kaufman and Wallace Sayre, *Governing New York City, Politics in the Metropolis* (New York, Russell Sage Foundation, 1960), Ch. 19.

the range of possibilities in New Haven, though the likelihood of finding still other patterns could not be excluded a priori. During our investigation of New Haven two possible variations on the five patterns became obvious. First, the prevailing pattern might vary with different combinations of issue-areas. For example, the pattern of integration applying to nominations and elections might not be the same as the pattern applying to education and redevelopment. Second, patterns of integration might vary over time. The variations might be long-run changes, such as the decline of the patrician oligarchy; they might be short-run changes; conceivably, one might even encounter more or less regular fluctuations in integrative patterns associated with, say, periodic elections.

Except for the first pattern (covert integration by Economic Notables), which it now seems safe to reject, all of these possibilities appear to be entirely consistent with the evidence so far. In the [sections] that follow I shall demonstrate, from an examination of particular decisions, that all of the remaining four patterns have actually existed in New Haven in recent years. Before 1953 there existed a pattern of independent sovereignties with spheres of influence, which I shall call Pattern A. This gave way briefly to a coalition of chieftains and then, under Mayor [Richard C.] Lee, to an executive-centered "grand coalition of coalitions," which I shall call Pattern B. Standing quite apart, the pattern of integration with respect to the political parties has been that of rival sovereignties fighting it out, which I shall call Pattern C.

PATTERN A: SPHERES OF INFLUENCE

The characteristic pattern of integration in New Haven before Lee's victory in 1953 seems to have been one of independent sovereignties that managed to avoid severe conflict by tacit agreements on spheres of influence. Because the boundaries were by no means perfectly defined, conflicts and disputes sometimes had to be settled by negotiation. But with the exception of the political parties, most of the time each of the petty sovereignties went its way without much interference from the others.

For example, under Mayor [John W.] Murphy (1931–45) once the basic decision on school appropriations had been made, the public school system was substantially autonomous and largely under the control of the superintendent. Under Mayor [William] Celentano, appropriations were increased and a new superintendent was appointed, but the decentralized pattern continued, and the locus of power remained in the hands of the superintendent. Zoning was substantially autonomous; in practice it was hardly coordinated at all with the work of the City Plan Commission or the Redevelopment Agency. Appointments to the Board of Zoning Appeals were among the most coveted political prizes in the city, since the capacity to grant or refuse variances to zoning regulations could be used to induce payoffs of various kinds. The Board of Fire Commissioners, the Parking Authority, the Housing Authority, the Department of Health, the Department of Public Works and the Building, Plumbing, and Housing Inspectors were each in a different part of the forest.

There was no dominant center of influence over these agencies. The Mayor and the Corporation Counsel constituted whatever center of coordination and control existed. When conflict occurred these two men were usually drawn sooner or later into the negotiations, and their wishes carried weight. But Celentano was not an executive who sought to develop his full influence over the various departments. He was disturbed by public criticism and highly sensitive to the views of the aging owner of the city's two newspapers. Hence after a brief flurry of reform in the school system following his election, the Mayor did not exercise and did not seek to exercise a decisive role in the decisions of the various petty sovereignties that made up the official and unofficial government of New Haven.

Survival of the system of independent sovereignties was aided by three factors. First, because most citizens are indifferent about public matters unless public actions encroach upon their own primary activities (which is not often or for long), control over any given issue-area gravitates to a small group which happens to have the greatest interest in it. Second, because political resources are fragmented . . . , no one except the mayor has enough resources at his disposal to exert a high degree of influence over all the issue-areas. In short, given the distribution of resources, if the mayor cannot or does not coordinate policy, then no one else can do so by the deliberate and direct exercise of influence. Thirdly, in this case the Mayor evidently believed that interference with the decisions of properly constituted agencies was undesirable; hence he saw no reason to exploit his available resources to the full in order to gain influence over their decisions. The petty sovereignties, then, enjoyed a large measure of autonomy.

Under some conditions the pattern of petty sovereignties might have produced such total deadlock or such a rapid increase in city outlays for various agencies as to be politically self-destructive. For several reasons, however, the pattern was relatively durable; indeed, New Haven may well revert to the pattern again. Because there is little basic disagreement over policies, the political parties do not divide the community into two warring sets of bitter-end partisans. On the contrary, attitudes among the voters, the active participants, and the subleaders usually pile up so much in one direction that leaders in both parties must struggle to present themselves as the true believers in the only policy that nearly everyone seems to agree on.

One recurring source of disagreement, to be sure, is the proper level of expenditures a particular agency is to be allowed. On this matter the petty "sovereignties" were not sovereign and disagreements had to be settled by *ad hoc* negotiations among the leaders, the most important of whom were the mayor and the members of the Board of Finance. Even then, however, because the largest element in legitimacy is precedent no matter how accidental or seemingly irrational the relevant precedent may be, agreement is relatively easy if an agency is prepared to accept without increase whatever appropriation it had during the preceding year. When other conflicts arose, as they occasionally did, these too were settled by *ad hoc* negotiations.

The system worked by negotiation, then, because the costs of an attempt to enlarge any one domain of influence appeared greater than the highly uncertain gains that might accrue. The system tended to a natural equilibrium in which each of the sovereigns was relatively well contented with his sphere of influence and unwilling to jeopardize his position by seeking to extend his sphere or curtail that of another. It was to this equilibrium that the system returned after a disturbance brought on by a brief controversy.

The Pattern Displayed : The Metal Houses

Since our investigation did not begin until 1957, concrete evidence on how the system of independent sovereignties worked is rather fragmentary. Fortunately, however, a case study made in 1953 of a political incident that occurred that year provides us with a vivid picture of the system in operation.[6] The story is worth telling here not only for the light it throws on the pattern of political coordination but because it illustrates many other aspects of the system as well.

In the winter of 1953, Benjamin and Milton Lebov, two brothers who had grown wealthy from a junk business located at the foot of Truman Street in the Hill section of New Haven, bought some metal houses from the New York Housing Authority, which sold them for scrap. The Lebovs did not intend to use the houses as scrap. Earlier that winter they had obtained a permit from the office of the New Haven Building Inspector to put up sixty-five metal houses in an area not far from the junk yard that was zoned for industry and had no restrictions on the structures that might be erected.

The Lebovs seriously misjudged the response of the neighborhood. The residents of the Hill, which was the heart of the state senatorial district in which George DiCenzo had established his control over the Republican party, were predominantly Italian and of the working classes. The Sixth Ward, where the Lebovs proposed to erect their metal houses, might easily have been mistaken by hasty observers for a run-down and disintegrating area. Ninety per cent of the Sixth's labor force consisted of

[6]Originally written as a senior honors essay at Yale, the case study later appeared in considerably shorter form as one of the Cases in Public Administration and Policy Formation of the Inter-University Case Program: William K. Muir, Jr., *Defending "The Hill" Against Metal Houses*, ICP Case Series, No. 26 (University, Ala., University of Alabama Press, 1955).

manual laborers, skilled artisans, service workers, and a few clerks and salesmen. Only seven other wards out of the city's thirty-three had so few white-collar workers. The average person over twenty-five had not completed the eighth grade; in the number of college graduates, the Sixth was third lowest in the city. A fifth of the population was foreign-born; of these half had been born in Italy and about a fifth had been born in Russia. The Italians were, of course, Catholics. The Russian-born residents were largely Jewish. The Eighth Ward, adjacent to the Sixth, had about the same characteristics. Here, the hasty observer might easily conclude, was a likely spot in which to find the politics of a mass society.

Despite surface appearances, however, neither ward was a slum area. The average family income in both wards was a little above the median for the city. The population was relatively youthful, vigorous, hard-working. The two wards contained almost no Negroes. The residents were by no means defeated or spineless. They took pride in their homes, in their work, in their children, and in their neighborhoods. In the residential area in the vicinity of Truman Street near the spot where the Lebov brothers intended to put up their metal houses, the largely Italian population maintained a strong and vigorous community life that made it possible to mobilize the neighborhood when the residents felt themselves threatened, as they did when they began to hear about the metal houses.

The proposal to erect the metal houses, parts of which began to appear in the junk yard, seemed to nearby residents to constitute a clear threat to the neighborhood. The cheap unorthodox housing seemed to imply slums, an influx of Negroes, a decline in property values, a sharp change in an area in which many of the residents had lived their entire lives. In short, their primary concerns were adversely affected by men whose actions they could not hope to influence—except perhaps through politics. And so these essentially apolitical people turned briefly to political action to avert the danger they thought confronted them.

In 1953, as a result of ticket splitting in the 1951 elections, the city executive was in the hands of Republicans while a slender majority of the thirty-three aldermen were Democrats.

The Sixth was a Democratic ward. For years it had given lopsided majorities to Democratic candidates, local, state, and national. When Celentano ran the first time for the mayoralty in 1939, the ethnic loyalties of the Italians overpowered their partisan loyalties, and the ward split almost exactly even. When Celentano ran again in 1945 and was elected, the Sixth supported him; thereafter it returned to the Democratic fold in mayoralty elections. In 1953 its alderman was a Democratic Irishman named James Slavin.

The Eighth, which had been as overwhelmingly Democratic as the Sixth, went for Celentano in 1945, for his Italian opponent in 1947, and then for Celentano again in the next two elections. Its alderman was an

Italian Republican named Montalto who had managed to slip into office in 1947 and had won by narrow margins in the subsequent three elections.

Miss Mary Grava, a spinster who had lived all her life on Truman Street and was outraged at the prospect that the metal houses would change the character of the neighborhood, took the lead in fighting against the Lebov brothers. Although she had never been active in politics, as a lifetime resident of the ward she had some acquaintance with her alderman, James Slavin. When she phoned Slavin and protested about the houses, he agreed to get together with Montalto to see what could be done.

After examining the city charter, Slavin and Montalto finally prepared an amendment the effect of which was to prevent houses of unusual materials, including metal, from being erected in New Haven without the permission of both the City Plan Commission and the Board of Aldermen. Early in May the amendment went to the Committee on Legislation of the Board of Aldermen.

Meanwhile the Lebovs had decided to seek another permit to build more metal houses in a nearby residential area. Because this neighborhood was zoned for residence and the plans for the metal houses did not meet zoning standards, the Lebovs were turned down by the Building Inspector. They appealed to the Board of Zoning Appeals. At the meeting of that Board in late May, Miss Grava, other residents of the neighborhood, and four aldermen, including Montalto and Slavin, appeared in opposition to the request for a variance from the zoning regulations. The Board unanimously rejected the Lebovs' application. The Lebovs had lost the first round.

But the danger to Miss Grava and her neighbors in the vicinity of Truman Street remained alive as long as the Lebovs were free to proceed with their project at the site they had originally chosen in the area zoned for industry. Political activity on Truman Street mounted; Alderman Slavin was subject to endless telephone calls; Montalto, in desperation, took to fleeing the city on weekends or remaining hidden inside his house; and "Miss Grava herself was everywhere, dropping words of warning, or the lastest rumor of some alleged Lebov malfeasance, in stores, on street corners, from her porch, or on the telephone."[7]

Early in June the Committee on Legislation of the Board of Aldermen met to consider the charter amendment proposed by Slavin and Montalto. The Committee was made up of two Democrats and a leading Republican, all of whom were sympathetic to the protests of the neighborhood. Moreover, in executive session the Director of the City Plan Commission testified to the undersirability of cheap metal houses; after all, the New York Housing Authority had never intended the metal houses to last more than three to five years and they were in danger of turning into slums almost from the

[7]Ibid., p. 12.

start. The Committee decided, however, that no amendment to the charter was necessary, since the existing charter gave the Board of Aldermen ample power to prevent the construction of the houses if they so wished.

One week later, despite a promise to the contrary the Lebovs' lawyer had made at the Committee hearing, the Lebovs began construction. The Chairman of the aldermanic Committee of Legislation immediately filed a resolution demanding that the license issued by the Building Inspector be revoked.

At this point, however, the Lebovs ran up some fresh battalions, consisting of no less than Mayor Celentano and his corporation counsel, George DiCenzo. In response to a request from two Democratic aldermen on the Board who were sympathetic to the Lebovs, on July 3 DiCenzo announced it as his considered legal opinion that "the Board of Aldermen does not have the legal power to order abatement of existing metal houses on the ground that they constitute a nuisance." The Lebovs had won Round Two.

On the night of July 5, twenty-five Democratic and Republican aldermen assembled in an unofficial meeting at which most of them agreed to support the resolution against the Lebovs, despite the opinion of the Corporation Counsel. On the following hot summer evening, over two hundred anxious and excited citizens from the threatened neighborhood gathered in the aldermanic chambers at City Hall for the regular monthly meeting of the Board of Aldermen at which the crucial vote was to be taken. After caucusing separately for several hours while the tension mounted among the sweaty and anxious citizens in the hot aldermanic chambers, the Democrats and Republicans finally descended from their caucus rooms to vote. The resolution passed over the opposition of a minority of three aldermen— all of them Democrats. The neighborhood had won the third round.

They had not yet won the fight however. The Lebovs could still win if the Mayor were to veto the resolution and if the opposition on the Board could be increased enough so that the veto would not be overridden. If twelve aldermen could be persuaded either to stay away or to vote in support of the Mayor, the veto would stand. The Lebovs sought to decrease the number of their opponents on the Board in two ways: by threatening to sue the aldermen individually for allegedly "illegal" action and by appealing to liberal opinion on the ground that their project promised housing for Negroes, who were notoriously subject to discrimination in their search for better homes.

Aware of these dangers, Miss Grava worked to improve the position of herself and her neighbors. She called upon one of the leaders in the New Haven League of Women Voters who, being anxious to broaden the narrow upper- and middle-class membership of the League, responded with a promise to support Miss Grava's efforts; later the leader in the League even offered a thousand dollars to help the neighborhood retain a lawyer to represent both the neighborhood and the aldermen in any legal actions that might take place. Miss Grava also got in touch with Richard C. Lee, who had been defeated in his second try as Democratic candidate for mayor two years earlier and was now the most likely Democratic candidate in the mayoralty election just four months away. Lee counseled Miss Grava to keep up the pressure on the members of the Board of Aldermen, to organize, and to maintain a steady flow of favorable publicity. The lead in organizing a neighborhood association was taken by Miss Grava's sixty-three-year-old brother, Dominic Grava. Although he had prospered and moved away from the Hill to a middle-class neighborhood, he still maintained his affections for his old neighborhood—in addition to which he owned several houses there. He had known the Mayor since Celentano's boyhood; he was, in fact, both Celentano's godfather and his neighbor, and the Mayor had appointed him to the Capital Projects Programming Commission. Grava became the organizing spirit behind the Hill Civic Association; he saw to it that the officers and the Board of Directors, of which he himself was chairman, were suitably balanced among Italian and Jewish residents of the neighborhood. (The Lebovs were Jewish, and it was obviously important that the battle should not turn into an ugly ethnic conflict that might split the neighborhood and weaken the public standing of those who fought the Lebovs.) One of the first acts of the Association was to hire a lawyer, Joseph Koletsky, who agreed to serve for a fee of a thousand dollars; that the sum was collected within five days from the residents of the embattled neighborhood is testimony to the passion of the citizens.

Meanwhile, however, the residents lost the fourth round in the continuing battle. In mid-July, the Mayor vetoed the aldermanic resolution.

For a brief moment, it looked as if the residents had suffered a grave, perhaps even a decisive blow. But their intense political activity, their passion, their organization, and their appeal to home and neighborhood against the deliberate invasion of social decay and slums, all now began to have their effects. The Lebovs' victory, like the Mayor's veto, was ephemeral. Within two weeks the tide of battle turned forever against the Lebovs and their allies.

A sign that the tide was turning was furnished by the support the residents now won from Henry DeVita. DeVita was the Republican minority leader on the Board of Aldermen and . . . leader of a faction of the party hostile to the domination of DiCenzo and Celentano. Though he did not come from the Hill, DeVita was of Italian stock; the base of his influence in the party lay in another area of the city, around Wooster Square, which was even more densely populated by working-class Italians. He may have felt that the conflict presented him with the possibility of undermining DiCenzo's control over the Tenth Senatorial District. Moreover, when Celentano was first elected in 1945 the Mayor had opposed the choice of DeVita as majority leader, ostensibly on the ground that it would give a too Italianate aspect to the party; Celentano was rebuffed by the Republican aldermen, and DeVita won the post. Whatever DeVita's motives may have been, he now announced that he was wholly opposed to DiCenzo's opinion. His action was a major victory for the residents, for Celentano and DiCenzo could no longer count on any votes from the Republican minority on the Board of Aldermen.

Because of a procedural contretemps, at a special meeting of the Board of Aldermen in July the Mayor's veto was not overridden. But at the next regular meeting of the Board in August, the veto was overturned 25-2 by a bipartisan coalition.

Though the Lebovs continued to press their case in the courts and in the press, for all practical purposes they had lost. The houses were never built. In time the rusting parts met the fate the New York Housing Authority had originally intended for them—they were turned into scrap.

Aware that they had suffered a major defeat with an election a few months away, the city administration sought to recover some of the ground it had lost. After a fire set by an arsonist turned one of the "fire proof" metal houses into a twisted frame the Fire Inspector promptly withdrew his approval. At the height of the mayoralty campaign in October, the Mayor announced that he would never allow the Lebov houses to come into the city. Even DiCenzo reversed himself. "I have come to the conclusion," he said, "that the Lebov Corporation . . . had not proceeded in accordance with the law . . . I will resist the development of this metal house project in this area by every legal means."

A few weeks later, Celentano lost the mayoralty election to Lee. The contest over the metal houses probably had little to do with the outcome, for it involved only a few hundred people. Even in the Sixth and the Eighth Wards, Lee's vote was only one per cent higher than it had been in 1951; Lee won in the Sixth and lost in the Eighth, just as he had in 1951. It is possible, however, that the publicity about the conflict in the local press created the impression among some wavering voters that the Celentano administration suffered from a lack of drive and coordination.

Some Observations on the Incident

The struggle of the people on the Hill against the metal houses illustrates several aspects of the political system.

To begin with, it displays three *durable* characteristics of the system. First, the residents of the Hill became active politically not from a sense of duty nor out of a sustained interest in politics but only because primary goals at the focus of their lives were endangered, and political action was thought to be the only way to ward off the danger. The metal houses directly threatened a variety of values basic to the residents of the neighborhood around Truman Street—or so, at least, they thought. Few of them had participated much in politics before; after the threat disappeared, few of them did anything again.

Second, even in this case where the primary values of several hundred citizens were involved, leadership quickly developed. What at first consisted mostly of spontaneous responses to a threat and uncoordinated direct actions by different residents soon changed in character as the struggle went on. Leaders began to give guidance and coordination; leaders recruited subleaders; and subleaders were carefully recruited from among both Italians and Jews in order to conform to the most salient characteristics of the constituents whose support was needed. The Association, though ephemeral, had already taken on by the time the aldermen voted in August most of the characteristics of political associations that have become familiar to us in the course of this study.

Third, conflict of this intensity is a rarity. Ordinarily, political decisions move along in an atmosphere of apathy, indifference, and general agreement. Even in this case, the conflict may have resulted largely from a serious miscalculation by the Mayor and his Corporation Counsel as to the amount of support available to the Lebovs, for the final coalition that defeated the Lebovs was overwhelming and seems to have rested on a very broad base of support. The community, it appears, was never really split, for among these leaders, subleaders, and active participants, support piled up almost wholly on one side; the rest of the community probably did not much care.

Although these characteristics of the system seem to be highly resistant to change, the pattern of integration that prevailed was more ephemeral. It displayed many characteristics of the pattern of petty sovereignties with spheres of influence. Yet open conflict could not be averted, and the course of the conflict suggests three important characteristics of the pattern of petty sovereignties.

First, despite the absence of great cleavages in New Haven, to avoid conflict altogether requires a very high level of political information and skill. Mayor Celentano and Corporation Counsel DiCenzo evidently made a strategic miscalculation when they supported the Lebovs, a miscalculation they tried to correct after the fight had already gone against them. A higher level of skill and more information might have enabled them to ward off the conflict before it got out of control: probably they need have done no more than to adopt at first the very policy that in fact they finally felt they had to adopt anyway.

Second, there was no clear center of dominant influence in the order. No single group of unified leaders possessed enough influence to impose a solution. There was not even a unified coalition with that much influence. The coalition that finally won was created *ad hoc;* it represented the temporary convergence on a common policy of different leaders drawn from a number of different centers of influence. That winning coalition fell apart as soon as victory was secure.

Both the winning and the losing coalitions were unstable compounds.

The losing coalition consisted mostly of two wealthy junk dealers; the Republican Mayor and his Corporation Counsel; the Mayor's appointee, the Building Inspector; and several Democratic aldermen. It also had the wavering support of the local press. The winning coalition consisted of several hundred residents of the Hill; leaders of a rival Republican faction; Lee, a Democratic leader; the Board of Zoning Appeals; and the remaining aldermen, both Republican and Democratic.

Third, the pattern of independent sovereignties with spheres of influence was incapable of providing centralized, deliberate coordination over a wide range of city activities—and hence was unsuited to the task of carrying through urban redevelopment and renewal on a massive scale. The relatively slow pace of urban redevelopment under Mayor Celentano was at least in part an inevitable result of the decentralized political mechanism through which the mayor had to operate. If the size and pace of redevelopment and renewal were to be stepped up, the political order itself would have to be changed.

PATTERN B: THE EXECUTIVE-CENTERED COALITION

During Mayor Lee's first term the political order was swiftly transformed. The pattern of petty sovereignities he had inherited soon gave way to another of the five patterns mentioned earlier, a coalition of chieftains. However, this pattern proved to be transitional, and we need not concern ourselves with it here. The executive-centered coalition that followed proved to be more durable. In this pattern, only the Mayor was a member of all the major coalitions, and in each of them he was one of the two or three men of highest influence.

. . . [L]ee first came into office as a protégé of John Golden, the Democratic leader . . . . [H]e formed a coalition with Golden and another Golden man, Arthur Barbieri, the town chairman of the party, and . . . this coalition substantially decided nominations in the Democratic party. . . . [L]ee inherited a sprawling collection of agencies and processes that determined the physical and social patterns of the city . . . . [H]e formed a new redevelopment coalition, and . . . this coalition enabled him and his collaborators in redevelopment to assume influence over local policies on redevelopment and renewal. [Moreover,] . . . out of some twenty-seven instances of successful action on policies bearing on the public schools in the years between 1953 and 1959, fifteen were traceable to the Mayor or to officials who were members of his educational coalition, while all the rest were scattered among a variety of individuals and agencies.

During Lee's tenure as mayor, control over urban redevelopment became much more highly centralized in the hands of the mayor and his redevelopment team than it had been in the previous administration.

Control over public education became slightly more centralized, though the pattern was, as we shall see, rather complex. Control over nominations in the Democratic party actually became somewhat more decentralized, for Golden's one-man rule gave way . . . to a triumvirate in which Golden shared his power with Lee and Barbieri. To a considerable extent, the growth of the new mayor's influence in the Democratic party and in public education was a function of his influence in redevelopment and renewal. It was the need for redevelopment that created the need for an executive-centered order, and it was widespread agreement on the need for redevelopment that generated widespread acquiescence in the creation of an executive-centered order.

Urban Change and Patterns of Influence

The pattern of petty sovereignties is perfectly adapted to piecemeal changes, which are typically produced by one or several intensely interested individuals who believe they stand to gain from some relatively small alteration in the physical pattern of the city. The number of people involved varies. The alteration may be sought by a single dentist who wants to convert a residence into a dental office, a family seeking to put up a neighborhood store, or an alliance of builders and merchants who want to construct apartments and shopping facilities. Because these people stand to gain, they are charged with energy: they scheme, plan, negotiate, haggle, bring pressure, make illicit payments, and otherwise use their influence to get what they want. Sometimes they encounter only light resistance because everyone else is apathetic or indifferent. At other times there is sharp skirmishing with other small, unified, hostile groups. In these short, tense battles the side less well-organized, less numerous, less resourceful, less affluent or otherwise less effective gets defeated. If the antagonists are more or less equal, there may be a stalemate or a compromise.

A city constantly undergoes change of some sort. But piecemeal changes often merely reduce some tensions while they generate others. As in the classic case of the onset of an economic depression, when the actions each individual businessman takes to save his own skin by laying off employees and living off inventories only speeds the depression on its way, so in the case of the city, the sum total of piecemeal actions may end up creating a city that very few people would choose to design if they were capable of anticipating a wider range of consequences and had some means of avoiding these consequences without immediate loss.

Because changes in the physical organization of a city entail changes in social, economic, and political organization, the larger the area altered the greater and more varied are the effects: on housing, neighborhoods, schools, shopping areas, churches, property ownership, incomes, employment, taxes, social standing, ethnic relations, business opportunities, and political influence. Rapid, comprehensive change in the physical pattern of a city is a minor revolution.

In the political context of a city like New Haven, such a revolution requires a distribution of costs and benefits nicely adjusted so as to command the support of a powerful coalition. There is no reason to suppose that such a happy balance of costs and benefits exists, even in principle, in every city. Moreover, even if this broad combination of actions, this strategic plan, does exist in some abstract sense, it must be discovered, formulated, presented, and constantly reinterpreted and reinforced. The skills required for discovering and formulating the grounds on which coalitions can be formed, the assiduous and unending dedication to the task of maintaining alliances over long periods, the unremitting search for measures that will unify rather than disrupt the alliance: these are the tasks and skills of politicians. It is obvious too, that in order for comprehensive action to succeed, the influence over the decisions of the city government exerted by the coalition that supports the broad strategic plan has to be greater than the influence of any opposing coalition. Consequently, no matter what their official positions may be, if indeed they have any at all, the leaders of an alliance capable of large-scale alteration in the physical shape of a city must be, by definition, among the de facto political leaders of that community.

When Lee took office in January 1954, there was evidently latent agreement within the political stratum of New Haven on the need for redevelopment. . . . [L]ee converted this latent agreement into active support for a huge program; in this effort the creation of the CAC [Citizens Action Commission] was an inspired act.[8] But the program that the political stratum almost unanimously supported could not be executed under the old highly decentralized pattern of petty sovereignties. In effect, then, Lee converted support for redevelopment into acquiescence in a new pattern of influence, the executive-centered order.

Thus the executive-centered order was legitimized by the need for coordinating decisions on redevelopment. And since redevelopment touched so many aspects of the life of the city, few public agencies and associations wholly escaped the demand for more coordination and control. To take a single example, operating under the old ground rules the Board of Zoning Appeals could slowly undermine in fact some of what was agreed on in theory in any strategic plan of redevelopment. Now, for the first time, representatives from the City Plan Commission and from redevelopment were heard when a zoning variance was requested. Behind them stood the Mayor, persuading, insisting, threatening. In February 1959, he finally

---

[8]. . . Some of the techniques used in gaining support are described in detail in Raymond Wolfinger's forthcoming volume, *The Politics of Progress*.

appointed a completely new Board of Zoning Appeals composed of leading citizens who could be counted on to reject variances at odds with the basic objectives of the city plan. (Paradoxically, by appointing members who could not be pressured, the Mayor lost much of his *direct* influence over the Board; but perhaps he felt he no longer needed it.)

However, although the Mayor became highly influential over many sectors of policy, it would be a mistake to interpret the executive-centered coalition as a completely hierarchical arrangement. Perhaps most integrative mechanisms that appear strictly hierarchical on first view would prove on closer examination to be much looser, less neatly patterned, more riven by internal contests over authority, frequently disordered by ambiguous and uncertain relations of influence, and subject to a good deal of internal negotiation and bargaining. In any event this was true of the executive-centered order in New Haven.

In urban redevelopment, the constraints on centralization were weak. In public education, they were much stronger; the area of latent agreement was less inclusive, the opposition was more powerful, and decisions were marked by extensive negotiation, conciliation, and bargaining. In the remainder of this [section] I shall illustrate, by means of some decisions on educational policy, the differences between the older pattern of petty sovereignties and the newer executive-centered order.

Chief Executive or Chief Negotiator?

The extent to which the mayor of New Haven can safely intervene in decisions involving the public schools is ambiguous. No doubt everyone in the political stratum takes it for granted that a mayor may legitimately have an important influence on the level of appropriations and expenditures. He will also influence the level of teachers' salaries and school construction, as mayors have done in New Haven for the last thirty years. He is necessarily involved, too, in major appointments. On the other hand, intervention on minor appointments and promotions would antagonize many of the citizens most interested in the schools; when mayors and other party leaders intervene in minor appointments and promotions, therefore, they usually do so covertly. Traditionally a mayor maintains a hands-off attitude on problems of curriculum and internal organization. However, the mayor is ex officio a member of the school board; and his support for one proposal or another can be decisive not merely because of his vote but because some members can usually be counted on to follow his lead. Hence different factions on the Board of Education will sometimes turn to the mayor for support. In this way he can be drawn into gray areas where the propriety of his intervention is unclear.

Different mayors interpret their role in different ways. . . . [M]ayor Celentano, after his election in 1945, supported an increase in school appropriations, in teachers' salaries, and in school buildings, and made sure that some of his key supporters in the school system received satisfactory jobs. In one significant respect, however, the system remained substantially unchanged. In the school system that Celentano inherited, control was evidently parceled out in three ways. School appropriations were the province of the mayor. Educational policies were the province of the superintendent. Appointments and promotions were subject to negotiation between politicians and school administrators. Amid these forces, the school board appointed by the mayor was little more than an instrument of the superintendent. With slight modifications these spheres of influence continued under the Celentano administration.

Under Lee, however, the pattern was altered. Control over key decisions of all kinds came to rest more and more with the mayor and his new appointees on the Board of Education and correspondingly less with the superintendent (who was held over from the Celentano administration) and other leaders in the old system.

This change in the locus of control was achieved in two ways. First, new appointments to the Board made it possible for the mayor's appointees to dominate the Board; second, the Board gradually increased its influence over the superintendent and school administrators. Even in Lee's administration, however, a division of labor existed. When decisions had to be made involving leaders *within* the school system, the new Board members took charge, knowing they could call on the mayor to back them up if they needed it. When decisions involved negotiations with leaders *outside* the school system, the mayor took charge, knowing that he could count on his appointees on the Board to back him up if he needed it.

In this respect leadership on school matters mirrored the general pattern. The mayor was the only individual who was highly influential in all the coalitions, in education, urban redevelopment, political nominations, welfare, police, and others. If it were possible to single out any one person as the leader of the "grand coalition of coalitions," the mayor was unmistakably that man.

Yet it would be grossly misleading to see the executive-centered order as a neatly hierarchical system with the mayor at the top operating through subordinates in a chain of command. The mayor was not at the peak of a pyramid but rather at the center of intersecting circles. He rarely commanded. He negotiated, cajoled, exhorted, beguiled, charmed, pressed, appealed, reasoned, promised, insisted, demanded, even threatened, but he most needed support and acquiescence from other leaders who simply could not be commanded. Because the mayor could not command, he had to bargain.

The centrifugal forces in the system were, in short, persistent and powerful; the fullest and most skillful use of all the resources available to the mayor added barely enough centripetal thrust to keep the various parts from flying off in all directions. Or, to change the image again, the system was like a tire with a slow leak, and the mayor had the only air pump. Whether the executive-centered order was maintained or the system reverted to independent sovereignties depended almost entirely, then, on the relative amount of influence the mayor could succeed in extracting from his political resources.

Sometimes his resources were too slender, and despite his efforts he was unable to create or sustain a grand coalition; he tried and failed, for example, to obtain a new city charter.[9] More often, however, his bargaining produced roughly the results he sought. The building of the high schools will serve to illustrate the mayor's role as the chief negotiator in the executive-centered coalition.

Struggle over the High Schools

After Lee was elected in 1953, but before he was fully caught up in redevelopment, he may have intended to make the rebuilding of the school system the dramatic central action of his first term. If so, the high schools were a good place to start. There were three of them—one academic, one commercial, one for manual arts—and they all sat tightly together on a little island engulfed by Yale. The school survey sponsored by Mayor Celentano in 1947 had recommended that two of the buildings be torn down, that if possible the third should be sold to Yale, and that two new high schools should be built on new sites.[10] The Board of Education subsequently agreed on a building program providing for one new high school about 1960; nothing was said about a second.

When Lee entered office . . . one of his first acts was to create a Citizens Advisory Commission on Education. The mission assigned to the CACE by the Mayor, a leading member later recalled, was "to look into the school situation and advise the Board of Education and arouse the community interest in better schools for New Haven." The first chairman . . . took great pains to organize the CACE as an effective pressure group. Meanwhile the Mayor appointed two new members to the Board of Education. In 1954–55, as the CACE and the League of Women Voters engaged in a vigorous campaign to generate public support for new high schools, the Board of Education—where the Mayor's new appointees were beginning to exercise their influence—revised its earlier building plans in order to speed up the day when new high schools would be built.

Yet there was one crucial limit to the Mayor's freedom of action—financial resources. The Mayor was firmly convinced that political success depended on his ability to reach his policy objectives without raising taxes. To follow this strategy and at the same time to build new high schools, the

[9]An extensive account of the rejection of the revised charter will be found in the forthcoming volume by Wolfinger, *The Politics of Progress.*

[10]*New Haven's Schools: [An Investment in Your City's Future, Report of a Survey of the Public School System 1946–47* (New Haven, 1947)], Ch. 13.

Mayor had to solve three problems: he had to find a source of funds outside the tax structure, turn up two low-cost building sites, and keep construction costs within modest limits.

In meeting the first problem, Lee was aided by circumstances. ("I think it may be true," Machiavelli once wrote, "that fortune is the ruler of half our actions, but that she allows the other half or thereabouts to be governed by us.") Over the years the governing authorities at Yale had come to regard the high schools as a blight in the midst of the university. Moreover, the university needed land for expansion. And if these were not already good and sufficient reasons, the daily migration of a horde of New Haven high school students through the Yale campus created frictions.

The Mayor had known the new president of Yale in the days when the one was director of public relations for Yale and the other was a history professor. The Mayor had invited the President to serve as vice-chairman of the Citizens Action Commission; the President had agreed; now they encountered one another frequently at these meetings. One day the Mayor casually broached the idea of selling the high schools to Yale. The President was intrigued. Encouraged, the Mayor subsequently came forward with a definite proposal. The President accepted. Soon only the price remained to be settled.

Both sides were anxious to consummate the deal. To the Mayor, Yale's offer to purchase the old schools was a heaven-sent source of funds which he could use to build two new high schools; hence he could ill afford to push the price so high as to scare Yale away. To the authorities at Yale, the chance to buy the schools was more than they had ever really hoped for; therefore they dared not insist on driving a bargain so hard that the Mayor might find it politically unpalatable. The compromise figure the two sides finally agreed on—$3 million—was higher than Yale's appraisal of the value of the buildings; one of the Yale officials involved in the final negotiations on the price said later, "As the university sees it . . . we paid the city more for those schools than either they were worth intrinsically or than the city could have got from any other purchaser." Yet the difference of a few hundred thousand dollars was less important to Yale than the possession of the land and buildings. As for Lee, despite the accusation in the next mayoralty campaign that he had sold out to Yale, and despite a persistent if politically unimportant body of citizens who held firmly to the belief that the city had indeed sold the schools too cheaply, probably he gained in political stature from the exchange, for now he could proceed with the high schools.

It was the Mayor, you will note, who carried on all the negotiations with Yale. It was the Mayor who persuaded the Board of Finance and the Board of Aldermen to accept Yale's offer. And a few months before the sale was completed, it was the Mayor who informed the Board of

Education of the plans afoot. There was never much doubt that the various Boards would accept what he arranged, though in his negotiations with Yale he used the difficulties he might run into in getting the deal accepted by the various other city authorities as part of his argument for a higher price than Yale had wanted to offer.

Now that Yale's cash brought the new high schools within reach, the Board turned to the question of sites. The only way to obtain low-cost sites, and thereby comply with the Mayor's over-all strategy, was to build the schools on city-owned property—which in effect meant park land. The authors of the 1947 school survey had, in fact, proposed two sites for new high schools in parks on opposite sides of the city. The Board now made this proposal its own.

But the members had not allowed for resistance from the Board of Park Commissioners. This Board, one of two anachronistic political institutions in New Haven,[11] consisted of eight unpaid members and the mayor ex officio. Under a section of the city charter passed three-quarters of a century earlier . . . , three commissioners were permanent members; two of these filled the vacancy caused by the resignation or death of the third. Three commissioners were appointed by the mayor for three-year terms; at the time of the conflict over school sites two of these were holdovers from the preceding administration. Finally, two commissioners, one from each party, were chosen for one-year terms by the Board of Aldermen.

To the consternation of the Mayor and the Board of Education, the Park Commissioners rejected both of the proposed sites. Because the three permanent members and the Republican appointees to the Board were in a majority, obviously the Mayor had to negotiate.[12] The Park Commissioners proposed two alternative sites. Although several of the Mayor's appointees to the Board of Education were anxious to fight out the issue in the public press, the Mayor himself urged caution. One of the alternative sites proposed by the Park Commissioners was in a redevelopment area; hence some costs might be shifted to the federal government. The Mayor assured his appointees on the Board of Education that if the Board accepted that site he could probably persuade the commissioners to accept the Board's first choice for the other school.

The Board's first choice, however, was a site in East Rock Park, a handsome area of woods, trails, cliffs, and a high bluff of red sandstone that is the city's most striking landmark. The park is a favorite and easily accessible spot for walking, a view of the city, family picnics, and lovers'

[11]The other was a committee of the "Proprietors of Common and Undivided *Grounds*" that dated from 1641. . . .

[12]A few years after the conflict described here, one of the permanent members of the Board resigned. One of the other two permanent members happened to be in Europe and unable to return immediately; under a hitherto unused section of the charter, the absence of a quorum of two made it possible for the Mayor to appoint a permanent member. . . .

trysts. Its excellent winding roads to the top enable the visitor to drive to the summit for a fine view of the city. One of the roads, English Drive, was paid for by [a] nineteenth-century entrepreneur . . . , James English.

Philip English, his grandson, was now a permanent member of the Board of Park Commissioners. English may have felt a special personal interest in maintaining East Rock Park intact, and he was supported by the other permanent members and several of the appointive ones. The Mayor had to bargain, but he had little to bargain with. The alternative site proposed by the Park Commissioners was in an area of increasing industrialization which the Mayor and the Board of Education firmly believed was unsuitable for a high school. The haggling dragged on month after month during a period when construction costs were rapidly climbing. Finally, the Mayor and the Park Commissioners both yielded. The site they agreed on was in the Park, as the Board of Education wanted; it was well situated not far from what sociologists (and real estate agents) classified as a Class I residential neighborhood. But it was on low, marshy land that could not be made suitable without vast amounts of fill and piling— and hence additional, unanticipated expenses.

The Park Commissioners had therefore enormously increased the Mayor's third problem—keeping costs low enough so that Yale's cash payment for the old high school buildings would cover most of the cost of the new high schools.

The Mayor's original estimate of costs had been, to say the least, preliminary—"a kind of wishful underestimate of the cost by Dick himself," one of the Mayor's supporters described it later. The inadequacy of those estimates, the costly preparation of the sites, and the extended delay during a period of rapidly rising building costs now converged abruptly toward one stark conclusion: if the Mayor was to adhere to his political strategy and avoid a tax increase, the outlays for building and equipment required under the Board of Education's plans would have to be slashed. The Mayor took the members of his educational coalition into his confidence and assigned to his Development Administrator the task of finding economies. The Mayor's supporters were convinced, as one of them put it, that with some savings turned up by the Development Administrator through the substitution of materials which they "had every reason to believe were of the same quality but in some cases cost a third less" and some cutting "from the ideal proportions that had been set according to the wishes expressed by heads of departments, principals, and so on," they "could still have good schools and so there didn't seem to be any alternative at all." Possibly the other members of the Board, as one participant later suggested, never "really caught on quite to what the score was." Anyway, the cuts were made. In the end, however, the schools cost nearly twice as much as the city received from Yale and it took a good deal of budgetary juggling to prevent a rise in taxes.

The Mayor, then, was the central figure in the negotiations over the schools. But he was a negotiator rather than a hierarchical executive. He could rarely command, but he could apply his political resources and skills to the task of negotiating and bargaining. Given the distribution of political resources in New Haven, perhaps he achieved about as much centralization as the system would tolerate.

Victory and Defeat

If the Mayor was the chief negotiator when decisions required the integration of policies in several different issue-areas, he followed the course of his predecessors and deliberately adopted a more passive role on internal educational questions. Aware that his direct intervention might be politically dangerous, he relied on the judgment of his new appointees—who in any case were men of stature hardly willing to take orders even if he had been so inept as to issue them. The Mayor's first appointee to the Board, in 1954, was Maynard Mack, professor of English at Yale and the first Yale faculty member appointed to the Board in generations. That same year the Mayor also appointed Mitchell Sviridoff, state head of the CIO (later of the merged AFL-CIO) and the first trade union man ever appointed to the Board. In 1956 he appointed John Braslin, who had been the first chairman of the CACE. The Mayor himself was an eighth member, ex officio; hence he and his new appointees had half the votes if they needed them. In addition, whenever the Mayor made his position known, the new appointees could count on William Clancy, the chairman of the Board. Though she stood outside the coalition, Mrs. Harry Barnett, wife of an executive of a downtown department store, usually agreed with Mack, Sviridoff, and Braslin.

The Mayor could have had no way of knowing how easily his appointees would work together. Mack, Sviridoff, and Braslin had never met before they were appointed. Except for a determination to improve the schools, which they all shared, when they were appointed they had no plans, no definite policies. As for the Mayor, one of them later remarked, "all that he ever said to me was that he wanted good schools and would back us."

By accident, then, rather than design, it turned out that Mack, Sviridoff, and Braslin worked in harmony. Believing that the Board had abdicated its legitimate influence to professional administrators, they were determined to restore the Board to what they felt was its rightful place in the determination of educational policy. They admired Lee and liked his policies. Although they sometimes needed his authority as a backstop, he needed their prestige, their political untouchability, and their vigor, if his administration was to develop and carry out a school program that would win approval from teachers and parents, whose support, the elections of 1945 had shown, was as vital to a candidate for mayor as their hostility was dangerous. One of the new appointees reflected later on the working partnership that developed:

> It was not organized in advance. It had no agreed program. It just evolved. By the like-mindedness of two people, to whom a third was eventually added of *their* own choice, it *became* a coalition, by its own volition rather than the Mayor's, and was never in any sense the Mayor's instrument except in so far as he would consent to back what *we* wanted: we were never a coalition in the sense of backing what *he* wanted unless we wanted it, too.

The Board's earlier status was nicely symbolized by the fact that no agenda was circulated before it met. Hence members came unprepared, allowed the superintendent and the chairman of the Board to determine what was to be taken up, and acted on information supplied almost exclusively by the very administrators the Board was supposed to supervise. Although that arrangement was altered without much difficulty after the new appointees came on the Board, their attempt to influence other policies met greater obstacles.

Squeezed among competing factions, the Board itself lacked allies among administrators and teachers, was sometimes deliberately misinformed as to what actually transpired in the schools, and could not be sure that its own policies would be faithfully executed throughout the system. The heart of the Board's difficulty was that promotions and appointments were used to build up factions, loyalties, and dependencies in the school system. Many teachers took it for granted that advancement depended entirely on "pull." In 1957 one of the members of the Board told the following story:

> My kid came home one day. . . and told me that in their guidance class they were discussing careers. This was a seventh or eighth grade class and one of the girls got up and said she was interested in a teaching career and particularly in becoming a principal. And how do you become a principal? And the teacher said—and she wasn't joking, "Well, you have to know the mayor." This was the common view and still is the problem.

A direct attack on promotions and appointments, however, would challenge two formidable sets of forces. To leaders in the Democratic party, an increase in the Board's influence over major appointments must only produce a diminution of their own. To Superintendent Justin O'Brien, an appointee of the previous mayor, the implications were probably more subtle. By the professional standards of a school administrator, it would be desirable if the Board reduced outside political influences on appointments and promotions within the school system, but such a step might also curtail the Superintendent's own influence and even weaken the coalition he had built up to counter factions still hostile to him.

The issue first confronted the Board directly in 1955 when an opening occurred for an assistant superintendent for elementary education. Mack and Sviridoff settled on Miss Mary White. A member of the New Haven school system for forty years, she had been Sviridoff's sixth-grade teacher. Now she was the highly respected principal of the laboratory training school at the State Teachers College, a post she was not anxious to leave as she looked forward to her imminent retirement. Miss White was Irish, Catholic, and a Republican.

Lee's Democratic cohorts, Golden and Barbieri, backed a junior high school principal, James Valenti. Valenti was Italian, Catholic, and an independent Democrat. Although Valenti was an old friend of Barbieri, Golden and Barbieri probably were animated by objectives more complex than mere amiability. Valenti's appointment would provide a handsome gesture to the Italian community, quiet Valenti's political aspirations, and provide Golden and Barbieri with an ally in a high position within the school system.

The Superintendent, who technically had the power of appointment subject to the Board's approval, had his own candidate. So did the Chairman of the Board. There were half a dozen other applicants, none of whom had much backing though many of them tried to create support. Of one of the applicants a Board member recalled later: "Even the guy who sells me gasoline was, I remember, urging me to take a beneficent view of his candidacy. These people get around. How be ever knew where I got my gasoline, God only knows, but anyway there it was."

Though the Superintendent indicated his hostility to the other candidates, he hesitated to press his own. (Soon his own reappointment would be coming up.) Hence the battle narrowed down to a contest between Miss White and James Valenti. The Mayor, who was hospitalized because of his ulcers during much of the controversy, was caught in a position of great delicacy: Miss White was his first choice, but by supporting her he would oppose the candidate of Golden and Barbieri. At the critical meeting of the Board when the first vote was taken, the Mayor was in the hospital, and no candidate received a majority. Confronted with a stalemate when he emerged from the hospital, the Mayor made the decisive choice. He called the Chairman of the Board of Education and expressed his support for Miss White. At its next meeting the Board voted unanimously for Miss White. (Four years later Valenti was the Republican candidate for mayor against Lee. He lost again.)

With this victory in hand, the Mayor's new appointees next launched a frontal attack on one of the major sources of factional influence by trying to neutralize the process of promotions. Now, however, they were playing on their own. "We never asked for his [the Mayor's] aid," one of them said later; "It never occurred to us, for we were frankly green, that it would be required, or useful." Whether, in a pinch, they could have obtained the full support of the Mayor on this matter as they had on the appointment of Miss White is uncertain; complete neutrality on promotions was not necessarily an unmixed blessing to the Mayor. In any case, after leaving the hospital the Mayor was preoccupied with an accumulation of pressing problems, and the dispute over promotions was not one of them.

In essence, the proposal developed under the auspices of Mack and Sviridoff involved two critical changes. The procedures used in promotions to the rank of principal or higher were to be clarified and made explicit; and all candidates for promotions were to be screened by a special committee, which would then make its recommendations to the superintendent. The membership of the screening committee was carefully spelled out; in addition to the superintendent and several other specified officials, it was to include several members of the Board—and also a teacher.

In preliminary meetings the proposal evidently evoked wide enthusiasm—not least, it seems, from the official representative of the Teachers' League. Only the Superintendent expressed doubts. Nonetheless, between a Saturday morning, when the proposal was enthusiastically approved in committee, and the following Moday night, when the Board met to consider it, the Teachers' League shifted from support to opposition. An explanation offered by some participants in the struggle is that the Superintendent of Schools and the leaders in the Teachers' League got together and concluded that to preseve their joint influence from the threat of erosion they had better oppose the proposal. The Superintendent's interpretation is that the leaders of the Teachers' League finally concluded over the weekend that one teacher serving on a committee to recommend the promotion of another teacher would be embarrassing to everyone concerned.

At a Board of Education meeting well attended by representatives of the diverse organizations concerned with school policy, only the representative of the Teachers' League spoke in opposition. In spite of the League's opposition, the proposal passed the Board unanimously.

Yet the policy was never put into effect. Later, the Teachers' League was joined in its opposition by the Principals' Club. Members of the Board began to get cold feet. Finally the entire proposal was tabled. Five years later the Board was still considering the idea of codifying procedures on promotions, but the proposal for a screening committee was dead. One of the supporters of the plan concluded later,

> We were defeated more because we were green at the game, not anticipating the kinds of influence that could be brought to bear over a weekend . . . than for any other reason. I think too, with hindsight, that our plan had the demerit of not being simple: it was somewhat complex, therefore extremely easy to misunderstand and to misrepresent. Finally, if anybody let us down, it was the teacher groups: if they had had the courage to stand up for these reforms, which in private they had inisted they wanted, nobody could have withstood them, or would have dared to politically.

Why did the Mayor's coalition win on the appointment of Miss White and lose on promotions procedures?

Mainly, it appears, because of the way the Mayor employed his influence. In the matter of Miss White's appointment he had made his stand clear and had put his influence behind her appointment. In the matter of promotions, he neither opposed the members of his coalition nor gave them his unequivocal support. There is little doubt that if he had vigorously insisted on the promotions policy they sought, the Board would have stood its ground; if the Board had remained firm, the Superintendent would have complied.

Had he failed to support Miss White the Mayor might have permanently alienated important support: the candidate of Golden and Barbieri would have been appointed; their influence within the schools and within the party would have increased relative to his own; and his highly favorable public image would probably have been damaged. The proposal on promotions was a different story. This time the Mayor's appointees made no effort to invoke his authority; they too were dismayed by the opposition their proposal had stirred up among the teachers. The Mayor was a busy man; he could not be expected to intervene every time his appointees on the Board ran into a snag; if he did so too often he might easily step over the ill-defined boundaries beyond which his intervention would appear to many persons as illegitimate political interference in the school system.

Thus, although the executive-centered order of Mayor Lee had drastically curtailed the independence of the old petty sovereignties and had whittled down the relative influence of the various chieftains, that order was no monolith. The preferences of any group that could swing its weight at election time—teachers, citizens of the Hill, Negroes on Dixwell Avenue, or Notables—would weigh heavily in the calculations of the Mayor, for the executive-centered coalition was not the *only* important pattern of influence in New Haven. The unending competition between the two political parties constituted another pattern of influence; thanks to the system of periodic elections, the Mayor and his political opponents were constantly engaged in a battle for votes at the next election, which was always just around the corner.

PATTERN C: RIVAL SOVEREIGNTIES

The leadership of the two political parties presents a pattern strikingly different from those that have prevailed in other parts of the political system in New Haven. . . .

In brief, the pattern . . . is one of petty sovereignties in periodic conflict in campaigns and elections. The men who control the nominations and manage campaigns in the Republican party are ordinarily a somewhat different set from those who control nominations and manage campaigns in the Democratic party. The two parties are to a great extent independent and competitive. Probably the competition between them has always been rather vigorous. Although rotation in office is not decisive proof of competition, in the past three-quarters of a century only once, during Mayor Murphy's fourteen-year span from 1931–45, has a single party held the office of mayor for more than a decade. In that same period there have been only four occasions when one party has held the mayor's office for as long as eight years; there have been two six-year periods of control by one party and two four-year stretches. In all the other elections, or almost exactly half, the incumbent party was defeated after only a single two-year term in the mayor's office.

The Grounds of Party Competition

In the years following the defeat in 1953 of the Republican mayor, William Celentano, competition between the two parties was somewhat weakened. The defection of many Republican business leaders to Mayor Lee deprived the Republicans of a traditional source of campaign funds and provided Democrats with larger financial contributions than they had ever before enjoyed. The shifting loyalties of the larger businessmen may in turn have temporarily softened the opposition of Celentano and DiCenzo to the administration of Mayor Lee. But there were other, probably more telling considerations. Celentano evidently felt that he could not defeat Lee; at the same time (so it was said by his critics within the Republican party), he did not wish anyone else to make so big a showing against Lee as to become the party's natural choice to run if and when Lee finally declined in popularity or moved on to the governor's mansion or the Senate. Hence, according to his critics, his support of Republican candidates against Lee was sometimes little more than perfunctory. As for DiCenzo, his ties with the Lee administration grew closer as the chances of a Republican victory waned. In 1957 he was appointed by Lee as chairman of a commission to revise the city charter, a task in which he endorsed most of the proposals suggested by Lee's lieutenants; in 1959, when a new system of state circuit courts was created, he was appointed by Governor Ribicoff, a Democrat, as a judge of the Circuit Court of Connecticut; subsequently he resigned from his position as state central committeeman for the Tenth Senatorial District and avowed his determination to cut all ties with partisan politics. Thus an influential opponent was out of the way.

Even so, party competition continued. The Lynch-DeVita wing of the Republican party ran mayoralty candidates who sharply attacked Lee's record. The Republicans on the Board of Aldermen, though a tiny minority, maintained a barrage of criticism in lengthy speeches written for the benefit of the newspapers by Henry DeVita, the Republican town chairman. Republican leaders kept up a steady fire through the local press. If they failed to make much of a dent in Lee's popularity at the polls, it was not altogether through want of trying.

The battlegrounds of competition during these years could be classified under three headings; unfortunately for the Republicans, Lee and the Democrats were considerably better off than the Republicans in every category.

The first was an appeal to ethnic loyalties and interests. The Republicans sought to attract Italian voters by nominating candidates of Italian background. In this they attained a fair degree of success, as Table 1 shows. The Democratic triumvirate (one of whom, Arthur Barbieri, was particularly well cast to handle appeals to the Italian voter) sought to counter this strategy by offering appointments, patronage, contracts, a comprehensive plan of urban redevelopment and renewal in DeVita's stronghold (the Wooster Square neighborhood), and extensive plans for rehabilitation of the Hill area, where DiCenzo had held sway; all of these benefits helped the Democrats to gain support among the Italians. By 1959, as Table 1 suggests, voters of Italian origin split about evenly between Lee and his Republican opponent, James Valenti. . . . [T]he Democrats maintained a considerable following among all the other major ethnic groups except the small minority of Yankee Protestants. Thus on New Haven's traditional battleground of party competition—ethnic loyalties and interests—the Democrats managed to secure an advantage despite lingering Republican predispositions among the largest ethnic group, the Italians.

The second ground of competition has just been alluded to, namely, covert policies relating to jobs and contracts. On this ground, the party that controls local government has a clear advantage—as the bosses of political machines in many American cities demonstrated for generations. Just as the Republicans had the advantage when they controlled local government from 1945 to 1953, so from 1953 the Democrats benefited from their capacity to channel city jobs and expenditures to their supporters. In New Haven, outright illegality in disposing of jobs and contracts seems

Table 1   Support for Republican candidates for mayor among Italians, 1953–1959

Election	Republican candidate	Ethnic background	Percentage of Italian vote cast for Lee
1953	Wm. Celentano	Italian	39
1955	P. Mancini, Jr.	Italian	43
1957	Edith V. Cook	Yankee	59
1959	J. Valenti	Italian	47

Source: Adapted from a table in Donald E. Stokes, *Voting Research and the Businessman in Politics* (Ann Arbor, Mich., Foundation for Research on Human Behavior, 1960), p. 14. Stokes based his table on surveys by Louis Harris and Associates, New York City.

to be rare. The great bulk of what is done covertly by political leaders in New Haven is not illegal; within the code of professional politicians concerned with maintaining party organizations and electoral coalitions most of their covert policies are not even reprehensible, though many of them would offend the sensibilities of a large number of citizens, particularly those who possess what are sometimes called middle-class morals. When political leaders reward friends and punish enemies, it is not so much a conflict with law as a conflict with normal moral standards that encourages them frequently to act circumspectly in order to avoid public disclosure.

The third ground of competition was, of course, overt policies. By giving prominence to his program of urban redevelopment and renewal, on which . . . there existed widespread latent agreement, Mayor Lee made it difficult for Republican opponents to compete with him on overt policies. Either they had to attack a highly popular program or they had to capture attention on issues far less dramatic and infinitely less interesting to the voters. Neither alternative was workable, and time and again the Republicans found themselves contesting with Lee where he was least vulnerable. The best they could reasonably hope for was that economic disaster, undue delay, or scandal would occur in the redevelopment program, but during the period covered in this study, at least, none of these occurred. Under the circumstances, probably any other strategy would also have failed, as Celentano no doubt foresaw when he cautiously rejected Republican overtures to run for mayor against Lee.

The Effects of Political Competition

To what extent did competition for votes between leaders and parties at periodic elections actually matter in the determination of the policies and actions of local government during these years? This question . . . poses formidable problems of observation, measurement, and analysis. It is therefore tempting to adopt the simplifications embodied either in optimistic interpretations of democracy according to which elected leaders are hardly more than agents of the electorate or in pessimistic or hostile interpretations that portray elected leaders as the agents of a small ruling elite. The evidence and analysis introduced so far strongly argue that neither of these furnishes a satisfactory description of New Haven.

The extent to which political competition at elections actually influences policies is evidently a function of a number of closely interrelated and rather complex factors, of which four are particularly important:

1. *The extent to which elections, political competition, and the desire for elective office (whatever may be the psychological basis of such a desire) tend to produce political activists whose strategy is to win office by shaping their overt and covert policies in whatever ways they think will gain the greatest number of votes at some future election— usually the next one.* In New Haven the number of such activists, the professional politicians, is moderately large.

2. *The extent to which this effort on the part of competing politicians actually leads to policies that reflect more or less accurately the political values of large numbers of voters and thus produces a measure of "democratic control" over policies.*

This is a function of many different factors.[13] One is the extent to which citizens vote, a proportion in New Haven local elections that runs around 50–60 per cent of the adult population. Another is the extent to which those who vote differ in their values and interests from those who do not vote. Additional factors are the extent and intensity of approval or disapproval of various policies among citizens and the extent to which these attitudes are activated, articulated, channeled into action, and perhaps even changed by new experiences. The political leaders themselves play a critical role in activating, channeling, and sometimes in changing latent attitudes. Thus Celentano and DiCenzo helped the Teachers' League and the League of Women Voters to reinforce feelings of discontent among parents and teachers over the state of the public schools, and they succeeded also in channeling the expression of these attitudes into votes against the incumbent mayor and for Celentano. Likewise, with the help of the CAC, Lee managed to activate widespread but largely latent feelings of discontent about the state of the city and latent attitudes of approval toward redevelopment; he channeled these attitudes into support for him at the polls.

The extent to which the policies of competing politicians reflect voters' preferences is also a function of one other highly critical factor—the way in which the outcome of an election is interpreted by members of the political stratum, particularly the professional politicians. The relation between an election outcome and the preferences of voters can be highly complex, and interpretations can—perhaps often do—err. If so, then voters do indeed influence policies—but not necessarily in ways they intend.

3. *The extent to which competing elected leaders actually succeed in determining the policies of government.* Their success depends on their influence over government policies in comparison with the influence of officials who are not elected, Social and Economic Notables, small pressure groups, and others. The relative influence of elected officials is in turn a function of their political resources, the rate at which they use their resources, and their political skills. As we have seen, under Mayor Lee the influence of the chief elected official, the mayor, was considerably higher than it was under Celentano.

4. *The extent to which the policies of government affect important rather than merely trivial values of citizens.* This in turn depends upon the role government plays in the life of the community. Some aspects of a community that many citizens would agree were highly important—employment, for example, or the distribution of incomes—lie pretty much beyond the reach of local government. Then too, in the United States most goods and services

---

[13]I have deliberately chosen to use somewhat loose language at this point to deal with an exceedingly complex problem. I have discussed some of these complexities in greater detail in *A Preface to Democratic Theory* (Chicago, University of Chicago Press, 1956).

are provided by nongovernmental rather than governmental agencies. Nonetheless it is probably true that directly or indirectly, by action or inaction, the policies of local governments have significant consequences for an extremely wide range of values. Thus the fact that the city of New Haven does not own and operate factories, department stores, or hospitals clearly does not mean that its policies have not had some impact on local factories, department stores, and hospitals.

What can we conclude about the specific effects of political competition in New Haven?

First, the elected officials of New Haven have had a significant influence on many policies—on schools and redevelopment, for example. And whatever may be the relation between elections and the preferences of citizens as to local policies, elections do determine—sometimes by an exceedingly small margin of votes—*who* is elected to office. Thus even if recent elections in New Haven were interpreted only as a choice of individuals to hold elective office, the effects on some policies were considerable.

Second, political competition and elections, at a minimum, lead to the rejection of a great range of possible policies, some of which may be discussed in campaigns but many of which are never discussed at all. Thus the assumption . . . among members of the political stratum that the essential characteristics of the socioeconomic system should remain substantially unchanged means in effect that every election is an implicit rejection of all policies that would entail sweeping changes in the social or economic structure of New Haven.

Third, the attempt of political leaders to win the votes of the various ethnic groups in New Haven has had a sizable effect on many policies that are not openly discussed in campaigns—on the ethnic and social characteristics of the men and women nominated for public office and on decisions concerning appointments, contracts, and other public expenditures. Two important side effects of these efforts to appeal to ethnic groups have probably been (1) to speed assimilation, transmit political skills, and gain acceptability among them for the American creed of democracy and equality, and (2) to inhibit the growth of distinctive working-class political identifications, ideologies, and political parties.

Finally, from time to time elections clearly have had a decisive effect on specific policies. Rightly or wrongly—but probably rightly—the election of Celentano in 1945 was interpreted throughout the political stratum as a vote in favor of spending more money on the schools. Rightly or wrongly—but probably rightly—the re-election of Lee in 1955 was taken as a sign that the voters had given overwhelming approval to urban redevelopment.

In short, New Haven is a republic of unequal citizens—but for all that a republic.

CHAPTER FOURTEEN

ROLES AND SYMBOLS IN THE DETERMINATION OF STATE EXPENDITURES

THOMAS J. ANTON

Despite growing appreciation of the significance of state government expenditures, relatively little is known about the manner in which state officials decide to spend public money. The few available reports, however, reach remarkably similar conclusions in different states, at different times. Agency or department officials, budget review officers, governors and legislatures take actions which appear to vary within rather narrow limits, regardless of the peculiarities of the state under consideration. These similarities of behavior on the part of financial officials in several states suggest the possibility of developing a model of expenditure decision-making that may have widespread relevance. My first purpose here, then, is to develop such a model, using the concept "role" to summarize actions which occur repeatedly and which appear to be structured by essentially similar goals. My second purpose is to assess the significance of the symbols around which these roles appear to be organized. Though necessarily tentative, such an assessment may help to clarify the characteristic responses of state actors to a common financial predicament.

ROLES

State Agency Officials

I take it that no one will be shocked by the proposition that the goals of those who administer operating agencies will vary along a continuum ranging from maintenance of currently-available resources to expansion of those

Reprinted from "Roles and Symbols in the Determination of State Expenditures," *Midwest Journal of Political Science*, Vol. XI (February, 1967), pp. 27–43, by Thomas J. Anton by permission of the Wayne State University Press. Copyright © 1967 by Wayne State University Press. Mr. Anton is Associate Professor of Political Science at the University of Michigan.

resources as much and as quickly as possible. At the moment this proposition rests mostly on faith, since adequately documented accounts of agency budget preparation in the states are exceedingly rare. On the other hand, my data provide supporting evidence with regard to agency officials in Illinois;[1] Allen Schick has reported findings of a similar nature in his survey of several eastern states;[2] and Rufus Browning has documented both extremes of the continuum in his study of two Wisconsin departments.[3] Browning quotes officials in the more expansive of his two departments as follows:

> We don't hesitate to lay our problems on the line. I would not refrain from reflecting a need.

> The budget is supposed to reflect the judgment of the administrator. There is no point in playing it cozy in trying to second-guess everybody along the line. The budget should reflect only felt needs, nothing more, or less.

> I usually put in something even if it has little chance of being approved. I think we should put all our needs before the department.[4]

I do not want to suggest that all agencies will be equally expansive; the data collected by both Browning and others demonstrate some considerable variety in agency aspirations. But I do have a good deal of confidence in the assertion that very few responsible agency administrators will be likely to request *less* money than is currently available to them. This is not simply because standards of service are rising, along with the increasing professionalization of state government. It is also, and in some sense more fundamentally, because budget requests are prepared by people whose organizational status is tied to, and reflected in, publicly available budget figures. To request a smaller budget than the current budget is to suggest that the job being done by the agency is not sufficiently important to warrant a greater claim on state resources and that the administrator in charge of that job is not sufficiently aggressive (or competent) to make the claim. Agency personnel, whose salaries are paid by public funds because they are presumably performing a needed public service, are threatened by the former implication, while the latter constitutes a direct threat to the agency administrator himself. As a budget officer once remarked to me, "We pay some of these men [hospital superintendents] better than twenty thousand each year and we expect them to be knowledgeable enough to know where and how things could be done better and to come in here with

[1]Thomas J. Anton, *The Politics of State Expenditure in Illinois* (Urbana and London: The University of Illinois Press, 1966), pp. 44–75.

[2]Allen Schick, "Control Patterns in State Budget Execution," *Public Administration Review* XXIV (1964), 97–106.

[3]Rufus P. Browning, "Innovative and Non-Innovative Decision Processes in Government Budgeting," Prepared for delivery at the 1963 Annual Meeting of the American Political Science Association, New York, September, 1963.

[4]*Ibid.*

requests for improved and expanded programs. If they didn't, we'd probably think that we needed to get new people."[5]

The pressure for agency budget expansion is intensified by the public nature of budgetary decisions. However secretive the process of preparing requests may be within agencies, the final disposition of those requests will either be made in public or reflected in public documents such as budget books or appropriation bills. This forces the agency administrator to be attentive to several different public audiences. One audience is composed of the agency's employees, who will look to the agency budget for some indication of how well the chief administrator is protecting their—and his—status. Another audience is composed of the agency's clientele group, if there is one, who will judge the agency in terms of a budget in which they have a direct financial interest. The third, and probably most important audience, is composed of those officials who must review the budget request— particularly those officials who are elected to office.

Requesting an increase in funds is the surest method available to the administrator to satisfy each of these audiences. Such action affirms the significance and protects the status of agency employees, assures clientele groups that new and higher standards of service are being pursued aggressively, and eases the burdens felt by reviewing officials in dealing with programs about which they may have little knowledge. Should the proposed increase be eliminated, the agency administrator can hold reviewing officials to blame, without any harm to his own position, precisely because he has made an effort that is publicly documented. Should the increase be granted, the administrator can properly take credit for the expansion resulting from his initiative.

Budget Review Officers

Whether or not agency administrators are in fact expansive in the preparation of budget estimates, it is reasonably clear that the persons who review estimates believe them to be expansive. Once again we are indebted to Allen Schick's paper for the best evidence on this point. Schick's multistate examination of budget practices revealed what he called "the control orientation." Responding to the question "Which of these two functions do you consider *more* important for your budget office: (1) To serve as watchdog of the Treasury, or (2) To assist the agencies to perform their responsibilities more economically and effectively?" the officials interviewed by Schick indicated that the watchdog function was a more accurate description of actual budget practices. "According to this view," writes Schick, "there is so much built-in pressure for expansion that there must be a specialized agency with the task of saying 'No'. This responsibility falls upon the budget office which then must bear the onus of cutting depart-

[5]Anton, *op. cit.*, p. 56.

mental requests, curbing expenditures, and otherwise asserting central control."[6]

Recognizing the strength of built-in pressures to expand budgets, then, and believing that these pressures will be reflected in budget requests, reviewing officials naturally see themselves as "cutters." Having experienced the results of this orientation, agency administrators react in a time-honored fashion that Schick describes succinctly: "The agencies, anticipating a cut, over-estimate their needs and pad the budget, while the budget office, in the conviction that the budget is padded, make deep cuts in the agency estimates."[7]

To explain the apparent negativism of budget review officials solely in terms of their mistrust of agency budget estimates, however, would be to overlook the personal and political stake they have in doing what they do. Review officers, too, must play to several audiences, including agency administrators, the governor, and the legislature. Their failure to make the cuts others expect them to make would challenge the grounds for the existence of specialized review agencies and thus threaten the jobs they hold. Moreover, so long as agency administrators cooperate by requesting increases over current appropriation levels, review officers can cut away at those increases, secure in the knowledge that they are doing no damage to ongoing operations. Budgetary reductions administered in this fashion may not reduce the cost of state government but they do protect the status of reviewing officials and they do help to generate public assurance that the diet of those who feed at the public trough is not overly rich.

These speculations about the meaning of budget review are buttressed by the general absence of an alternative philosophy of budgeting among the states and the general absence of the informational and institutional means of developing an alternative philosophy. Paul Appleby's justly-famous defense of budgetary negativism asserts the utility of special institutions to represent the values of "fiscal sense and fiscal coordination," but makes no attempt to specify the meaning of these values—apart from the assertion of strong opposition to "program and expenditure expansion."[8] Appleby calls this "a specialized way of looking at problems in decision-making," thus providing a rationalization for the convenient division of labor which I suspect exists in most American states: Agencies press for expansion using programmatic criteria while budget review officers attempt to negate expansion using financial criteria. But neither set of criteria produces the expected consequences. Significant programmatic and budgetary expansion takes place when money is available to fund it, while significant expenditure reductions take place when there is sufficient hostility

---

[6]Schick, *op. cit.*, p. 99.

[7]*Ibid.*, p. 100.

[8]Paul Appleby, "The Role of the Budget Division," *Public Administration Review* XVII (1957), 156.

to programs to force a cutback in expenditures. Meanwhile, since neither dramatic expansion nor dramatic reduction takes place very often, programmatic and financial justifications are used less as criteria for decisions than as symbolic shields, behind which agency administrators and budget officials both play a game of organizational status maintenance.

Governors

What does a governor have to do with the process by which his state's expenditures are determined? The best answer, it seems to me, is "very little." This conclusion is based, in part, on Shadoan's report that governors in some of the states she visited were singularly uninterested in what went into the state budget.[9] A far more important source of support, however, derives from documented accounts of the behavior of governors who were vitally interested in expenditures for which they were responsible: Freeman,[10] Harriman,[11] Rockefeller[12] and Kerner.[13] Fragmented and incomplete as these reports may be, they do offer some striking insights into the kinds of predicaments governors are likely to face and the regularities of their responses to such predicaments.

We all know, of course, that nearly all of the states have long since adopted the executive budget system, which authorizes governors to review agency spending proposals and holds governors responsible for preparation of what is supposed to be a comprehensive spending program. The preeminence granted by these formal arrangements, however, is seldom easy to achieve. The governor will probably come to his position without any direct experience in dealing with state finance. His own inexperience will thus provide a sharp contrast to the wisdom of the old hands who occupy administrative and legislative positions of influence, and who will probably regard the governor as an outsider—a "new boy," come to muddle in their affairs. Moreover, since the average length of service for most governors is less than five years,[14] the old hands can confidently think of the "new boy" as someone who is likely to be gone from the scene far in advance of their own departure. Neither the governor's lack of financial sophistication nor the ambiguity about his staying power is likely to encourage a warm reception from the old hands. The new boy must prove himself first, and he must do so in the face of a formidable array of obstacles.

[9]Arlene Theuer Shadoan, *Organization, Role, and Staffing of State Budget Offices* (Lexington: Bureau of Business Research, 1961), mimeo, p. 59.

[10]Thomas Flinn, *Governor Freeman and the Minnesota Budget* (University, Alabama: University of Alabama Press, ICP Case Series, No. 60, 1961).

[11]Donald G. Herzberg and Paul Tillett, *A Budget for New York State, 1956–1957* (University, Alabama: University of Alabama Press, ICP Case Series, No. 69, 1962).

[12]Clark D. Ahlberg and Daniel P. Moynihan, "Changing Governors—and Policies," *Public Administration Review* XX (1960), 195–204.

[13]Anton, *op. cit.*, pp. 112–146.

[14]Joseph A. Schlesinger, "The Politics of the Executive," in Herbert Jacob and Kenneth N. Vines, eds., *Politics in the American States* (Boston: Little, Brown and Co., 1965), p. 209.

The first—and probably most important—obstacle is the truly staggering complexity of the state's system of financial bookkeeping. Constitutional limitations, marvelously incoherent divisions of financial accountability, incomprehensible budget documents and, worst of all, an intricate maze of general funds, special funds, revolving funds, loan funds, trust funds, federal funds, local funds, all conspire to shroud the state's financial situation in mystery. Illinois, with only forty or so (the number changes from biennium to biennium) special funds to worry about in addition to the general purpose fund, is perhaps more fortunate than most states in this respect. But consider Connecticut, which finances expenditures from roughly 100 funds (only 5 of which are included in the budget), or Wyoming, where no less than 168 special funds are used to support state spending.[15] The governor who hopes to fight for financial righteousness in these circumstances will surely be hard-put to locate the battlefield, let alone lead his forces to victory.

Given time, of course, any governor can come to some reasonably adequate understanding of these matters. But time is precisely what the governor does not have, at least in his first term. Presentation of the governor's budget typically is required at some point early in the legislative session following the governor's election to office and is typically the first major action taken by the governor. He will thus have no more than six to twelve weeks in which to learn what he must learn and incorporate that learning, if he can, into his first budget. Difficult enough in its own terms, this problem is made enormously more difficult by the realization that the old hands will be watching the new boy for signs of his political skill—as will the governor's political enemies and the general public. In view of the relative brevity of the governor's stay in office, impressions generated by his handling of his first budget are likely to remain influential during his entire tenure. Should these first impressions suggest less-than-adequate skill, the governor will have lost a good part of the battle almost before it began.[16]

Even assuming a willingness and competence to learn, however, the governor will probably conclude that there is very little he can do to control state spending. Other elected state officers, the legislature and the courts will be beyond his reach. Similarly, expenditures from special funds will be practically, if not always legally, impossible to control. Some idea of what this can mean for a governor may be gleaned from the fact that three-fifths of the states finance upwards of 50 per cent of their total expenditures from such special funds.[17] What is left, then, is general fund expenditures, but since these are typically concentrated in two or three large programs or agencies—welfare and education, primarily—which cannot

[15]Tax Foundation, Inc., *State Expenditure Controls: An Evaluation* (New York: Tax Foundation, Inc., 1965), p. 74.

[16]Ahlberg and Moynihan, *loc. cit.*, p. 195, offer a similar view.

[17]Tax Foundation, Inc., *op. cit.*, p. 74.

be abandoned, the proportion of the general fund open to significant influence by the governor may well turn out to be a minuscule part of total spending. And even this may be affected more directly by national economic trends than by anything the governor does or doesn't do; witness the experience of both Harriman and Rockefeller in New York.[18]

These situational constraints help to explain the curiously unreal quality of gubernatorial action. Governors typically campaign on platforms stressing, among other things, increased service (i.e., program expansion) and increased economy. Once in office, however, they typically find it impossible to accomplish either of these objectives. Freeman in Minnesota, Harriman and Rockefeller in New York, and Kerner in Illinois all promised to initiate new programs; all found, or claimed to find, their states in a condition of near bankruptcy; each had all he could do to find sufficient revenues to finance current operations, *after* putting aside plans for expanded activities.[19] A major factor in their inability to implement new programs, of course, was the built-in increase in the cost of existing programs. They all struggled to find more money for education because more students *were there*, waiting to be educated; they all struggled to find more money for state agencies because state personnel *were there*, waiting for salary-step increases; they struggled variously to find more money for activities such as welfare or capital construction because more clients *were there*, waiting to be serviced. Nothing the governors did or said affected these conditions. Instead, precisely the reverse was the case, for these conditions eliminated the possibility of either new programs or significant economies. The public statements of the governors nevertheless continued to use the rhetoric of "increased service and greater economy"—a curious and significant fact to which I will shortly return.[20]

By and large, then, governors do not "determine" expenditures, in the sense of looking at most state activities and deciding to reduce, continue or expand them. Rather, the exigencies of their situation force them to focus most of their attention on revenue, which typically must be increased just to keep pace with existing programs. This is an important—indeed crucial—problem, but it need not entail a very close examination of where state money goes. The need for more money can be established without difficulty in most states and, once established, the governor's attention is necessarily drawn to what he must regard as the more sensitive problem. Most states, after all, legally require a balanced budget. But even if legal obligation is

[18]Ahlberg and Moynihan, *loc. cit.*, p. 199, write: "The national economy, both on the downturn and the upsurge, fixed the limits of the real policy alternatives for these new governors as must be true in nearly all states."

[19]Flinn, *op. cit.*, provides a particularly effective account of the processes which forced Governor Freeman to abandon most of his new programs.

[20]Herzberg and Tillett, *op. cit.*, p. 30 write: "The public expression of these controversies often does not reflect candid consideration of governmental goals. To some extent, legislative and executive budget releases to the public have an academic character."

absent, public concern for "fiscal integrity" will control the image pursued by the chief of state. Governors may be regarded as "money providers" or as "budget balancers"; only infrequently can they be viewed as "decision-makers" in the determination of state expenditures.

Legislatures

Like governors, state legislatures tend to focus what attention they give to state finance on the problem of revenue, and for similar reasons. Lacking the staff personnel required to cope with the intended and unintended complexities of state financial documents, legislatures typically know very little about what is contained in such documents. Constrained by constitution or by custom to dispose of major appropriations within a limited period of time, legislatures have little opportunity to do anything but approve the expenditures recommended by the governor. Occasionally a legislature will rise up, axe in hand, and begin chopping away indiscriminately at a governor's budget recommendations. However, such behavior is primarily aimed at the general public, which expects legislators to be "economy minded," and is easily circumvented by the executive. Thus, whether in Kentucky, where the last budget was introduced on Tuesday and passed by the following Friday,[21] or in New York, where the legislature normally requires only two days to approve the budget,[22] or in Illinois, where defeat for *any* appropriation bill is almost unheard of,[23] legislative participation in the determination of state expenditure is virtually non-existent.

On the other hand, legislatures are being drawn increasingly into the search for new revenue. For legislators, as for governors, the question of "who shall pay?" is more sensitive than the question "for what?" precisely because it fits more easily into the conventional platitudes which structure public expectations about state finance. Above all, legislatures must act in a "responsible" manner, by providing the governor with sufficient funds to operate the government—or else provide a publicly acceptable rationale for failing to do so. Since the general public knows very little about state programs, either choice (i.e., approving or not approving the revenue requested by the governor) can be rationalized as something which "provides necessary services," at "the most economical level," consistent with "efficient and sound management practices," taking care all the while to "maintain a favorable tax climate for industry" without sacrificing "equity" in the revenue structure. And since either choice can be so rationalized, the choice that is ultimately made will turn less on the activities to

[21]Douglas Kane, "Our Steamrollered Assembly," *The Courier-Journal Magazine*, Sunday, February 20, 1966.

[22]Frederick C. Mosher, "The Executive Budget, Empire State Style," *Public Administration Review* XII (1952), 73–84.

[23]Anton, *op. cit.*, pp. 147–177.

be supported at some higher level than on the question of who will be given credit or blame for providing that higher level of support. A legislature controlled by the opposition party can be expected to attempt to prevent the governor from receiving the credit for expanding activities or to blame him for increasing taxes—hence the common executive-legislative disputes over revenue. Legislative actions thus help to provide the money necessary for budgetary expansion, though the grounds for such actions seldom have anything to do with the activities to be financed by such expansion.

TOWARD A DRAMATURGICAL VIEW OF STATE EXPENDITURE POLITICS

These speculations persuade me that there are significant uniformities in the behavior of officials involved in determining expenditures for American state governments. A peek into the decision-making black box in most states, I submit, would probably reveal a system in which operating agency heads consistently request more funds, executive and/or legislative reviewers consistently reduce agency requests, governors consistently pursue balanced budgets at higher expenditure levels, and legislatures consistently approve higher appropriations while engaging in frequent disputes with the governor over revenues. From a process point of view, the operations of most of these systems could probably be summarized in terms which would closely resemble the "incrementalism" model developed by Professor Lindblom and others: marginal rather than fundamental changes, determined by piecemeal rather than comprehensive calculations.[24] From a structural point of view, the operations of these systems would probably not be inconsistent with the widespread belief that decision-making power has become concentrated in the hands of actors in the executive rather than the legislative branch of American governments.

Perhaps the most significant aspect of such systems is the contrast between what state officials actually do and the public statements or symbols used to rationalize their behavior. Agency administrators, I suggested, typically justify proposed budgetary increases on programmatic grounds, yet the frequency with which they propose increases for which they do not expect approval belies a rather difficult goal: protection against the adverse consequences of cutting a request that contains no increases that can be cut. In similar fashion, review officers—including the governor—justify the reductions they impose in terms of economy and efficiency, but their failure to prevent rapid and large-scale appropriation increases suggests that they, too, have a different operating goal: preservation of their peculiar status

[24]Charles E. Lindblom, "Decision-Making in Taxation and Expenditures," in *Public Finances: Needs, Sources, and Utilization* (Princeton: National Bureau of Economic Research, 1961), pp. 295–329; Aaron Wildavsky, *The Politics of the Budgetary Process* (Boston: Little, Brown and Co., 1964).

within an environment that knows no other justification for such a status. Governors and legislatures make use of both programmatic and management symbols, though their principal activities are aimed at increasing revenues in order to balance budgets which seldom show any evidence of either new programs or management efficiency. From budget request to final appropriation, every action is rationalized in terms which mask its true meaning.

In this sense the symbols themselves are deceptive, but it would be quite unfair to accuse state officials of a conscious intent to deceive. The realities of state politics are more complex than that. Reality number one is that states have lost effective control over their expenditures. Complex structures of special funds that are difficult to understand and more difficult to change, coupled with heavy investment in existing activities that must be continued, make up an expenditure base that leaves little room for innovation, particularly since this base contains built-in pressures for increases that strain state tax resources. Increases beyond those that are built in typically occur as a result of circumstances that, from the state point of view, are fortuitous: Congress passes a massive federal-state highway program that pulls the state to dramatically higher highway expenditures, a riot in the streets triples a state's expenditure for human relations programs, a massive campaign to "do something" about state mental health hospitals, led by private citizens, doubles state appropriations for such hospitals.[25] Initiative for such changes comes from actors in the external environment, who pull state actors along after the fact. Not infrequently, disagreement among state actors over the question of revenue enables the state to exercise a veto over the rate of expansion desired by external actors. But even here, the possibility of appeal to other sources of public funds—particularly federal aid—frequently permits these actors to soften the effects of a state veto. Thus state actors not only have given up a great deal of their power to initiate major changes in expenditure, but they also have lost much of their power to act as a brake on public spending.

Because the power to control the course of financial events has been lost, state actions designed to influence those events take on a peculiar quality of uncertainty.[26] A budget reviewer eliminates a request for funds submitted by an agency only to discover (perhaps) later that the activity for which the funds were requested has been carried on anyway, using some of the "free floating" money made available to the agency by the federal government. Who was responsible? Was it the agency head? Was it the federal government? Or was it the budget office, which failed to keep track of what was going on in the agency? A governor of the sovereign State of New York submits a budget full of new and expanded services, only to dis-

[25]All these examples are taken from recent Illinois history.
[26]This discussion owes a great deal to Schlesinger's perceptive argument. *Op. cit.*, pp. 207–217.

cover later that a moderate economic depression has eliminated the new revenue with which he had planned to finance the new services. Who was responsible for the failure to implement the governor's plans? Was it the governor, whose estimates of revenue turned out to be so wrong? Was it the Federal Reserve Board, or General Motors? Was it anybody? A governor of Illinois, anxious to conserve his state's dwindling financial resources, orders a "freeze" on the hiring of new employees, but discovers later that his order has reduced neither employees nor expenditures. Should the governor be held responsible for the failure of his directive? Should uncooperative agency heads bear the blame? Or perhaps it is the state's constitutional and legal system, which tolerates the existence of eighteen different personnel systems, many of which are beyond the scope of gubernatorial influence.[27]

These examples, of course, have been simplified to the point of caricature, but the caricature itself has a point, for in none of these cases is it at all clear that the actions of state officials had any significant impact on future events. Nor is it at all clear that future events would have been different in the absence of those actions. Expenditures for state employment might have been the same, whether or not the governor ordered a freeze; the activities of the State of New York might have been the same, whether or not new programs were proposed by the governor; agency activities might have been the same, whether or not a budget office reduction was imposed. From a public point of view, uncertainty about the effects of actions taken by state officials means that fixing responsibility for such actions is impossible: an appeal to some environmental force or internal complexity is always available to an official seeking to avoid responsibility, while his attempt to assume responsibility can always be challenged on the same grounds. And from the point of view of the actors themselves, uncertainty about the effects of their actions deprives them of an important source of feedback from the real world. How is a budget officer or governor to evaluate his judgments if they are not carried out? How can a governor evaluate his plans for new programs if they are not implemented? What, indeed, are the criteria of "success" or "failure" in a world in which budgets are balanced or unbalanced and programs initiated or stopped at least as much by uncontrollable external events as by the conscious actions of the officials who are presumably in charge?

The answer, it seems to me, lies precisely in the symbols used by state actors to rationalize and justify their public behavior: the budget as a symbol of Responsibility; the cut, as a symbol of Economy; and the increase, as a symbol of Service. What is at stake in the performance of the roles discussed above is not so much the distribution of resources, about

---

[27]See Thomas Page, "The Employment Systems of the State of Illinois," *Illinois Government* (Urbana: Institute of Government and Public Affairs), No. 7 (1960).

which state actors have little to say, but the distribution of symbolic satisfaction among the involved actors and the audiences which observe their
stylized behavior.[28]

To a mass public which has been taught to believe that there is
"someone" in charge of the government and that there must be a "reason"
for every governmental act, the budget document itself provides reassurance
that these beliefs are valid. Prepared by a gubernatorial staff agency,
presented with a ceremonial flourish that typically involves a joint legislative
session to receive the governor's budget message from his own lips, and
widely publicized by the mass media as "the governor's" program, the
budget is popularly identified with a single official, who is presumed to be the
"someone" in charge. The guarantee that this program has been rationally
conceived is provided by the great masses of figures contained in the document. Whether these figures result from careful calculation or, as is frequently
the case, from more or less wild guesses is beside the point, for it is the
specificity of the number rather than its source which warrants its rationality.
However fuzzy the thinking behind any given figure may have been, its
representation as a specific dollar-and-cents figure implies precise measurement of quantifiable factors, leading to this—and no other—sum.

For those who are closest to the centers of decision—and who are
therefore in a position to know how unscientific the budget can be—it
is not the document which offers symbolic satisfaction, but the process of
putting it together. The constantly recurring cycle of financial activity
provides an anticipated series of occasions for action, as well as a series of
settings in which such action will take place. Visitations in the director's
office, or the governor's office, legislative chambers, committee hearing rooms,
and public forums of various kinds all provide settings in which the actors
can display the behavior appropriate to their respective roles. The busyness
of such activities together with the official secrecy which shrouds the decisions made in many of these settings reinforce the public impression that
important matters are being dealt with by powerful men. It is similarly reinforcing for the actors themselves, whose long hours and frequently feverish
work help to maintain their belief that the roles they play are in fact both
powerful and important. In all these respects the budget, as document and
process, creates symbolic satisfaction built upon the idea that affairs of state
are being dealt with, that responsibility is being exercised, and that rationality prevails.

As the principal symbol of economy, the cut is especially favored
by legislative actors, though it is in fact utilized more frequently by governors and budget officers. Governors and budget officers, however, have
recourse to other powerful symbols of responsibility (i.e., the balanced

[28]The discussion which follows is stimulated by Murray Edelman's exciting work,
The Symbolic Uses of Politics (Urbana: The University of Illinois Press, 1964).

budget, or "prudent management"), whereas legislative actors do not. The satisfactions derived from the cut are therefore largely monopolized by legislators. Grounded in the folklore of "rampant bureaucracy," building "empires" through "padded budgets" which "waste the hard-earned dollar of the taxpayer," and fed by the demand for "a dollar's worth of service for every dollar spent," the cut symbolizes a popular check on governmental excess. The cut may be specifically aimed at a program or a payroll, or it may be a meat-axe reduction designed to reduce all requests by some stated percentage. In either case it provides reassurances to legislators and to the mass public that their joint concern for economy has been implemented.

The overt and stylized distrust of public spending creates the need for another symbol to account for the obvious inability of state actors to prevent expansion of total state expenditures. The need is met by resorting to the imagery of "services" provided by the recurring increases. Since additional revenues are frequently required for the support of these expanding "services," opportunities for conflict are regularly provided. But since there is seldom disagreement over the propriety of performing the services (recall that most increases arise from built-in pressure for expansion), the issue involved in such disputes is not "what will be done?" but "who will receive credit?" for services that everyone accepts as necessary. A classic case involves the problem of state aid for local schools. When the governor and the legislature are on opposite sides of the political fence a good deal of maneuvering can be expected before the "credit" issue is resolved. Thus, a premature announcement by Republican legislative leaders in New York of a school aid plan more generous than the governor's forced Harriman's hand. According to Herzberg and Tillett, Harriman " . . . felt betrayed and explained with some heat that he did not want to be parsimonious toward the localities and certainly did not wish to appear less favorably disposed toward local education than the Legislature." Harriman's solution may be regarded as symbolic perfection: "The Governor immediately endorsed the Republican proposals publicly in a statement which seemed to suggest that he had expected such proposals, had agreed to them in advance, and had shared in their origin."[29]

Because revenues are so inherently unpredictable, their involvement in the symbolism of "increased services" frequently provides opportunities for the manufacture and distribution of an important subsidiary symbol: competence, or the lack of it. Revenue predictions can always be attacked as too high or too low, particularly where there exists a past record of inaccurate projections. The stylized forms in which such attacks and counterattacks are expressed typically involve legislative charges that (a) revenues have been miscalculated by the governor, (b) needed programs can be

[29]Herzberg and Tillett, *op. cit.*, p. 26.

carried on without additional expenditures, and (c) gubernatorial incompetence or deceit explains the new revenue requests. Gubernatorial responses typically involve charges that (a) legislators are "playing politics" with the poor, the school children, etc., (b) new revenues are required to provide necessary services, and (c) legislators are not fully informed (i.e., are incompetent).[30] An example taken from the most recent legislative season in Illinois provides a nice illustration of these symbolic themes.

Governor Kerner's budget for 1965–67 included the sum of $27 million for state participation in a federally-aided program of special education for the culturally disadvantaged. There was no disagreement about the desirability of the program but at the end of the session the Republican-dominated Senate deleted the $27 million state appropriation. Democratic reactions predictably lamented the failure to meet the needs of the people. Justification for the cut was summarized later in a press release issued by the Republican leader of the Senate. That release is worth quoting in some detail:

> Legislation establishing a special education program for underprivileged children was strongly supported by the Republican Senate during the past session and has become law.

> This program is wholly financed by federal funds but is administered by the State of Illinois. The Federal Education Opportunities Act passed recently provided $61.7 million for this program in Illinois this year. An additional $72.6 million is authorized for next year, bringing the total for the biennium to $134,300,000.

> The Democratic administration in Illinois did not understand the financing of this program during the last session of the Legislature and apparently still does not. The Republicans in the Senate passed the bill establishing the program but deleted the state appropriation attached because of the massive allocation of federal funds. No state matching funds are required and in fact, if any state money were appropriated it would jeopardize future federal monies. The Federal law specifies that once state money is used, the same amount must be appropriated every year in the future for the program or the federal funds will be cut off.

> Governor Kerner continues to lament that the program suffered when in truth, instead of the $27 million he would have allocated, the Republican Senate assured that Illinois will now receive over $134 million for the biennium without matching obligations.

---

[30]Murray Edelman offers an apt comment on the repeated use of cliches such as these, and others noted earlier: "Chronic repetition of cliches and stale phrases that serve simply to evoke a conditioned uncritical response is a time-honored habit among politicians and a mentally restful one for their audiences. The only information conveyed by a speaker who tells an audience of businessmen that taxes are too high and that public spending is waste is that he is trying to prevent both himself and his audience from thinking. . . " Edelman, *op. cit.*, pp. 124–125.

> Governor Kerner was uninformed about the relevant federal legislation and unaware of the financial operations of the program. The Republican task force will try to keep him better informed in the future.

Whatever the merits of the partisan position expressed in the press release, its significance here lies primarily in the symbols used to justify Republican behavior. Implicitly, the Republican cut is justified because it reduces the state's financial burden. Explicitly, it is justified because it results in an even higher expenditure for this program than was proposed by the governor. Credit for this increased service is fully assumed by the Republicans, whose greater financial sophistication permitted them to overcome the incompetence attributed to the governor. What the program does, for what persons, is not an issue. Who can claim credit for the program is an issue— indeed, the only issue.

The willingness with which a traditionally conservative Republican leadership embraced federal participation in local education may seem surprising, but it provides a useful insight into the ambiguity with which state actors view the federal government. Virtually all state actors are verbally opposed to federal encroachment on state affairs, but on the other hand are quick to accept federal aid and the controls that are part of federal aid. In this case it is difficult to see what part the state can play in a program financed entirely from federal funds and utilized by local school boards who, we may surmise, are likely to be more responsive to federal requirements than to state officials who have no financial stake in the program. To the extent that the program narrows the scope of effective state responsibility it is a retreat from the principle of state control over state affairs. Yet the Republican senators who led the retreat mask it as a victory by alluding to their "sharpness" in getting something for nothing—"134 million . . . without matching obligations." Not unlike their small-town cousins, who pride themselves on their ability to "outwit" the "city-slickers," these state actors turn defeat into victory by "sharp deals" which "outwit" the slicksters in Washington.[31] Implicit symbolism of this sort, by preventing a full appreciation of state dependence on federal aid, helps to maintain the conviction that state actors have power. The reality behind the symbolism is quite different but, because it is not consciously recognized, it has little effect on state action.

To interpret state expenditure politics in symbolic terms is not to say that state actions are inconsequential. The consequences are real enough, but they are not the consequences we normally look for. Actors on the various stages of state politics are forced to act in situations which offer only a severely limited number of appropriate roles, none of which

---

[31]For an analysis of these themes in a small-town setting, see Arthur J. Vidich and Joseph Bensman, *Small Town in Mass Society* (Garden City, N. Y.: Doubleday & Co., Inc., Anchor Books edition, 1960).

permit the exercise of full control over state finance. Lacking such control, but driven by the desire to maintain office and status, actors behave *as though* they are powerful by following a script written in terms of easily understood symbols. Rationally derived Responsibility, Economy and Service are the principal symbols for which state actors compete and around which they organize their stylized behavior. If the tangible outcome of such behavior seldom corresponds to the symbols by which it is justified, nothing is lost, for it is not at all clear that tangible outcomes can be significantly influenced by anything done, or not done, by state actors. In this context use of these symbols provides a net gain, for they reassure actors and their audiences that powerful figures are engaged in important activities, in a significant governmental context. The extent to which these assurances have no basis in fact is both the source of state symbolism and the measure of the state financial predicament.

CHAPTER FIFTEEN

THE CITY MANAGER IN LEGISLATIVE POLITICS

RONALD O. LOVERIDGE

I. INTRODUCTION

The "Lost World of Municipal Government" has been rediscovered. Nothing less than an expansive assertion of research has rescued urban politics from the backwater of political science. Instead of a preoccupation with formal and prescriptive statements about "good government," urban politics has witnessed important developments in theory, method, and empirical studies.

The first discovery of municipal government dates to the Progressive Era when the politics of the city, under indictment by journalists and reformers, became the object of concerted popular reform. The political ideology of the reform movement was the ethos of "good government"— efficiency, honesty, impartiality. Many political scientists participated in the hue and cry for political change; scholars like Goodnow, Merriam, White, among others, both studied city politics and promoted its reform.

From the ferment of change, perhaps the outstanding structural

Reprinted with permission of publisher and author from Ronald O. Loveridge, "The City Manager in Legislative Politics," *Polity*, Vol. 1 (Winter, 1968), pp. 214–36. Mr. Loveridge is Assistant Professor of Political Science at the University of California at Riverside.

Most of the data examined in this paper have been drawn, either directly or indirectly, from research of the City Council Research Project, Institute of Political Studies at Stanford University. I am especially indebted to two colleagues, Charles Adrian and Francis Carney, for useful criticisms and suggestions on an earlier draft of this paper, which was delivered at the 1967 annual meeting of the Western Political Science Association in Tucson, Arizona.

legacy is the council-manager plan.[1] (First adopted by Dayton, Ohio, in 1914, the plan is now in effect in over 1,750 cities with a total population of approximately 45 million.) The plan became the immediate focus of scholarly attention. Early evaluations were almost uniformly favorable; these sentiments were well expressed by Harold Alderfer: "No system is perfect, but the council-manager form allows the best possible combination of democracy and efficiency in local government."[2] In much of the early writing and research, the major concern was to discuss, even "prove," why manager government is the best form of local government.

But after World War II, the city manager lost his pre-eminent status. The council-manager plan was initially conceived, justified, and popularly accepted on the premise of separation of politics and administration. The city manager was to be the administrator, the city council, the policy maker—so the advocates proposed.[3] When the dichotomy between politics and administration was debunked, the policy role of the city manager was open to close evaluation. While commending his administrative performance, political scientists frequently criticized the policy values of the city manager. Edward Banfield and James Q. Wilson in *City Politics*, for example, note that "managers . . . tend to be conservative, unenterprising, and devoted to routine [and] . . . the typical manager's mentality is probably still a good deal closer to that of the engineer than to that of the politician."[4] The recurring theme in most of the critiques is that the city manager exerts little or no policy leadership on nonroutine decisions, is unresponsive to the needs and demands of the people, and in general acts to depoliticize the allocation of city values.

The "behavioral persuasion" further relegated the city manager to the sidelines of community research. Questions about the community political system, decision-making process, and leadership structure took priority

[1]"The origin of the council-manager plan," wrote Leonard White, "is imbedded in the revolution of the civic and business interests of the American city, aided and abetted by various forward-looking groups, against the waste, extravagance, and sometimes corruption which characterized 'politician' government of the last century." Leonard White, *City Manager* (Chicago, 1927), p. ix.

[2]Harold Alderfer, *American Local Government and Administration* (New York, 1956), p. 308. And even the pre-1945 great men of political science were enthusiastic about the successes of the council-manager plan; for example, Charles Merriam commented: "Permit me to say in language as plain as I can make it that city managers have made the outstanding contribution to public administration in the United States in the twentieth century." See Charles Merriam, "The City Manager of Today," *Public Management* (February, 1950), p. 28.

[3]The administration-politics dichotomy has had a strange yet important life history. Embraced by early writers as sound causal and normative theory, the dichotomy is now wholly rejected in academic circles. For a succinct perspective on the administration-politics dichotomy, see Wallace Sayre, "Premises of Public Administration: Past and Emerging," *Public Administration Review* (Spring, 1958), pp. 102–105.

[4]Edward Banfield and James Q. Wilson, *City Politics* (Cambridge, Massachusetts, 1963), pp. 173, 174.

over questions of "efficiency and economy" or of what is the preferred structure of local government. At best, the city manager was seen as one of many forces which act to mold public policy. The city manager was, in short, a favorite of traditional political science. To those of a different generation, the city manager is viewed more as another paramenter in the urban political environment.

Why then should we as students of urban politics be interested in the policy role of the city manager? In council-manager cities, the city manager appears often in study after study as the most influential public official, elected or otherwise.[5] More than a popular administrator or a hired hand for the "power structure," a city manager emerges as a full-time professional committed to direct intervention in community affairs:

> To begin with, a major source of innovations are those professional occupational roles centrally concerned with community institutions. Part of the job of certain occupations is to constantly propose changes in community institutions. Such professionalized roles as city manager... carry within themselves the notion of constant improvement in the services involved.[6]

The prominent place of the manager in community decisions can be attributed to reasons beyond career obligations to report city problems and propose policy solutions. The manager's recognized expertise, position at the apex of city administration, and virtual monopoly of technical and other detailed information propel him, willingly or unwillingly, into a pivotal policy position. And, as suggested by a colleague, the city manager is probably the one local actor able to take a comprehensive view of the public interest *and* to exercise an important influence on other policy participants.

Because he provides executive leadership for the city's policy process, the analysis of the city manager's policy role is important for the study and practice of urban politics. If we assume that the behavior of political actors is conditioned by the conception of appropriate roles for themselves, how a city manager participates in the policy process should depend, in some measure, on values and expectations held for the manager's policy role. And as observed by Karl Bosworth: "Not only is he [city manager] inevitably in public view, but the range of his operations is broad, and the

---

[5]"Rule by amateurs," write Williams and Adrian, "is likely to mean that under most conditions, persons outside the legislative body must be depended upon to make the essential policy decisions in all but the formal sense." Oliver Williams and Charles Adrian, *Four Cities* (Philadelphia, 1963), p. 292; see pp. 305–308 for an excellent discussion of the manager as an influential outsider. Also, see Aaron Wildavsky, *Leadership in a Small Town* (Totawa, New Jersey, 1964); he concludes, "As a matter of course, therefore, we would expect a city manager who takes a broad view of his responsibilities, in a town without full-time elected officials, to be the most general activist and to appear in more decision areas than anyone else."

[6]Peter Rossi, "Theory, Research, and Practice in Community Organization," in *Democracy in Urban America*, eds. Oliver Williams and Charles Press (Chicago, 1961), p. 388.

fate of his community may be determined in part by the public goals his thoughts lead him to set for his government."[7]

II. PROBLEMS AND PROCEDURES

Two definitions of the manager's policy role are especially crucial to its normative content and its influence on behavior—those of city managers *and* of city councilmen. First, city managers are the occupants of the focal position. How they interpret the policy role obviously conditions their policy-making activities; but more important to this paper, their conceptions of what a city manager should or should not do provide the central direction to the role's normative content. *The first objective is to examine the normative character of the policy role as defined by city managers.*

The city manager, unlike most political executives, is appointed and thus serves at the pleasure of the council. As expressed by one writer, "the manager is one of the most dispensable men in any political community."[8] Moreover, the content of a manager's policy activities has to be at least generally endorsed by the city councilmen. The dependence of the city manager on their approval guarantees councilmen a prominent place in defining what a city manager can do. *The second objective is to explore the expectations of councilmen for the city manager's policy role.*

The third and final objective is to analyze the role conflict between city managers and city councilmen. Is there disagreement? If so, what is the extent and kind of the disagreement? And what is the significance of such a disagreement for the city manager's involvement in the policy process?

To investigate the above objectives, the policy role conceptions of city managers and city councilmen will be examined. Such data are available for city managers and city councilmen in the San Francisco Bay region.[9] Of some 72 "centralized managed" cities, role data have

---

[7]Karl Bosworth, "The Manager is a Politician," *Public Administration Review* (Summer, 1958), p. 216. For a further discussion of the importance and implications of the city manager as a political executive, see the symposium is *Public Administration Review* (Summer, 1958): Charles Adrian, "A Study of Three Communities," pp. 208–213; Dorothea Strauss Pealy, "Need for Elected Leadership," pp. 214–216; and Karl Bosworth, "Manager is a Politician," pp. 216–222.

[8]Gladys Kammerer, Charles Farris, John DeGrove, and Alfred Clubok, *City Managers in Politics* (Gainesville, Florida, 1962), p. 81.

[9]This paper is based on data to be used in a monograph—tentatively titled "City Managers in Legislative Politics"—on which I am currently working. The monograph is one in a series to be published by memebers of the City Council Research Project, Institute of Political Studies at Stanford University, Heinz Eulau Director. The Project, financed by a grant from the National Science Foundation, is investigating decision making in small legislative groups. Focusing primarily on city councils, we have been collecting interview data from over 400 councilmen in the San Francisco Bay region (that is, the counties of Alameda, Contra Costa, Marin, Napa, San Francisco, San Mateo, Santa Clara, Solano, and Sonoma). However, my monograph is based not only on data from interviews with city councilmen but also on a questionnaire sent to all Bay Area city managers in December, 1965, and to a lesser extent on 40 field interviews conducted with Bay Area managers in the summer of 1964.

been collected on 59 managers (82% of those possible) and 338 city councilmen (84% of those possible). An interest in policy conceptions is particularly
suited to survey research, for role conceptions can be tapped by asking rather
than observing—to this end, structured interviews and written question-
naires were both used.[10]

III. INTRAPOSITION CONSENSUS AND THE POLICY ROLE: THE CITY MANAGER

In contrast to most American political executives, city managers should
have relatively well-defined and agreed upon conceptions of their policy
role.[11] There are several reasons for clarity of role definition. First, the city
charter or enabling ordinances provide a formal and often detailed specification of the duties of the city manager. Second, every city manager makes
decisions on problems which directly commit the city government and which
affect the community in important ways. The proper policy role is thus
a normative question a city manager cannot really avoid. And third,
because of the long standing controversy over the proper policy activities
of the manager, the content of the policy role is frequently discussed at
graduate school, at conferences, in the municipal literature, or at council
sessions. For example, in commenting on an annual conference of the
International City Managers' Association, two city managers observed:
"The familiar, never answered questions concerning the philosophy of
professional city management, the proper role of the council and manager,
and the dearth of political leadership were discussed time and again."[12]

Agreement on the central values of the policy role result from three
conditions peculiar to the city manager as a political executive. To begin,
city managers view themselves and participate as members of a profession.
The implications of being a professional are suggested by Banfield and
Wilson:

[10]See the rationale of *The Legislative System* for relying on interview data in studying role
conceptions: John Wahlke, Heinz Eulau, William Buchanan, and LeRoy Ferguson, *The
Legislative System* (New York, 1962), particularly pp. 31–33. (The concept of role is especially
prominent in American sociology, social psychology, and cultural anthropology.) Important summaries of the concept of role can be found in Neal Gross, Ward Mason, and Alexander McEachern, *Explorations in Role Analysis* (New York, 1958), pp. 11–69; and Theodore
Sarbin, "Role Theory," in *Handbook of Social Psychology I*, ed. Gardner Lindzey (Reading,
Massachusetts, 1954), pp. 223–258. Two useful introductions to the relationship of expectations and behavior can be found in Robert Bierstedt, *Social Order* (New York, 1957) and
Arnold Rose, ed., *Human Behavior and Social Process* (Boston, 1962). More seminal works on
the implications of the concept of role include George Mead, *Mind, Self, and Society* (Chicago,
1934), Ralph Linton, *Study of Man* (New York, 1936), and Talcott Parsons, *Social System*
(Glencoe, Illinois, 1951).

[11]Where a study taps central, clearly defined expectation sets, role analysis becomes an
especially valuable explanatory tool. See, for example, Alvin Gouldner, "Cosmopolitans and
Locals," *Administrative Science Quarterly* (December, 1957; March, 1958), pp. 281–306; 444–
480.

[12]C. A. Harrell and D. G. Weiford, "City Manager and the Policy Process," *Public
Administration Review* (Spring, 1959), p. 102.

Whether or not he regards managing cities as his life's work, he knows that it is a profession and that what is "right" or "wrong" both for him and the council is to be found in the professional Code of Ethics and in the "common law" that has grown up around it.[13]

A member of the city manager profession is exposed to new ideas, programs, and techniques. Such exposure occurs through print and through face-to-face contact at meetings, conferences, or conventions. The International City Managers' Association, for instance, holds national conferences, publishes a monthly journal as well as a variety of handboods, offers training courses, supplies technical advice or materials, and reports on new municipal developments. And in California, the League of California Cities acts as a clearinghouse for city managers. The League, among other things, sponsors an annual state-wide convention, hosts semiannual conferences in northern and southern California, and encourages frequent county meetings. The effect of these activities is to lessen the parochialism of the city managers and to provide them with a set of general norms to guide public policy making.

Table 1   Key career choices and experiences of San Francisco Bay Area city managers

Career Patterns	Percentage of City Managers (N = 59)
College Education (BA Completed)	78 (46)
Social Science Major	58 (34)
MA Work (or Law School)	44 (26)
Appointment Outside of City Staff	76 (45)
Prior City Management Experience When Appointed	68 (40)

The second reason for policy role agreement lies in the sequence of career choices and experiences common to many managers. Though not prescribed by a legally sanctioned professional education or apprenticeship, a set of common recruitment and socialization patterns now characterize the city manager. Furthermore, all evidence indicates that these patterns are becoming increasingly important criteria in city manager appointments.[14]

City managers tend to be college educated, usually with an undergraduate major in the social sciences—the most popular being political science. Especially, the younger managers have begun or completed MA work in public administration. For example, a manager in his early thirties gave this response: "While I was at University of California, I had intended to go to law school. For my undergraduate major in political science, I

[13]Banfield and Wilson, op. cit., p. 174.
[14]See, for example, *Directory of City Managers 1964*, published by International City Managers' Association (1964), pp. 6–19.

picked public administration as an option. During my senior year, I became acquainted with Howard Gardner of the League of California Cities. I took a seminar from him and decided that this was the field for me. Upon graduation, I did a year of graduate work at UC in public administration." And it is at graduate school where the prospective city manager is exposed to professional concepts, emphases, and values. (See Table 1.)

Two other patterns reinforce a comparable policy ideology. One is that most city managers are appointed from outside the city staff. And when appointed, they usually have had previous city management experience. Because most city councils review many applicants before hiring a manager, these professional credentials of mobility and experience loom as important. It should also be added that the high turnover rate—average tenure in a city is less than five years—further encourages a cosmopolitan rather than a local policy perspective. These career choices and experiences should fashion a set of general norms to guide participation in the public policy process.

The third and final reason—the city manager as a policy actor has been the subject of continuous exhortation. The two most important sources are the International City Managers' Association and the municipal journals. The ICMA, parent body of the city manager profession, circulates good government memoranda and pamphlets. Probably though, the most conspicuous and influential exhorters are the municipal magazines: *American City, Mayor and Manager, National Civic Review, Public Management, Western City*. These magazines repeatedly tell the city manager how he can or should be a more active and effective policy maker.

Any content analysis of commonplace themes would reveal almost unanimous agreement that the city manager should be a policy innovator and leader. As an innovator, the expectation emphasis is on new programs, policies, or problems. And as a leader, the focus is on the manager as a change agent, a professional activist responsible for making what Selznick calls critical decisions.

To examine the policy role expectations held by the city managers, we used nine closed questions. These items were designed to discover the direction and content of city manager defined policy role conceptions.[15] We asked: "Now, ever since the council-manager plan was first adopted, there has been much disagreement over what a city manager should or should not do. Here are nine questions on the job of being a city manager. Read each question and then decide which one of the four answers most closely describes how you feel—do you strongly agree, tend to agree, tend to disagree, or strongly disagree?" (See Table 2 for a recapitulation of results.)

---

[15]The policy expectation items were devised and selected from an evaluation of the study's objectives and after a review of the city manager literature—in particular, some questions were drawn from Jeptha Carrell, *Role of the City Manager* (Kansas City, 1962).

Table 2   City manager expectations for the policy role

1. *City manager as policy innovator*
   (A city manager should assume leadership in shaping municipal policies.)

Agree			Disagree		
SA	TA	%	%	TD	SD
22	28	88	12	4	3

2. *City manager as policy advocate*
   (A city manager should advocate major changes in city policies.)

Agree			Disagree		
SA	TA	%	%	TD	SD
22	25	81	19	8	3

3. *City manager as budget consultant*
   (A city manager should consult with the council before drafting his own budget.)

Agree			Disagree		
SA	TA	%	%	TD	SD
4	14	31	69	17	23

4. *City manager as policy administrator*
   (A city manager should act as an administrator and leave policy matters to the council.)

Agree			Disagree		
SA	TA	%	%	TD	SD
4	9	22	78	33	12

5. *City manager as policy neutral*
   (A city manager should maintain a neutral stand on any issues on which the community is divided.)

Agree			Disagree		
SA	TA	%	%	TD	SD
4	10	24	76	33	11

6. *City manager as political advocate*
   (A city manager should advocate policies to which important parts of the community may be hostile.)

Agree			Disagree		
SA	TA	%	%	TD	SD
6	26	55	45	21	5

7. *City manager as political leader*
   (A city manager should work through the most powerful members of the community to achieve policy goals.)

Agree			Disagree		
SA	TA	%	%	TD	SD
8	23	53	47	18	9

8. *City manager as political recruiter*
   (A city manager should encourage people whom he respects to run for city council.)

Agree			Disagree		
SA	TA	%	%	TD	SD
4	21	44	56	20	12

9. *City manager as political campaigner*
   (A city manager should give a helping hand to good councilmen who are coming up for re-election.)

Agree			Disagree		
SA	TA	%	%	TD	SD
1	14	25	75	33	11

The level of consensus among city managers on many policy expectations is striking. While some disagreement exists, most city managers see themselves as active participants in the public policy process.[16] To be specific, on items 1–5, there is overwhelming agreement that the city manager should exercise executive leadership. And policy leadership is viewed as more than the staff role of advice giving. As expressed by one manager:

> A city manager is obligated to bring his expertise, experience, and ability to the council. He should actively take part in policy recommendations. Common sense would seem to indicate that a full-time manager trained and experienced in municipal affairs should make recommendations to what is essentially an amateur, part-time council.

The managers believe they should be policy innovators and policy advocates. The municipal budget is regarded as an executive budget—and, as is often the case, many of the more important community decisions are embodied in that executive budget. Three out of four managers reject the classic administration-politics dichotomy which assigns the manager only administrative responsibilities. And managers feel they should be involved in the resolution of controversial issues, which means taking a position rather than retiring behind the cloak of professional neutrality.

Somewhat less agreement is evinced on more politicized and community related activities (item 6–9). On matters of community controversy, especially when there is powerful opposition, city managers are more reluctant to act as policy advocates. Nevertheless, over one half of the managers believed they should take policy positions even in the face of important opposition. As to possible tactics of manager involvement in controversial questions, one manager responded as follows:

> The real distinction is what you should do publicly in contrast to what you must do privately. A city manager should be more than a council adviser. He should urge and recommend policy. He should write policies for others to present. A city manager should definitely lead behind the scenes. But he should not lead publicly. . . . I think a city manager should be a faceless man in the community.

As to political leadership vis-à-vis the community power structure, a comparable distribution resulted. A slight majority of managers felt that the city manager should be a community leader and not simply a municipal executive, that he should work directly with the influential people of the community to facilitate the achievement of policy goals. Perhaps a more significant indicator of the strong policy role adopted by many managers is the normative expectation among 40 percent of the

[16]See Ronald O. Loveridge, "Role Orientations of an Urban Policy Maker," Dittoed Paper, University of California, Riverside (1965).

managers that they should "encourage people . . . to run for city council." In other words, 25 out of 58 respondents believe a proper function of the city manager is to influence the cast of legislators. But, finally, there is overall agreement on one prohibition: a city manager should not get involved in the political campaigns of city councilmen—though some city managers privately said they have written speeches and planned strategies for incumbent councilmen. Yet, in general, the one political activity most managers believe they should avoid is electioneering. Beyond this, the city manager has apparently few normative restrictions on the breadth or style of his involvement in the public policy process. The expectation portrait of the city manager's policy role that emerges, therefore, from the distributions of the nine questions is that of a strong political executive, expected to exert policy leadership on most demands or issues before the civic agenda.[17]

IV. INTRAPOSITION CONSENSUS AND THE POLICY ROLE: CITY COUNCILMEN

If a city manager also shapes his policy activities by taking into account the expectations of others with whom he interacts, no "other" is likely to be more concerned with or important to the city manager's policy role than the city council.[18] The policy-making style and discretion of the manager are, for one thing, largely contingent upon the council. And because the manager is dependent on council acceptance of his innovative and leadership activities, the city council should be able to exert strong demands on him for conformity to its goals, interests, and norms.

But why should the council be so crucial for the policy role of city managers? For most policies are, by and large, initiated from sources outside the council, and councils themselves tend to demonstrate little political leadership. As observed by one writer: "The evidence now available does not show the council to be a very strong agency and its major power does appear to reside in the fact that its acquiescence is needed."[19] Nevertheless, the council is still the critical group with whom the city manager must interact. Perhaps of most importance, the city manager's career depends on the desires and satisfactions of the legislative body, namely the city council. At any time, the city manager can be dismissed by the council. The success of the manager depends on his rapport with the council, itself a product of highly personalized relations. In council meetings,

[17]For a general description of the "most essential and characteristic functions" of a chief executive, see Edward Banfield, "The Training of the Executive," in *Public Policy*, eds. Carl Friedrich and Seymour Harris (Cambridge, Massachusetts, 1960), pp. 27–28.
    [18]For further and more detailed explanation, see Ronald O. Loveridge, "City Manager and Role Analysis" (unpublished doctoral dissertation, Stanford University, 1965), pp. 123–127.
    [19]Duane Lockard, *The Politics of State and Local Government* (New York, 1963), p. 325.

informal working sessions, private meetings, or personal communications, the manager is subject to the continuous face-to-face influence of the council. On top of that, managers spend an estimated 30 to 40 percent of their time in meetings with the council, carrying out instructions of the council, and preparing reports for the council.

To examine city councilmen's expectations, we used both interview and questionnaire data. Before proceeding to analysis, we must comment on a problem of inference. First, it is unlikely that the expectation demands of the council are the sum of the expectations of city councilmen; certain councilmen, for instance, are more important than others. And second, the expectations of councils vary from city to city; that is, in one city the council may expect the city manager to act as public leader and chief executive, while in another he may be expected to act as the chief administrator and council errand boy. Nevertheless, for lack of an alternative measure and because of the emphasis on general expectations, we will use the combined responses of city councilmen to measure the direction and content of their expectations for the city manager's policy role.

The focus first is on the general functional expectations expressed by city councilmen to one open-ended question: "Now, what about the city manager? What should he do, or not do, to be most effective in his relations with the Council? How about on policy matters?" Responses were coded into sanctioned policy activities for the city manager, with up to five major functional expectations counted per councilman. (See Table 3.)

Table 3   Councilmen expectations for policy role of city manager

Expectations for Manager	Percentage of Councilmen Who Mention Each Expectation (N = 348)	
Be a Good Administrator	45	(156)
Leave Policy (and Politics) to Council	43	(148)
Give Good Advice	41	(142)
Keep Council Informed	34	(119)
Work with Council as a Policy Team	26	(091)
Identify Policy Problems	24	(085)
Be a Good Diplomat for City	22	(078)
Be a Good Public Relations Man for Council	19	(066)
Be a Professional	19	(065)
Avoid Intra-Council Politics	13	(044)

The policy image held by councilmen for the city manager seems much closer to a staff administrator than a political executive. The four most frequently mentioned expectations clearly support this interpretation. The city manager is first to be a good administrator; that is, he should maintain a smooth-running city administration and effectively carry out council policy. Second, in one way or another, many councilmen said a city manager should avoid direct involvement in the policy or political process of the city. Sometimes a councilman would curtly reply, "Carry out policies as determined by the council majority. Period." More commonly, however, councilmen would find cause to point out the subordinate or adviser role of the manager. The priority given to the third and fourth expectations again tends to stress the adviser role of the manager. He should be prepared to answer all questions and be able to give first-rate policy advice and to keep the council informed on all problems facing the city. The most accepted policy role as generalized by city councilmen for the city manager is that of the staff officer hired to give advice and information on city affairs as well as to implement council-passed policy.

Perhaps a better measure of the expectation map of city councilmen would be closed items, comparable to those asked of city managers. To this end, we will examine the results to nine general expectation questions. We asked: "Here are some statements which reflect different viewpoints about the job of city manager or top administrator. We would like to know how you feel about these viewpoints. Would you please read each one and then check just how much you generally agree or disagree with it?" (See Table 4 for a recapitulation of results.)

Again, most councilmen seem agreed upon the policy image of the city manager as a staff administrator as opposed to a political executive. Particularly noteworthy is that councilmen reveal greatest consensus on the classic dichotomy between politics and administration. To most councilmen, the city manager is viewed as the administrator, the council, the policy maker. Overall, the councilmen delimit the proper policy activities of the manager to those of council adviser. They object to claims of community or political leadership. A majority of councilmen even oppose any involvement which is represented as policy innovation or policy leadership. And, finally, one of the most vigorously pressed prerogatives of the city managers is that of the executive budget—which in fact is—written into the statutes or charters of many of the cities. However, even on this activity, only a hairline majority favored such arrangement. City councilmen, then, tend to define the policy role in a "narrow context" with the primary emphasis on the city manager as a source of information, not as a policy—much less political—leader.

V. EXPECTATIONS FOR THE POLICY ROLE: AN INTERPOSITION COMPARISON AND INTERPRETATION

City managers and city councilmen hold pointedly different conceptions for the policy role of the city manager. In itself, the lack of interposition consensus should not be unexpected. For role consensus between most focal and counter positions is far from unanimous. What is important is the kind and extent of disagreement. City managers largely share the policy values of the political executive—they are interested in formulating and defining the purposes of city government. City councilmen, for the most part, regard the city manager as their man in city hall who administers the city and who is on tap for advice, information, and recommendations. We thus have two quite dissimilar sets of expectations of how the city manager should function as policy maker.[20]

For two sets of political actors who interact continuously on a face-to-face basis the general lack of consensus is surprising. To highlight this conflict in policy role ideologies, let us look at Table 5 and examine the differences in responses to six comparable items answered by both managers and city councilmen.

The disagreement percentages illustrate clearly the conflicting role definitions for the manager's policy activities. These disagreements center on the fundamental character of the city manager's participation in the policy process and, as such, cannot be dismissed as unimportant role conflicts. Rather, it would appear that managers and councilmen subscribe to two contrasting views of the city manager's policy role.

Whether attributing the policy role conflicts between managers and councilmen to differences in socialization and recruitment, development of language, standards of evaluation, or reference groups, the tendency of most writers is to dismiss such role disagreements as "image versus reality" conflicts. That is, while councilmen justify and explain the council-manager prerogatives in terms of the image of the manager as dealing primarily with administrative matters and leaving policy matters to the council, city managers, in practice, participate in most stages of the community policy process.[21] Furthermore, most political scientists see the city manager as acquiring actual leadership and dominance in the determination of public policy. From this conclusion, the city manager is continuously exhorted to "assume new responsibilities for leadership." An example—John Pfiffner writes: "From now on the city manager will have to become more of a human or social engineer and less of an efficiency engineer in the traditional sense."[22] Almost all of these evaluations or recommendations ignore or

---

[20]Between managers and councilmen the clash in role conceptions appears consistent regardless of the structural or cultural characteristics of cities. Such variables as, for example, city size, socio-economic status, or even political values do not generally change the conflicting interpretations of the policy role of the city manager.

[21]For example, B. James Kweder in a study of 21 North Carolina cities states: "The perceptions of managers, mayors, and councilmen of the policy-making process in their cities clearly refutes the idea that policy making is something performed exclusively by the council. Not only do the managrers participate actively in the process, they participate actively in every one of the six phases into which the policy-making process has been divided for this study. Moreover, in many cities the manager clearly emerges as the person who has the greatest influence over what is happening at every stage of the policy-making process." James Kweder, *The Roles of the Manager, Mayor, and Councilmen in Policy Making* (Chapel Hill, North Carolina, 1965), p. 31.

[22]John Pfiffner, "The Job of the City Manager," *Public Management* (June, 1961), p. 123.

Table 4   City councilmen expectations for the city manager policy role

1. *City manager as policy administrator*
   (The city manager should act as an administrator and leave policy matters to the council.)

Agree			Disagree		
A	TA	%	%	TD	D
205	54	87	13	32	7

2. *City manager as political leader*
   (The city manager should work through the most powerful members of the community to achieve his policy goals.)

Agree			Disagree		
A	TA	%	%	TD	D
9	26	12	88	85	176

3. *City manager as political campaigner*
   (The city manager should give a helping hand to good councilmen who are coming up for re-election.)

Agree			Disagree		
A	TA	%	%	TD	D
21	33	18	82	48	195

4. *City manager as policy adviser*
   (The city manager should work informally with councilmen to prepare important policy proposals.)

Agree			Disagree		
A	TA	%	%	TD	D
141	95	80	20	27	33

5. *City manager as political recruiter*
   (The city manager should encourage people whom he respects to run for the council.)

Agree			Disagree		
A	TA	%	%	TD	D
31	36	23	77	63	165

6. *City manager as policy neutral*
   (The city manager should maintain a neutral stand on any issues which may divide the community.)

Agree			Disagree		
A	TA	%	%	TD	D
121	68	64	36	45	61

7. *City manager as policy innovator*
   (The city manager should assume leadership in shaping municipal policies.)

Agree			Disagree		
A	TA	%	%	TD	D
48	77	42	58	59	112

8. *City manager as political advocate*
   (The city manager should advocate policies even if important parts of the community seem hostile to them.)

Agree			Disagree		
A	TA	%	%	TD	D
80	57	46	54	72	86

9. *City manager as budget consultant*
   (The city manager should consult with the Council before drafting his own budget proposal.)

Agree			Disagree		
A	TA	%	%	TD	D
91	53	49	51	60	92

Table 5   Policy expectation disagreements between managers and council

1. City manager as policy administrator

City Managers (%)		Percent Disagreement	City Councilmen (%)	
Agree	Disagree	%	Agree	Disagree
22	78	66	88	12

2. City manager as policy innovator

City Managers (%)		Percent Disagreement	City Councilmen (%)	
Agree	Disagree	%	Agree	Disagree
88	12	46	42	58

3. City manager as political leader

City Managers (%)		Percent Disagreement	City Councilmen (%)	
Agree	Disagree	%	Agree	Disagree
53	47	41	12	88

4. City manager as policy neutral

City Managers (%)		Percent Disagreement	City Councilmen (%)	
Agree	Disagree	%	Agree	Disagree
24	76	40	64	36

5. City manager as political recruiter

City Managers (%)		Percent Disagreement	City Councilmen (%)	
Agree	Disagree	%	Agree	Disagree
44	56	21	23	77

6. City manager as budget consultant

City Managers (%)		Percent Disagreement	City Councilmen (%)	
Agree	Disagree	%	Agree	Disagree
31	69	18	49	51

discount the policy expectations of the council for the city manager. This writer, on the other hand, contends that the policy role conflict between the manager and council is central to any explanation of the city manager's behavior as a policy maker.

To judge the importance of the policy role conflict, let us look at two kinds of responses made by city managers. First, the council is the city manager's most important reference group. One prominent manager has explained the relationship in these words: "I regard myself as the hired hand of the city council. In the last analysis I don't work for the public; I don't work for the individual citizens of the city; I work for the council." To identify the audience before whom a city manager tries to maintain or enhance his standing, the question was asked:

A city manager's reputation is said to be dependent on the approval of a number of different publics. Some publics, however, are probably more important than others. How would you rank the following on the importance to your reputation as a city manager:

administrative staff_____	council_____
fellow city managers_____	community groups_____
public-at-large_____	professional management groups_____

Of the 58 managers who responded, 42 managers (73%) ranked the council first and an additional 13 (23%) ranked it second. The data suggest that city managers are very sensitive to and dependent upon favorable council appraisal and that no other reference group is a serious rival to the council.[23]

Second, perhaps the most direct measure of the frequency and intensity of the policy role conflict can be found in the expressed frustrations of city managers. In field interviews with a sample of 40 Bay Area managers, the question was asked: "What would you say are the two most pressing problems or frustrations you face as city manager?" Although responses could run the gamut from community problems to policy matters to personnel questions or to more personal feelings, over 60 percent (25) of the managers identified conflict with the city council as one of their two most important problems or frustrations. Conflict between managers and councils can result from sources other than policy role conflict; however, upon a rereading of the interview protocols, the main frustration of the managers appears to center on various aspects of the policy process.[24] For example, here are several illustrative responses:

> I find it frustrating that you have a highly trained professional, proficient in efficient and economic operations of city government, subject to the approval of a lay council. A group of men who typically have less education, who are affected by political pressures, who are relatively uninformed, and who invoke personalities will often reject almost out of hand ideas carefully developed and presented by the city manager.

> The council is my number one gripe. When anything goes wrong, I am to blame—it is my judgment, my policies. I am the scapegoat when something goes wrong. . . . The council, too, often feels it is the expert on everything. Yet, they spend little time in studying problems.

> The first problem would be the city council. Councilmen are not on the council long enough to become oriented into the job, to become aware of the need for open-minded evaluation of problems. . . . Councilmen often demonstrate the inability to recognize the long-range implications of some of their actions.

Effects of the differences in policy conceptions between managers and councilmen take myriad forms.[25] Tentative analysis of available data

[23]Gladys Kammerer suggests that elected mayors or political bosses would also be important interpreters of the manager's policy role. See Gladys Kammerer, "Role Diversity of City Managers," *Administrative Science Quarterly* (March, 1964), pp. 421–442.

[24]For example, Jeptha Carrell distinguishes between six major sources of conflict between managers and councilmen: power prerogatives, personality clashes, political setting, policy-expediency differences, manager's inflexibility and rectitude, and communication and cognition difficulties. See Jeptha Carrell, "The City Manager and His Council: Sources of Conflict," *Public Administration Review* (December, 1962), pp. 203–208.

[25]Obviously the policy environment of city politics is inordinately more complex than the interactions between manager and councilmen. The city is not a blank check on which the manager and his council can together or separately write their policy preferences. For an excellent essay on why cities adopt varied decisions and policies, see Robert Alford, "The Comparative Study of Urban Politics," in *Urban Research and Policy Planning*, eds. Leo Schnore and Henry Fagin (Beverly Hills, California, 1967), pp. 263–304. Also, see James Q. Wilson, *City Politics and Public Policy* (New York, 1968); and a recent evaluative venture in the community power literature, Richard Merelman, "On the Neo-elitist Critique of Community Power," *American Political Science Review* (June, 1968), pp. 451–460.

suggests the direction and character of certain general consequences. The city manager in confronting the gap between personal and council-sanctioned policy activities cannot react as an elected chief executive. Rather, publicly and to the council, he presents himself as a professional administrator. Policy activities of any legislative significance have to be camouflaged accordingly or carried out in an informal and indirect manner. Thus, it is behind the scenes that the city manager strives to build, utilize, and husband his political resources to influence public policy decisions.

More important, evidence indicates that the normative expectations of city councilmen influence *how* the city manager expends his political resources on *what* policy questions. A pronounced impact on the direction and foci of policy innovation and leadership activities by city managers is the result. The overall effect was well explained in one city manager study as follows:

> Managers were in substantial agreement on the areas where they should push hard for managerial policies and the areas where they should remain neutral or stay out altogether. They agreed that managers should assert themselves strongly on technical questions where the best policy is strongly or entirely dependent on factual data. They also strongly defended the responsibility of managers in fields of internal management.
>
> The areas where the managers play a more limited role or stay out altogether include: partisan political issues; moral and regulatory issues; public versus private ownership; the internal operations of the city council; relations with independent boards and commissions and other governments, except as guided by council instructions; and issues where the city council is divided within itself.[26]

The city manager, in brief, is most likely to act as a political executive primarily in "safe" areas. But on policy problems of a controversial variety, he is expected by the council to act as staff adviser. In many ways, therefore, the city manager is a consensus politician par excellence; high priority is given to avoiding friction, criticisms, or opposition. Bounded by council sanctions and alert to their anticipated reactions, the city manager cannot initiate, fix priorities, or bargain for acceptance of policies as he believes he should. The city manager cannot introduce major policy decisions onto the civic agenda which do not have the implicit approval of the city council. Moreover, besides a real antagonism to the city manager as a community change agent, the city council expects the city manager to participate in a policy decision in accordance with the wishes and prejudices of the council —and not the abstract values of the public interest or of the city manager profession. One councilman put the expectations of many into these words:

> The job of the city manager is carrying out the administration of city affairs within the policies laid down by the council. He shouldn't become involved in

[26]Clarence Ridley, *The Role of the City Manager in Policy Formulation* (Chicago, 1958).

the political atmosphere of the community. For his job is carrying out council policies regardless of his personal feelings. . . . The council is an elected group supposedly reflecting the desires of the electorate. The manager is appointed by the council—it's a paid position; he is an employee of the city council!

VI. CONCLUSION

City managers reveal a near consensus on the appropriate policy role orientation. Almost all managers believe they should participate in the initiation, formulation, and presentation of policy proposals. The textbook stereotype of the city manager as viewing himself as an "efficiency and economy" administrator is no longer accurate. Various changes ranging from differences in socialization and recruitment patterns to the complex needs and requirements of city governments have worked together to fashion a new set of general norms to guide the policy behavior of the city manager, namely those of the political executive.

In contrast, city councilmen cleave to the image of the city manager as a staff administrator. The city manager's participation in the policy process tends to be delimited to those activities of adviser and political agent for the council. For city councilmen do not see the city manager as an independent policy participant; quite the contrary, he is more likely to be conceived as the "servant" of the council, acting at their pleasure and for their interests.

Probably the most important finding of this paper is the unusually dissimilar conceptions of the policy role held by city managers and city councilmen. Anyone who occupies a particular position has role partners who are differently located in the social structure and who, as a result, have differing values and expectations. But the kind and extent of disagreement between managers and councilmen—given the power of councilmen, their close and continuous interaction with the city manager, and the relative visibility of the city manager's policy activities—make this incidence of role conflict especially crucial. How the city manager resolves his conception of the political executive with the council's conception of the staff administrator probably takes a number of forms. We have developed two. One is the camouflaging of policy activity or confining all such activity to behind-the-scenes politicking. The other is ready involvement in "safe" policy areas and cautious retreat or withdrawal from more controversial questions. This question of role resolution deserves more extensive and systematic analysis because it explains much of the dynamics of the policy exchange between managers and councilmen.[27]

"If responsible management of economic development and the find-

---

[27]For two excellent statements on the importance and mechanisms of the resolution of role conflict, see Robert Goods, "A Theory of Role Strain," *American Sociological Review* (August, 1960), pp. 483–495; and Robert Merton, *Social Theory and Social Structure* (New York, 1957), pp. 225–386.

ing of the resources necessary to conduct desired programs for economic and social improvements are to be successfully achieved, we shall need," writes Duane Lockard, "great political ingenuity, courage, and leadership. ... In short, the courage to plan ahead, the wit and leadership required to make enough people see the need of facing the realities of mass society may turn out to be the crucial challenge facing state and local government."[28] The city manager met the demand for improved administration of city goods and services—and still does. However, the data we have examined raise doubts as to the probable success of the manager in the areas of social conflict and economic progress and more generally the quality of city life. Though the city manager shares the values of the political executive tempered often with the best training that academics can provide, the role collision between manager and council severely handicaps his exercise of innovative public leadership on nonroutine decisions.[29]

[28]Lockard, op. cit., pp. 20, 22.

[29]To foster community leadership, California managers now frequently propose an elected mayor or at least a mayor with greater responsibility and authority. This change violates a basic tenet of the Model City Charter of the National Municipal League but is seen as necessary to meet emerging community conflicts. A strong mayor—the managers hope—can speak out on political issues, build support for new policy directions, and focus attention on social questions. (To a 1968 ICMA Goals Questionnaire administered by the California League of Cities, almost 70 percent of the managers who responded said they favored a strong mayor who can exercise political leadership.)

THE POLICY-MAKING PROCESS: JUDICIAL RULE-MAKING AND NORM-ENFORCEMENT

Almost all important political conflict is, at some point in its evolution, translated into terms that make it susceptible to the adversary proceedings of the courts. Individuals, groups, political parties, and government officials whose claims are not satisfied by state legislatures or city councils, or by governors, mayors, and other administrative officials often have the option of presenting their grievances for judicial consideration. Thus, the courts have many opportunities to resolve disputes, to redistribute resources, to enforce the norms of society, and, generally, to influence policy in significant ways. Apart from its importance in the policy-making process, the court system itself possesses many other status and material benefits to dispense to those who actually play a role in the administration of justice.

These are among the points treated by Wallace S. Sayre and Herbert Kaufman in their discussion of judicial politics in New York City. The authors describe the city's judicial structure, the broader implications of court decisions, and the roles judges play in the settlement of disputes and the distribution of rewards. They note that judges are themselves contestants for the "prizes" government has to offer, suggesting that jurists enjoy a somewhat unique position compared to other governmental decision-makers. They are more insulated from the types of control to which other officials must submit, and their independence is accented by the formality of the judicial process and by certain ethical norms that other governmental actors and the public accept. In New York City the courts and the political parties enjoy a symbiotic relationship. The courts aid the parties by dispensing jobs to loyal party workers, adding to party coffers, and protecting party interests, while the parties provide ambitious lawyers and resourceful District Leaders with the passkeys to judicial office.

Sayre and Kaufman are not concerned with delineating the significance of the courts in the formulation of public policy, a task that Kenneth M. Dolbeare undertakes in his selection. Dolbeare examines court decisions in an urban county near New York City to determine the courts' impact on major controversies within the county. He is interested primarily in analyzing the areas of public policy that are subject to court influence and in estimating the proportion of the courts' attention devoted to major, as opposed to less salient, political issues. Conflicts within the county over zoning and land use, education, taxation, nominations and elections, and local governmental organization are found to occur with the greatest regularity and intensity. The extent of court influence varies among issue areas, but it appears to be most significant in shaping governmental organization and the locus of power within government. Dolbeare next turns to the courts' impact on disputes in three substantially different types of communities within the county. He finds considerable variation in the quality and direction of court influence, with the courts tending to reinforce the social, economic, and political norms of each community. Clearly, however, the judiciary is not called upon to adjudicate the full range of issues that intrude upon county and local politics.

S. Sidney Ulmer is also interested in the courts' contribution to the policy-making process, but his "laboratory" is the state of Michigan, and his observations are centered specifically on the State Supreme Court's handling of workmen's compensation cases. Ulmer points out that the Michigan Supreme Court operates within a highly politicized context and that the political party affiliation of its justices is sometimes the critical variable in the disposition of cases reaching the Court. Given the ideological orientation of the two parties in Michigan, Ulmer expects to find—and does find— Democrats to be considerably more sympathetic than their Republican colleagues to workers' claims in workmen's compensation cases. He notes that during the period 1954 to 1960 a sharp increase in the percentage of cases decided in favor of workers' claims paralleled the increase in Democratic representation on the state's highest court. In all ten nonunanimous compensation decisions handed down by the Court from 1958 to 1960, for example, the eight justices consistently split along party lines, with five Democrats outvoting three Republicans in virtually every instance. Thus, the judges' party affiliation, combined with their apparent homogeneity of social attitudes along partisan lines, was critical to the outcome of a particular class of disputes.

CHAPTER SIXTEEN

COURTS
AND POLITICS
IN NEW YORK CITY

WALLACE S. SAYRE AND HERBERT KAUFMAN

THE PLACE OF THE COURTS IN THE POLITICAL CONTEST

Their Dual Role

Like all other governmental officials and employees engaged in the quest for the stakes of political contest, judges and their staffs are both claimants and distributors. The special character of the judicial process sets them apart from those whose primary functions are the formulation and management of government programs, so they are most conveniently treated separately. Nevertheless, they are participants in the political contest, involved as fully as all the others who take part in it. Many individuals and groups expend a great deal of energy trying to influence court personnel (from judges down); judges and other court personnel, in turn, exert all the influence they can bring to bear upon some other contestants when certain questions are to be decided. Judges and their staffs are not without their modes of exercising influence, nor are they invulnerable to the pressures of others.

No Courts Are "Local"

In a strict sense, there is no such thing as a wholly local court in New York State. As regards federal courts, this point requires no elaboration. As regards all other courts, even the lowest ones in the state judicial hierarchy are governed by state legislation covering jurisdiction, procedure, and method of selection and removal and tenure of judges; moreover, all courts are at least

Reprinted with permission of publisher and authors from Wallace S. Sayre and Herbert Kaufman, *Governing New York City: Politics in the Metropolis* (New York: The Russell Sage Foundation, 1960), pp. 522–54. Mr. Sayre is Eaton Professor of Public Administration at Columbia University. Mr. Kaufman is a Senior Fellow of The Brookings Institution's Governmental Studies Program.

mentioned, and many of the higher ones are treated quite specifically, in the state constitution itself. Even most nonjudicial court personnel lie beyond the powers of the city; some are provided for in statutes, some are placed loosely under the jurisdiction of the state Civil Service Department, and many are entirely under the discretion of the judges they serve. Most court expenses are mandated upon the city, with judicial salaries usually set by state law and nonjudicial salaries often fixed by the judges themselves. While the city pays, it does not itself decide what the size of its bill will be. Currently, the court system costs the city over $30 million a year.

To be sure, the city has some discretion. State law permits it to fix the number and the boundaries of the districts of Magistrates' Courts, for example, and to set the salaries of these judges and administrative staffs. And the city is permitted to and does increase the salaries of many judges over and above the figures set in state law. The power of the state over the court system, however, is so extensive, and the measure of freedom allowed the city is so restricted, that all courts other than federal are generally regarded, and most realistically considered, as organs of the state.

The Court System in New York City

Jurisdictions   Although it is something of an oversimplification, it may be said that there are in New York City eight courts of original jurisdiction, three of which are criminal courts, three of which are civil, and two special.

Table 1   Federal courts of importance to New York City, January 1, 1959

Court (Jurisdiction national unless otherwise noted)	Total number of judges	Number of judges from New York City[a]
U.S. Supreme Court	9	..
U.S. Court of Claims	5	..
U.S. Court of Customs and Patent Appeals	5	..
U.S. Customs Court	9	..
U.S. Court of Appeals, Second Circuit[b]	6	4
U.S. District Court, Southern District[c]	18	19
U.S. District Court, Eastern District[d]	6	5
Tax Court of the United States	16	1
Total	74	29

[a]Estimated   [b]Connecticut, New York, Vermont.
[c]Counties of Bronx, New York, Columbia, Dutchess, Greene, Orange, Putnam, Rockland, Sullivan, Ulster, and Westchester.
[d]Counties of Kings, Queens, Nassau, Richmond, and Suffolk.

The criminal courts, listed in ascending order according to the severity of the maximum penalties they may impose, are the Magistrates' Courts, the Court of Special Sessions, and the County Courts.[1] The civil courts, arranged

[1]Called the Court of General Sessions in New York County.

Table 2 State courts and judgeships of importance to New York City, January 1, 1959, arranged in ascending order by size of territorial jurisdiction

Territory	Civil	Criminal	Other
Less than county	118 Municipal Court: 28 districts, plus special "parts"	68 Magistrates' Courts: 32 district and special courts, plus special units 50	6
County	29	23 County Courts (in New York County—i.e., Manhattan—called Court of General Sessions)	Surrogates' Courts
More than county, less than city	63a Trial, Appellate, and Special Terms of the Supreme Court. First (New York and Bronx Counties), Second (Kings and Richmond Counties), and part of Tenth (Queens County) Judicial Districts are in New York City	63a Appellate Division of the Supreme Court. First Department and part of the Second Department are in New York City. Must be sitting Supreme Court Justices.	
City	69 City Court	22 Court of Special Sessions	24 Domestic Relations Court 23
State	15 Court of Appeals	7 Court of Appeals	8 Court of Claims
Total	294a		

aDoes not include vacancies or justices from Nassau and Suffolk Counties (that are in the Tenth Judicial District), which together total 12 seats.

in ascending order according to the authorized maximum dollar amount of claimed damages they may handle, are the Municipal Court, the City Court, and the Trial and Special "Terms" (divisions) of the Supreme Court, which also possesses, but rarely exercises, jurisdiction in criminal cases. The special courts are the Surrogates' Courts, for wills, estates, adoptions, and guardianships, and the Domestic Relations Court of the City of New York.

Appeals lie from these tribunals to either the Appellate Term of the Supreme Court, the Appellate Division of the Supreme Court, or the Court of Appeals. The Appellate Term hears appeals from the judgments of the Municipal Court and the City Court, and litigants may appeal further to the Appellate Division and ultimately to the Court of Appeals, the highest

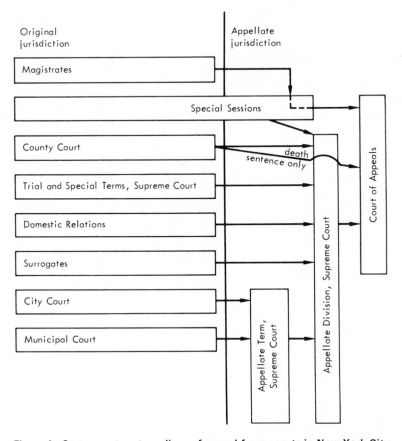

Figure 1. State court system : lines of appeal from courts in New York City

court in the state. With but two exceptions, appeals from all other courts lie to the Appellate Division, and hence to the Court of Appeals. The exceptions are appeals from decisions of magistrates, which lie to the Court of Special Sessions (making this a court of appellate as well as original jurisdiction) and thence directly to the Court of Appeals; and first-degree murder cases, which are appealed directly from the County Courts (the Court of General Sessions in New York County) to the Court of Appeals.

The vast bulk of the litigation in, or affecting, the city takes place within this hierarchy. In addition, however, there is a state Court of Claims that handles suits against the state, and the federal courts[2] that hear cases in which city residents and officers are frequently involved. By volume, the preponderance of litigation originating in or affecting the city that is handled in these special state courts and in the federal tribunals is substantially less than that disposed of in the courts discussed earlier, but they are in no sense less important, whether evaluated by the social and political consequences of their decisions or by their prominence in the government and politics of New York City.

The Manpower of the Judiciary   As of the beginning of 1959 there were 380 seats on the benches of all these courts of immediate relevance to the government and politics of New York City. A total of 271 of them are in

Table 3   **Mode of selection of judges**[a]

From wholly within city			*From a territory in which the city or a part of the city is contained*		*Total*
Appointed: By Mayor:			By Governor:		
	Magistrates	50	Court of Claims	8	
	Special Sessions	24	By President:		
	Domestic Relations	23	Federal Courts	74	
Total		97	Total	82	179
Elected: Municipal Court		68	New York Supreme Court	20[b]	
	City Court	22	New York Court of Appeals	7	
	County Court (and				
	General Sessions)	23			
	Surrogates'	6			
	New York Supreme				
	Court	55			
Total		174	Total	27	201
Grand Total		271		109	380

[a]Figures as of January 1, 1959.
[b]Although all 20 are elected from the Tenth Judicial District (Queens, Nassau, Suffolk Counties), 8 are regularly from Queens.

[2]The United States District Courts for the Southern District, in which New York and Bronx Counties lie, and for the Eastern District, in which the remaining three counties are located; the United States Court of Appeals for the Second Circuit; and the federal courts of nationwide jurisdiction, including the Court of Claims, the Court of Customs and Patent Appeals, the Customs Court, the Tax Court, and the Supreme Court itself.

districts wholly within the boundaries of the city and are therefore filled by city residents. The remaining 109 (including the 74 federal judgeships) have districts of which the whole city or sections of the city are part; of these, at least 44 places are occupied by city residents. There are thus 315 places currently held by New Yorkers. In the course of time, this figure varies somewhat because of the 109 seats from jurisdictions not wholly within the city. It rises as additional city residents are appointed to vacancies in this category, falls as city residents die or depart and are replaced by personnel from other parts of these areas. By and large, however, the total does not deviate extensively from the present one.

A great deal of maneuvering and bargaining attends the filling of any of the 380 places as New Yorkers of all factions of all parties compete with each other and with party organizations outside the city to obtain as many as they can of the 109 places on courts with jurisdiction extending beyond the city, and with each other alone for the 271 places inside the city. Not counting interim appointments to vacancies on elective courts, the Mayor appoints 97 of the 380 judges, the Governor, 8, the President, 74, for a total of 179. Of the 201 elected judges, 174 are elected from constituencies entirely within the city, 27 from constituencies extending beyond the city. Localism and popular election thus predominate in the composition of the judiciary in the courts discussed here.

Table 4   Constituencies of elective courts

Constituency	Court	Number of judges[a]
Smaller-than-county districts	Municipal Court	.. 68
Counties	County Courts	23
	Surrogates Court	6
	City Court	22
Larger than counties, smaller	Supreme Court[b]	51
than city (Judicial Districts)	First District	36
	Second District	19
	Tenth District	20
		75
Entire city		.. ..
Entire state	Court of Appeals	7
Total		201

[a]As of January 1, 1959.
[b]First District: New York and Bronx Counties; Second District: Kings and Richmond Counties; Tenth District: Queens, Nassau (L.I.) and Suffolk (L.I.) Counties. Only eight of the justices from this District currently come from Queens.

The Governmental Importance of the Courts

Collectively, the decisions of all these courts and of all these judges mean a great deal to the community as a whole. The freedom, the security, the welfare, the health, the fortunes of people are greatly affected by what the judiciary does; the impact of 380 judges is considerable. Moreover, there are so many of them that they are of enormous significance to the parties, to the institutions of the legal profession, and to the careers of lawyers. Finally, when they act in concert in pursuit of their common interests, the judges often have major effects on particular segments of public policy. In all these respects, they are part of the political and governmental processes.

JUDGES AS DISTRIBUTORS OF PRIZES

As Umpires Between Other Contestants

In particular, judges settle disputes—disputes involving money, services, office, reputations, and even life and liberty, disputes between litigants invoking governmental powers to implement their claims upon each other, upon the parties, and upon governmental officials and employees. Judicial decisions thus determine, in part, who gets what. Private citizens and nongovernmental groups may be contending with one another, or they may contest the action, or inaction, of officials or employees at any level of government. Government officials often bring suit against one another, or, when this is precluded by existing law (the city, for example, is unable to sue the state), may achieve the same effect by staging taxpayer suits. Law enforcement officers of all kinds represent the state in litigation with alleged law violators.

Table 5   Judicial salaries, January 1, 1959
In thousands of dollars

Court	Associate judge's salary	Presiding judge's salary
Magistrates'	$16	$19
Municipal	17	19
Special Sessions	19.5	21
Domestic Relations	19.5	21
Claims (New York State)	22	..
U.S. District	22.5	..
U.S. Tax	22.5	..
U.S. Customs	22.5	..
U.S. Claims	25.5	..
U.S. Circuit	25.5	..
U.S. Customs and Patents Appeals	25.5	..
County (and General Sessions)	34.5	..
Surrogates'	34.5a	..
Supreme Court (state)	34.5b	..
U.S. Supreme Court	35	35.5
Appellate Division	36.5c	38d
Court of Appeals	37.5e	40e

a$33,000 in Richmond.
b$21,000 by the state, the balance by the city or appropriate county.
c$23,000 by the state, the balance by the city or appropriate county.
d$23,500 by the state, the balance by the city or appropriate county.
eIncludes $5,000 for expenses.

Public officials and employees sometimes bring actions against their employers; the city, being a corporation rather than a "sovereign" power, is especially vulnerable to attacks of this kind. Voters, candidates, and party members frequently challenge party leaders—sometimes within their own parties, sometimes in other parties—in the courts. At one time or another, virtually every possible combination of those identified as contestants for the rewards of governmental action appears in the courts. And the judges, in deciding the questions at issue, in effect employ governmental authority in such a way as to allocate some of the prizes. Most of the time, judges are umpires rather than players. But, after all, how a contest comes out depends in large measure on what the umpires do.

As Interpreters of the Rules

Judicial decisions often do much more than settle the immediate question in litigation. They often determine the content and scope of the constitutional and statutory provisions . . . characterized as "the rules of the game," and they may sometimes upset state legislation, local legislation (far more frequently), or administrative rules and regulations, instead of merely invalidating a specific governmental act under a particular rule. The way in which judges dispose of election cases has far-reaching effects on the relationships among the parties and especially among the factions within parties. Judicial attitudes and actions of both kinds generally strengthen the positions of some contestants seeking to influence governmental policy and reduce the leverage of others—rarely does an interpretation of the rules of the game affect equally all who are concerned with them—sometimes regardless of what the judges intend or prefer, but effectively just the same. Thus, for example, when the courts construe narrowly the meaning of the phrase "government, property, and affairs of the city" in the Home Rule Act, the Home Rule Law, and the home rule provisions of the constitution . . . , they permit state officers to intervene more extensively in the governance of the city than a different construction of the language would allow. When they ruled that the principle of separation of powers does not apply to governments of cities,[3] they denied to the Mayor powers and immunities associated with the chief executives in Albany and Washington, particularly in his relations with the City Council. When they refused to invalidate inequalities of representation growing out of failure to reapportion the lines of the old aldermanic districts,[4] they buttressed the Democratic majority that benefited from the prevailing situation; when, on the other hand, they refused to hold proportional representation unconstitutional,[5] they strengthened the hands of the minority parties in the city. When they upheld the power of the city, under

[3]*Matter of La Guardia* v. *Smith*, 288 N.Y. 1 (1942).
[4]*People on Relation of Boyle* v. *Cruise*, 189 N. Y. Supp. 338 (1921).
[5]*Matter of Mooney* v. *Cohen*, 272 N.Y. 33 (1936).

permissive state legislation, to enact rent control laws,[6] they won the plaudits of the tenants and the condemnation of the landlords, and the net result was to increase the popularity of the Democratic officers who were responsible for the measure. When they declared municipal employees were subject to the federal income tax, the result from the point of view of these persons was a reduction in salary. It has been said the law is what the judges say it is; while this assertion, without qualification, is unquestionably an exaggeration, it reflects the fundamental truth of the proposition that the distribution of rewards among the contestants striving to influence governmental decisions is shaped to a large extent by what judges say the rules are.

As Appointing Officers

The 315 judges in or from the city are the formal appointing officers for several thousand employees constituting the nonjudicial staffs of the court system. The exact number of such appointees outside the competitive civil service is difficult to ascertain, but it apparently amounts to some four or five hundred. A relatively small number of appointees, in turn, are themselves appointing officers who formally name staffs of their own.

From the standpoint of salary, prestige, responsibility, and prominence, the most important of the judicial appointees are the County Clerks and the Public Administrators. The County Clerks, appointed and removable by the Appellate Division of the Supreme Court, receive $15,000 a year, except in Richmond, where the County Clerk gets $10,500; as custodians of all the books, records, and papers of their respective counties, and as clerks of their respective County Courts and of the Supreme Court when it sits in their counties, they have substantial staffs of their own. The Public Administrators are appointed by the Surrogates; they administer estates for which, for one reason or another, no other executor is available, and they have employees to assist them. The Public Administrator in New York County is paid $15,000; in Kings, $10,750; in Queens, $8,750; in Bronx, $4,000 and fees; in Richmond, $5,925.

Even the less visible positions, however, are frequently highly remunerative. The Chief Clerks of some of the courts receive as much as $20,000, while many fall in the range from $9,500 to $11,500, and their deputies normally are not far behind. Individual judges frequently have clerks who earn as much as $10,500, and some have confidential attendants in addition who get from $5,000 to $7,000. Three courts have Commissioners of Records in the same salary bracket as the clerks, and the Commissioners' deputies are proportionately well paid. There are also secretaries and law assistants who may be paid from $5,000 to $15,000. At the lower levels stand the clerks to the Justices of the Municipal Court, whose salaries

[6] *Molnar* v. *Curtin*, 273 App. Div. 322 (1948).

are about $3,800 a year for each, and some courtroom personnel. Many of these salaries are set by the judges themselves, and are mandated upon the city by state legislation. Furthermore, there are numerous appointments as commissioners in mortgage foreclosure which yield substantial fees, as administrators of the estates of persons who die intestate, as guardians, and as referees, all of these quite apart from the appointments to positions on the public payrolls. The judges are thus formal dispensers of jobs and benefits, many of them highly rewarding.

Not all the appointments to public positions are wholly at the discretion of the judges. Most are under the jurisdiction of the city or state personnel agencies, and the appointments must be made from lists of the names of people who have passed a competitive, or at least a qualifying, examination. Party considerations play significant parts in the selection of personnel for some posts. And the necessity of having competent personnel to perform many of the duties incidental to the judicial process is an imperative which cannot be ignored; hence, as a matter of common practice, law clerks in the federal courts, the Court of Appeals, the Appellate Division, and many parts of the State Supreme Court are selected by the judges from the top law school graduates without reference to political recommendations. So the judges are not without restrictions, both legal and practical, on their range of choice. But they are the formal appointing officers in all these instances, and their discretion, if not unlimited, is still quite broad. Their appointing authority places them squarely and prominently in the political struggle.

JUDGES AS CONTESTANTS: THE REWARDS OF JUDICIAL OFFICE

Honorific Rewards

Judges do not merely distribute the rewards of politics, however; they also share in them. They occupy places of great prestige; both in the courtroom and outside, they are deferred to by their legal colleagues, by the social groups in which they move, and by the rest of officialdom. Attorneys engaged in trial work constantly feel the weight of the authority of the jurists who sit on the bench above them, ruling on their efforts, controlling the procedure, and occasionally subjecting them to criticism and caustic comments to which they are in no position to reply. Even the most prominent lawyers appearing before the most obscure judges cannot escape the fact that the latter are their superiors in the courtroom. And the habits—indeed, the obligations—of deference accorded by tradition to those who sit in the highest positions in an old and esteemed profession carry over; in court and out, judges are automatically part of the legal élite, and it is not surprising that so many lawyers yearn to sit on the bench. The sense of the majesty of the law and of the judges who represent it is even more impressive to laymen involved in judicial proceedings, even for nothing more important than traffic viola-

Table 6   Judicial salaries, January 1, 1959, by salary range

Salary range	State judges		Federal judges		Total
$16,000–$19,999	All Magistrates	50			
	All Municipal Court justices	68			
	Associate Special Sessions justices	23			
	Associate Domestic Relations justices	22			
	Total	163			163
$20,000–$24,999	Chief Justice, Special Sessions	1	Judges of District Courts	24	
	Presiding justice, Domestic Relations	1	Judges of Tax Court	16	
	All judges, Court of Claims	8	Judges of Customs Court	9	
	Total	10	Total	49	59
$25,000–$29,999	Justices of City Court	22	Judges of Customs and Patent Appeals	5	
			Judges of Court of Claims	5	
			Judges of Circuit Courts	6	
	Total	22	Total	16	38
$30,000–$34,999	Judges of County Courts (and General Sessions)	23	..		
	Surrogates	6			
	Supreme Court Justices	62			
	Total	91			91
$35,000 or over	Justices of Appellate Division	13ᵃ	Justices of U.S. Supreme Court	9	
	Justices of Court of Appeals	7			
	Total	20	Total	9	29

ᵃPlus one from the Ninth Judicial District.

tions; the robes, the formalities, the authority of these men elevate them to something apart from ordinary human beings. Judges, like physicians, are surrounded by an honorific aura that to many is both awesome and wonderful.

Salary and Working Conditions

So, too, are the material rewards. Of the 380 judgeships treated in this analysis, none brings a salary of less than $16,000 a year, and one—the Chief Judge of the State Court of Appeals—earns (including a $5,000 allowance for expenses) $40,000. More specifically, 163 are paid $16,000 or over, but less than $20,000; 59 receive $20,000 or more, but less than $25,000; 38 have salaries of $25,000 or more, but less than $30,000; 91 get $30,000 or over, but less than $35,000; 29 are paid over $35,000. This puts virtually all of them in the highest income brackets in American officialdom, and many of them well above federal cabinet officers, Representatives, and Senators. Moreover, constitutional provisions forbid reductions in the salaries of judges while they are completing a term of office (not at all, therefore, for lifetime appointees while they continue to serve). Finally, many of them are covered by rather liberal pension plans.

Working conditions are relatively pleasant. The work is taxing, it is true, for the strain of intense concentration and heavy responsibility in the courtroom is wearing. Moreover, work in the courtroom is only part of the job; many additional hours are spent poring over briefs, perusing legal literature, and trying to achieve agreement between litigants in informal sessions in judges' chambers. Still, judges have greater freedom in allocating their time than many other officials. Court sessions do not normally begin until ten o'clock, and are commonly recessed by four in the afternoon. During the summer months, some courts virtually suspend operations, and some have only abbreviated sessions presided over by a small percentage of the full judicial staffs. Vacation periods are generous. Most judges have comfortable offices, adequate professional assistance, and ample secretarial help.

Table 7   Judicial terms of office

Term in years	Court	Number of judges	Per cent of total number
9	Claims (State)	8	2.1
10	Magistrates', Special Sessions, Domestic Relations, Municipal, City	187	49.2
12	U.S. Tax Court	16	4.2
14	County, General Sessions, Surrogates, Supreme (State), Court of Appeals	111a	29.2
Life	U.S. District, U.S. Customs, U.S. Circuit, U.S. Customs and Patent Appeals, U.S. Claims, U.S. Supreme	58	15.3
	Total	380	100.0

aIncludes those Supreme Court justices serving five-year terms in the Appellate Division.

Finally, to a larger extent than most other public officials, judges may be said to be their own bosses. To be sure, there are administrative and procedural requirements they must observe. And they may be assigned by their chief judge to categories of adjudication they find not especially attractive. Most important of all, the opinions of virtually every judge are subject to review by higher courts, and no judge likes to be reversed. Nevertheless, each judge is in full command of his own courtroom, sets his own pace, and is insulated from many of the external pressures and imperatives that sometimes come to control the public lives of other public officials.

In an increasingly frenetic, bureaucratized world, this feature of judicial positions is probably sometimes even more alluring than the unusually favorable salaries, hours, and working conditions.

Tenure and Advancement

Judges have exceptionally long terms of office compared with other public officials. Just under 50 per cent of the 380 treated here have ten-year terms; over 29 per cent have fourteen-year terms; more than 15 per cent have life tenure. Four per cent have twelve-year terms. Only 2 per cent have terms of less than ten years; the eight judges of the State Court of Claims are appointed for nine years. Thus many judges span several administrations, enjoying a degree of security unmatched by few other elective or appointive officials of comparable salary and stature. Not even the so-called permanent civil servants, few of whom ever attain to salaries even approaching judicial compensation, are, in practice, more secure in their jobs.

Table 8   Democratic and Republican district leaders in non-judicial state court positions as of January 1, 1952

County	Total leaders	In court posts, 1952		In court posts, 1952 or previously	
		Number	Per cent	Number	Per cent
	Democratic				
New York	35	16	46	18	51
Bronx	14	2	14	4	29
Kings	23	10	43	13	57
Queens	25	4	16	7	28
Richmond	5	2	40	3	60
Total Democrats	102	34	33	45	44
	Republican				
New York	31	2	6	7	23
Bronx	13	6	46	6	46
Kings	24	9	38	9	38
Queens	24	6	25	9	38
Richmond	5	0	–	0	..
Total Republicans	97	23	24	31	32
Total for both parties	199	57	29	76	38

Source: New York State Crime (Proskauer) Commission, Public Hearing No. 4, 1952, vol. 6, p. 54, mimeographed.

A number of informal practices tend to lengthen the already impressive duration of judges' formal terms. The Mayor and the Governor frequently reappoint judges who have satisfactorily completed their terms of service; and both major parties customarily endorse sitting judges running for reelection without regard to party, except in the most unusual circumstances. Consequently, anyone who enters the judicial hierarchy knows there is a very high probability that he can remain as long as he wants. Furthermore, the ranks of the higher courts are to a substantial extent filled by advancement of the incumbents of lower judicial posts; this is true of the patterns of both appointments and nominations. Thus, although the number of vacancies filled each year exceeds what would be expected if every judge served out his full term, this does not mean the positon of the judges is fraught with uncertainties. Many vacancies are created by the resignations of judges moving up to higher courts, the retirement of judges who have reached the (state) mandatory retirement age after long years on the bench, and by the illness and death of men who have grown old in the judicial branch. In practice, men and women who enter the judiciary frequently remain there as long as they are able to function and would like to stay. There are, of course, exceptions to this generalization, but it applies to a large number of the judges considered in this chapter.

For some, judicial office is the capstone of a political career. Among the judges sitting in 1958, not only were there individuals who once occupied comparatively minor posts in one or another of the branches and levels of government, but there are also former congressmen, an ex-Mayor, former District Attorneys, a former Borough President, a former Deputy Mayor, and at least two former city department heads. For others, the courts have been primarily safe way-stations on the road to other political offices. In recent years two judges have left the bench to run for Mayor, and others have resigned to accept other appointive offices, or to seek other elective offices. Six of the fourteen men who have been Mayor or Acting Mayor of the Greater City since its formation in 1898 were judges at some point in their prior careers, and several moved directly from the bench to City Hall. Judicial office thus functions as both a fitting climax to a life in politics and as a snug niche in which to bide one's time.

Bargaining Position

A further reward of judicial office is the bargaining leverage it affords its incumbents. As referees between other contestants, as interpreters of the rules, and as appointing officers—in short, as distributors of prizes—judges are often in a position to give other people what they want, and they can presumably employ this opportunity to obtain in exchange what they, the judges, want for themselves. Actually, there is little probative evidence that judicial prerogatives and privileges are used for this purpose, although the Seabury Investigation of the Magistrates' Courts in New York City in 1932, as well as the exposure of some individual judges in other courts in the past, demonstrate that this was not always the case. Today, however, although surveillance of the courts by professional associations of lawyers and by civic groups has grown more thorough and more stringent than ever before, one only occasionally hears the charge that a judge conducted a trial or decided a case on the basis of a favor done him by one of the litigants or because of a request denied him by one of the parties at suit. There is reason to suspect that practices of this kind occur, but the supposition is unproved.

In the matter of nonjudicial court appointments, things are quite different. There can be little question that (excepting the federal courts and the higher state courts, as noted above) most of the jobs over which judges have broad discretion are filled not so much on the basis of the competence of the candidates as for the value of particular appointments in paying political debts to the party leaders responsible for the judges' election or appointment and in position to affect their future careers. The same is true of the appointment of referees in foreclosures, special guardians, commissioners in incompetency proceedings, and referees to hold hearings. Indeed, it appears likely that many more nonjudicial postions in the court system have been created than are necessary to perform the work of the courts, that many of those who occupy these positions have little idea of their responsibilities, and that some of them never actually report to their duty stations except on payday. Naturally, some of these discretionary appointees are highly competent and hard working, or the judicial system would break down; this is perhaps especially true of merit system appointees under the supervision of the state or city personnel departments. (In the federal courts, where there is a well-developed centralized institution for judicial administration, the standards are particularly high.)

Prominent among the rewards of judicial office, then, stand the opportunities for bargaining that accompany elevation to the bench. Although the powers of judicial decision are not often employed for this purpose, the powers of appointment are, and it will become apparent in later discussion that the use of this bargaining implement is one of the factors accounting for the high rewards in the judicial branch.

DIFFERENCES BETWEEN JUDGES AND OTHER CONTESTANTS

While judges, since they share in the distribution of the stakes of politics and can use their control over the distribution of other prizes to buttress their own claims and those of their allies, may thus be treated in much the same fashion as other governmental participants in the contest for these stakes, the distinguishing features of the judicial process and judicial institutions must not be overlooked. On the whole, the distinctions between the courts and other governmental institutions and practices are differences in degree rather than in kind. But the differences are sufficiently pronounced to warrant particular attention.

Take, for instance, the Anglo-Saxon juridical principle of judicial independence. This tradition is reflected in the deliberate insulation of judges from many types of control exercised by legislatures and chief executives over other public officers and employees; hence, the security of tenure, the unusually strong safeguards against suspension or removal, the constitutional and statutory bans on reductions in the salaries of sitting judges, and the weakness of overhead agency controls upon the courts. The procedures that keep the other agencies of government responsive and "accountable" to elected legislators and executives have purposely been rendered inapplicable to the courts; they contravene the principle of judicial independence. Some administrative agencies, it is true, achieve substantial autonomy, sometimes by the way they are structured (as, for example, in the case of regulatory commissions, public corporations, and public authorities), sometimes by accident, and sometimes by virtue of the personalities and strategic skills of their leaders. But no other agencies are shielded as are the courts by so many built-in protections, by such strong constitutional and statutory and traditional bulwarks. Even judges are not totally immune to pressure and retaliation, but successful assaults on their redoubt are less frequent. Figuratively speaking, they can follow the dictates of conscience almost to the extent of thumbing their noses with impunity at those outside the judicial hierarchy. Other things discussed in this chapter make it most improbable that they will feel so inclined, but the fact that they could conceivably do so sets them apart from most of their governmental colleagues.

In addition, the formality of judicial procedure, the weight of legal traditions, the ethical norms instilled through professional training and policed in a general way by professional organizations, and supervision of lower courts by higher ones appointed by other chief executives or elected from other constituencies, all combine to restrict the avenues of access to judges and to limit both their opportunities and their willingness to use their decision-making powers for bargaining purposes. Again, this is only a relative proposition; it is not impossible to negotiate with, or bring pressure to bear upon, a judge, but it is rather more difficult to reach a judge this way than to reach other public officials who are regarded, and who regard themselves, as having a primarily "representative" function in contrast with the emphasis on judicial independence.

Taking account of these qualifications (which apply primarily only to the processes of judicial decision and less to appointments by judges), it may be said that the factors identified in the foregoing paragraphs tend to reduce the vulnerability of judges to the pressures of other claimants on the prizes of politics, and to limit (but by no means to eliminate, particularly in the lower courts) the responsiveness of judges to some influences from outside the courts and the legal profession.

The distinctions between judges and other participants in the contest for the rewards of politics can easily be overdrawn. All the participants have much in common, and judges are participants. But it is important to bear in mind that the independence of the judiciary is one of the central values around which our court system is organized, and that judicial procedure is less flexible, less hidden from scrutiny, more circumscribed by expectations of neutrality and impartiality and by the traditions of the legal profession, than most of the other institutions involved in the governmental process.

COURTS AND THE PARTIES

The Importance of the Court System to the Parties

Incentives to Party Workers   The court system provides much of the fuel for party engines. It is true . . . that many party workers are satisfied with relatively nominal material rewards. But almost invariably, predominant among the ranks of those who give unstintingly of their time and energy and money to their party are lawyers striving for positions on the bench, and both lawyers and nonlawyers endeavoring to establish claims on other court posts. On the one hand, this enables the parties to recruit, hold, and motivate a large body of willing, industrious, and often able workers in their cause. On the other hand, it helps the parties maintain a measure of discipline in their ranks and among officeholders who owe their positions to their respective parties.

Positions in the court system are not the only ones furnishing motivations for party workers, of course. But one must climb to the highest echelons of the executive branch in any level of government before the scale of remuneration begins to approach that which obtains for even minor judgeships. In the legislative branch, with the exception of Congress, salaries do not compare at all (although the pay of city councilmen, relative to the time and effort their jobs require, are exceedingly generous though less than half in absolute figures of the pay of a city magistrate). At the same time, judges need not be concerned, except at long intervals, about the ordinary vicissitudes of politics or the recurrent financial crises and economy drives that sometimes sweep other public officials and employees from office or result in cuts in pay. Furthermore, as noted earlier, even many nonjudicial employees of the court system—County Clerks, court clerks, judges' clerks, and Public Administrators, for example—commonly receive salaries rivaling those of bureau chiefs and Deputy Commissioners and far exceeding the pay of local and state legislators. For jobs of this kind, people are willing to work and wait, to accept the onerous chores of party activity, to fill for a time less prized posts and less rewarding ones, and to follow their leaders. The unusual attractiveness of court system emoluments thus plays a large part in the maintenance of party organizations.

Not only does the judicial system provide strong incentives, and in relative abundance, but it does so on a continuing basis. In the first place, 322 of the entire 380 judgeships (and 286 of the 315 occupied by New York City residents) have fixed terms, and the terms are staggered so that part of the membership of each such court comes up for reappointment or reelection annually; each year, therefore, some vacancies are sure to occur.

In the second place, despite efforts to keep the number of expirations roughly equal each year, retirements, deaths, resignations, and the intermittent addition of new posts disrupt the regularity of the cycle and increase the actual number of vacancies to more than the expected number. (Retirement at the end of the year in which a judge turns seventy is mandatory under the state constitution. Furthermore, elevation to the bench often comes relatively late in life. Still further, since judgeships are, as observed earlier, convenient positions from which to wait for still greater opportunities, there are voluntary resignations.) Thus, from 1947 to 1957, a total of 500 vacancies—a figure far in excess of mathematical prediction—were filled in the 380 places. With as many as 40 to almost 50 openings a year, it is not difficult to advance many judges to higher courts and simultaneously to introduce perhaps 15 or more deserving and qualified party workers into the judiciary. In any four-year period, this source of high-level jobs is likely to prove richer than any other; the legislative and executive branches help keep the parties going with many lesser rewards, but they provide fewer big prizes. The plenitude of choice jobs in the courts increases enormously the ability of party leaders to reinvigorate the loyalties of the congeries of Assembly District and clubhouse organizations of which the parties are composed. District Leaders play key parts in the accession to office of both appointed and elected judges, and they work hard for their parties in order to justify their claims to as many of these positions for their followers as they can. One factor holding the parties together despite powerful centrifugal tendencies is the number of judicial offices available, which helps the County Leaders placate every area and every unit of their parties in the long run.[7]

The profusion of court positions also facilitates the satisfaction of many demands by religious, ethnic, and national elements in every party in the city. Dealings of this kind are neither clandestine nor unconscious. Party officers have testified to seeking out Irish or Italian or Jewish candidates for appointment or election to judicial office, and, more recently, Negroes and Puerto Ricans have begun to take their place in the judiciary. The demands are overt; ethnic groups have high regard for the prestige of the courts, and for the opportunities for professional and social advancement offered by judicial offices. The efforts to satisfy these demands are candid. This does not mean there is any formula for the automatic partitioning of the prizes, or that there is any mathematical balance among the claimant groups. On the contrary, the calculus of adjustment is intricate, so that one or two high judicial offices allocated to one group may offset the nomination of a member of another group for executive or legislative office, or the appointment of a

[7]Two factors limit the freedom of party leaders in their efforts to fill all the demands upon them. One is the residence requirements for elective judgeships, and for some appointive judgeships. The other is the unusual concentration of judges in Manhattan, a concentration far out of proportion to this borough's population. This imbalance may be explained in part by the accidents of history, the clustering of business and governmental activities in the downtown area, and the customary failure of governmental districting to keep pace with population shifts.

member of another group to an administrative position. The number of judgeships thus permits the parties to diversify the basis of their electoral strength.

It also enables the parties to reconcile individuals politically eligible for high office, who, denied a top spot on a ticket, might decide to run independently or negotiate with the opposition. And it gives party leaders a chance to repay the loyal party workers who cannot easily be given more prominent positions. (Thus, for example, two former Mayors—Hylan and Impellitteri—accepted judicial posts after being denied renomination for the mayoralty.) Moreover, a judgeship is sometimes a convenient way of neutralizing a District Attorney or other law enforcement officer whose zeal in his enforcement practices offends important party supporters.

The attraction and the number of judicial offices is probably one reason for the abundance of lawyers in politics. Even without the stimulus of positions on the court, politics would probably become the vocation of many lawyers. Their skills equip them to perform the legal services of which the political clubs and their members seem always to stand in need, their profession often allows them to allocate their time as they see fit, and their training tends to encourage the versatility needed for negotiations among contending and competing individuals. If they are partners in large law firms, they may continue to share in the profits of the firm although they direct the major part of their energies to their political pursuits (partly because these often work to the financial benefit of the firm). When to all of this is added the allurement of numerous, highly valued judgeships for which only lawyers are eligible, the magnetism apparently becomes almost irresistible. So lawyers come eagerly to politics. Except for the general requirement that every judge be an attorney admitted (from three to ten years earlier, depending on the judgeship) to the bar of the state, the statutes are virtually silent on the professional qualifications of judges. Nevertheless, professional legal standing is always requisite, thereby removing nonlawyers from competition for many of the best positions the political system can offer, and putting on this occupation a premium that brings its practitioners to the parties.

Added to the judgeships themselves are the remunerative appointments as referees, guardians, administrators, and executors of estates mentioned above. There are enough rewards of this kind—particularly in the hands of the Surrogates—to make working for the parties worthwhile.[8] Even lawyers with small hopes of becoming judges themselves are thus

[8]Indeed, it has been said that control of the Surrogates in New York County sustained the Democratic party in the county during the lean years of the thirties. The long terms of the Democratic Surrogates electd prior to the accession of Mayor La Guardia saved these positions for Tammany Hall in the defeats it suffered at the polls in that period. With the rewards thus available to its supporters, it was able to hold itself together despite the fact that it was displaced in City Hall, cut off from federal support by President Roosevelt (whose nomination Tammany fought in the 1932 Democratic National Convention), who favored Edward J. Flynn's Bronx organization, and was treated coldly by Governor Lehman (who identified with the Roosevelt-Flynn alliance).

drawn to the parties. But, it must be added, the hope of becoming a judge does not die easily in those who once set their sights that high.

While the incentives of judicial office appeal particularly to lawyers, they are important also to nonlawyers in the parties. As noted earlier, the courts employ, in addition to judges, several thousand individuals to perform the work of the judicial system. All but several hundred of these are in the competitive civil service. These hundreds add substantially to the reservoir of rewards party leaders can use to attract and motivate followers, and it is not unlikely that at least a portion of the classified positions are filled by the party faithful through manipulation of the provisions of the Civil Service Law. Some of this patronage is used by some judges to provide employment for relatives and personal friends. By and large, however, the judges accept the recommendations of District Leaders in filling the choicer posts. Indeed, many District Leaders and County Chairmen themselves have found well-paid judicial clerkships a convenient source of income to sustain them while they perform their demanding party services. The New York State Crime Commission reported that in 1952, 29 per cent of the 199 District Leaders of both major parties in the city were employed in the court system, and that 38 per cent of them were either serving at that time or had served there in the past. Although most of the jobs entailed legal work, almost three quarters of the District Leaders holding them were not lawyers. A more recent study by the Citizens Union of the clerks to the resident Justices of the Supreme Court alone revealed that more than one third are District Leaders or County Chairmen, with both parties being well represented. District Leaders are not the only party functionaries to find sources of personal income in the court system; Captains and other organization workers are also frequently employed here. However, the fact that so many District Leaders are employed by the judiciary is a rough indication of the importance to the parties of nonjudicial posts in the court system, and the District Leaders constitute only the visible segments of the iceberg, no studies having yet been made that penetrate much below this level. But there is little doubt that the grip of the parties on judicial patronage is quite firm. Indeed, there are instances on record of judges submitting to demands by some party leaders that they discharge the secretaries in their employ and replace them with appointees suggested by the faction in ascendancy. So it is not just the judiciary per se that makes the court system important to the parties; rather, it is all that goes with the judgeships as well as the judgeships themselves that helps the parties build and maintain their organizations.

The Judicial System as a Source of Party Revenue   A man who wants to be a judge must normally be a party insider, and, in addition, must be prepared in many cases to donate substantial sums of money to the organization of the appropriate party leader whose influence will be the chief factor in his nomination for appointment or election. This practice obtains even when the aspirant has worked long and hard for his party and is well qualified for the post. And he is expected, once in office, to contribute generously to his party in its fund-raising campaigns.

Some District Leaders can apparently extract as much as a year's salary plus an additional "campaign fund" of several thousand dollars.[9] For *elective* office, the amount is frequently set on the basis of a fixed sum (from $50 to $100) for each Election District in the judicial area. The smallest of these territories, Municipal Court Districts, normally encompass between 145 and 180 Election Districts, and the prospective candidate is therefore expected to furnish up to $20,000 over all. The charges are higher for judgeships on higher courts having larger constituencies. Practically no reliable evidence is available on the finances underlying judicial *appointments*, but since it is demonstrable that the appointing chief executives tend to rely very heavily upon their party functionaries to supply them with the names of men to be appointed to fill judicial vacancies, it is possible, if not probable, that similar practices prevail.

Not much is known, either, about what happens to payments of this kind. By and large, it would appear that the District Leaders take a substantial part of it themselves for their own and party uses, and divide the remainder among their workers in the Election Districts. This is apparently regarded in party circles as an ordinary part of the revenues of the District Leader and of the party workers in the field; presumably, for shouldering the burdens of party work, and for their services to their parties and to their candidates, the members of the party hierarchies are widely regarded as entitled to this form of party resource and personal compensation. Most candidates for elective office, and even for appointive office, outside the judiciary as well as in it, give money to their respective party units for putting forth their names and assisting them in their quests; in addition, some of the money donated by the general public for election campaigns ends up in the hands of local party personnel. In this fashion, the party organizations manage to "pay" their regular "staffs." A substantial part of this recompense comes from those who would like to be judges.

Moreover, since those who attain the bench or nonjudicial court posts generally seek to strengthen their chances for advancement and to ensure that, if they are not promoted, they will at least be renominated or reappointed at the expiration of their term, they can almost always be counted upon to contribute generously to all fund-raising efforts and to heed the advice of their party mentors in matters of appointment and perhaps even of decision.

Like all organizations of the modern world, parties need money to operate. Clearly, one of the primary reasons the court system is of such

[9]It is rumored among lawyers that there is a "going rate" for judgeships, currently the equivalent of two years' salary for that office.

profound concern to the parties is that this is where a part of their money comes from.

Protection of Party Interests   In one additional and final respect, the court system is important to the parties. In the Supreme Court, where many decisions about electoral conduct and procedure are in practice decided (though subject to appeal which infrequently materializes), judges who are beholden to party organizations will probably be less sympathetic to challengers to party discipline and authority than would critics of "machine politics." The method of selecting judges greatly reduces (if it does not preclude altogether) the likelihood that party organizations will often be confronted with hostile judges. The pattern of judicial rulings interpreting Election Law provisions governing designating and nominating procedures and the use of party names by insurgent groups in any of the parties seem to bear out this inference. So, too, do other more isolated decisions in other courts—as, for example, a magistrate's dismissal of the charges against members of a Democratic club who were arrested for gambling and for using loud and boisterous language. The magistrate ruled that "political organizations are to be allowed to meet without interference." Admittedly, the evidence that the party obligations of the judges are controlling in these cases is far from conclusive, and there are certainly important judgments one would not anticipate on the basis of party loyalty. Many other elements, which the judges themselves do not control (such as the working of statutes), are operative here. Nevertheless, one reason the parties display such deep interest in the judiciary is that their own organizational security rests to a significant extent in the hands of the judges.

The Importance of the Parties to the Judiciary

Parties and Judicial Selection   Except perhaps for the highly skilled court jobs, such as court stenographer, nobody gets one of the better judicial or nonjudicial positions in the court system without going through party channels.

When a judicial appointment, whether for a full term, the remainder of a term, or until the next election, is to be made by a chief executive, the usual procedure is for the County Leader in whose territory the court sits (or who is acknowledged by other County Leaders as a result of some earlier bargain to have first claim on the filling of the next vacancy) to determine which of his District Leaders is entitled to nominate the appointee for this post. An able County Leader generally succeeds in balancing the distribution of these prizes among his constituent units so that his decisions are accepted by his party subordinates. While most County Leaders manage well enough in this regard, even the best of them may run into strong objections from clubs that feel they have been victims of discrimination or neglect. When this happens the County Leader may relieve the tension by promising future openings to the offended groups, or by reallocating the existing vacancy to the plaintiffs and mollifying the deprived groups with a lesser prize, or with the promise of a better one in the future. Occasionally a group of District Leaders may get together and agree among themselves on the distribution of nominations and appointments; in such cases, their County Leader commonly endorses their decision. Once agreement is reached in one fashion or another, the name of the candidate is put before the appointing executive, who, in most cases, promptly appoints the organization choice. The procedure is roughly the same in each of the major parties, whenever it has captured the office of the chief executive at City Hall, in Albany, or in Washington, while the third parties can hope at best to be granted one or two places (for which their own party hierarchies, like those of the major parties, select the candidates) in return for their support in the elections—particularly in close elections. (Only the highest federal positions seem to be more or less exempt from these practices.)

The hold of the inner cores of the parties on nominations for elective judgeships is, as was noted in the discussion of the nominating process, equally strong, if not stronger. Almost all the nominations made by the rank and file of the parties in direct primaries are dominated by the Assembly District Leaders in each jurisdiction; the primaries are little more than ratifications of the individuals the Leaders select. For Municipal Court nominations it is primarily the Leaders whose Assembly Districts fall within each Municipal Court District who bargain with each other and arrive at decisions on their slate of nominees. For the County Courts (including the Court of General Sessions in New York County), the City Court, and the Surrogates, it is the Courty Executive Committees, made up of all the Assembly District Leaders in each county, negotiating with each other and with their County Leaders (who are occasionally overruled by coalitions of their District Leaders), who are chiefly responsible for the choices. The county committeemen routinely go along with the Leaders, and the voters in the parties are seldom offered alternatives in the primaries, although the contests are usually energetically fought when they do occur.

Similarly, the nomination of candidates for the Supreme Court by party conventions in each of the Judicial Districts of the state is controlled by the County Leaders in those areas; the convention delegates almost invariably accept the names presented by them. Even the nominees for the Court of Appeals, selected by the state conventions of the several parties, are chosen largely by bargaining among County Leaders from all parts of the state. (As a result, at least three or four of the justices are virtually certain to come from New York City, the remainder from upstate and suburban sections.) In short, no part of the judiciary, however high, is divorced from the parties.

The parties are important, too, to those who seek to or do occupy nonjudicial offices in the court system as well as to judges. Most judges maintain amicable relations with their party sponsors (past, present, and future) by employing their discretion in making appointments to install in office people recommended by District Leaders, which, as noted above, frequently means appointing the District Leaders and County Chairmen themselves, among others. Indeed, one judge is reported to have been so assiduous in satisfying claims made upon him by a District Leader that he accepted the Leader's recommendation for every appointment without regard to the qualifications of the candidates, and then found himself compelled to engage competent assistants at his own expense. Appointed court officers with appointive powers of their own adopt in the same manner and for the same reasons their party organizations' suggestions as to whom to select. It may therefore be said that nearly everybody in a more important position in the court system owes his position in good part to the support of some party functionary, and that even some holding lesser posts (probably including a number of posts nominally protected by Civil Service Law and regulations) are similarly indebted.

Few are the aspects of government in which the influence of the parties is never felt at all. Nowhere in government, however, is that influence more pervasive and profound than in the court system.

Judicial Election Campaigns   Candidates for elective judgeships find the parties especially important to them because of the character of judicial electoral campaigns. For one thing, campaigning has somehow come to be considered inconsistent with the dignity and the duties of judicial office—a rather strange myth in the light of the way judicial candidates are chosen, but one that helps obscure the realities of judicial politics from the eyes of many voters and that is therefore scrupulously observed. Candidates for judicial office do not ordinarily make "political" speeches, do not appear regularly at campaign rallies and demonstrations, or engage in the usual campaign practices designed to bring candidates into personal contact with as much of the electorate as possible; indeed, the statements of campaign expenditures by judicial candidates generally (and, in a technical sense, no doubt accurately) show no personal outlays. Barred from the opportunity of applying their own energies and talents and personalities to their own election, the candidates for judgeships are forced, even more than colleagues running for places in the other branches of government, to rely on the established party machinery for vote-getting. The "citizens' committees" that spring up to promote the election of a particular candidate are occasionally made up of persons who for professional or personal reasons are willing to work for his victory. Far more frequently, these are merely the parties in other guises, establishing these auxiliary associations to avoid legal limitations on campaign expenses, to obtain donations from people reluctant to give money to political parties themselves, and to exploit the myth that their judicial candidates have independent rather than merely partisan support. Organizing in this fashion is not by itself sufficient to guarantee election, but lack of it is enough to make defeat virtually certain in a close contest.

In the second place, nominees for judicial office commonly enjoy the endorsements of both major parties; this is one of the reasons for their security of tenure. Originally, the custom of joint nomination apparently applied only to judges who had completed a full term on the bench. Judges appointed to fill vacancies in an elective court until the next election, and candidates running for judicial office without any prior service in the positions at stake, ordinarily encountered an opposing candidate from the other major party. Over the years, however, the parties began to make bargains with each other involving temporarily appointed incumbents and even nonincumbents, so that many more candidates for judicial office make their runs uncontested than the "sitting-judge" tradition would lead one to anticipate. For example, twice since the end of World War II, more than 80 per cent of the judicial seats to be filled by election were won by candidates having both Republican and Democratic nominations. On the other hand, there is nothing fixed about this ratio, the number of joint endorsements by the major parties having fallen as low as 2 out of 14 elective judgeships in 1952. Indeed, in one case in 1955, another in 1956, and two in 1957, one or the other of the major parties refused to endorse an elected sitting judge renominated by the other party and instead put up a candidate of its own. The number of dual nominations clearly depends on a great many delicate adjustments. This point is underscored by the bipartisan deals behind the creation of new judicial posts. In 1931, 12 new court positions were created in the Second Judicial District. None of them, however, was contested in the election. Democratic leaders agreed to endorse Republican candidates for 5 of the 12 new seats in return for Republican support in getting the Republican-dominated state legislature to establish the positions, and the Republicans in the Judicial District completed the bargain by endorsing seven Democrats for the remaining seven vacancies. A similar understanding underlay the passage of bills in 1956 creating new seats on the Supreme Court in the First, Second, and Tenth Judicial Districts. This measure was opposed by Mayor Wagner (allegedly on the grounds that the city would be unable to finance its share of the additional costs) and Governor Harriman vetoed it, but a new agreement between the parties dividing the seats (by joint endorsement) resulted in the establishment of seven additional seats in the Tenth District in 1958. Since bipartisan endorsement makes election a certainty, and since it also depends upon agreements reached by the County and District Leaders of the regular party organizations, every judicial candidate doubtless awaits tensely the outcome of negotiations regarding his own situation. He cannot help being aware that the decision is his party's and not his to make. Candidates from districts that are strongholds of their own party need not, of course, worry about this phase of the electoral process. In doubtful districts, and in districts where the opposition party is in firm control, what the party functionaries do is of deep concern to the candidates.

In sum, aspirants to elective judicial posts, after having surmounted the obstacles to nomination, are not freed from dependence on the parties for the attainment of their objectives.

The Emoluments of Office   Since World War II, judicial salaries have risen rapidly. In large measure, this must be ascribed to inflation and to the widespread consensus that levels of judicial compensation should keep pace with the rest of the economy. To a lesser extent, it must be attributed to the skill of the judges themselves. Although the traditions and public expectations of dignity and reserve have somewhat hampered their quest for higher pay, they have managed to press their claims quietly and discreetly through their own groupings (such as Magistrates' Associations, the County Judges' Association, and others). They have had some assistance from professional associations of lawyers and civic groups, but the initiative has not come from this quarter. The real thrust, the driving force, and the strategies behind increases in the compensation of judges have originated to a large degree in the party hierarchies, which have strong incentives to elevate salary levels, and which (as was noted earlier) have the influence in the legislature and the Executive Mansion to attain their objectives.

The interest of the parties in judicial salaries is clear. The better the pay, the more attractive the office; the easier it is to get willing workers, to get generous contributions from office seekers and officeholders. So bills providing increases for the judges of now one court, now another, are introduced virtually every year. This is not to say, on the one hand, that judges do not welcome these raises, or, on the other, that they do not deserve them. But they get many of them because party leaders, for reasons of their own, fight for them. In a sense, the benefits to sitting judges are more or less incidental. Just the same, their debt to party leaders is real.

Similarly, judges on the bench enjoy the advantages accruing from increases in the number of seats in the higher courts. For them, it means additional possibilities of advancement. But this is not the principal benefit to party leaders; for party leaders, new judgeships mean more rewards to distribute to party workers and, therefore, more compliant party units. To be sure, most courts of civil jurisdiction have been swamped by litigation, and some cases take several years to come to trial; under these conditions, there are reasons other than pure partisanship and sources other than party leaders behind proposals for additional judgeships. The main drive, however, seems to originate with County and District Leaders; the incidental benefits are more or less accidental. To judges, these incidental benefits are often important, and so, consequently, are the party organizations responsible for them.

Mutual Accommodation

The relationship between courts and parties—as, indeed, between the parties and all elected or politically appointed government officials and employees—is thus one of mutual benefit and accommodation. The court system is important to the parties; the parties are important to the judiciary. As things are now constituted, this is an inevitable and an indissoluble bond.

COURTS AND CHIEF EXECUTIVES

The power of appointment is useful to the appointing officer in two ways. He may employ it to install in office individuals of his own choosing. He may also use it to install in office someone favored by somebody else in return for a favor or a series of favors by that "somebody else."

The appointment of judges by chief executives is more widely used for the second purpose—bargaining—than for the first. For chief executives are generally not in a position to *direct* their legislative bodies to do what they, the executives, want. Nor can they easily *compel* party organizations to do their bidding. Nor, for that matter, are they always able to *command* all administrative agencies; many of these are quite autonomous. So the executives, lacking adequate sticks, must employ carrots whenever they can. Hence, they make appointments recommended by legislators or party leaders in return for support for their programs or candidacies, and they move administrators into choice jobs if the administrators are faithful to the chief executives. But the programs of chief executives are more dependent on the actions of administrative officers than of judges (although there are important exceptions). Executives, as a result, seem more inclined to try to induct the persons they individually prefer into many high administrative positions and to use judicial office to bargain with legislatures, parties, and with administrators hoping for seats on the bench eventually. The two purposes often merge, but they are distinguishable.

The President, the Governor, and the Mayor are equipped to bargain with varying degree of effectiveness in the political contest in New York City. From this special point of view, the Mayor may well be in the strongest formal position of the three. The President appoints to vacancies in all of the federal judgeships whose respective jurisdictions include New York City, but the names he proposes must win the consent of the Senate. Because of the practice of senatorial courtesy, he is obliged to come to terms with the Senators of the states affected when he appoints men to United States District Courts, and he must reach agreement with the Senate committee on the judiciary and other senatorial leaders when filling vacancies on higher courts. As for the Governor, the only court appointed by him is the State Court of Claims, and he, like the President, must obtain the consent of the upper house of his legislature before his appointments to vacancies take effect. The Governor is also empowered to make interim appointments— that is, appointments effective only until judges elected at the next general election can take their seats—to fill vacancies on the City Court, the County Courts (including General Sessions in New York County), the Surrogates' Courts, the Supreme Court, and the Court of Appeals. (If the state Senate is in session when he makes the appointments, the consent of that body must be obtained.) In addition, from among the sitting Supreme Court Justices, the Governor names seven to the Appellate Division in each of the two Judicial Departments that include the city (and five in each of the other two Judicial Departments into which the state is divided). But the Mayor fills all unoccupied seats in a total of 97 appointive judgeships, and he makes interim appointments to vacancies in the ranks of the 68 Municipal Court Justices, all without the necessity of concurrence or approval by any other governmental institution. (Although the "sitting-judge rule" did not originally cover interim appointees, some of these judges receive bipartisan endorsement at election time. Power to elevate men to the bench for short periods is thus more useful to chief executives than the brief duration of the initial interval suggests.)

The chief executives freely use their powers of judicial appointment as currency in political negotiations. This enables them to do many of the things they were presumably elected to do. It also enables party leaders to exert great influence over the choice of appointed judges. The executives thus gain some control over policy; the parties thus get jobs for their people.

COURTS AND OTHER CONTESTANTS

Besides the party leaders and chief executives, only professional associations of lawyers, the Citizens Union, and the press exert any significant, visible influence on the composition of the court system. Insofar as the claims of ethnic, national, and religious groups and of neighborhood consciousness affect the courts, they make themselves felt through the party hierarchies, or, in a general way, through the voting behavior of the electorates, both discussed earlier. The impacts of the lawyers, the press, and the Citizens Union are more direct and distinct.

There are many professional associations of lawyers in New York City. Especially prominent is the Association of the Bar of the City of New York, which is a citywide organization. In addition, there is a bar association in each of the five counties (the New York County Lawyers' Association being the largest in the metropolitan region and second in size in the country only to the American Bar Association). Each year the Association of the Bar rates all the candidates for judicial office, after their nomination, as "outstandingly qualified," "qualified" or "unqualified." Each of the county bar associations does the same most of the time for all judicial nominees within their respective areas. These findings are printed in moderate quantities and distributed to the membership of the organizations and to the press, ordinarily receiving something more than routine attention but less than front-page coverage from the latter. There is also a Metropolitan Trial Lawyers' Association, but it is generally more concerned with court organization and procedure than with the choice of judges.

The actions of the bar associations have had little, if any, effect on the choice of nominees for judicial office. Indeed, until 1956 the parties made only sporadic efforts to solicit the opinions of the bar associations regarding prospective nominees; the bar associations were thus in no position to bring any weight to bear on the selection of candidates. In that year, in response to the persistent urging of the Association of the Bar and of *The New York Times*, the New York County Leaders of both major parties pledged themselves to seek systematically the opinions of the bar associations about all prospective candidates prior to nomination. Whether this will have any discernible effect, and whether the party organizations in the other counties will follow suit, remains to be seen; the complaints that led to the adoption of this policy constitute convincing evidence that the professional legal associations have heretofore been largely ineffective in their efforts to influence the nominating process.

Their impact on elections also appears to be limited. Were this not the case, they would not feel compelled to try to intervene at an earlier stage; they would be content, if they could assure the defeat of a candidate by withholding their approval, to punish the parties in this fashion if the parties put forth unqualified candidates. But their ratings apparently do not sway electorates (perhaps because almost all the candidates are called "qualified"). Consequently, if they are to influence the composition and caliber of the judiciary to a larger extent than they have managed to affect in the past, the bar associations must somehow manage to intervene in the selection of nominees. Otherwise, they become little more than helpless bystanders.

If their role in nominations should become more prominent, the lawyers in the parties would probably move in to take over the leadership of the bar associations. The charge has already been leveled that the Bronx and Kings (Brooklyn) County Bar Associations are dominated by Democrats, and that the New York County (Manhattan) Lawyers' Association is controlled by Republicans, with the alleged result that the endorsements more closely reflect political preferences than professional judgments. If party domination is not the case now, it is likely to develop should the bar associations become more influential. Thus the prevailing situation is unlikely to change significantly in the immediate future.

The Citizens Union operates in much the same way as the bar associations, except that it uses a four-category rating scale ranging from "unqualified" through "qualified," "qualified and preferred" to "endorsed." Its influence on the nomination and election of judges, however, is no greater than that of the bar associations, particularly since it tends to follow the lead of the Association of the Bar.

Some of the daily newspapers grumble editorially about the process of judicial selection, and all of them express editorial preferences for judicial along with other candidates, but their recommendations sometimes cancel each other out. Anyway, it is doubtful that they control the voting behavior of their readers. Consequently there are no indications that the parties vie for their suppost when choosing nominees for judicial office.

Thus the dominance of the party hierarchies over the selection of elected judges is virtually uncontested by the only respectable nongovernmental groups in the community that consistently pay any attention to this phase of politics. The ascendancy of the inner cores of the parties over the selection of appointed judges is even more complete, for there is customarily no evaluation by nongovernmental groups at any stage of the appointive process, and only the most egregious incompetence or dishonesty is likely to attract any significant attention from them at all.

In the organization and procedure of the courts, as contrasted with the actual naming of judges, groups other than the parties have had greater (though not necessarily decisive) influence. The two issues are not completely separable, of course; while emphasis on *how* the courts are structured and *how* they operate may be distinguished from *what* they decide and *who* makes the decisions, these are related to each other. Nevertheless, it is on the *how* that groups other than the parties ordinarily concentrate, placing their greatest stress on increased speed, lower costs, and more symmetrical patterns of organization.

Agitation among lawyers' associations and civic groups and the press for modernizing the whole court system of the state resulted in the creation by the state legislature in 1953 of a Temporary Commission on the Courts (the "Tweed Commission"), appointed by the Governor. When the Commission brought in its report in 1956, proposing sweeping revisions of the system in order to achieve greater standardization and order, it provoked a storm of controversy. In general, civic groups and the press backed the recommendations, several of the lawyers' societies cautiously supported large parts of them but took exception to others, Mayor Wagner appointed a Citizens Commission on the Courts in New York City and subsequently endorsed this body's approval of most (but not all) of the provisions of the Tweed Commission plan. On the other hand, social welfare agencies tended to oppose the proposed abolition of special Youth Courts they had been instrumental in establishing, the State Association of Towns (and other such associations of public agencies and officials) attacked the revamping of inferior courts of local jurisdiction, associations of Magistrates and of County Judges, among other judicial officers, criticized the portions of the report affecting them, and the Chief Judge of the Court of Appeals urged caution. The Commission modified its plan to satisfy many of the critics, but in the end the opposition of many Republicans throughout the state, speaking through their representatives in the legislature, coupled with a lack of enthusiasm on the part of Democratic leaders, led to the defeat of the recommended reorganization, and the Commission went out of existence. It would appear from this that the parties play a large part even in matters of court organization and procedure, although no other aspects of the court system result in the active participation of so many groups. Organization and procedure and discussions of efficiency bring the nonparty groups out; they do not always prevail, but more is heard from them on these questions than on the selection of individual judges.

Efficiency is also a primary target of the Judicial Conference of the state, which consists of the Chief Judge of the Court of Appeals, the presiding Justices of the Appellate Division of the Supreme Court in each of the four Judicial Departments in the state, and, for terms of two years, one Supreme Court Justice (not in an Appellate Division) chosen by their associates in each Judicial Department. The Conference compiles and publishes judicial statistics, surveys "jurisdiction, procedure, practice, rules, and administration of all of the courts of the state," reporting its findings annually to the legislature and recommending legislation to improve the administration of justice. In addition, it studies the operation of the courts and tries to win the cooperation of judges throughout the state in improving court performance, speeding justice, and reducing waste and inefficiency. In New York City, the Association of the Bar and the Citizens Union have made studies of possible economies in judicial administration in recent years, and the City Administrator has advanced suggestions for consolidating Municipal Courts to save personnel, equipment, and space, and to effect other improvements.

The control of the party leaders over judicial *machinery* is thus shared with a great many other contestants in the political arena. It is in the naming of court *personnel* that their ascendancy is all but unchallenged in practice.

Clandestinely, however, one element of the population outside the parties in New York City plays a role in the selection of some judges: the underworld. The extent of underworld influence is difficult to assess and is probably limited, but it is unquestionably present and probably extends to both elective and appointive posts. Both the New York State Crime Commission (the Proskauer Commission) and the Special United States Senate Committee to Investigate Organized Crime in Interstate Commerce (the Kefauver Committee) elicited testimony from witnesses about the connections between known gangsters and racketeers on the one hand and some judges on the other. The leaders of large-scale unlawful enterprises— gambling, prostitution, narcotics handling, and extortion through counterfeit labor unions and spurious trade and industrial associations—generally have a good deal of cash on hand, and, since some of it finds its way into units of each party, it occasionally influences some choices of nominees and finances parts of some campaigns.

Yet the underworld, like the other nongovernmental and nonparty groups interested in the judiciary, stands on the periphery of the arena.

At the center are the party hierarchies and the judges and other court personnel. The roles of all the others in the staffing of the court system are secondary by comparison.

CONCLUSION: THE COURTS AND PUBLIC POLICY

Judicial decisions, like the decisions of other governmental institutions, are vehicles of public policy. Inevitably, therefore, judges are targets of influence exerted by other contestants in the struggle for the stakes of politics. The strategies of the contestants are the same as they are with respect to other policy-forming institutions: (1) efforts to determine the choice of policy-making personnel, and (2) attempts to sway the decisions of the personnel who actually come to occupy office.

The methods of influencing policy decisions made by judges are somewhat different from those applied to other organs of government. Tenure, tradition, procedure, and myth render them less susceptible than other officials to many of the standard techniques of political pressure. They are, to be sure, not impervious to pressure, but they are in especially favored positions to resist if they choose, and find fewer imperatives to bargain or cultivate support than the members of the other governmental branches. Policy decisions of judges are thus made in a field of forces in which many contestants are of limited effectiveness at best, and from which many are excluded for all practical purposes. This probably tends to skew their decisions in a different direction from the decisions of officials who face competitive elections far more frequently, or who depend on alliances with a functional constituency for strength. At any rate, the influences on judicial decisions are not obvious.

One natural channel of influence of this kind would be the parties. The bonds between courts and the parties are numerous and strong. The willingness of party leaders to transmit to the courts the requests of constituents is widely recognized; except when the interests of the parties themselves are at stake, party leaders tend to be more concerned with the jobs, the revenues, and the loyalty supplied by the men they put in office than by the substance of court decisions and, as far as policy goes, are apparently as happy to press one way as another as a favor to a supporter. To what extent party hierarchies actually employ their dominance over selection of court personnel for such purposes is not known, but the opportunities certainly exist, and the temptations must be very strong.

Thus, whereas much of the maneuvering and negotiation elsewhere in government are overtly and explicitly oriented toward shaping the substance of decisions, the visible foci of judicial politics are selection of personnel and design of organization and procedures. The forces concerned with the substantive aspects of political questions are hampered; the forces with the greatest influence are commonly neutral with respect to content.

Professional associations of lawyers and civic organizations must be content to direct their attention to raising the general professional standards of appointment and to improving judicial machinery. Public policy is often affected or formed by judicial decisions, but the policy questions are rarely highly perceptible or widely discussed. In appearance, at least, judicial politics is a politics of personnel and procedure rather than of program. Although policy flows out of it, the policy seems often to be an unwitting by-product of other considerations, and sometimes to be the work of contestants who see in the special processes of the judicial world opportunities to escape from the competition in the other branches of government. The full significance of the courts in the formulation of public policy still remains to be explored.

CHAPTER SEVENTEEN

TRIAL COURTS AND PUBLIC POLICY IN AN URBAN COUNTY

KENNETH M. DOLBEARE

This chapter combines two related but quite different analyses. First, it sets up a specification of the major issues and problems which make up County politics and then examines the impact of the courts on these matters. Second, it looks at the totality of court decisions to determine the extent to which the courts are involved with all *other* possible public matters. The purpose of juxtaposing an analysis with an issues-of-politics focus against an analysis with a total-output-of-courts focus is to produce a comprehensive answer to the question: Which areas of public policy within the County are subject to court control or influence (and in what ways), and which are *un*affected by the courts? The second analysis is necessary in order to determine what the courts *are* doing (in addition to or instead of dealing with the major issues) as well as to provide a sense of perspective regarding how much of the courts' attention is directed at the major issues.

THE ISSUES OF COUNTY POLITICS

We need a defensible characterization of the important issues and problems in the County from which to start. A four-stage procedure was adopted, striking a rough balance between what would be necessary for utter comprehensiveness and what was practical for the purposes involved. "Issues and problems" for this purpose were defined as (a) those matters which involved numbers of people in a controversy of a continuing nature or

Reprinted with permission of publisher and author from Kenneth M. Dolbeare, *Trial Courts and Urban Politics: State Court Policy Impact and Functions in a Local Political System* (New York: John Wiley & Sons, Inc., 1967), pp. 87–105. Mr. Dolbeare is Associate Professor of Political Science at the University of Wisconsin.

(b) significant decisions involving public funds or affecting the economic or social character of the County, whether or not they gave rise to controversy of a public nature.

Initially, the relevant literature on local and urban politics was searched, both for summaries of the issues found to exist in such contexts and for characterizations of the basic cleavages usually associated with them. Leading writers' interpretations were combined to establish a working set of categories for attention while collecting data. These categories served as a means of alerting the investigator to subjects and not as precast conclusions about the issues here.

Second, two newspapers were searched in different ways for reports of actual issues and controversies of a public nature. The New York Times, which makes no effort at comprehensive coverage of this County and whose entries probably reflect the availability of space as well as the human interest qualities of the story, was entered through its index items for this period and a record of the subjects of public controversy made. A much more valuable source was the leading local newspaper which does make a serious effort to present full coverage of news events in the County. It is not indexed, so the procedure was to search its pages for the entire sixteen-year period and to establish the record of issues in this way. This appears to have been a satisfactory means of locating matters which received some attention, and the minutiae which do reach print lend confidence that few items of importance would be missed by this procedure. Issues located in this way were organized into categories by general subject area and the much sparser New York Times entries integrated with them.

Third, under the assumption that some matters of real importance do not emerge as public controversies, three other analyses were made: a comparison of expenditure-revenue patterns by means of budget analysis; a tabulation of nominations, elections, and appointments; and a review of the enactment of local ordinances applying sanctions and controls (by reference to the proceedings of the major units of government). Certain trends, developments, and decisions of significance involving public funds or affecting the economic or social character of the County were added to the emerging itemization of the component substantive elements of County politics in this way.

Fourth, in a series of interviews with major figures representing a cross section of viewpoint toward County politics, specific inquiry was directed toward adding to or otherwise improving this itemization. No additions were made in this way, but a fuller sense of the relative importance of various issues and the character of their development was gained. This varied approach appears to have resulted in a reasonably full presentation of the issues and problems making up the substance of County politics. Its results are summarized briefly in the following paragraphs.

The literature of urban politics shows substantial areas of concurrence in identifying issues.[1] These tentative categorizations provided a beginning orientation for the approach to the data sources. The actual gleanings from the newspaper search are summarized in categories derived from the data in Table 1. This itemization is very important, for it reflects all those matters which created some public controversy or notice, or which appeared to involve decisions of the level of significance described previously.

Two of the other areas which appeared to be such integral parts of the substance of County politics as to necessitate special concentration were developed next. The first of these is the area of nominations, elections, and patronage distribution—the "who shall hold office" problem. Between 1948 and 1963 elections were held for the purpose of filling the following major offices the number of times indicated:

Supreme Court Judge	19
County Court Judge	7
Family/Children's Court Judge	5
County Executive, Sheriff, Comptroller, and Clerk	5 each
Congressman	14
State Senator	20
State Assemblyman	40

In addition, three Towns, two cities, and literally hundreds of incorporated villages, school districts, and other districts were also regularly electing officials. These represent only a fraction of the activity really involved because a contest for the nomination may precede the election and in every instance after the election is concluded several patronage appointments must be decided upon. Thus there is a substantial amount of choice-making by authoritative elements in the system, of which the electorate is but one, and this must be included as an important component of the substance of County politics.

The final subject area for supplementary consideration is the conferring of benefit and burden implicit in the changes in the expenditure-revenue patterns which occurred during this time period for each unit of government taken independently. Decisions which form a component of the substance of County politics are defined as those relating to (a) increases in the absolute amounts to be expended in each category of responsibility, (b) the shifts in the share of available funds allocated to each

---

[1]Particularly useful for this purpose and drawn on here were: Scott Greer, *Governing the Metropolis* (New York: John Wiley and Sons, 1962), pp. 90–96; Charles R. Adrian, *Governing Urban America* (New York: McGraw-Hill Book Co., 1961); Robert C. Wood, *Suburbia: Its People and Their Politics* (Boston: Houghton Mifflin Co., 1959), p. 164; Wallace S. Sayre and Herbert Kaufman, *Governing New York City* (New York: Russell Sage Foundation, 1960), pp. 39–64; Edward C. Banfield and James Q. Wilson, *City Politics* (Cambridge: Harvard University Press, 1963), pp. 35–46, 18; Robert Agger, et al., *The Rulers and the Ruled* (New York: John Wiley and Sons, 1964).

Table 1   Major specific issues of county politics, 1948–1963, according to local newspaper reports

Transportation	Education	Location of Improvements	Housing	Zoning	Racial
Railroad breakdown (1948)	Shopville segregation (1949–51, 54, 1961–63)	Village C incinerator (1948)	Regulation of builders (1948)	Flower City offices (1948)	Newtown rentals (1949, 1950, 1952–53)
Railroad bankruptcy (1949)	Village A merger (1955)	Area 1 incinerator (1950)	Services for GIs (1948)	Shopville business (1948)	Shopville zoning (1948)
Railroad reorganization (1950–53)	Community College (1956–58)	Intracounty Expressway 1 (1951–52)	Slum clearance and urban renewal:	New College (1950–51)	City B sit-ins (1963)
Bus lines' routes (1950)	Newtown policy dispute (1960–63)	Boulevard widening (1952–54)	(1) Village D (1949)	Conversion of airfield (1954–55)	(See also Education)
Railroad investigation (1957)	Village B segregation (1963)	Aircraft plant runway extension (1952–53)	(2) City A (1955–60)	Nicetown synagogue (1954–55)	
Railroad strike (1960)	Segregation, other schools (1963)	Parkway extension (1953)	(3) City B (1956–62)	Flower City synagogue (1956)	
Aircraft noise (1960–63)		Intracounty Expressway 2 (1955)	(4) Village E (1957–60)	Industrial Pk. (1952–59)	
Bus lines' franchise (1963)		Demotown incinerator (1958–63)	FHA bribery scandal (1956)	Town Zoning Plan (1959)	
			Apartment development (var.)		

Table 1 (continued)

Local Laws and Ordinances	Obsolete Air Force Property	Labor Relations	Conflict Intraparties	Disputes with-in Local Govts.	Tax Levels and Assessment
Village F aircraft altitude (1952–53)	New runway (1956)	Major union probes and scandals (1950–56)	Individual Republicans (1954)	City B (1948)	School tax levels (1948–63)
Village G traffic (1952)	Closing urged (1958)	Strikes:	Republican factions (1959)	City B (1952)	Utility Co. assessment (1961)
Sand pit regulation (1957–58)	Closing agreed upon (1960)	(1) Instrument Co. (1955)	County Leader replaced (1959)	City A (1952)	Shopping Plaza assessment (1963)
Employment agencies (1958)	Study proposed uses (1961)	(2) Aircraft Co. (1956)	Liberal Party frauds (1960)	City B (1958)	
Sunday Laws (1950–55)	Private air field (1963)	(3) Railroad (1960)	County Leader replaced (1961)		
	Disposition (1963)				

Annexation and Incorporation
Village H (1952)
Village J (1958, 60–61)

Miscellaneous Major Issues
Raceway scandal (1953–54)
County government party conflict (1961–63)
Savings banks enter County (1960)

category, and (c) the sectors of the available taxable resources which will be tapped to provide the requisite funds. "Decisions" for the most part have to be inferred from the changes found to have occurred, and in many instances events and circumstances may have mandated governmental response so insistently that no real choice was involved at all. Nevertheless, over a sixteen-year period sufficient opportunity exists for the application of values and priorities (about which various segments of the community might well hold differing convictions or possess varying interests) to make this inquiry suggestive of the existence of decisions of significant impact on the County. Where such decisions have in fact been made and are of such a character as to affect the economic or social character of the County, we have entered the bounds of our definition of the substance of County politics and must therefore include them.

The most noteworthy item, of course, is the sharp increase in absolute amounts raised and expended by all units of government. By 1963 the total sum expended by all units of government in the County was around $600,000,000. In the case of the County, the total budgetary increase was more than 600% from 1948 to 1963, when it approached $200,000,000. The School Districts eclipsed all other units of government, however, with a 2800% increase in total expenditures, from less than $13,000,000 in 1948 to more than $334,000,000 in 1963; at one point in this era, County school construction accounted for 25% of all school building in New York State. Town expenditures and budgets also rose spectacularly, with the special districts showing large capital outlays. The property tax sustained all these increases, with only the School Districts receiving any major share of their budgets from the State. The increases were felt most heavily by residents of newer, unincorporated areas.

The elements identified in the course of these three approaches to the characterization of the substance of County politics may now be drawn together. . . . [T]he individuals, groups, and organizations of the County [have been] differentiated along certain economic, religious, and social lines, and [have been seen] as possessing correspondingly disparate interests, values, and aspirations. The two basic motivations of status aspiration and economic self-interest [have been] seen as fundamental political activators, with the search for power as a partly independent, partly enabling or secondary motivation. As these participants act in accordance with these motivations, they intrude upon the interests, values, and aspirations of others and the resultant clashes give rise to conflicts requiring accommodation or authoritative resolution. Such clashes occur or significant determinations are made with sufficient regularity at identifiable places and over identifiable matters to permit us to say that the politics of the County focus primarily on certain specific conflict-points or display certain specific issue-vehicles. These appear, from the evidence so far assembled, to be characterizable under five headings, as follows:

Conflict-Point	*Illustrative Aspects of the Basic Motivations Displayed*
1. Zoning and land use	Status: Prestige involved in house and address, quality of surrounding community, amenities available, absence of undesirable business or commercial uses, lower-class elements, etc. Economic: Profit from best use of property, easing of tax burden by shift to industry, efficiency, rationality of master plan.
2. Education	Status: Prestige from reputation for high quality of education, attainment of middle-class ideal, entrance to upper-echelon colleges. Economic: Class mobility and financial betterment, minimum cost levels associated with basic education.
3. Taxation	Status: Threat to home ownership. Economic: Burden of home ownership, shift of burden to industry, financial needs for governmental services.
4. Nominations, elections, and control of political party	Status: Traditional route of mobility for lower-class groups, rise to first acceptance and then control by newer ethnic and religious groups. Economic: Income from position of stature and public visibility, inside knowledge of future events, patronage, control of contracts. Power: Influence on character of community, patronage, opportunity for service.
5. Forms of governmental organization, locus of power within government	Status: Prestige from being associated with high-status communities (by means of annexation or incorporation). Economic: Advantages of tax avoidance, efficiency in government, jobs and contracts from government. Power: Determinative of access to decision-makers, responsiveness of government, patronage.

These are, of course, only the points at which conflict converges with the greatest regularity and with the highest intensity. The first three are in the nature of policy outputs of the political process, whereas the last two categories are progenitors or inputs into the decision-making system. Some other policy areas, such as transportation, are important focusing issues but do not display the regularity or intensity of the basic five and so have not been raised to an equivalent level. Also, occasional ad hoc issues not in these categories arise and generate great bitterness or involvement and may invoke the basic motivations on the part of the disparate elements, without being classifiable as part of the basic continuing content of County politics. An example of such an occasional issue, nevertheless of major importance, was the problem of disposition of a surplus airfield.

The purpose of this five-part categorization of major conflict-points is to integrate the issue classifications derived from the original newspaper search with the refinements drawn from the review of electoral contests and the implications of the expenditure-revenue pattern changes. Each of these five categories includes items from all three of the empirical source areas and is in effect a fusion of them. Distributing the items from the newspaper-produced classification scheme (Table 1) and introducing relevant items from the two supplementary presentations produces a sharpened sense of the actual substance of County politics in defined areas of primary importance. We take this to be the substance of County politics for our purposes.

THE IMPACT OF THE COURTS ON THE ISSUES

With these five primary issue areas established, an analysis of the way in which the local courts impinge on them and affect policy outcomes in each may proceed to contrast these issues with the actual decisions of the courts in each area. The number of cases in each area varies sharply:

Zoning, land use	200
Education	25
Taxation	9
Nominations, elections	16
Govt. powers, forms	34

It is clear that zoning and land use is the area in which the courts have the greatest involvement and thus potentially the most continuous (although not necessarily qualitatively the most significant) opportunity for influence over policy. This would not be inconsistent with the formulation just developed because the zoning and land use area would appear to offer the largest number of opportunities for status and economic interests to collide. Let us examine the policy role of the courts (if any) in each of the areas in sequence by comparing the totality of issues which actually arose with the decisions of the courts, after the dual analysis fashion described at the outset of this chapter.

Zoning and Land Use

The volume of cases in this category and the differences in land uses involved require that a distinction be made between issues involving the location of public improvements and those concerning zoning and land use matters. The rather surprising result of the comparison regarding the location of public improvements is that, with the single admittedly spectacular exception of the Demotown incinerator issue, the decisions on where to locate public improvements were not affected by courts at all. Opposition was substantial in every one of these instances, and in the case of Intracounty Expressway 1 was strong enough to cause the project to be abandoned, and yet none was carried to court until the Demotown incinerator episode. The success of the latter technique suggests that courts were not without some utility, but they were in fact not used. Decisions about some highway projects are made by the Public Works Department of the State and appear to be less vulnerable than the actions of local governments, but there were only two of these among the ten major issues.

The pattern in the zoning category is distinctly different from that in land use. The courts are consistently active in reviewing the day-to-day decisions of local boards, with particular concern for the economic rights of individuals and small businesses. The nature of the courts' impact appears to be interstitial rather than comprehensive in that the courts are decisive in a large number of individualized cases but without establishing over-all policy guidelines and probably without considering alternative land use policies as such.

Education

The record shows very slight contact by the courts with the major issues. A total of three proceedings each in regard to budgets and contracts is negligible in view of the vast sums raised and expended by the school districts, and in any event all six were unsuccessful. Court contact with educational matters was for the most part limited to reinstatement proceedings by teachers and efforts by parents to obtain some specialized request from the schools; only in the latter category were school decisions reversed by the courts. Possible reasons for this limited effect include the extensive provisions for review of local school decisions within the educational system itself, reaching up to the Commissioner of Education, an exclusive set of procedures fostered by State legislation. Some issues which do rise through the administrative process within the Education Department would then come under the jurisdiction of the courts of Albany County, whereas some claims such as segregation are litigated in the federal courts. In any event, the result is minimum contact between the courts and education.

Taxation

Few specific tax matters reach the level of public controversy, although the general subject of tax levels is never far from the forefront in any governmental jurisdiction. School tax needs engendered particularly violent reactions and determined opposition during the course of this study (partially reflected in budget contests in the education area), but there is no way to create a court contest over the *level* of tax imposed (as distinguished from the legality of the tax itself).

Much lies beneath the surface in this area, however. There were some determinations of significance, for example, which were never subjects of public controversy, nor is the significance of tax policy decisions reflected in the number of cases in the field. The trend is toward a major role for the courts but without much public notice. The cases which were litigated before 1960 were largely individual efforts to avoid local assessments for improvements, and it was only in the latter years that the large taxpayers challenged the County's assessment policies. Initial complaints gave rise to a County study project and then successes in court action began to encourage further litigation. A special section in the County Supreme Court had to be set up to handle tax certiorari and condemnation cases; at stake was a significant element in the County revenue structure and the Justice assigned to this specialized function happened to be convinced of the scientific character of the appraisal business, so that modifications of specific assessments would not appear to be barred by considerations of deference to legislative or administrative discretion.[2] The insertion of judicial determinations into the revenue structure of the County is not limited to the County's's assessments on the larger shopping centers and industrial plants, for the small merchants of Shopville, believing their assessments to be excessive in the light of customer drift to the shopping centers and consequently reduced income from their stores, also successfully challenged their Village assessments and received substantial reductions.

Nomination, Elections, and Control of Government or Control of Political Party

Comparison of the issues identified with the cases decided leads to the impression that the most vital matters are concluded within the parties without invoking the courts. Despite the number of major offices contested during this sixteen-year period, not one of these involved the courts of the County. Indeed, except for one area, there is an inverse relationship between the importance of the office and the propensity to involve the courts. Nine of the decisions in this field deal with individual nominating petitions, usually of party committeemen rather than candidates for office, and the Board of Elections was upheld in all but one. The courts *have* provided authoritative definitions of potentially ambiguous statutory provisions, so that the legitimate authority of Board actions or local government incumbents could be established, and this appears to be a primary function in this area. The character of the decisions in this area is distinctively technical, apparently a product of the obvious partisan political implications of any result and the concern of the judges for the public reaction to any decision.[3] The conflict between the political parties for control of the

[2]In an article in the local bar association journal, this judge reports that ". . . today's appraiser never has to guess. . . . It can truly be said that appraising has become a science." He defines the problem in an assessment case as being the statutory limitations on the kind of proof acceptable in proof of valuations, that is, the taxpayer must show that the ratio of value to assessment is different in his case from that of other properties. Taxpayer and County each select a set of sample properties whose ratios support their cases and the Court is obligated to fix values, average out a Countywide ratio for them, and compare to the case at hand. The "Countywide ratio" found is different for each case, depending on the samples submitted.

[3]Interviews with judges confirm the acute awareness of partisan implications in Election Law cases, and also the tendency to bury oneself in the obscurity of legalisms as a means of avoiding the charge of partisan motivations. The trend on appeal would appear to be away from technicalities and toward common sense as the case rises on the appellate ladder away from its origin and toward the more protected courts.

County government mechanisms in 1962–1963, . . . is the major exception to this pattern of involvement with minor matters only . . . .

Forms of Governmental Organization, Locus of Power within Government

This category is an outgrowth from the previous one, but is formulated separately because it involves the structure and powers of government rather than the obtaining of office. From the data, the courts appear to be more closely involved with the major issues in this area than in any of the others, probably because the very nature of the subject calls for authoritative legal determinations. The Towns' resistance to annexation of adjoining property by villages within the Towns has led to litigation as the only recourse on several occasions; annexation appears to provide the kind of fusion of status and economic motivations which brings out spirited demands and intransigent resistance, and offers no basis for resolution other than litigation. Court applications of policy here have been wholly determinative of the outcome in this area. The City *A* and City *B* disputes were not exclusively over the powers of institutions of government and were probably more amenable to adjustment within and between parties and factions. They might with equal propriety have been classified with the "control of party, control of government" issues.

Certain categories of issues emerged from the search of the newspapers that have not yet been examined for their relation to the courts of the County. The field of transportation, vital as it is to the economy of the County and replete as it is in Table 1 with entries indicating public concern, has not led to a single court decision in the sixteen years involved. The explanation probably lies in the fact that State public service and franchise commissions occupy that part of the field not already pre-empted by federal commerce power regulations. The Rail Road's operating and financial problems were handled by the ICC and by State reorganization legislation, and a single abortive move was made in the local courts in response to all its difficulties.

Labor relations is represented not by cases reflecting the celebrated issues but by decisions centering around the questions of NLRB jurisdiction and regulation of picketing. Eight of the nine cases in this area fit the foregoing description and the exception deals with internal union affairs. The Sunday closing law issues are represented by a total of five cases, four of which uphold convictions for violations, but the litigation appears to have been at least partially successful in that it drew attention to the statutes and aided in bringing about their ultimate moderation.

The final category drawn from the identification of issues was that of the imposition of sanctions and controls by means of local ordinances. In this area, largely one of the regulation of businesses in behalf of public convenience or in fulfillment of status-related objections to the business, the volume of court activity far outstrips the public controversy over the ordinances or their application. The most widely agitated local ordinance question, that of the Village *A* low-altitude ordinance, was litigated in the federal courts, but the next most important one, sandpit regulations, was upheld in a series of local court decisions. In addition, six cases deal with efforts by units of government to enforce standards of propriety on bars and restaurants by denying or withholding licenses; others range from antinoise ordinances aiming at eliminating private schools to traffic regulations which would preclude the conduct of a business to denials of the right to engage in a business on essentially aesthetic grounds. The economic interests of the business are pitted against the status concerns of the legislative body in all of these cases, and in twelve out of fourteen of them the decision favors the pursuit of economic gain.

THE IMPACT OF THE COURTS ON LOCAL GOVERNMENT POLICIES: THREE CASE STUDIES

In an effort to add further dimensions to this analysis of the ways in which local courts bear upon the issues of County politics, we can consider the impact which they have on the policies established within different types of local governmental units. Envisioning each of these units of government as responding to a distinct political environment, faced with different complexes of demands, resources, and powers, and possessed of varied alternatives in the way of policy choices—in other words, facing disparate fields of political forces—we seek to specify how the courts affect the substance of policy applied within those jurisdictions.

Three units of local government have been selected for this purpose. Shopville was chosen because it is a heavily populated commercial and apartment center, with the most government (in the sense of employees, services, expenditures, etc.) of all the County's villages, and with significant problems representative of urban life such as declining business, urban renewal, and a substantial (27%) nonwhite population. The unincorporated area of Newtown was chosen because it offers insight into the problems of recent rapid growth and resultant demands for services and schools. It is also a community of over 50,000 persons governed jointly by a Town government and a collection of autonomous special districts; it has no real identity except as a School District, a post office address, and in a similarity of home design and construction, and these factors might give rise to distinctive impact by the courts. The Village of Flower City was selected as the third case study because it represents the other type of local government in the County: the wealthy, well-ordered, exclusively residential, country club, commuting type of village which constitutes the "ideal" of suburban living. Flower City functions by "gentleman's agreement" (uncontested rotation of the Mayoralty among the four property owners' associations) and by plan. Rigid enforcement of zoning and other ordinances has kept Flower City an oasis in the eyes of its residents, and the role of local courts could well be different (as is everything else) in regard to Flower City.

In each case, the totality of issues of public concern or importance was compared with the substance of court decisions, just as was done for the issues of County politics previously. The entire range of controversy and significant decision-making within each jurisdiction thus again provides the basis for characterizing the impact of the courts in each of these three settings.

Shopville A long-established center of population, Shopville stood out during the 1920s and 1930s as the commercial and transportation hub of the County. It contained more retail establishments, including branches of major department stores, than any other community and was the focal point for all major bus lines. With the advent of decentralized shopping centers in the postwar years, however, it began to decline in terms of proportion of retail sales and in terms of the quality of its businesses in comparison with the branches of the New York City stores which were springing up nearer the new centers of population. At the same time new residential development shifted from single-family homes to apartments as a result of limitations of available land and the need for increased tax revenues to meet demands for services. Shopville had a population of 29,000 in 1950 and 34,000 in 1960; its Village budget for 1963 was over $2,400,000, the largest of the villages in the County, and it still ranks first among all localities in the County in number and volume of sales of retail and service establishments, being in these respects comparable to such middle-sized cities as Albany, New York, and Corpus Christi, Texas.

The character of the issues agitated and significant decisions made clearly reflects the urban and commercial character of Shopville. A total of twenty-three issues and problems involving the commercial aspects of the Village were identified during this time period and ten of these reached the courts in some form. In seven instances, the right to engage in business was upheld against Village policies or efforts at regulation which threatened to reduce profits, in two cases Village land development policies were upheld, and in one case court action was inconclusive. A relatively commercial ethos obtains in Shopville: an uneasy accommodation between the merchants (with their Chamber of Commerce, Rotary, Lions, and other means of group representation) and the small home owner (with the taxpayer's concern for status-related respectability and order in the community) makes the Village Board a regulator of the excesses of the market place and the arbiter of the means toward profit. Fully half of the issues and problems found here is the product of the presence and proclivities of business, and one-third of these resulted in court decisions reversing Village policies. The implication is clear that regarding the circumstances of Shopville and its propensity for regulatory action in the economic area, the courts are a major means of maintaining an unhindered market. The economic motivation and its thrust toward profit thus are aided in its role of structuring the community and directing its development.

The impact of the courts on the twenty issues and problems not connected with the commercial side of the Village is slight. In one case, Board denial of rezoning for apartment purposes was upheld and in another a mantle of legitimacy was cast over a condemnation action where two members of the Board were stockholders of the corporation owning the land. The other issues, such as school segregation, political control of Village government, and other zoning changes were dealt with by the State's administrative hierarchy, open electoral decision, and pressure group activity, respectively. At the same time, the courts handled six cases not rising to the level of public controversy or major significance, all in the area of land use. Five of these involved use of land for business purposes and in all five Village policy was reversed in furtherance of economic opportunity; the one instance where a zoning ordinance was upheld was in a case where the owner had not exhausted his opportunities to obtain a variance under existing law. The uses of the courts in defense of economic rights could hardly be more decisively documented.

Flower City Settled in the late nineteenth century as a development literally designed as a "garden community," Flower City has continued the emphasis on planning and rigidly enforced its standards. Its population was 14,500 in 1950 and 24,000 in 1960. Very little industrial or commercial development was permitted until the last few years, although many of the highest echelon New York City department and specialty stores have branches on its primary business street.

The residential emphasis in Flower City is faithfully represented by the distinctive pattern of its community conflicts as compared to its immediately adjacent neighbor, Shopville. Only eleven issues and problems were identified, and these deal primarily with the task of preserving the high-status residential character of the community against the pressures of rising taxes and costs of services. The temptation to use lands at the peripheries of the Village for industrial or commercial purposes in order to lighten the tax burden is always present and just as consistently opposed by those who will pay any price for purity. With the single exception of the 1948 dispute over increases in gas rates, every one of the issues and problems identified relates to the defense of status against the broadening of the tax base or, with regard to the Jewish Center and street-widening instances, against the intrusion of outsiders. Interestingly, only the attempt to prevent the synagogue from locating within the Village reached the courts; a decision was deferred for some time until an authoritative precedent from the Court of Appeals in a similar case was available, at which time the permit was ordered. Even then, further recourse to the courts was necessary to prod a reluctant Board into action. The pattern of the courts' other decision-making is distinctive too: five cases were decided in all, and in all three in which the Board had enforced zoning standards it was upheld.

The Board was upheld also in its assessment policy and reversed only where it sought to limit the number of seats in a local college grandstand (not prevent them). The pattern in the case of Flower City is one of local resolution first, with slight propensity to challenge a determination once made, and then of court support for Board enforcement of standards. The courts' role shifts from defending economic rights to supporting community status. In part a reflection of the character and approach of the community itself, there is still a sense from the courts' performance that Shopville is viewed as a place to do business and Flower City as a place to reside in comfort.

Newtown   The development of Newtown presents a picture sharply at variance with the two previous Villages. There was no Newtown until a mass developer went to work after the war. By 1960 there was a community of over 50,000 persons, a School District serving 18,000 pupils and expending almost $11,000,000 in public funds annually, and all the other services which a suburban community expects. Newtown is governed by a Town government, due to its unincorporated status; this means that most decisions affecting it are made by the Town Board, a body of six elected by the 800,000 residents of the Town on an at-large basis. For this and other reasons, there is relatively less consciousness of community in Newtown than in the two Villages and also less direct contact between voters and officeholders.

Because it is not a self-governing community, it is sometimes hard to find Newtown as a social entity except when it focuses around its deep and bitter school controversy. This division arises out of philosophical and religious differences which line up educationally traditionalist, highly tax-conscious, politically conservative, predominantly Irish Catholic residents against educationally "progressive," liberal, largely Jewish elements of the community. It has been an enduring split and shows every sign of continuing. Thousands of dollars are invested in School Board election contests, unheard of in other parts of the County, and most events are interpreted in terms of the school situation. After Newtown was initially organized and the first burst of idealism and self-realization had run its course, this controversy seems to have been the only major issue. Other matters are probably dissipated before they can crystallize because the structure of Town government succeeds in diffusing political power and responsibility across so vast a terrain.

The issues and problems of Newtown may be seen in three categories: the early stage of community organization and idealistic efforts at its definition, a subsequent mature state of settled-in suburbanism, and The Great School Controversy. The first stage includes the period through

1953 in which a total of fifteen issues arose including such matters as district organization and access to facilities, racial and religious discrimination, and services. Three issues reached the courts, with the result that both racial (lease provision) and religious (Sunday closing laws) antidiscrimination efforts were blunted. A third case resolved a fire district boundary question. No other decisions were made affecting Newtown in this era. The second stage reaching from 1950 to the present includes only three major issues, probably due in part to the diffusion effect previously noted, and all of these are in the area of zoning and boundaries. None of these ended in litigation, but three less important matters did engage the courts; in two of them Town zoning was upheld and in the third a teacher was denied reinstatement. The third stage of school controversy produced six high points of noteworthy public conflict and each election to the School Board should be added to this list. None of these, however, have produced a court decision, again largely because of the magnitude of administrative machinery involved in the area of education.

The case of Newtown suggests that one of the by-products of large-scale Town government may be a lessening of local pressures on legislative bodies and reduced assumption of responsibility on the part of citizens. This apparently lower level of controversy may be due also to the lower-class character of the population or the fact that all such energy is used up in fighting the school battle. It might be the product of a lower sense of involvement as a result of the newness of the resident in the community, but the experience of the early years would tend to refute this—unless those early community-minded settlers have moved on to higher-status communities and been replaced by newer migrants from the city, for which there is some evidence. In any event, the courts have not been relevant to the issues and problems of Newtown in any important way.

We have then differential impact on the governance of a community resulting from the socio-economic character and governmental form the community displays. These differences appear to create for the courts a distinctive role with reference to each community and to point up distinctive aspects of judicial effects on policy.

SUMMARY: THE ISSUES AND THE COURTS

This chapter has sought to identify and analyze the issues and problems which make up the substance of politics in the County, and to evaluate the effects of the courts on the resolution of these issues. These issues and problems were defined as those matters which involved numbers of people in controversy of a continuing nature or significant decisions involving the use of public funds or affecting the economic or social character of the community, whether or not they gave rise to public controversy.

There were some areas of major public controversy identified in the search for issues which appeared not to have involved the courts in any important way: transportation and labor relations, for example. A listing of the five most significant issues of public concern during the period involved in this study, determined by the amount of attention paid to them in newspaper reports, would include the Rail Road (reorganization, performance, and fares), the Raceway scandal (ownership, taxation), the major union labor empire and its operations, the closing and disposition of the surplus airfield, and the battle for control of County government in the years 1962 and 1963. Only the latter, by far the least important of the five, has reached the court in any form.

The impact of the courts on the substance of policy determinations in the major issues of County politics is narrow, specialized, and distinctively individualistic. Where the economic opportunity of an individual or a business in terms of maximized profits, free competition, use of property, or return on investment are involved, the law and the courts are invocable and effective. There is thus a kind of "private rights" emphasis to court determinations and impact, primarily, but not entirely, made up of "rights" in the economic dimension, and this can be seen running through zoning, particularly in the areas of nonresidential land use and nonresidential use of residentially zoned land, taxation, education, and the Shopville case study. The courts thus contribute to the shaping of public policy in those areas where the (largely) economic rights and opportunity of individuals and businesses are involved, and the effect of this particular kind of contribution is to defend or assert the inviolacy of these rights and hence the primacy of the free market over efforts at social control. This appears to be of no small importance in structuring the outcome in those areas where these economic rights are assertable, but it does not mean that all economic matters are subject to court control. It means that (simply) in the continuing conflict between status-related actions and economically related actions, the courts will normally be available and effective in tilting the outcome in behalf of the economic side; where status opposes status motivations, or economic opposes economic motivations, the impact of the courts is less clear but likely to support an individual's claim over that of the community.

The courts have a nonindividualized, public function also and this is found largely in the forms of government area. In matters of annexation, incorporation, Charter interpretation, and the respective powers of component parts of government, the decisions of the courts are primarily determinative of major substantive matters and crucial to the outcome of the County political process. No clear pattern of the direction of such involvement emerges, except to note the emphasis on procedural fairness and adherence to statutory authorization which results.

There is a further implication arising from this survey of issues and decisions, and that has to do with the manner of the courts' participation.

It does not appear from the evidence here assembled that the courts establish a specific policy which must be adhered to within the County even in the areas where they have been most involved; their involvement is more in the nature of setting the outer boundaries beyond which the legislative body may not go and (with the exception of the field of tax assessments and certain other specific situations) then accepting a legislatively selected alternative within the area. The result of this approach is that substantial initiative is retained in the legislative body and although an occasional alternative may be vetoed, ultimately legislative will can be expected to be made effective by virtue of the number of alternative means available for reaching the same practical result.

The net result of this analysis is an image of the courts as totally uninvolved in some major controversies and some highly significant areas, engaged in busy work of limited significance in many areas (the over-all pattern of which may add up to a substantial policy role over time), and primarily determinative in a few key areas. When the courts are invoked, they tend to be defensive of economic rights, responsive to the character of the community, and possibly means of partisan shaping of the basic forms and rules.

THE POLITICAL PARTY VARIABLE IN THE MICHIGAN SUPREME COURT

S. SIDNEY ULMER

This study of the Michigan supreme court was undertaken for several reasons. In the first place, it is convenient to study a court in the state in which one happens to live and work. But of greater importance is the fact that the Michigan supreme court (1) is the highest court in the seventh largest state in the Union (2) is composed of elected members whose political affiliations are known and (3) operates in a highly politicized context as a result of the relative balance of the Republican and Democratic parties in the state. Moreover, the policies followed by the two major parties in the state seem more closely tied to the interests of those sociopolitical groupings which generally are affiliated in the public mind with one or the other party as the case may be.[1] The parties also appear ideologically more homogeneous in Michigan than their national images would suggest. Thus, while the Democrat party in Michigan is probably to the left of the national party, the ideological spectrum spanned by state party policy seems somewhat more narrow than at the national level. The same can be said of the Michigan Republican party if we substitute right for left in the comments above.

One consequence of this is that the lines of ideological conflict may be

[1]*E.g.*, labor interests—Democratic party; large-scale economic enterprise—Republican party.

Reprinted with permission of publisher and author from S. Sidney Ulmer, "The Political Party Variable in the Michigan Supreme Court," *Journal of Public Law*, Vol. 11 (No. 2, 1962), pp. 252–62. Mr. Ulmer is Professor of Political Science at the University of Kentucky.

Political party variable refers to membership in the Republican or Democratic party by Michigan supreme court justices. Thus party affiliation is conceptualized as representing a set of values sufficiently internalized to become, psychologically, qualities of the individuals under study. This enables us to view political party affiliation as a dichotomous, qualitative variable.

expected to follow party lines more closely than in national politics. And, of course, the fact that Michigan supreme court judges are elected serves to reinforce these tendencies insofar as Michigan judicial politics is concerned.

The involvement of the Michigan supreme court in state politics stems in part from article VII, section II of the 1908 constitution which established the election of the justices at the regular biennial spring elections. The same section requires a chief justice and associate justices, the number of which is left to the legislature. Acting under its authority, the legislature in 1903 set the number of justices at eight, serving eight-year terms.[2] Since 1954, the chief justice has been chosen by the justices themselves from among their number.[3] Once chosen, he serves until the expiration of that term for which he was elected as chief justice of the supreme court.

From 1908 to 1939, Michigan supreme court justices were nominated by political party conventions and elected by the people at large under a party label. There seemed to be little complaint about this procedure up to 1932. The Republicans dominated the court as well as state politics. When a Republican justice died, a Republican justice was appointed by a Republican governor to fill the unexpired term. Subsequently, the appointee would be nominated by the Republican convention and re-elected under a Republican party label. With the Democratic resurgence, however, came agitation for an appointive system. This is not to say that the change was favored because it appeared that the Democrats might increase their representation in the court. But the coincidence of the two events is not without interest.

The political role of the Michigan supreme court cannot be separated from the constitutional and statutory requirements governing selection of court personnel or from the political history of the state. The historical chronology of party balance, in particular, is helpful in understanding judicial politics in Michigan in 1961. It must be remembered that the Republican party was organized in an oak grove at Jackson, Michigan, in 1854 and reflected at the time the political ideology of the region. The same year Kinsley S. Bingham was elected the first Republican governor in the state and the nation.[4] From 1854 to the constitution of 1908, only one Democrat was elected to the governor's office—Winans gaining the office in 1890. During the same period, the Republicans elected fifteen different governors. In the period since 1908, the Republicans have won the executive office in fifteen of twenty-six elections.[5] It is obvious that the Democratic party has fared somewhat better in the latter period, but

---

[2]Act 250 of Public Acts of 1903. The number of justices has varied: five in 1850, (6-year terms), four in 1857 (8-year terms), five in 1887 (10-year terms) and eight in 1903 (8-year terms).

[3]Act 142 of Public Acts of 1954.

[4]BAIRD, THIS IS OUR MICHIGAN 83 (1959).

[5]MICHIGAN MANUAL 94 (1959-1960).

the gain of the party has not been spread evenly over the sixty years of this century. On the contrary, the improvement is due almost entirely to a Democratic resurgence which began in the thirties and culminated with the tenure of Governor G. Mennen Williams from 1948 to 1960.

Thus, from 1908 to 1930, a period of Republican domination, the Democrats elected one governor. From 1930 to 1940, the two parties alternated with the Republicans taking the executive office in 1930, 1934 and 1938, and the Democrats winning the position in 1932, 1936 and 1940. This was a period of party balance. The third period, 1948 to the present, has been an era of Democratic dominance in the executive branch of state government, although that dominance has not carried over to the state legislature. The salient feature of Michigan judicial politics since 1948 has been the attempt of the Democrats to broaden their dominance from the executive branch to include the judiciary thus circumventing in many respects a legislature in which Republican dominance is maintained. This dominance is based on malapportionment of numerical representation —a vestige from an era characterized by somewhat different population patterns.

As the strengths of the two parties have approached a relative balance in state politics, competition for judicial office has involved that office in the basest kinds of political struggles. As a consequence, in 1939 a constitutional amendment made supreme court justices elective on a nonpartisan basis. The method of nominating the candidates, however, was left to the legislature which in turn has left it to the political parties. Thus, Michigan has, for some years, nominated judicial candidates at party conventions and elected them to office on a nonpartisan ballot. If such a system was designed to "take the politics" out of the selection of justices, it has not succeeded. In the first place, each candidate is identified by party affiliation in almost every newspaper covering judicial elections. A considerable amount of publicity is also given the actions of the candidate and the party during the nominating period. From this alone, no one in the state need have any doubt as to who is what. But if this were not enough, the candidates themselves have chosen to inject political considerations into their campaigns for office. Thus, the *Detroit News* reported the following remarks on February 24, 1957:

> Justices George Edwards, Detroit; Tablbot Smith, Ann Arbor; Black, and Voelkner have announced that they will shun court tradition and campaign as partisan Democrats.
>
> Justice Smith told a Democratic caucus that an entire arm of State government—the courts—is up for capture in the April election.
>
> In a manner unprecedented in previous conventions, the State Supreme Court justices wove in and out of night-long party caucuses. In each, they asked outright political support in the designated court contest.[6]

[6]Detroit News, Feb. 24, 1957, p. 2A.

The justices themselves do not deny partisan activity, Justice Kavanagh has remarked that "no election is actually non-partisan." And in discussing the 1939 amendment in 1957, he said, "the people knew we were not expected to change our stripes after a party had nominated us."[7] Thus, he appealed for the election of Democrats to the court in order to get "equal justice." This blatant assertion that "Democratic justice" is not the same as "Republican justice" has not only gone undisputed but other members of the court (both Democrats and Republicans) have expressed the same view. In 1953 Chief Justice Dethmers (Republican) was reported as asking: "[C]an judicial officials be expected to hand down impartial decisions when those decisions may affect their re-election? . . . Can we, under our present system of election of judiciary officials, find men who are courageous enough to stand against the will of the mob?"[8] And in 1956 Justice Black (Democrat) charged that when supreme court justices are nominated at political conventions, "[T]hey have a responsibility to partisan delegates who nominate them, and I don't feel this is in keeping with the dignity of the Supreme Court."[9]

No doubt, each of the justices mentioned was criticizing "the other fellow." Yet, enough smoke is produced by such comments to inquire whether fire is also present. This paper, therefore, starts from the premise that Republican justice and Democratic justice do, indeed, differ; that the political party variable is a crucial cutting edge in certain cases; that the justices of the Michigan supreme court have pronounced tendencies to group in certain politicized situations in terms of their political party affiliation. This does not mean that any judge ever takes any position because his party wants him to do so. It is to suggest that certain voting and opinion groupings can be explained by party affiliation, that in some specific subject-matter areas Democrats go in one direction and Republicans in another. In short, we ask: To what extent can differences in the judicial behavior of the judges in the court be explained by the political party variable? The analysis that follows is designed to delineate some answers to this query in certain selected areas of decision-making.

The only study made of judicial politics in Michigan was published by Glendon A. Schubert in 1960.[10] The motivation for Professor Schubert's brief analysis stemmed from the observation that the Michigan supreme court near the close of the 1954 term was splitting along party lines in workmen's compensation cases. After characterizing the workmen's compensation issue as "an acceptable criterion of judicial liberalism-conservatism in the United States,"[11] Schubert examined all workmen's compensation cases decided by the Michigan supreme court in the period 1954–1957.

[7]*Id.*, March 14, 1957, p. 7.
[8]Lansing State Journal, April 30, 1953, p. 17.
[9]Detroit News, Aug. 19, 1956, p. 8A.
[10]SCHUBERT, QUANTITATIVE ANALYSIS OF JUDICIAL BEHAVIOR 129–42 (1960).
[11]*Id.* at 132.

Such a focus is particularly important in view of the fact that the settlement of workmen's compensation disputes by a court of law is obviously
a political matter. That is, in most instances the question reduces to who
gets what and how much. Moreover the conflicts taking place in this area
have overtones of a class struggle. For normally the forces or representatives
of labor are arrayed against the forces or representatives of management.
And the stakes in this game are of great magnitude often involving the very
question of subsistence or sustenance during crisis periods in the lives of
those protected by workmen's compensation statutes.[12]

An order for the payment of workmen's compensation is the end result
of a series of decisional processes. The initial hearing in a dispute is presided over by a hearing referee whose decision is subject to review by an
appeal board of three members (no more than two of whom may be from
the same political party). The decision of the appeal board in turn may be
reviewed by the Michigan supreme court by writ of certiorari.[13]

Recognizing the importance of these final decisions made by the Michigan supreme court in workmen's compensation cases, the present study
extends the Schubert analysis from 1957 through the 1960 term. The period
1958–1960 is set off from the period studied by Schubert by virtue of
the fact that the Democrats attained a five-to-three majority in the court
for the first time in 1958. This event is unusual in more ways than one.
For Democratic representation on state supreme courts has not, in general,
exceeded that of Republicans except in the South. In 1955 a breakdown of
the party affiliations of the 304 supreme court justices serving in forty-
eight states showed 153 Democrats, 118 Republicans and 33 with party
affiliation unknown. When the seventeen southern states were eliminated,
it was found that 65 per cent of the justices in the thirty-one northern states
were Republicans. And nine supreme courts in the northern states had no

**Table 1   Composition of the Michigan supreme court 1954–1958 by political
party affiliation of the justices**

	1954	1955	1956	1957	1958
Republicans	6	6	4	3	3
"Old Line" Democrats	2	1	1	1	
"Williams" Democrats	0	1	3	4	5

Legend: "Old Line" Democrats were elected or appointed prior to the Williams era (1948–1960) and generally voted with the Republican majority.
"Williams" Democrats were elected or appointed during the era of Governor G. Mennen Williams and
generally voted en bloc and in opposition to the Republicans in workmen's compensation cases.

[12]For example, in the fiscal year ending September 30, 1960, compensation paid
(excluding medical payments) totaled over 35 million dollars for the 107,778 employers under
the Workmen's Compensation statute.
[13]See WORKMEN'S COMPENSATION DEPARTMENT, WORKMEN'S COMPENSATION ACT
AND RULES OF PRACTICE 56 (1960).

Democratic representation at all.[14] Thus the Democratic majority attained in Michigan in 1958 deserves special notice.

The change in the composition of the Michigan court resulted from the retirement of Justice Sharpe on December 31, 1957, and the election of Justice Kavanagh who took office January 1, 1958. This event was the culmination of a trend which commenced at an earlier date. The changing proportion of party representation in the court in the period 1954–1958 is summarized in Table 1. As the table indicates, the Republicans steadily lost ground in the period 1954–1958 and by the latter date were reduced to a minority of three. We may ask whether the addition of the fifth Democrat in 1958 was of consequence for the behavior of the justices or the court in the workmen's compensation cases. In Table 2 we present the voting statistics for the period 1954–1960.

Table 2   Votes in favor of workmen's compensation claimants: supreme court of Michigan, 1954–1960

Term	1954	1955	1956	1957	1958	1959	1960	1958–1960
Number of Cases	18	10	16	15	11	11	7	29
				(Percentage)				
Black (D)			100	100	81	90	57	79
Edwards (D)			100	100	81	90	57	79
Smith (D)		85	100	100	81	90	71	82
Voelker (D)				100	90	88	50	79
Kavanagh (D)					72	90	71	79
Souris (D)							75	75
The Court	33	30	87	100	81	90	57	79
Kelly (R)	35	30	81	80	63	63	14	51
Dethmers (R)	27	30	62	86	63	63	14	51
Boyles (R)	31	30	76					
Butzel (R)	41	50						
Reid (R)	27	30	62					
Bushnell (OD)	50							
Sharpe (OD)	22	30	62	40				
Carr (R)	33	30	62	40	63	63	14	51

If we compare the figures for the pre-1957 and post-1957 periods, several discrepancies are notable. In the first place, the total number of workmen's compensation cases being decided by the court each year was somewhat less in the latter period. Thus, if we examine comparable three-year periods, 1955–1957, and 1958–1960, the total workmen's compensation cases decided was forty-one in the first period and twenty-nine in the second. A large part of the difference, however, is attributable to the remarkably low figure for 1960. The court not only decided only seven

[14]Nagel, *Unequal Party Representation on the State Supreme Courts*, 45 J. AM. JUD. SOC'Y 62 (1961).

workmen's compensation cases in 1960, but through April 25, 1961, had not decided a single additional case. This raises a question: Why such a sudden drop in the workmen's compensation cases being decided by the court? A hypothetical answer may be based on the fact that the percentage of workmen's compensation cases being decided favorable to the worker's claim increased from 33 per cent in 1954 to 90 per cent in 1959, the year before the sudden drop. This increase actually coincided rather closely with the increasing number of Williams Democrats coming on the court. In 1954, there were no Williams Democrats in the group and the court found for the workman's claim in 33 per cent of the cases. Smith was added in 1955, a year in which 30 per cent of the claims were decided in favor of the workman. In 1956, however, when two additional Williams Democrats came to the court, the percentage increased to 87 per cent. In 1957 the court found for the claimant in every one of fifteen cases. And in 1958 and 1959, with the Democrats in the majority at last, the percentage of claims decided for the workman was 81 and 90 per cent respectively.

In view of these figures and the changing composition of the group which seems to have been responsible for the statistical variation, it is plausible to hypothesize that the decline in the number of cases decided in the 1958–1960 period was due to a decrease in the number of cases lost by management at the lower levels and appealed to the supreme court. For once the percentage of outcomes favorable to the claims reached 100 per cent in 1957, management, it may be expected, would recognize the inevitable and begin to be more selective in choosing cases to be appealed. The appellate process, after all, is expensive, and one is not likely to be interested in litigating in an area in which the chances of success are 10 to 20 per cent. Thus, it may be that the lower figures for 1958–1960 merely reflected the recognition by management forces in Michigan of the operating role of the party variable in the Michigan supreme court.

If our hypothesis is correct, the percentage of management appeals from adverse decisions at the lower administrative and judicial levels should have decreased from the former period to the latter. In 1954, out of eighteen workmen's compensation cases decided by the Michigan supreme court, thirteen, or 72 per cent, were appealed by management. The ratio of successful appeals was 69 per cent. In 1955, management appealed seven of the ten workmen's compensation cases decided during the year, a ratio of 70 per cent. The appeals were successful in five, or 71 per cent, of the cases. In 1956, management appealed fourteen cases, 86 per cent, and won a verdict in only three, or 21 per cent. The reversal of form here is obvious. Whereas in 1954 and 1955 management had been successful in about 70 per cent of their appeals, in 1956 the success ratio was less than one-third of that figure. The drop is accounted for by the fact that two new Democrats joined the court and in conjunction with Justice Smith supported the workmen's claim 100 per cent of the time. The court, however, was for the claim in 87 per cent of the cases.

One might have expected management to get the message implicit in the increase in the ratio of decisions favorable to the claim from 30 to 87 per cent in one year. But the myth of objectivity apparently dies hard even among hardheaded business executives. In 1957 every one of fifteen appeals, 100 per cent, was made by management from losing decisions at a lower level. The percentage of success was zero since every case was affirmed, and every decision was for the worker. This development was made possible by the accession of a fourth Williams Democrat, Justice Voelker, to the group. This gave the Williams Democrats one-half the membership of the bench. It should be noted, however, that while the court voted for the workmen's claim in every case, in only two of the fifteen cases was decision for the worker based on a four-to-four split, which had the effect of affirming the decision below.

After the experiences of 1956 and 1957, one might have predicted a reduction in the percentage of management appeals coming to the court raising workmen's compensation issues. Yet in 1958, management appeals originated ten of eleven cases, or 91 per cent. In 1959, however, the message finally seems to have penetrated, for management appealed only five, or 45 per cent, of the eleven cases decided during the term. In 1960 the ratio was four in seven, or 57 per cent. Thus, in 1959 and 1960, we find management appealing workmen's compensation decisions at about one-half the previous rate. On the other hand, workmen have been encouraged to appeal decisions against them at the lower levels by the obvious improvement in their chances in the supreme court. Thus, the data is consistent with our hypothesis that the fewer number of cases in more recent times reflects less inclination on the part of management to appeal a losing decision at the lower level.

We cannot, however, be certain that other factors are not operating in this situation. It may be that recognition of supreme court attitudes on the part of the decision-making agencies at the lower levels, *i.e.*, the board of appeals and the circuit courts, served to make these agencies a little more sensitive and somewhat more sympathetic to the claims pressed by aggrieved workmen. In such case, a higher percentage of decisions for the workmen at these levels would decrease the number of appeals to the supreme court in workmen's compensation cases. That one or both of these hypotheses are valid is suggested by the fact that of those cases heard and decided by the court in 1960, the ratio of support for the workmen's claim among Democrats and Republicans was considerably lower than in previous terms. The Democrats supported such claims in 1960 at least 30 per cent less than formerly. And the Republicans did so about 50 per cent less frequently than in the preceding four years. Thus, Justices Black, Edwards and Voelker, who had supported workmen's compensation claims in at least 80 per cent of the cases in each of the three terms of the 1957–1959 period, dropped to 57 per cent in the case of Justices Black and Edwards, and 50 per cent in the case of Justice Voelker. Justices Kelly, Dethmers and Carr, who in 1958 and 1959 supported such claims 63 per cent of the time, dropped to a support rate of 14 per cent in 1960. It is not to be thought that after all these years the attitudes toward these claims which seemed to prevail in the period 1956–1959 suddenly underwent such drastic change. We infer on the contrary that the change occurred in the type of case being appealed. Such a hypothesis would also explain the fact that the rate of support for workmen's compensation claims by the court as a whole reached only 57 per cent in 1960 for the lowest ratio since 1955.

In one respect, however, it can be said that no change occurred between the two periods examined—that is, as the figures make clear, the Democrats continued more favorably inclined to workmen's compensation claims than Republicans. The difference is in the percentage: between 51 per cent for the Republicans and 75 to 82 per cent for the Democrats in the period 1958–1960. Thus, we see that party affiliation serves to distinguish two groups of judges who behave differently in workmen's compensation cases, such behavior being entirely consistent within each group. The extent of this intragroup consistency is better grasped by looking at the data summarized in Table 3.

Table 3   Voting patterns in workmen's compensation cases 1958–1960

	SM	ED	KA	VO	BL	DE	KE	CA	Number
Type I	+	+	+	+	+	+	+	+	14
Type II	+	+	+	+	+	−	−	−	10
Type III	−	−	−	−	−	−	−	−	5
Total + ...	24	23	23	20	23	14	14	14	

Legend: + is a vote for workman's claim
             − is a vote against the claim
Note: Discrepancies in total + votes reflect non-participations for Justices Kavanagh and Voelker and a single inconsistent vote for Justices Black and Edwards.

This table contains the three types of voting patterns identified in the twenty-nine workmen's compensation cases decided in the period 1958–1960. Of all votes cast, only two were cast inconsistent with these patterns. Thus, for all practical purposes, we may say that these three patterns summarize the voting behavior of the court in the twenty-nine cases. Two of the patterns show a unanimous court, either for or against the workmen's compensation claim. These account for 65 per cent of the total votes cast with fourteen of nineteen cases being decided unanimously in favor of the claim. The remaining ten cases (35 per cent of the votes) however, show a five-to-three split, with five Democrats for the claim and three

Republicans opposed. Such near-perfect intragroup consistency is rarely seen in social science research and certainly is not what one would expect to find in such a controversial subject-matter area as workmen's compensation. This is brute testimony to either the strength of party affiliation in Michigan judicial politics or the unusual homogeneity of social attitudes among those judges who wear the party labels.

Table 4   Voting patterns in unemployment compensation cases decided by the Michigan supreme court 1958–1960

Voting Patterns	SM	ED	SO	KA	VO	BL	DE	KE	CA	Number	Votes
I	+	+	+	+	NP	+	+	+	+	1	8–0
II	+	+	NP	NP	+	+	+	+	+	2	7–0
III	+	+	NP	+	−	+	+	+	−	1	6–2
IV	+	+	NP	+	+	+	−	−	−	3	5–3
V	+	+	+	−	NP	−	−	−	−	1	3–5
VI	+	−	NP	+	−	−	−	−	−	1	2–6
VII	−	−	NP	−	−	−	−	−	−	1	0–8
VIII	−	−	−	−	NP	−	−	−	−	2	0–8
Inconsistencies. . . .			1	1						12	94

Legend : + = a vote for compensation claim
          − = a vote against compensation claim

In the related area of unemployment compensation, we find that the same basic voting patterns persist. That is, Democrats are more favorable to the claim for unemployment compensation than are the Republicans. Table 4 presents the data for the twelve cases decided in the period 1958–1960. In these cases, the three Republicans were solidly opposed to the claim on eight occasions. And, one of the Republicans, Justice Carr, was opposed in one of the four remaining cases. The Democrats on the other hand were solidly in favor of the claim in six of the twelve cases and solidly opposed in only three cases. These figures show that the same basic dichotomy between Republicans and Democrats exists in the handling of unemployment compensation as in the handling of workmen's compensation cases: i.e., the Republicans favor such claims less than the Democrats to a significant degree.

The consequences of all this may be good or bad, desirable or undesirable. It is clear that in workmen's compensation and unemployment compensation cases, Democratic justice is more sensitive to the claims of the unemployed and the injured than Republican justice. Whether such a finding suggests a need for reform is, of course, the most basic kind of political question. For, in effect, it is the question of who gets what, when and how. In the past the worker got "less"—at present he gets "more." This change is directly related to the resurgence of the Democratic party in the state and in the court. It is a by-product of the election of the justices, reliance for nomination on the political parties and the absence of life tenure subject to good behavior. It furnishes the critics of present methods of judicial selection in Michigan with hard empirical evidence for consequences they, for whatever reasons, have long predicted.[15]

[15]On the whole such predictions have focused on the effect of popular election on the independence of the judge. In testifying before the state constitutional convention on November 7, 1961, Justice Eugene Black called for a complete divorce of "degrading politics" from the state supreme court. He went on to suggest that judicial independence is not consonant with a "partisan-nominated" judiciary. Lansing State Journal, Nov. 8, 1961, p. 1, at 2.

PART SIX

THE STUDY OF STATE AND LOCAL GOVERNMENT: CHANGING EMPHASES

During the last two decades the study of state and local government has undergone important shifts in emphasis and direction. Students of state and local governments are today asking probing questions applying concepts and modes of analysis previously utilized for the study of other political phenomena and adapting sophisticated statistical and other techniques to answer the significant questions they have raised. As the authors of this reader's final chapter point out, "the study of state and local politics has reentered the mainstream of political research."

Herbert Jacob and Michael Lipsky summarize the new directions recent research has taken while reviewing some of the major contributions social scientists have made in these areas. They also suggest an agenda for future research calculated to fill the more important gaps in our understanding of the field. The authors note, for example, that findings about the relationship between policy outputs and socioeconomic and political variables are still quite tentative. The same can be said about the relationship between inputs and the conversion or decision-making process. Ambiguities continue to plague students of community power, and there are few concrete findings available concerning the forces governing political interactions among nonelites. Finally, the authors consider the need to develop and to employ more sophisticated classification schemes, without which the product of comparative analysis is relatively unrewarding. If there is a common thread running through the chapter, it is the demand that theoretical or pretheoretical frames of reference be generated. And this, perhaps, is the most telling indication that students of state and local government are catching up with other specialists within the political science discipline.

CHAPTER NINETEEN

OUTPUTS, STRUCTURE, AND POWER: AN ASSESSMENT OF CHANGES IN THE STUDY OF STATE AND LOCAL POLITICS

HERBERT JACOB AND MICHAEL LIPSKY

State and local politics as a field of political science is no longer a "lost world" or the site of "Dullsville."[1] Rather than being the laggard of the discipline that some political scientists perceive it to be, the study of state and local politics has reentered the mainstream of political research. Much of the work in political science which has influenced the drift of the profession has been within its domain. V. O. Key's *Southern Politics*[2] quickly became a classic for the discipline. Robert A. Dahl's *Who Governs?*[3] as well as other community power structure studies have raised significant questions for other spheres of the discipline. *The Legislative System*[4] by John C. Wahlke *et al.* has remained the model for investigations of the roles of political actors; Thomas R. Dye's *Politics, Economics, and the Public*[5] is a landmark in the systematic analysis of public policy.

[1]Lawrence J. R. Herson, "The Lost World of Municipal Government," *American Political Science Review*, 51 (1957), 330–45; Coleman Ransone, "Revolt in Dullsville," *Public Administration Review*, 27 (1967).

[2]V. O. Key, Jr., *Southern Politics in State and Nation* (New York: Alfred A. Knopf, 1949).

[3]Robert A. Dahl, *Who Governs?* (New Haven: Yale University Press, 1961).

[4]John C. Wahlke, Heinz Eulau, William Buchanan, and LeRoy C. Ferguson, *The Legislative System* (New York: John Wiley & Sons, 1962).

[5]Thomas R. Dye, *Politics, Economics and the Public* (Chicago: Rand McNally, 1966).

From Herbert Jacob and Michael Lipsky, "Outputs, Structure, and Power: An Assessment of Changes in the Study of State and Local Politics," in Marian D. Irish, editor, *Political Science: Advance of the Discipline*, © 1968 by the Southern Political Science Association. Reprinted by permission of Prentice-Hall, Inc., Englewood Cliffs, New Jersey. Mr. Jacob is Professor of Political Science at Northwestern University. Mr. Lipsky is Assistant Professor of Political Science at the University of Wisconsin.

We are grateful to James Davis, John Gardiner, and Kenneth Vines for comments on an earlier draft.

Although we can confidently say that the state and local politics field is no longer a lost world, we cannot be equally confident that it is a unique field of study. Political activity which occurs at these levels of government is not very different from that which occurs at the national level, in other nations, or on the international scene. Because the focus of study has shifted from particular institutions, defined in legalistic terms, recent research has universal implications. Consequently the large body of literature on political phenomena in state and urban political systems has important implications for the understanding of political behavior in general. Conversely, the field must be evaluated by the standards of the discipline rather than by the parochial concerns of a sub-field.

Our focus in the following pages will therefore be on the potential contributions of recent literature to the concerns of the discipline writ large. Further, we shall concentrate on questions which recent research has opened for investigation rather than engage in a laudatory review of settled issues. We shall be concerned with the gaps that remain unfilled and the potential for future research based on the substantial advances of the past quarter century.

We shall focus on problems in four areas: (1) potential for policy analysis; (2) political behavior in institutions where policy decisions are made; (3) utilization of the power structure model of urban politics; and (4) the need for development of pre-theoretical typologies. Our concentration on four areas critical for the advance of the discipline precludes analysis or mention of some studies which would be prominent if we had a different perspective. The recent literature includes studies of the philosophy of federalism, of voting behavior, of parties and elections systems, of particular issues such as urban renewal and of intergovernmental relations, most of which are peripheral to our concern in the following pages. They should be—and are—included in any thorough bibliography of the field.[6]

I. RELATIONSHIP OF POLICY OUTPUTS TO SOCIAL, ECONOMIC, AND POLITICAL VARIABLES

The most marked innovation in the study of state and local politics has been the investigation of the relationship of policy outputs to social, economic and political variables as undertaken by Richard E. Dawson and

[6]See, e.g. James Herndon, Charles Press, and Oliver P. Williams, *A Selected Bibliography of Materials on State Government and Politics*, Bureau of Government Research, University of Kentucky, Lexington, Kentucky, 1963; Leo F. Schnore and Henry Fagin (eds.), *Urban Research and Policy Planning* (Beverly Hills, Calif:. Sage Publications, Inc., 1967), pp. 603–630; and bibliographical notes in John C. Bollens and Henry Schmandt, *The Metropolis* (New York: Harper and Row, 1965).

James A. Robinson,[7] Thomas Dye,[8] Richard I. Hofferbert,[9] Lewis A. Froman,[10] and Ira Sharkansky[11] in the state field. Their work follows the earlier efforts of economists, notably Fisher,[12] and Sachs and Harris[13] who were concerned with the relationship of socio-economic variables to the level of governmental expenditure. Similar investigations have examined urban policy outputs.[14]

The investigations at the state level have produced a number of important, indeed startling, results. Three independent investigations, using slightly different analytic techniques, have concluded that legislative malapportionment has not been related to a distinctive pattern of outputs.[15] Policies which might be heavily favored by the under-represented urban majority are no more in evidence in well apportioned than in poorly apportioned states. The substantial differences in the level of outputs are accounted for by a variety of other variables, not by legislative malapportionment.

Secondly, at least three independent investigations reject the hypothesis that party competition is related to the level of governmental

[7]Richard E. Dawson and James A. Robinson, "Interparty Competition, Economic Variables and Welfare Politics in the American States," *Journal of Politics*, 25 (1963), 265–289.

[8]Dye, note 5 above.

[9]Richard I. Hofferbert, "The Relation between Public Policy and Some Structural and Environmental Variables in the American States, *American Political Science Review*, 60 (1966), 73–82.

[10]Lewis A. Froman, Jr., "Some Effects of Interest Group Strength in State Politics," *American Political Science Review*, 60 (1966), 952–961.

[11]Ira Sharkansky, "Correlates of State Government Expenditures," paper prepared for delivery at the 1966 Annual Meeting of the American Political Science Association, September, 1966 (mimeo.).

[12]Glen W. Fisher, "Determinants of State and Local Government Expenditures: A Preliminary Analysis," *National Tax Journal*, 14 (1961), 349–355; "Interstate Variation in State and Local Government Expenditures," *ibid.*, 17 (1964), 57–64.

[13]Seymour Sachs and Robert Harris, "The Determinants of State and Local Government Expenditures and Intergovernmental Flow of Funds," *ibid.*, 17 (1964), 75–85.

[14]See especially, John H. Kessel, "Governmental Structure and Political Environment: A Statistical Note about American Cities," *American Political Science Review* 56 (1962), 615–620; Leo F. Schnore and Robert R. Alford, "Forms of Government and Socio-economic Characteristics of Suburbs." *Administration Science Quarterly*, 8 (1963), 1–17; Robert R. Alford and Harry M. Scoble, "Political and Socio-economic Characteristics of Cities," *The Municipal Year Book*, 1965 (Chicago: The International City Managers' Association, 1965), 82–97; Raymond Wolfinger and John Osgood Field, "Political Ethos and the Structure of City Government," *American Political Science Review*, 60 (1966), 306–326; Thomas R. Dye, Charles S. Leibman, Oliver P. Williams, and Harold Herman, "Differentiation and Cooperation in a Metropolitan Area," *Midwest Journal of Political Science*, 7 (1963), 145–155; Lewis A. Froman, Jr., "An Analysis of Public Policies in Cities," *Journal of Politics*, 29 (1967), 94–108; Amos H. Hawley, "Community Power and Urban Renewal Success," *American Journal of Sociology*, 68 (1963) 422–431; Oliver P. Williams, Harold Herman, Charles S. Liebman and Thomas R. Dye, *Suburban Differences and Metropolitan Policies: A Philadelphia Story* (Philadelphia: University of Pennsylvania Press, 1965).

[15]Herbert Jacob, "The Consequences of Malapportionment: A Note of Caution," *Social Forces*, 43 (1964), 256–261; Thomas R. Dye, "Malapportionment and Public Policy in the States," *Journal of Politics*, 27 (1965), 586–601; Hofferbert, note 9 above.

activity.[16] More competitive states are not more liberal in welfare or education expenditures when one holds wealth, industrialization, education, and urbanization constant. In addition, Dye has shown that it makes little difference whether a state is dominated by Republicans or Democrats or whether there is a high or low level of electoral participation.[17] Variations in state policy outputs are principally related to socio-economic variables according to these studies.

These investigations also represent a substantial advance in methodological sophistication. Using simple and multiple correlation techniques, they permit assessment of the relative importance of a large number of variables in accounting for variance in the level of outputs. These techniques also allow truly comparative analysis since there is no technical barrier to the consideration of data from 25, or 50 states or several hundred urban communities. In the near future we shall no doubt see further methodological advances with the use of causal modelling, factor analysis, and time series analysis.

Yet despite the methodological sophistication of these studies, we are troubled by some conceptual simplifications. Each investigator appends a theoretical framework to his study, usually a version of systems theory. The theory, however, rarely guides the research. This is because of the way in which key concepts are operationalized and the manner in which linkages between inputs, the conversion processes, and outputs are conceptualized.

These problems can be illustrated by Dye's work, the most extensive output analysis yet published. Dye outlines a model in which inputs are operationalized as socio-economic variables, the political system is operationalized in terms of the party system, legislative malapportionment, and electoral participation, and outputs are operationalized by levels of expenditures for a wide variety of programs, impact measures, and measures of the program quality. He then posits linkages which connect inputs to the political variables and then to outputs, and alternatively, inputs to outputs while by-passing the political process.

The first problem with this operationalized model is that income, urbanization, industrialization and education are not in themselves inputs. The measures have little substantive relationship to the phenomena they are supposed to represent. We might conceive of them as environmental factors which may lead to the articulation of demands and support and their communication to political authorities. Demands are verbalizations or behavioral articulations of satisfaction or dissatisfaction with the status quo.[18] The relationship between demand-behavior and environment may

[16]Dawson and Robinson, note 7; Hofferbert, note 9; Dye, *Politics, Economics, and the Public*, note 5.

[17]Dye, *Politics, Economics and the Public*, note 5.

[18]David Easton, *A Systems Analysis of Political Life* (New York: John Wiley & Sons, 1965), pp. 38 ff.

in some circumstances be high but it is certainly neither 1:1 nor constant. We know that in apparently dissimilar environments, political controversy centers around the same issues. Corruption is a controversial and central issue in both Massachusetts and Louisiana.[19] In both Montana and Wisconsin air pollution control was an issue in the 1967 legislatures.[20] Social structure, political culture, political institutions, and elite perceptions intervene between a given environment (as measured by Dye) and the articulation of demands.

Further the operationalization of the political system is generally primitive. In Dye's work, party competition, electoral participation, and legislative apportionment are used; they do not represent the whole of the political system nor perhaps even its most significant elements. In Dye's defense, it must be pointed out that much of his work was intended to test specific hypotheses derived from earlier investigations by Key,[21] and Lockard,[22] on the role of party competition and electoral participation. Dye himself admits that these measures are incomplete representations of the political system.[23] What we need then are synoptic measures of political systems or their most significant elements. Such measures will have to include, as a minimum, consideration of the organization of the executive branch, the organization of the legislature, the strength of interest groups,[24] the linkages between state systems and their federal and local counterparts. Perhaps the characteristics of party systems should also be considered although their influence is doubtful on the strength of the evidence accumulated thus far.

Considerable further work also needs to be done in conceptualizing the dimensions of policy. Most of the analyses we have cited use measures of several dimensions indiscriminately without showing an awareness that more than one dimension is involved. Most frequently used are measures of the level of expenditure, program quality, and program impact.[25] In addition, we can identify at least one other dimension: the distribution of benefits among a population. The distribution of benefits or sanctions is perhaps the most significant output dimension for political scientists, since

[19]For Massachusetts, see Edgar Litt, *The Political Cultures of Massachusetts*, (Cambridge: MIT Press, 1965); Murray B. Levin, *The Alienated Voter* (New York: Holt, Rinehart, 1960); Duane Lockhard, *New England State Politics* (Princeton: Princeton University Press, 1959), pp. 119–176; for Louisiana, see Alan P. Sindler, *Huey Long's Louisiana* (Baltimore: Johns Hopkins Press, 1956).

[20]Douglas C. Chaffey, *Legislative Party Leadership: A Comparative Analysis*, unpublished Ph. D. dissertation, University of Wisconsin, 1967.

[21]Key, note 2 above, pp. 298–310.

[22]Lockard, note 19 above.

[23]Dye, *Politics, Economics and the Public*, note 5 above, pp. 296–297.

[24]An early attempt to provide such a measure of interest group strength is in Belle Zeller (ed.), *American State Legislatures* (New York: Thomas Y. Crowell, 1954), pp. 190–191.

[25]The level of expenditure is the most frequently used dimension. Examples of quality measures include teacher/pupil ratios, doctor/patient ratios, and per pupil expenditures. Impact measures include school drop-out rates, literacy rates, and crime rates.

much of the conflict preceding adoption of a program is not about whether it should be embarked upon but who will pay and who will benefit. Even programs that apparently benefit most of the population—such as education and highway construction—have a variable incidence of benefits. Thus to understand the politics of education at the state level one must understand how grants-in-aid are distributed to school districts. To comprehend the bitter in-fighting about education in an urban community one needs measures of the inequalities in the distribution of schools, teachers, and teaching aids throughout a city. Measures of distribution unfortunately are rarely available in public records (an interesting political fact in itself). But the lack of data cannot deter political scientists from investigating what may be the most important dimension of policy outputs. Just as it became necessary to spend much money to generate data about voting behavior, it is necessary to allocate resources to collect data about the distribution of program benefits.

Once more adequate measures of the dimensions of outputs have been collected, it will be possible to analyze separately the linkages between these several dimensions and the input and conversion-process variables. It is likely that these linkages will be different for each dimension. For instance, it seems probable that quite different conditions will be associated with the level of expenditure and with the impact of a program. As administrators sadly know, high expenditures may have little impact. The level of expenditures may be closely associated with demands while the impact of a program may be more closely related to structural characteristics of political institutions.

The manner in which Dye infers linkages also raises serious problems and challenges for the future. Dye's method is to account for the variance rather than to use regression coefficients to indicate how much a change in one variable is associated with a change in another variable. Thus for the most part Dye is unable to make causal inferences although he and others often imply causality. He shows convincingly, confirming the findings of others, that socio-economic and political variables are highly correlated. However, because they are highly correlated, by holding one constant, the variance of the other is reduced.[26] Thus he is not able to infer quite as exactly as he claims that one set of variables is more important than another.

Dye also leaves unexplored the nature of the linkages that he asserts exist between economic development and programmatic outputs. We conclude from reading his analysis that by some magic a high level of economic development becomes transformed into high levels of expenditure. The processes by which this transformation takes place remain in the

---

[26]We are indebted to Charles Cnudde and Donald McCrone for making this point to us. In a forthcoming article, they illustrate the use of regression coefficients with Dye's data.

shadows although it has been the traditional task of political scientists to illuminate them.

Policy studies which grew out of an entirely different conceptual framework—the process-oriented studies such as *State Politics and the Public Schools*,[27] *Schoolmen and Politics*,[28] and *The Politics of State Expenditures in Illinois*[29] —illuminate some of the linkages which are missing in the statistical studies. Each of these books deals with the immediate as well as distant antecedents of the policy under analysis. Thus, Masters, Salisbury and Eliot are concerned with interest group structure and activity, the activity of institutions such as the State Department of Education and the legislature, and with the partisan complexion immediately prior to the adoption of a policy decision. The significance of intervening institutions is illustrated by Anton's finding that the rate of growth of governmental expenditure in Illinois is positively related to the budget-cutting norms of the Illinois Budgetary Commission.[30] The rate of growth of educational expenditures in Illinois has been related to the norms and functions of the School Problems Commission;[31] where such an articulating agency is absent (as it was in Michigan), the rate of growth will be slower even in the presence of greater environmental resources.[32] What is needed are studies in which the two traditions of analysis reinforce each other. The results of the statistical investigations may provide criteria for the selection of cases for intensive analysis and sensitize case studies to variations in the dimensions of policy outputs. The case analyses may suggest new measures of input, process, and output for further comparative statistical analysis.

Case studies also suggest another conceptual difficulty with the statistical analyses. Researchers generally posit a single political system which operates in the same fashion in the educational, welfare, transportation, recreation, public health, and regulatory areas. As Dahl showed in New Haven[33] and other policy studies imply, policy arenas have quite separate sets of decision makers associated with them. It is probably erroneous to expect that input and process variables are associated in the same way to each policy output. What we need are maps of the sub-systems which are responsible for output decisions in various subject areas. The state-wide political system that many have sought to describe may in fact not

[27]Nicholas A. Masters, Robert H. Salisbury, and Thomas H. Eliot, *State Politics and the Public Schools* (New York: Alfred A. Knopf, 1964).

[28]Stephen K. Bailey, Richard T. Frost, Paul E. Marsh, and Robert C. Wood, *Schoolmen and Politics* (Syracuse: Syracuse University Press, 1962).

[29]Thomas J. Anton, *The Politics of State Expenditures in Illinois* (Urbana: University of Illinois Press, 1966).

[30]*Ibid.*

[31]Masters, *et al.*, note 27 above.

[32]*Ibid.*

[33]Dahl, *Who Governs?*, note 3 above.

exist.[34] What we perceive as the ongoing political process may be a series of relatively autonomous processes occasionally linked on the floor of the legislature, in the chief executive's office, and by the fact that political events tend to be concentrated in the capitol and city hall.

Another aspect of the problem of linking the environment, the political process, and outputs is illuminated by Froman's article, "Some Effects of Interest Group Strength in State Politics."[35] Froman related interest group strength in the early 1950's to the characteristics of state constitutions which were written between 1789 and 1965. He finds some slight relationships. The presence of these relationships, however, should not deter us from asking what theoretical justification there is for relating a phenomenon occurring in the mid-twentieth century with outputs spanning nearly two centuries. Sharkansky provides us strong reasons for rejecting this approach. He traces the growth of governmental expenditures and enters into his regression equations the previous level of expenditures. He finds that the level of expenditures in 1962 is closely related to that of 1957 and that of 1957 is closely related to that of 1952.[36] He thus provides supporting evidence for the hypothesis that governmental policy making is incremental in nature; sharply innovative decisions are rarely made. If Sharkansky is correct, then we might expect the same pattern of decision-making to characterize state constitution-making and present day constitutions would be more closely related to input and conversion characteristics of earlier eras than they would be to contemporary phenomena. Sharkansky's investigations initiate the study of the change dimension of political outputs, a subject rarely examined by political scientists.[37]

These problems with output analyses reflect more on the state of the discipline than on the particular investigators. Concerned with a narrow range of problems and utilizing measures at hand, this group of scholars has made a considerable contribution. In part that contribution

[34]It is interesting to note that most of the state-wide studies published in the last 20 years are in fact limited to one or two segments of the political system; none deal systematically with outputs. See, for instance, Leon D. Epstein, *Politics in Wisconsin* (Madison: University of Wisconsin Press, 1958) [elections]; Lockard, *New England State Politics*, note 19 above [elections and legislative politics]; Key, *Southern Politics*, note 2 above [elections]; Sindler, *Huey Long's Louisiana*, note 19 above [elections]; William C. Havard and Loren P. Beth, *The Politics of Misrepresentation* (Baton Rouge: Louisiana State Univeristy Press, 1962) [legislative apportionment]; John Fenton, *Politics in the Border States* (New Orleans: The Hauser Press, 1957) [elections].

[35]Note 10 above. Cf. recent "Communication" from Thomas L. Thorson, *American Political Science Review*, 61 (1967), 478–479.

[36]Sharkansky, note 11 above.

[37]For a different kind of longitudinal analysis, see H. D. Price, *The Negro and Southern Politics* (New York: New York University Press, 1957), pp. 41–44, who relates Negro registration in 1950 with the percentage non-white in 1900. This is reiterated by Donald R. Matthews and James W. Prothro, *Negroes and the New Southern Politics* (New York: Harcourt, Brace, and World, 1966), pp. 115–120.

consists of specific findings which undermine hypotheses long a part of the folklore of political science. But the greater part of their contribution lies in illuminating research gaps which stand in the way of testing more theoretically sophisticated models of the relationship between outputs on the one hand and inputs and the conversion processes on the other.

II. SYNOPTIC INDICATORS OF THE POLITICAL PROCESS

One of the gaps highlighted by policy studies is the lack of synoptic indicators of conversion processes. Concern for these processes characterizes much of the work in state and local politics, but decision-making in institutions has usually been studied as a political process complete in itself. The research is rarely directed to the task of isolating those characteristics of a decision-making process which are essential to understanding the institution's ingestion of inputs or its production of outputs. Thus we have not advanced as far as we might wish in either the task of creating synoptic measures nor in understanding the relation of behavior in the institutional framework to the larger political world.

These problems can be easily illustrated with the research on legislatures. Scholarly interest in institutions since World War II has been overwhelmingly directed at state legislatures. These studies have several foci. The most widely noted has been the examination of the role perceptions of legislatures in four states, *The Legislative System*.[38] It explicitly adopted role theory as the framework for its research design. Its authors examined the backgrounds of legislators, the formal characteristics of their legislative assemblies, and the significance of the party systems in terms of how legislators perceived their roles. Somewhat akin to this study is James Barber's *The Lawmakers*[39] which more loosely uses the framework of role theory but also studies the activities of Connecticut legislators.

The Legislative System and *The Lawmakers* are both landmarks of political investigation. The former is explicitly theoretical in conception and comparative in its analysis. The latter probes more deeply into the relationship between self-perception and overt behavior. Both studies are careful in operationalizing their key concepts through questionnaire items which permit replication. Both represent the first important studies in political science relying heavily upon role theory.

Yet both leave us considerably short of our objective of understanding legislative behavior. *The Legislative System* is a bit like a hall of mirrors. It permits legislators to observe themselves and see how others perceive them, but it does not tell us how these perceptions affect overt behavior. Its authors fail to link the roles which they identify with behavioral patterns. Barber links his role categories more closely with behavioral patterns and

---

[38]John C. Wahlke, *et al.*, *The Legislative System*, note 4 above.
[39]James David Barber, *The Lawmakers* (New Haven: Yale University Press, 1965).

attempts to build a theoretical framework which helps explain why certain legislators choose particular role and activity patterns. However, he fails to take into account the role categories of *The Legislative System;* consequently, his work does not permit that cumulation of observation which would encourage broader generalization.

Other investigations focus entirely on behavior. The one form of behavior that has won most attention has been roll call voting.[40] Research in this tradition has come to a number of findings. In many legislatures most issues are decided without substantial divisions on roll call votes. In many legislatures significant divisions occur at stages other than the final roll call vote; in a substantial number of states, legislative rules are designed to obscure partisan and group differences and to transfer them from the floor of the legislature to committee meetings, committees of the whole, and party caucuses. Constituency characteristics are probably significantly related to deviant voting behavior on roll call votes. Where divisions occur in competitive states, they are usually along party lines and mark the most vital issues rather than routine ones.

What the roll call studies preeminently possess is methodological sophistication, ranging from relatively simple indices of block voting to factor analysis and scalogram analysis of voting behavior. What they almost uniformly lack is a theoretical framework which would place their findings more comfortably into the perspective of other political investigations. Thus roll call studies rarely examine a broad range of outside influences on the voting behavior of legislators[41] and they seldom have been comparative so that the impact of varying institutional arrangements could be assessed.[42]

A third but small set of investigations consists of case studies of legislative decision-making as exemplified by Gilbert Y. Steiner and Samuel

[40]Among others, see Duncan MacRae, "The Relationship Between Roll Call Votes and Constituencies in Massachusetts," *American Political Science Review*, 46 (1952), 1046–1055; ———, "Some Underlying Variables in Legislative Roll Call Votes," *Public Opinion Quarterly*, 18 (1954), 191–196; ———, "Roll Call Votes and Leadership," *Public Opinion Quarterly*, 20 (1956), 543–558; R. W. Belker, F. L. Foote, M. Lubega, and S. V. Monsma, "Correlates of Legislative Voting: the Michigan House of Representatives," *Midwest Journal of Political Science*, 6 (1962), pp. 384–396; Malcolm E. Jewell, "Party Voting in American State Legislatures," *American Political Science Review*, 49 (1955), 773–791; W. W. Crane, "A Caveat on Roll Call Studies of Party Voting," *Midwest Journal of Political Science*, 4 (1960), 237–249; and John G. Grumm, "The Systematic Analysis of Blocs in the Study of Legislative Behavior," *Western Political Quarterly*, 18 (1965), 350–362. See also the comprehensive review of this literature in Malcolm E. Jewell and Samuel C. Patterson, *The Legislative Process in the United States* (New York: Random House, 1966), pp. 414–452.

[41]Notable exceptions are MacRae, "The Relationship Between Roll Call Votes and Constituencies," note 40 above, and John G. Grumm, "A Factor Analysis of Legislative Voting," *Midwest Journal of Political Science*, 7 (1963), 336–356. For an excellent example of the focus on this relationship, see Oliver Garceau and Corinne Silverman, "A Pressure Group and the Pressured: A Case Report," *American Political Science Review*, 48 (1954) 672–691.

[42]But see Malcolm E. Jewell, *The State Legislature* (New York: Random House, 1962), pp. 48–76.

K. Gove's *Legislative Politics in Illinois*[43] and Edward C. Banfield's *Political Influence*.[44] Such studies are broader in scope than role analyses or roll call studies, but what they gain in scope they lose through theoretical diffuseness and generality. Steiner and Gove, for instance, keep their theoretical framework entirely implicit. Banfield's framework is likewise the examination of influence, although he is more concerned with how various actors exert their influence than with the decision-making process itself. These studies carefully examine the influence of parties, interest groups, and constituencies, and distinguish between one issue area and another in the manner in which the legislative process operates. They are rich in detail and provide us with the flavor of legislative battles. But they are difficult to generalize upon because they fail to operationalize their key concepts. As Dahl and others have made clear, influence and power are elusive concepts; studies which confront influence directly run the risk of stumbling on its operationalization.

The emphasis on legislative behavior and activity reflects the accessibility of legislators and the adaptability of research methods to their arena. Where decision-making is more obscured and where roll call voting and survey research are less applicable, far less work has been done. Consequently, although the mid-twentieth century is par excellence the age of the executive, few researchers have ventured into the cubicles of bureaucrats. Equally few have searched the halls of justice.

The principal study of the states' chief executive is *The Office of Governor in the United States* by Coleman Ransone.[45] Ransone comprehensively describes the politics of gubernatorial selection and the manner in which the chief executives of the states perform their duties. He notes great variations in the selection of governors, their functions, their staffs, and their formal and informal powers over the bureaucracy, but he does not attempt systematically to account for these differences. Although the gubernatorial office is much smaller than the presidential, Ransone stumbles on the same barriers as have scholars of the presidency—neither have developed reliable indicators of influence nor have they been able to isolate the chief executive's role in interactions with bureaucrats which lead to decision-making and policy initiation. Joseph A. Schlesinger's attempt to rank order the formal power of governors is the first at developing the kind of synoptic measures which are needed for comparative research.[46] But as Schlesinger himself recognizes, it is a weak measure because it concerns only formal powers

[43]Gilbert Y. Steiner and Samuel K. Gove, *Legislative Politics in Illinois* (Urbana: University of Illinois Press, 1960).

[44]Edward C. Banfield, *Political Influence* (New York: The Free Press of Glencoe, 1961).

[45]University, Alabama: University of Alabama Press, 1956.

[46]Joseph A. Schlesinger, "The Politics of the Executive," in Herbert Jacob and Kenneth N. Vines (eds.), *Politics in the American States* (Boston: Little, Brown & Co., 1965), pp. 207–237.

for a position in which many informal functions are very important. More-over, it is an ordinal scale which yields estimates of power vis-a-vis other governors but not relative to other institutions in the same state or in other political systems.

There have been very few studies of the state bureaucracy other than case studies of isolated incidents and investigations of the social back-grounds of key personnel in state agencies.[47] Even though it is generally recognized that most key decisions are initiated or made within executive agencies, the conditions under which they operate, those which are as-sociated with one kind of organizational structure rather than another, and the relationship between executive branch characteristics and legislative and judicial characteristics remain unmapped and challenges for future students of state politics.

The judiciary has been somewhat more frequently studied, but judicial research suffers often from the same insularity as legislative and executive studies. Recruitment patterns and appellate voting behavior have been the principal foci of investigation. The recruitment studies have achieved a preliminary understanding of the results of various judicial selection systems but they have not shown how these recruitment patterns are related to other political behavior—the party system, non-judicial elections, or court decisions.[48] Research on appellate voting behavior[49] has shown that most state appellate court decisions are unanimous, partially as the result of decision-making rules which lead to specialization among judges and limited participation by most judges in decisions before their appellate courts. Stuart Nagel asserts that the party identification of judges distinguishes their voting patterns, but his conclusions are based on extremely limited data for a few states.[50] Sidney Ulmer and Glendon Schubert make a more convincing case for the influential role of party identification among

[47]Deil S. Wright and Richard L. McAnaw, "American State Executives: Their Back-grounds and Careers," *State Government*, 38 (1965), 146–153; Deil S. Wright, "Executive Lead-ership in State Administration," *Midwest Journal of Political Science*, 11 (1967), 1–26. See also the case studies published by the Inter-University Case Program.

[48]Herbert Jacob, "The Effect of Institutional Differences in the Recruitment Process: The Case of State Judges," *Journal of Public Law*, 13 (1964), 104–119; see also the forthcom-ing study of the Missouri selection plan: Richard A. Watson, Randal G. Downing, and Frederick C. Spiegel, *The Politics of the Bench and the Bar*.

[49]Daryl R. Fair, "An Experimental Application of Scalogram Analysis to State Su-preme Court Decisions," *Wisconsin Law Review*, (1967), 449–467; Edward Ferguson, III, "Some Comments on the Applicability of Bloc Analysis to State Appellate Courts," paper delivered at the Midwest Conference of Political Scientists, 1961, mimeo. One of the few attempts to relate decisions by appellate courts to political behavior elsewhere is in Kenneth N. Vines, "Southern State Supreme Courts and Race Relations," *Western Political Quarterly*, 18 (1965), 5–18.

[50]Stuart Nagel, "Political Party Affiliation and Judges' Decisions," *American Political Science Review*, 55 (1961), 843–851. At the most, he relies on decisions from 13 states; in seven instances he relies on observations from less than five states.

Michigan Supreme Court judges.[51] Studies of state trial courts by political scientists are still more scarce.[52] Much interesting work on trial courts, however, has been done by legal scholars and sociologists who have examined the administration of bail,[53] the availability of defense counsel,[54] variability in sentencing,[55] and similar problems of immediate practical importance. But such scholars have not sought to associate these phenomena with other aspects of the political system.

As even this brief review makes clear, the discipline is a long way from providing the statistically-minded comparative analysts the kind of synoptic measures of the political process which they need to optimize the explanatory power of their regression equations. Nor should we define our task as simply providing such measures. Once we recognize the need for such measures, we can be certain that some energies will be devoted to providing them. In the meantime, a great deal of work remains to be done in understanding the legislative, executive, and judicial decision-making processes as they relate to extra-institutional political behavior. Analysis of roles needs to be joined to the analysis of overt behavior. Roll call analyses need to be joined to a more intensive contextual analysis. Much preliminary work remains to be done on the decision-making processes within the executive and judicial branches.

III. COMMUNITY POWER STUDIES

The local community potentially provides political scientists with a natural laboratory in which to examine the dynamics of political and economic resource allocation. This potential has been realized by community power studies which have left open the question of the exercise of influence by focusing attention away from public officials. These studies have shifted research in local politics from prescription of formal-legal arrangements to description of political constellations. They have supplemented other research efforts in American politics by highlighting the importance of the underlying value structure in determining the character of the political system.

[51]S. Sidney Ulmer, "The Political Party Variable on the Michigan Supreme Court," *Journal of Public Law*, 11 (1962), 352–362; Glendon Schubert, *Quantitative Analysis of Judicial Behavior* (Glencoe, Ill.: The Free Press, 1959), pp. 129–142.

[52]Herbert Jacob, "Politics and Criminal Prosecution in New Orleans," in Kenneth N. Vines and Herbert Jacob, *Studies in Judicial Politics*, Tulane Studies in Political Science, 8 (1962), pp. 77–98, and the study by Kenneth Dolbeare, *Trial Courts in Urban Politics: State Court Policy Impact and Function in a Local Political System* (New York: John Wiley and Sons, 1967).

[53]Charles Ares, Anne Rankin and Herbert Sturz, "Administration of Bail in New York," *New York University Law Review*, 38 (1963), 67–95.

[54]The most comprehensive study is Lee Silverstein, *Defense of the Poor* (Chicago: American Bar Foundation, 1965).

[55]Edward Green, *Judicial Attitudes in Sentencing* (London: Macmillan, 1961). For a study by political scientists, see Albert Somit, Joseph Tanenhaus, and Walter Wilkie, "Aspects of Judicial Sentencing Behavior," *University of Pittsburgh Law Review*, 21 (1959) 613–620.

Extraordinary energy has been invested in attempting to answer the four questions posed by Harold Lasswell. Debate concerning characterization of American communities as "elitist" or "pluralist" has occupied the attention of many scholars.[56] Yet there remains an unfortunate aridity to the discussion of community politics. This is attributable to at least three factors which will be elaborated here: a confusion of methodology with ideology; limitations of focus; and failures in the utilization of comparative techniques.

The debate between those investigators who discover various shadings of elite and pluralist configurations in American cities, which has encouraged the development of technical and theoretical advances, in some ways has proved unproductive. There has been confusion as to whether the designations "elitist" and "pluralist" refer to methodological approaches, empirical observations, or ideological postures. This confusion is manifested by lumping together investigators with dissimilar techniques and findings, and linking conclusions about influence distribution with a fixed ideological stance. For example, in an otherwise insightful critique of the literature on community power, Agger and his associates give an ideological caste to a variety of empirical research efforts by using phrases such as "Pluralists take the position . . . ," "As one pluralist puts it . . . ."[57] This usage obscures the debate over areas of disagreement and places it in an arena where tentative conclusions are assumed to be fixed, where disparate findings are discussed as if they were uniform, and where it seems that men conduct research in order to validate their own ideological stance.

Research may well reflect ideology to the extent that designs are informed by the kinds of questions in which investigators are interested. Indeed, even where alternative empirical formulations are not forthcoming, research has been subject to criticism because of the attributed ideological content of the work.[58] But the debate on community power has tended to

[56]The literature on community studies is vast. Bibliographical aids to this literature include Charles Press, *Main Street Politics: Policy-Making at the Local Level* (East Lansing: Michigan State University Institute for Community Development and Services, 1962), and Wendell Bell, *et al.*, *Public Leadership* (San Francisco: Chandler Publishing Co., 1961). The elements of the pluralist-elitist controversy are reviewed in Nelson Polsby, *Community Power and Political Theory* (New Haven: Yale University Press, 1963); Robert Presthus, *Men at the Top* (New York: Oxford University Press, 1964), chs. 1-2; Peter Bachrach, *The Theory of Democratic Elitism* (Boston: Little, Brown & Company, 1967); and Wallace Sayre and Nelson Polsby, "American Political Science and Urbanization," *The Study of Urbanization*, Philip Hauser and Leo Schnore (eds.) (New York: John Wiley and Sons, 1965), pp. 115-156. See also Norton Long, "Political Science and the City," *Urban Research and Policy Planning*, Leo Schnore and Henry Fagin (eds.) (Beverly Hills, Calif.: Sage Publications, Inc, 1967), pp. 242-262.

[57]Robert E. Agger, Daniel Goldrich, and Bert E. Swanson, *The Rulers and the Ruled* (New York: John Wiley and Sons, 1964), pp. 76, 91.

[58]For a recent discussion of these matters see Jack Walker, "A Critique of the Elitist Theory of Democracy," *American Political Science Review*, 60 (1966), 285-295, and a reply by Robert Dahl, "Further Reflections on 'The Elitist Theory of Democracy'," *American Political Science Review*, 60 (1966), 296-305.

ignore the precept of Dahl and others that operational concepts and observable data should characterize future research on community power.

A second difficulty with the studies of community politics has been their almost exclusive focus on elite activity and orientations. Certainly it is obvious that power is distributed unequally in American society, but the task of determining the extent and impact of that inequality (to paraphrase Nelson Polsby) cannot be undertaken by elite studies alone. The literature on community power in political science, whether employing a framework emphasizing decision-making, reputation for influence, or various combinations for assembling panels of potential influentials, has neglected consideration of the influence of other strata on local politics. For example, Dahl experiences considerable difficulty in explaining the linkages between the political behavior of masses and that of influential elites. Sporadic political pressures articulated outside the pattern in which governmental affairs are normally conducted receive little mention in *Who Governs?* or other prominent studies of city politics.[59]

Oliver Williams and Charles Adrian, who distinguished among city political systems by their orientations toward providing governmental services, also neglect the consideration that a city's service may be a function of its level of demand.[60] A city may provide a relatively high level of services for reasons of civic ethos, protest activity, organized welfare-oriented interest groups, or high income levels. Where the relationship between "demand" and governmental services has been noted, as measured by percentage poor and welfare expenditures per capita, research has not followed to ascertain the reasons for this confluence.[61]

The changes in city politics resulting from the Negro protest movements of the early '60's cannot be accommodated by the community power structure models of urban politics. The failure to trace out the impact of various decisions as they "feed back" to affect the political system has left political scientists with very little to say about Negro political activity in the last half of the decade. The conditions under which quiescence and

[59]See Dahl's discussion of "the case of the metal houses," *Who Governs?*, note 3 above, pp. 192–199, 302. See, e.g., the two studies of Chicago politics: Martin Meyerson and Edward Banfield, *Politics, Planning and the Public Interest* (Glencoe, Ill.: Free Press, 1955); and Banfield, note 44 above. Sayre and Kaufman, in their study of New York City politics, ascribe no role to ad hoc pressure groups. The ephemeral role of protest organizations in New York City politics is reiterated in the introduction to the paperback edition. Wallace Sayre and Herbert Kaufman, *Governing New York City* (New York: Norton and Co., 1965). See p. xlii. Compare the influence attributed to ad hoc neighborhood groups in J. Clarence Davies, *Neighborhood Groups and Urban Renewal* (New York: Columbia University Press, 1966).

[60]Oliver Williams and Charles Adrian, *Four Cities* (Philadelphia: University of Pennsylvania Press, 1963). The converse, of course, may also obtain. Protest activity may receive encouragement from civic organizations because they provide high service levels. It is precisely the nature of this ambiguity in charting input-feedback flows that requires extensive research.

[61]See Robert Wood, *1400 Governments* (Garden City, N.Y.: Doubleday and Co., 1964), p. 64. Problems with interpretations of "demand" have been previously discussed, Section I.

arousal of relatively deprived groups occur—to use Murray Edelman's terms—and the impact of governmental and elite behavior on these conditions, has emerged as a high priority research focus for the discipline. This is a priority poorly served by previous studies of community politics.

The failure to study non-elite behavior in the literature on community power has not been remedied by research concentrating on urban Negro politics. For the most part, these studies of Negro politics have exhibited the same shortcomings as characterize the literature on city politics. They have focused on elite behavior with little reference to the effectiveness of differential leadership patterns, or they have concentrated on case descriptions without the theoretical insights which would help explain a profusion of observations.[62]

In *Negro Politics*, for example, James Q. Wilson analyzes the relationship of Negro politicians to white politicians in considerable detail but omits consideration of the impact of these relationships on the Negro community.[63] Similarly, leadership studies which promulgate dichotomous typologies of Negro leadership in distinguishing between "militants" and "moderates" fail to analyse the impact of differential leadership styles on obtaining rewards.[64]

Like the research on community power, studies of Negro leadership would benefit from consideration of the systems in which political activity takes place. Greater understanding of the context of Negro politics might help account for some of the contradictions in the literature. For example, it might help explain findings that conflict among Negro leaders is functional in some cases, and apparently dysfunctional in others.[65] It might also assist in synthesizing contradictory findings that militant Negro leaders seek "status" goals in Chicago, but "welfare" goals in Atlanta.[66]

[62]These remarks on the literature on Negro politics are elaborated in Michael Lipsky, *Rent Strikes in New York City: Protest Politics and the Power of the Poor*, Unpublished Ph.D. dissertation, Princeton University, 1967, pp. 7–16.

[63]See James Q. Wilson, *Negro Politics* (New York: The Free Press, 1960). This study remains surprisingly pertinent in many of its insights, although it was written in the pre-sit-in era.

[64]This dichotomy pervades the literature, although some writers have preferred "protest leaders" to "militants," and "accommodation leaders" to "moderates." See, e.g., Wilson, *ibid.* pp. 214 ff.; Gunnar Myrdal, *An American Dilemma* (New York: Harper and Row, 1962), pp. 720 ff.; Lewis Killian and Charles Grigg, *Racial Crisis in America: Leadership in Conflict* (Englewood Cliffs, N.J.: Prentice-Hall, 1964), pp. 81–90; Jack Walker, "Protest and Negotiation: A Case Study of Negro Leadership in Atlanta, Georgia," *Midwest Journal of Political Science*, 7 (1963) 99–124.

[65]Those who have argued that conflict was functional include James Q. Wilson, "The Strategy of Protest: Problems of Negro Civic Action," *Journal of Conflict Resolution*, 5 (1961), 298; Horace Cayton and St. Clair Drake, *Black Metropolis* (revised edition) (New York: Harper and Row, 1962), p. 731; Walker, "Protest and Negotiation," note 64 above, 122; Kenneth Clark, *Dark Ghetto* (New York: Harper and Row, 1965), p. 156. An excellent review of the literature on Negro politics can be found in John Strange, *The Negro in Philadelphia Politics, 1963–65*, unpublished Ph. D. dissertation, Princeton University, 1966, ch. 1.

[66]See Wilson, *Negro Politics*, note 63 above, pp. 214 ff.; Walker, "Protest and Negotiation," note 64 above, 110.

One hypothesis that might be tested in an analysis of the context of Negro politics is that the efficacy of different patterns of minority group leadership is related to the internal division of local elites. Where fundamental community cleavages emerge as a result of minority group demands, leadership divided among those who demand and those who conciliate may produce favorable results. But where deep community division is absent, and conflict emerges over obtaining greater proportions of community resources, then unified leadership may be more effective in bargaining than one split by internal disputes.

Recently, some efforts have been made to transcend the decision-making approach and elite orientation of studies of urban politics by examining the relationship between political pressure and actual political outcomes.[67] These studies are unified by the fundamental conviction that research must be pursued beyond the point that decisions are announced and policies promoted. They attempt to discover what *in fact* happened to those most affected by governmental activity. They assume that only in this way can meaningful study of the relationship between political activity and participation, governmental action, and underlying political attitudes be conducted. In this context it is instructive that studies of political participation and activity conventionally have been pursued by inquiring into partisan preferences and electoral participation. Insight into the behavior of low-income groups might be different if inquiry into participation in welfare systems and perceptions of schools and police behavior were also foci of investigation.

A third difficulty with studies of community politics has been their failure to utilize successfully the opportunities for comparative systems research. Many studies of community power have been pursued in single cities. They have usually presented conclusions accompanied by invitations to other scholars to attempt replication of the studies. This has rarely been done, although some investigators have attempted to synthesize the decision-making approach of Dahl with the reputational approach of Hunter.[68] Some writers have followed their studies of single cities with attempts to generalize from their observations to a larger universe. Their constructs are not so much attempts to develop theory as they are observational frameworks at the pre-theoretical level. These include Banfield's study of Chicago, and Wilson's utilization of bargaining language in understanding protest politics.[69]

[67]See e.g., James Q. Wilson (ed.), *City Politics and Public Policy* (New York: John Wiley & Sons, 1968). Also Herbert Jacob, "Politics and Criminal Prosecution in New Orleans," note 52 above; William Keech, *The Impact of Negro Voting: The Role of the Vote in the Quest for Equality* (Chicago: Rand McNally, forthcoming); Strange, note 65 above; Lipsky, note 62 above.

[68]See Presthus, note 56 above. The structure of Atlanta elites has been studied in order to test some of the conclusions of Floyd Hunter. See M. Kent Jennings, *Community Influentials: The Elites of Atlanta* (New York: Free Press, 1964).

[69]See Banfield, note 44 above; Wilson, "The Strategy of Protest," note 65 above; Norton Long, "The Local Community as a Ecology of Games," in Norton Long, *The Polity*, Charles Press (ed.), (Chicago: Rand McNally and Company, 1962).

A number of studies have recognized the desirability of adopting the comparative case method.[70] However, the cases are selected frequently for reasons of convenience, and superficial similarities of size, location, or economic base. The reason for selecting cases has little to do with the subject of inquiry.

A promising development in the comparative study of urban politics is the recent trend toward utilizing aggregate data to try to explain statistically the incidence of governmental forms and policy outputs to various socio-economic community factors.[71] As with output studies, the alternative of integrating quantitative analytic techniques with the comparative case method remains to be explored. Significant variables may be isolated by quantitative techniques, while the case method may be employed to approach greater understanding of the appearance of significant correlations.[72]

IV. CLASSIFICATIONS IN THE STUDY OF STATE AND LOCAL POLITICS

The relative sophistication of theoretical formulations in the field is partially revealed in the schemes used for classifying political phenomena generally designated as "state and local." The classification systems used by state and local scholars are often untested as to their reliability, validity, and utility. Their reliability depends on the existence of operational guides for placing phenomena in exhaustive and mutually exclusive categories. Their validity depends on our knowing what they represent by applying them to actual data. Utility is related to the problem(s) and question(s) under investigation. To be useful, a classificatory scheme must distinguish on theoretical grounds between empirically different phenomena. Both theoretical relevance and empirical differentiation are characteristic of a successful classificatory scheme, but are criteria which are rarely met in state and local studies.

Political scientists continue to distinguish among systems by location and size. While Southern politics, following the investigations of V. O. Key,[73] continue to display unique political configurations related to racial discrimination and franchise limitations, it is by no means clear that other regional configurations are particularly salient. Research efforts subsequent to the publication of *Southern Politics* appear to have accepted regional distinctions for convenience, while actually expressing interest in other

---

[70]By comparative case method we are not referring to the common practice of studying many issues within single cities. See Presthus, note 56 above; Agger *et al.*, note 57 above; Williams and Adrian, note 60 above. See also Wilson, *Negro Politics*, note 63 above; and Wilson, *The Amateur Democrat: Club Politics in Three Cities* (Chicago: University of Chicago Press, 1962).

[71]See note 14 above.

[72]A start in this direction is provided in Martha Derthick, "Intra-State Differences in Administration of the Public Assistance Programs: The Case of Massachusetts," in James Q. Wilson (ed.), *City Politics and Public Policy*, note 67 above; and John Gardiner, *Police Department Policy-Making: The Case of Traffic Law Enforcement* (in manuscript).

[73]Key, *Southern Politics*, note 2 above.

phenomena. The most significant aspect of Lockard's *New England State Politics* relates to the impact of varying degrees of inter-party competition. John Fenton's *Midwest Politics* was undertaken to explore notions of goal orientations of state government.[74] A recently published collection of readings on state politics, utilizing a sectional framework, testifies to the continued assumed salience of regional patterns.[75]

Another classification which political scientists have adopted uncritically is that of size of city. Students of community power utilizing the comparative case method frequently attempt to "hold things equal" in part by studying communities of the same size. Perhaps one of the reasons that communities of relatively similar size appear so diverse in the literature is that investigators never specify what it is that they think they are holding constant. Controlling for size might mean controlling for resource availability, community heterogeneity, bureaucratic complexity, or frequency of elite social interaction. Failure to specify the meaning of size in community studies has left obscure the importance of size of place.[76]

One area in which classification based upon both size and place does seem fruitful is that of suburban politics. Schnore and Alford have identified three types of suburbs displaying patterns of governmental form and socio-economic characteristics.[77] Williams and his associates also usefully distinguish among three kinds of governmental units in the metropolitan area (excluding the central city).[78] This study is outstanding for its adherence to the standards of inquiry enumerated above. Somewhat similar distinctions are made by Leo Snowiss in his analysis of differences in congressional recruitment patterns in metropolitan areas.[79]

Studies such as these have helped to break down the notion, prevalent

[74]Lockard, note 19 above; John Fenton, *Midwest Politics* (New York: Holt, Rinehart and Winston, 1966); Fenton, *Politics in the Border States*, note 34 above; Frank Jonas (ed.), *Western Politics* (Salt Lake City: University of Utah Press, 1961).

A different rationale for using region as an independent variable outside the South is provided by Wolfinger and Field, note 14 above. In this study region is thought to "stand for" time of urban settlement. See also Schnore and Alford, note 14.

[75]Frank Munger (ed.) *American State Politics: Readings for Comparative Analysis* (New York: Thomas Y. Crowell Co., 1966). "Sectional differences have declined, but still exist." p. viii.

[76]Size of place does seem related to form of government and the adoption of various reforms associated with a "good government" orientation. Middle-sized cities, for example, have adopted the council-city manager form in much higher proportions than big or small cities. See Alford and Scoble, note 14 above. The limitations of studying the big city as a critical category are revealed in Edward C. Banfield, *Big City Politics* (New York: Random House, 1965), pp. 3–15; and Agger, *et al.*, note 57 above, pp. 760–779. The tendency to classify by size has not infected students of state politics.

[77]Note 14 above. A classificatory scheme based on anything other than governmental form is not explicitly promulgated in this study.

[78]Williams, *et al.*, *Suburban Differences and Metropolitan Policies*, note 14 above.

[79]Leo Snowiss, "Congressional Recruitment and Representation," *American Political Science Review*, 60 (1966), 627–639. For an analysis of public officials' roles based upon the size of constituency in metropolitan areas see Michael Danielson, *Federal-Metropolitan Politics and the Commuter Crisis* (New York: Columbia University Press, 1965).

in the 1950's, that the metropolitan problem was one of inferior management and inadvertent fragmentation. These studies view metropolitan governmental fragmentation as serving the function of providing different and separate environments for urban area residents.[80] One might speculate that it is the critical functions served by different metropolitan environments, rather than the areal or size dimension, which makes useful the typologies focusing on suburban differentiation.

A second perspective on classifying sub-national areal politics has been sought through a vague and uneven interest in underlying political attitudes. This may be called a focus on political culture, although nothing as systematic as the exploratory investigations of *The Civic Culture* is usually intended.[81] Rigorous research on underlying political cognitions and attitudes has not characterized studies of state or urban politics. Nonetheless, there has been an interest among students of these areas in "the 'internalized' expectations in terms of which the political roles of individuals are defined and through which political institutions (in the sense of regularized behavior patterns) come into being."[82]

Illustrative of this interest, Agger, Goldrich and Swanson propose a four-fold classification of urban political systems based upon two dimensions: 1) sense of potency among the electorate; and 2) the probability of illegitimate sanctions being employed against incipient efforts to alter the scope of government. These dimensions yield four regime types.[83] Pursuit of these considerations cuts across an areal pattern of observation, points to the similarities between the relatively closed systems of a southern middle-sized city and a small parochial western city, and encourages comparison of city political systems with systems at other levels of government. Further, the concentration of research efforts over a long time span permits the entertaining of possibilities of regime change within recognizable periods.

[80]Also contributing to this reorientation have been the writings of Robert Wood, esp. *1400 Governments*, note 61 above, and *Suburbia* (Boston: Houghton Mifflin Company, 1958). See also recent studies of metropolitan consolidation in Edward Sofen, *The Miami Metropolitan Experiment* (Garden City, N.Y.: Doubleday and Company, 1966); Frank Smallwood, *Metro Toronto: A Decade Later* (Toronto: Bureau of Municipal Research, 1963); Henry Schmandt, *et al.*, *Metropolitan Reform in St. Louis* (New York: Holt, Rinehart and Winston, 1961). Victor Jones anticipated many of the problems of metropolitan reform in *Metropolitan Government* (Chicago: University of Chicago Press, 1942).

[81]Gabriel Almond and Sidney Verba, *The Civic Culture* (Boston: Little, Brown and Company, 1965).

[82]Harry Eckstein, "A Perspective on Comparative Politics, Past and Present," in *Comparative Politics: A Reader*, Harry Eckstein and David Apter (eds.), (New York: The Free Press of Glencoe, 1963), p. 26.

[83]Agger, *et al.*, note 57 above. The four regime types are: developed democracy (high, low); guided democracy (high, high); underdeveloped democracy (low, low); and oligarchy (low, high).

There is an implicit reference to political culture in the elitist-pluralist dichotomy, particulary in the sense that citizens are alleged to anticipate the sanctions of those "really in power." Recent studies have abandoned this simplistic dichotomy. See, e.g., Presthus, note 56 above, p. 25.

Political culture considerations are at the foundation of Williams and Adrians' classification of urban government based upon governmental scope. They initially suggest a typology of "local community values" (p. 21) or "roles of local government" (p. 23), although in their discussion of the characteristics of their four cities they shift to classify cities "according to performance" (p. 187). Their typology, based upon the considered judgment of the investigators, yields cities classified as those 1) promoting economic growth; 2) providing or securing life's amenities; 3) maintaining traditional services; and 4) arbitrating among conflicting interests.[84] This presentation provides an excellent example of the utility of typology for organizing findings, although as the authors point out, their work is essentially descriptive and pretheoretical.[85]

The stimulating work of Edward C. Banfield and James Q. Wilson in attempting to demonstrate differential value orientations toward governmental expenditures by analyzing referenda data also suggests an interest in characterizing cities by citizen attitude toward governmental scope.[86] This refinement of the old machine-reform dichotomy has placed questions of ethnic politics again in the forefront of urban studies. Their further explorations in this area, as promised in their recent "Communication," will be awaited with interest.[87]

Two recent studies of state politics have employed political culture concepts—one implicitly, one explicitly—without providing the reader with the means to evaluate the classifications. John Fenton's study of six midwestern states attempts to explore the distinction between job-oriented and issue-oriented politics, although what in a sense is his major independent variable—issue-job orientation—is an assumption the validity of which is never established.[88] Daniel Elazar has written a mystifying book on American states, utilizing what he calls a "political culture" approach. Unfortunately the data which permit the author to distinguish among Individualistic, Moralistic, and Traditionalistic American political culture patterns are never presented.[89] Elazar is undoubtedly correct when he argues that a regional division of the states is not necessarily the best for political analysis.[90] But he fails to assess the utility of his classification.

[84]Note 60 above, p. 23, and *passim*.
[85]*Ibid*, pp. 312–315.
[86]James Q. Wilson and Edward C. Banfield, "Public-Regardingness as a Value Premise in Voting Behavior," *American Political Science Review*, 58 (1964), 876–887. See also Banfield and Wilson, *City Politics* (Cambridge, Mass.: Harvard University Press and the M.I.T. Press, 1963). The utility of the public-regardingness distinction has been forcefully challenged by Wolfinger and Field, note 14 above. See also the exchange of comments in the *American Political Science Review*, 60 (1966), 998–1000.
[87]*American Political Science Review*, 60 (1966), 999.
[88]*Midwest Politics*, note 74 above.
[89]Daniel Elazar, *American Federalism: A View from the States* (New York: Thomas Y. Crowell, 1966). See esp. ch. 4.
[90]*Ibid*., p. 114.

The most extensive typological developments in the study of state and local politics have been in areas of research where attempts have been made to confine analysis to some of the structural variables of the political system. This may be observed in reviewing classificatory efforts in the area of state party systems.

Following the seminal research of V. O. Key, political scientists have made considerable attempts so distinguish among states by the degree of party competition. For some purposes, classification has been based upon a combination of factors which accounts for both national and interstate variations in party competitiveness.[91] For other purposes, particularly a concern with testing the relationship between party competition and public policy outputs, classification has proceeded by concentrating exclusively on inter-state measures.[92] These efforts have thoroughly explored the classificatory problems of cut-off points, selection of time-dimensions, and application to various research problems.[93] The attempts to develop typologies of states based upon party competition serve as the most complete area toward which political scientists have focused systematic attention. The continuing utility of these classifications remains to be demonstrated as other studies challenge the notion that party competition is highly salient to public policy outcomes.

Related to interest in the degree of state party competition has been speculation concerning the structural-functional hypothesis that degree of interest group activity is inversely related to party competition. Where political parties fail to aggregate interest, in other words, this function will be assumed by interest groups.[94] One student of American politics has made an attempt to characterize state politics in terms of interest group

[91]Austin Ranney and Wilmore Kendall originally utilized a single index for classification, in *Democracy and the American Party System* (New York: Harcourt, Brace, 1956). See also Lockard, note 19 above. Joseph Schlesinger attempted to account for the distinction between states which experience long periods of one party government, followed by resurgence of the other party, from states in which party control alternates. See "A Two-Dimensional Scheme for Classifying the States According to Degree of Inter-Party Competition," *American Political Science Review*, 49 (1955), 1120–1128. See also Schlesinger, "The Structure of Competition for Office in the American States," *Behavioral Science*, 5 (1960), 197–210. Richard Hofferbert has offered an approach which combines the advantages of accounting for the "cyclical" problem with the statistical desirability of working with a single index, in "Classification of American State Party Systems," *Journal of Politics*, 26 (1964), 550–567.

[92]See Robert T. Golembiewski, "A Taxonomic Approach to State Political Party Strength," *Western Political Quarterly*, 11 (1958), 494–513, and Dawson and Robinson, note 7 above. For an attempt to relate party competition to other systemic factors in urban politics see Charles Gilbert and Christopher Clague, "Electoral Competition and Electoral Systems in Large Cities," *Journal of Politics*, 24 (1962), 323 ff.

[93]These difficulties are discussed by Leon Epstein in his evaluation of the applicability of the Ranney-Kendall classification for Wisconsin. See Epstein, *Politics in Wisconsin*, note 34 above, pp. 33–35.

[94]This is an alternative hypothesis to one promulgated by Key, who suggested that where party competition was weak, interest group aggregation increasingly was focused on the dominant party. See, e.g., V. O. Key, Jr., *American State Politics: An Introduction* (New York: Alfred A. Knopf, 1956), pp. 97 ff.

activity. He perceives four distinct state patterns.[95] This study forcefully illustrates the wide gaps in basic data availability in the field. It is dependent for an evaluation of interest group strength on the highly undependable characterizations by political scientists in the various states published more than a dozen years ago.[96] Testing of the usefulness of the typology must await basic data collection on various dimensions of interest group activity in the states.

Typological interest in other structural features of state and local politics has been neglected.[97] While the three forms of urban executive arrangements—mayoral, council-manager, and commission—are familiar to students of city politics, little systematic research has been conducted on the impact of these executive forms on other aspects of urban politics. Some research has revealed the kinds of cities likely to adopt various executive styles,[98] and in the case of the city manager, some research has suggested various conditions affecting the political behavior of urban executives.[99] These efforts, however, represent exceptions. Without assistance from substantive research, writers on city politics must resort to distinctions, such as the formal-legalistic, strong mayor–weak mayor dichotomy,[100] or the non-operational continuum of Influence Centralization–Decentralization.[101]

Implicit throughout this discussion has been the unwavering focus on the basic areal legal units of analysis—the cities and states. In part this is entirely sensible because the performance and characterization of these units remain critical research problems. But classification of political phenomena in terms of these units alone may obscure links with other categories of political behavior. Theodore Lowi's recent work provides a case in point.[102] By concentrating on three functionally coherent policy areas in city politics—distributive, redistributive, and regulative—Lowi

[95]Harmon Zeigler, "Interest Groups in the States," in Herbert Jacob and Kenneth Vines (eds.), note 46 above, pp. 101–147.

[96]Belle Zeller, note 24 above. These characterizations by political scientists—certainly a "reputational" measure—are also utilized by Lewis Froman in "Some Effects in Interest Group Strength in State Politics," note 10 above. See also the classification of nongovernmental groups by scope of activities and frequency of participation in decision-making in Sayre and Kaufman, note 59 above.

[97]An exception is the work on nonpartisanship by Eugene C. Lee, *The Politics of Nonpartisanship* (Berkeley, Calif.; University of California Press, 1960); and Charles Adrian, "A Typology of Nonpartisan Elections," *Western Political Quarterly*, 12 (1959), 449–458.

[98]See, e.g., Alford and Scoble, note 14 above.

[99]See Gladys M. Kammerer, Charles D. Farris, John M. DeGrove, and Alfred B. Clubock, *City Managers in Politics: Am Analysis of Manager Tenure and Termination* (Gainesville: University of Florida Press, 1962). This limited research on Florida city managers does not, strictly speaking, permit inferring of classificatory divisions.

[100]As does Charles Adrian, *Governing Urban America* (2nd ed.) (New York: McGraw-Hill, 1961), pp. 199–214.

[101]As do Banfield and Wilson, *City Politics*, note 86 above, pp. 104–111.

[102]Theodore Lowi, *At the Pleasure of the Mayor* (New York: The Free Press, 1964). See also his "American Business, Public Policy, Case-studies and Political Theory," *World Politics*, 16 (1964), 676–715.

has discerned distinct recruitment patterns which might never have been revealed if he had, say, researched comparative recruitment patterns in three cities. A willingness to transcend the areal, legal units in searching for classificatory meaning may prove fruitful at a time when other typological developments appear unrewarding.

V. CONCLUSIONS

In this brief survey we have attempted to review the development of the field of state and local politics over the last twenty years. We have concentrated on three areas in which notable contributions toward an understanding of political phenomena have been made—the study of outputs, of institutions, and of community power relations. We have focused attention on aspects of these subjects which remain to be explored, clarified, and re-examined, and have tried to highlight these problems through analysis of the adequacy of typological developments.

Political scientists in attempting to divorce themselves from the prescriptiveness and formal-legalism of former generations, have succeeded in taking on, and destroying, a number of clichés about American politics and problems. They have demonstrated that suburban fragmentation serves social functions that could not be easily challenged by purely administrative solutions. They have resurrected the reputation of machine politics by pointing out the integrative function performed by patronage and personalistic politics. They have forced investigators to search deeply to explain relative non-participation in conventional political activity by those segments of the population which would be most likely to benefit from certain public policies. They have substantially discredited two highly regarded precepts of American political life—that malapportionment and low levels of party competition are substantially related to the level of outputs.

In these pages we have reviewed some of the advances in the field, and suggested some of the areas in which research in state and local politics might profitably be initiated. These areas in a sense are mirror reflections of a field devoted to decision-makers and not decision-takers, to elites rather than masses, to the results generated by political stimuli and not the impact of those results on subsequent stimuli. Thus we look forward to future studies which will examine the impact of policies on individual attitudes and behavior. We look forward to studies in non-electoral politics and the impact of non-elite pressures on the policy process. These studies would include basic anthropological investigations of Negro and white lower class incipient political groups, and intensive analysis of police precincts, welfare offices, newspaper city rooms and other lower-level bureaucracies whose effects on the political system are so extensive. We look forward to studies of differential administration, so that we may begin to explain differences in the impact of a variety of public expenditures.